*f***P**

Tina and Harry

*Tina Brown,
Harry Evans, and
the Uses of Power*

Come to America

JUDY BACHRACH

THE FREE PRESS
New York   London   Toronto   Sydney   Singapore

THE FREE PRESS
A Division of Simon & Schuster Inc.
1230 Avenue of the Americas
New York, NY 10020

THE FREE PRESS and colophon are trademarks
of Simon & Schuster Inc.

Designed by DEIRDRE C. AMTHOR

Manufactured in the United States of America

10   9   8   7   6   5   4   3   2   1

Library of Congress Cataloging-in-Publication Data
Bachrach, Judy
    Tina and Harry come to America : Tina and Harry come to America :
Tina Brown, Harry Evans, and the price of power / Judy Bachrach.
        p.   cm.
    1. Brown, Tina.   2. Periodical editors—Great Britain—Biography.
3. Evans, Harry, 1928–   4. Publishers and publishing—Great Britain—
Biography.   I. Title.
PN5123.B68 B33 2001
070.5'1'092241 21—dcaB   2001040152
ISBN 0-684-83763-3

to Noah and Sam

CONTENTS

Tina and Harry Come to America

Introduction

Tina Brown was thirty the year she switched continents for good, but a very old thirty. Her husband, Harry Evans, was fifty-five, to all outward appearances a determinedly youthful and attractive figure, full of bounce and even a lingering naïveté. Not much was expected of either of them. Harry, the greatest editor Britain had ever known, had left his country a shattered man, fired and humiliated by Rupert Murdoch. He was headed—who knew where? Really, at that point, at what should have been the height of Harry's career, he was perceived in cruel and indifferent New York circles mainly as his young wife's consort.

In 1984, the year of the couple's arrival, Tina was made editor of a lame and halting magazine, recently revived: *Vanity Fair,* it was called; it was owned by Si Newhouse, the shy billionaire of Condé Nast. No one expected much out of that endeavor either. "Do you know anyone who reads it anymore?" it was asked. Two editors had, in quick succession, been hired and fired at *Vanity Fair* before her. Circulation stood at 274,000; advertising, although initially robust, had pretty much evaporated: fourteen pages in a single pallid issue that year; simultaneously, $14 million of Newhouse's money went straight down the drain.

And who was Tina Brown, anyway? Of what possible use could she be—in America, in the roguish eighties—to the pampered, brittle world she invaded? Nothing about her seemed prepossessing. She was a quiet person, small, pale, indifferently attired, with thick tinted glasses and short-cropped blond hair.

INTRODUCTION

Her new colleagues at *Vanity Fair* made the mistake of underestimating her. But this was a common failing.

Within exactly six years, Tina Brown had become the established Queen of New York, her magazine read by roughly two million people. Virtually every cover was a celebration of fame, beauty, and money. Inside, of course, there might be a multiplicity of compelling subjects: AIDS, poverty in Haiti, Moammar Kadafi, deposed tyrants, or yet more fame and money. But the magazine's brassy exterior mirrored exactly the aspirations and temptations of a nation. It took an Englishwoman to discover them.

"My job is one of seduction; I'm about entrapping the reader," Tina once said, and in this she was not alone. When Harry Evans became the head of Random House (also owned at the time by Newhouse), the arbiter there of who and what would get read, many of these same urgent strivings were given voice. You could argue—and many did—that too much literary power was thereby vested in the hands of a single couple during the seven years they simultaneously ruled two (and then three) publishing units; but you were tempted to do so only if willing to remain forever outside their gilded circle. Few were so inclined.

There was no more feared or powerful couple in the country than Harry and Tina, and for good reason. They controlled competing empires, dueling writers, vast budgets. They knew not only how to edit but how to market: indeed, as time went on, the line, once so sacrosanct, that separated these two functions, the editing and the selling, grew ever fainter until it disappeared altogether. General Colin Powell's coy, informal flirtation with the presidency was given a brilliant send-off, thanks to Harry, who deployed two publicity units and his glittering skills as a party thrower on behalf of the general, Random House's most munificently compensated author. And yet— this was the odd part—apart from Maureen Dowd of *The New York Times,* not many thought to dwell on the propriety or wisdom of such a venture. A British-born publisher was helping to sway an American electorate on behalf of one of his authors. It should have merited more comment. That it did not says a good deal about those who had the capacity, if not the will, to say a lot.

In the hands of Harry and Tina, the American press was an easy mark. They were, in one way or another, masters of destiny, molders of careers, gods if you like, but oddly secular, which probably accounts for a lot of mundane descriptions of them at the time. Tina was, wrote the smitten, "a brightly polished red Porsche," a "beauty," the leader of the "glitterati." She was part of a team known as "Teenanarry," last names unnecessary. Inside their circle, favored authors and editors found themselves blessed many times over: impressive salaries from Tina, large advances from Harry; and if one was especially lucky, both arriving simultaneously. There were parties, publicity, and contracts, a mild approximation of the celebrity featured on Tina's covers. For the longest time this sort of seduction worked. Then, very abruptly, it didn't.

But one thing is certain: between them, Tina and Harry managed to change forever the face of Grub Street, once quite literally a street—indeed, the teeming, squalid resort of London hack writers—and then subsequently an unhappy metaphor for the torpid insignificance of so many of these writer's hungry descendants. The eking out of precarious livings, the outstretched hand, the thrift and scrambling: all these vanished for the fortunate collected beneath the shelter of their American umbrella. And this generosity was by no means simply Harry's or Tina's way of improving their own prospects and ambitions by securing the labor and loyalty of the most talented, although that was certainly a factor. It stemmed as well from the fierce reactions of the couple to the England they had left, to the class system that, they believed, had shackled so many of their own cravings and aspirations.

Like everything, such beneficence came with a price tag, a big one. But America was such an exuberant, rollicking place in the eighties. How were writers to know at the outset what, in return for their improved paychecks, they would be relinquishing? How, for that matter, were Tina and Harry to understand, when they came to America, that the meritocracy they unquestionably championed was in its own way as brutal and unforgiving as the class system they had fled? That their chosen people and the country they embraced could pardon anything at all, however wrong-headed and meretricious, except failure?

I think of this trajectory, despite the origins of the two main characters, as an especially American story. Harry and Tina both were nature's Americans. They possessed the cool, uncluttered perceptions of the outsider, and yet the drive, the will to succeed at any cost, the ability to overwhelm so many of those they encountered here. It was only in America, a renaissance nation, that the couple could reinvent themselves successfully. Not long ago, Tina would describe as her "defining moment" a certain night on Liberty Island, the eve of a launch party that attracted almost every celebrity imaginable to Tina's side. And along with them: "The flickering candles, the Statue of Liberty illuminated and the flag fluttering in the light summer breeze, and being in America as an immigrant."

Well, there are immigrants and there are immigrants. Long before the decision to relocate—we are going back now three decades—there was a smaller world inhabited by a brilliant but once-plain young girl in her first days at Oxford, as well as a more expansive one, presided over by an ambitious son of a train driver. The two individuals who occupied these separate worlds would eventually meet and marry— but really theirs was more than a marriage: it was for a time a fusion of seemingly inexhaustible resources, enterprise, and striving. Then they settled, much to the surprise of everyone who knew them at the time, into a truly remarkable American journey, the only country that could contain them. It is an intriguing odyssey Tina and Harry embarked on, wonderfully crafted but hazardous, and it took them from there to here, and from there perilously close to the sun.

Chapter 1

Precocity

In the fall of 1971, a small, blond, and extremely voluptuous young woman named Tina Brown arrived at Oxford University's St. Anne's College—not unannounced. She was a month shy of eighteen, young for an undergraduate. A great deal of fanfare had preceded her somehow or other, so much so that Robin Leanse, writing the gossip column for *Cherwell*, the student newspaper, was swiftly apprised of the new undergraduate's attributes and superior connections, which he then duly reported to the student body. "Anyway, TINA's in St. Anne's and she's VERY NICE," he wrote in October 1971.

This reference to the young woman's college was no throwaway remark, but a useful indicator that could help a reader judge how far up the ladder Tina was. The answer: not very. St. Anne's, an all-girls college in Tina's day, was startlingly ugly in its spare, bloodless style, the building topped by an oddly glassed-in dome edged in brassy green. It was considered an upstart college, satisfactory enough as a landing site, but it provided an unfortunate contrast to the honey-colored stone, medieval chancels, and limewood carvings of cherubs, as well as the Victorian echoes of earlier eras that characterized its older, more gracious rivals. Lady Margaret Hall—staid, decorous, named after the scholarly Margaret Beaufort, mother of Henry VII—might have been a better selection: Benazir Bhutto was there during a portion of Tina's Oxford career; or Somerville, the most academically distinguished of the women's colleges: its alumnae included Margaret Thatcher. Those were the places for

5

women with aspirations to be in Tina's time. All the colleges were single-sex back then (although this would change in 1974), not that it mattered much—to Tina. The ratio of men to women at Oxford was a glorious five to one. Within less than a year, at least one of her boyfriends would be caught after hours in her residence.

The young woman loathed the look of her new place as much as anybody—"Kind of a Bauhaus telephone box—horrible!" was how she described her room, and St. Anne's as a whole was no less loathsome—"a multistory car park!" Tina Brown had arrived, as the gossip item on her made clear, coming as it did so delightfully early in her student career; but only just. She was neither beautiful nor especially studious. "I've got a first-rate second-class brain," would be her considered verdict. But like the rest of her, it worked overtime. She had always been, she would later explain, "precocious."

She was, as it turned out, the daughter of a pleasant and gentlemanly British film producer, George Hambley Brown, who lived with his wife, Bettina, in the pretty town of Little Marlow, halfway between London and Oxford, on the Thames. He patently adored his daughter: the student gossip columnist heard that he had actually named the family yacht after her. The name of Tina's father did not necessarily ring a bell with everyone at Oxford, but his profession was glamorous enough to lend cachet to the daughter.

Brilliantined, mustachioed, invariably courtly, George Brown was quite successful within the narrow movie world of Britain, but by no stretch of the imagination a great filmmaker. "Rather a dull man—frightfully John Bull. I think Tina was aware of the rather lowly opinion George Brown was held in by critics," said an old acquaintance. "Not as well known as Tina wants him to be," was how one of her lovers from her Oxford days classified her father, a deficiency, he believed, that dismayed and disappointed her. "There, I think Tina slightly felt a grudge against somehow having been overlooked in the great pattern of life. She had not been born into the nobility, or riches."

She had, however, been born into something nearly as exotic: Britain's slipper-thin version of Hollywood, which would mark her from the start as both a devotee and a dispatcher of illusions. "As far as I could see castles were always plaster, money was always funny and the nuns came off the set for a cigarette," she wrote in later years. George Brown was the son of Christopher Hawthorne Brown, a theatrical producer, and Nancy Hambley Hughes, an actress with the D'Oyly Carte Company.

He began his movie career as a stuntman, riding bareback in the nude, with only a pink jockstrap: he was supposed to be a Greek god, which he then very much resembled. As it happened, he had never before been on a horse, but he wheedled a group of Horse Guards cavalrymen to teach him to ride. Persuasion was Brown's forte. It served him well enough when he became a producer and formed a professional partnership with the actor-writer Peter Ustinov: among the films they made was *School for Secrets* (1946) a wartime tale, and *Vice Versa* (1947), a comedy about a father and son who magically change places. But he was a scrambling, artful moviemaker, not a hustler and certainly no mogul. When the British studio system broke down, Brown's career suffered.

Perhaps this reversal of fortune may have affected the producer more than most of his acquaintances realized. "He was a very different personage from what most people think," a family friend of the Browns concluded. "That bonhomie of George's was simply a veneer. He was more complicated than that. He could get very angry if thwarted. He could be a volcano. And he was highly able. His job as a producer meant *everything* to him. He was a very tense, anxious man who put on this John Bullish aspect. The real father was a twitchy, intelligent person."

In fact, Brown was fairly prolific. *Guns at Batasi,* the 1964 film starring Richard Attenborough and young Mia Farrow, was one of his better-known productions, along with *Hotel Sahara,* starring Yvonne De Carlo; *The Chiltern Hundreds;* and in 1961, a couple of Agatha Christie films starring Margaret Rutherford, who was initially hesitant about playing Miss Marple: she hated crime as a subject. If he was famous for anything, however, it was because years earlier, in 1939, he had been very briefly married to the red-haired film star Maureen O'Hara, who was exactly nineteen at the time of the wedding. Her very strict mother was present at the ceremony in a church outside London.

Nonetheless, O'Hara would soon have the union annulled. The actor Charles Laughton, a middle-aged father figure to her, whisked her off to America right before Britain entered World War II. Laughton had been O'Hara's co-star in the Alfred Hitchcock movie *Jamaica Inn,* which he had also helped to produce. He and his wife, the actress Elsa Lanchester, foresaw great things for the lovely young Irish girl in Hollywood. And as it turned out, once in the States, Laughton pushed O'Hara's career at RKO to great effect.

"Charles Laughton literally rushed my sister from the altar of the church where she and George were married to the town of South-hampton where the *Queen Mary* was sailing to the States—and off they went," O'Hara's younger brother, Charles FitzSimons, explained. "George Brown and my sister never saw each other again. In Hollywood, Maureen lived with our mother in the Garden of Allah Hotel." FitzSimons said he remains completely mystified by O'Hara's decision to end the marriage. His sister will not speak of it, either to him or to anybody.

In his actors, however, Brown appeared to have instilled a far higher degree of affection. "Oh, George was a very affable old boy," recalled the actress Joan Collins, who starred in a 1971 Brown production that underwent a fair number of baptisms. Initially entitled *Revenge,* the movie was subsequently redubbed *Inn of the Frightened People,* and then *Terror Under the House.* Collins played the luscious wife of a pub owner, so intensely desirable that she is attacked by a sex-crazed young man: "The son of the publican that I married gets the hots for me," was how the actress described the movie's most critical moment. It was actually filmed on the cheap at The King's Head, a spacious pub in Little Marlow with a sign sporting the impressively bewigged head of Charles I (who was in fact decapitated); it happened to lie next door to Greengates, the white cottage where young Tina Brown lived with her older brother and parents. The film was memorable, said Collins, mainly because of what she was asked to do for her art. "George was very persuasive, that I can tell you. I had to take off my clothes in the movie and strip down to my bra and panties, and it was George who persuaded me to do all that. I had just had a baby so I was not too keen on taking off my clothes. But George said it was essential. He was a nice old boy.

"Now ask me what I remember about Tina," Collins said after a delicate hesitation. "Well, I have to be charitable and say that as a young girl—and I saw her then on the set—she didn't stand out."

The Browns' only daughter was known as Cristina then. "Rather a strange child," was how her own father saw her. "Very withdrawn." He found remarkable her "almost fairy look" and "halo of pale blond hair." The child spoke little—until age two, George Brown insisted— "and then out came the most unexpected words like 'soporific' and 'clandestine.' One felt she was impatient to leave her babyhood behind, that she was biding her time and that there was a powerhouse going on there that hadn't quite switched on." The more attentive within her circle, however, could perceive very early indications of this power. Peter Ustinov, among others, would be one of the targets of the child's fast-developing gift for mimicry and withering observations. After guests left the house, "she'd reach for her pencil," George Brown recalled. Little Cristina was given a fur coat by parents who spent a fair amount of time doting on her. Here they had the field largely to themselves.

The Browns also had a son, Christopher Hambley Brown, three years Cristina's senior, also blond and quiet, but at least very handsome and tall. Cristina, denied these assets, was a girl of whom her teachers expected very little.

"A bit of a pudding, to be frank. If you want the absolute truth, I thought she was very dull and uninteresting; she had nice blond hair. . . . But she wasn't the sort of child you would remember well," said Audrey Waller, a teacher at the Rupert House School in Henley, which Tina left at ten. Just a few miles from her home in Little Marlow, the school was named after Prince Rupert of the Rhine, a nephew of Charles I. It boasted more than a hundred children at the time, all of them expected to curtsey to Sylvia Fawcett, the school's stout and exigent headmistress. She was a gray-haired lady with decided notions of comportment. Little girls had to wear party dresses on dance-instruction days, so they could "hold up their dresses for the polka." For every day, kilts and blouses were in order.

Most of the pupils were the daughters of the wealthy or the prominent: Lady Mountbatten's children and grandchildren; the heirs of biscuit and beverage companies; as well as a number of the offspring of other long-ago British film stars, many of whom lived near the Browns. These were the classmates against whom young Cristina, pale, bespectacled, silent, was measured by her earliest friends and teachers. "Plain is what I'd call Cristina," was the judgment of David Glennerster, the son of the Browns' longtime housekeeper, who knew Tina as an adolescent. "These thick glasses—she was nothing special, I thought."

"Maybe she had hidden depth," conceded an early teacher. "But *I* never saw any." Decades later, a couple of Tina's former instructors pored over a photograph of the neatly packaged and celebrated woman she had become, marveling at the transformation, the trim suit and hairdo that accompanied her success: "Good God, not her!" one marveled. "That little dumpling! That suet pudding! Talk about Cinderella!" Even Tina's best friend in her boarding school days appeared to have reservations about her: "Tina came back today," she wrote in her diary, "the frizzy-haired fart."

Her academic background prior to her arrival at Oxford was equally unexalted, but in its own way impressive. Coexisting with the young girl's shyness, her implacable reserve and stern quiet judgments, was what George Brown called, admiringly, "a great capacity for causing trouble." Tina had been twice expelled from boarding schools and once suspended before she was sixteen, in one instance because she had observed that the breast of a headmistress resembled "an unidentified flying object." Years later her father would remember, but entirely without rancor, that he had had to intercede on her behalf with an assortment of headmistresses. In his daughter he perceived all sorts of robust virtues invisible to school heads. "How depressing for you to know you have failed with this talented child," was George Brown's favorite line to those who despaired of his daughter. He found her difficulties with school authorities "all tremendously funny."

In fact, Tina managed to gain entrance to Oxford because eventually she went to what is known in Britain as a "crammer"—a school specifically designed to infuse indifferent or late-blooming students with the education necessary to pass university entrance examinations. Really, she felt, she had no choice in the matter. "In England there's Oxford and Cambridge and then there's everywhere else," Tina said, and in such a cliché, bald though it was, there was undeniable truth. How could Tina even consider being elsewhere? Everything about her was in abeyance in her early years, but she had no doubt that this was but a temporary withholding, a promise deferred.

From the start, she clearly felt singled out by destiny. "When I become famous after my first novel . . ." was the beginning of one of her earliest recorded entries in a notebook (later retrieved by the son of the Brown family housekeeper) when she was growing up. Her future, she decided, would be exceptional. It was her body that she found wanting. She kept a diary faithfully from the time she was twelve, a glaring but composed reflection on her own shortcomings. "Roger's Fancy Dress Party" began another entry, this one at sixteen. "I went as Scarlett O'Hara. Looked QUITE FAT." On the other hand, she did not quite despair of her imperfections. Tina bathed them in the flattering light of her own artless candor: "jodhpur thighs," she sneered in an article about herself. She knew who she was: "numero uno," and also "a lewd, vain-glorious creature who saw herself as the beleaguered sophisticate in a world of dullards. This secret knowledge— the Real Me—was something to be enjoyed in the writing. . . ." And so she wrote, quietly but steadily. "Moshe Dayan," she scribbled beneath the Israeli general's color photograph, "I wish you were here to ravish me with your single glittering green eye!"

By the time Tina arrived at Oxford, however, the long-awaited powerhouse was just beginning to switch on, the dull pudding undergoing a slow but purposeful transformation into a dish. The glasses that had once clouded her face were occasionally tossed aside, and it was observed at these moments that her eyes were huge, and of a devastating, irresistible blue. The painful shyness that had once characterized her was still there, but often masked by bouts of effrontery, wit, and provocation. Already then she possessed the talent that throughout her life would never leave her: the ability to inspire in both friends and rivals a feeling of deficiency, as though no one was quite worthy of her. "She was in fact quite sexy," an early friend recalled, "although she had a rather sulky expression, a face which was hard to please— unless of course you were someone she wanted to know."

In Oxford, Tina became almost instantly the object of the most intense and fascinated scrutiny. Male and female, members of her new, self-important student world took notice, although it seems that none of them really understood her. They simply recognized her skills, the dedication with which she marshaled burgeoning talents and desires. Dressed in large "principal boy" shirts, with huge bell-shaped sleeves, draped over black velvet trousers tucked inside knee-high boots with platform heels, and a gray rabbit fur that just skirted her rear, "she was always very keen to make an impression," as one Oxford woman recalled.

Indeed, the transformation of Tina Brown, while far from complete and somewhat unconvincing to many of her peers, was just under way. She was still slightly fleshy. "She was lumpy, exactly like Princess Diana was," said Simon Carr, a boyfriend from that era. It was a distraction to some whose ardor she wished to compel, and there were a few notable romantic flops among them. But not many. Wildly sensual ("She just oozed sex appeal," another admirer explained), she emerged from her long period of dormancy a commanding girl, with a clever, insistent suggestiveness that left a fair number of men bewitched.

There were some ten thousand students at the university, a good number of them anxious to make their mark there and then. "Hacks" and "gnomes," these itchy self-advancers were called. They were the people who ran for president of the Oxford Union, the debating society, or who studied in their rooms with demonic fervor. Tina did not occupy herself in such a manner; she possessed ambitions beyond Oxford.

"University is such a springboard to other things," was her reflection on her student years. "There's nobody you can't meet at Oxford if you want to enough and if you grab the opportunities. I mean if you were longing to meet Tom Stoppard, all you'd have to do is ring him up and invite him to speak at the Union or ask him for an interview." Her English literature studies, friends noted, while not ignored, were not quite at the epicenter of this existence. She loved Jane Austen. She was fond of the works of certain Victorian writers (George Eliot's *Middlemarch* particularly) because her tutor, Dorothy Bednarowska, "made me understand how modern they were in their themes." It is doubtful, Tina conceded, that she would have discovered such a truism about the Victorians on her own. "I don't think I would have ever taken the time and attention necessary to really get into them if she hadn't shown me how."

But however much she appreciated fine writing, there was a side to her, her fellow students saw, that clearly chafed under the restraints of Oxford. The medieval university town, with its river threading past those pale stone structures, boasted a fairly stratified environment. From some of its circles, Tina was pointedly excluded. From others, she excluded herself. A woman who dutifully invited her to "coffees," occasions when men "were invited to the girls' colleges," as well as tea afternoons ("Just ghastly rituals where girls invited men for tea—the idea was to have as many men to your room as possible"), swiftly realized that Tina wasn't interested. In fact, she had the knack of making those who *were* interested in such unambitious gatherings doubt their own judgment.

"I realized she was in a stratosphere way above me," one would-be friend concluded. "I got the impression she soon noted who was necessary, who was important, who was not—for her future career at Oxford."

Thus was Tina's ascent scrutinized, each victory noted, every failure jotted down by some of the very people she snubbed. Oxford, one of these would later explain, was in many ways open. "But it also has—because of the English class system—there's always been this sort of fast upper-class set, people who went to Eton. My impression of Tina when she first arrived was she first tried to be with the Eton public school set. And that that didn't work—because it never does.

Because they always in the end only take their own. They might have toyed with her a bit."

Clearly, this rejection stung, and in later years, Tina would dispatch these careless and unsatisfactory men of the upper classes with her own interesting version of events. "In my second year, I managed to shed all these freaks," she said, "and mixed with actors and writers, which was low-key but amusing." But her description of the second group of friends was equally inadequate. What she wanted, after her initial social setback, was something more substantial than mere low-key writers or actors: men of talent and stature, men who could teach her, were the ones she gathered around her. Even as a late adolescent, she had an expert collector's discrimination. Tina Brown, it was quickly perceived, rarely sought romance with the obscure—and then never for long. "I just bought a car. Would you like to come for a drive?" a young student, Alex Dufort, asked her one day.

"No, not really," came the languid reply. She felt no need to disguise rejection with insincere apologies. "Goodness me," the dismissed suitor remembered thinking, but without resentment, "she must have a lot better things to do with her life." And she did, he observed. "She seemed to have millions and millions of important and useful friends." As for Tina, "It wasn't clear what she was. An enigma is what she seemed." Within short order, he noticed, some of that mystery was dispelled as the young woman allowed a photograph of herself to appear in *Isis,* the student magazine.

TINA SELLS ISIS—WHY DON'T YOU? read the ad on March 12, 1972, in which the young woman was captured wearing a straw hat encircled with a thick dark ribbon, as well as her trademark glasses rimmed with plastic. "And everyone said to themselves: *Who on earth is Tina Brown?*" Dufort recalled. "It made quite a splash."

"You felt with Tina she was out there making contacts and using Oxford as a springboard, which was a clever move," an acquaintance would later say. "She had her own agenda. She was never one to avoid publicity. She was not one to waste her time. And the fact that she was the daughter of a producer certainly helped."

Within a year, the comedian Dudley Moore, then at the height of his fame and career, came courting at St. Anne's in his limousine, much to the amazement of Tina's classmates. Months afterward, Auberon Waugh, the son of the great British novelist Evelyn Waugh, became her most ardent champion, and a wonderful help to her burgeoning career as a writer. Martin Amis, the son of another famous novelist, Kingsley Amis, followed suit. None of these conquests—

with the exception of Amis—did she hold in awe. Privately, a few of them would become the objects of a coolly detached amusement. Later confidants claimed to have been informed by Tina that Dudley Moore, despite his attractions, had one leg shorter than the other; that Auberon Waugh washed frequently after sex.

At Oxford it was presumed, given her glamorous movie background, that she would be very beautiful. Here, however, there was some disappointment. "She was much plainer than I expected. It felt to me as though she had her looks on the debit side," Robin Leanse recalled. "She had a very big nose in those days. The balance of her face wasn't particularly elegant. I was surprised at the absence of immediate luster in her face, although there was luster in her eyes." Nonetheless, he was totally smitten with her—not so much for what she said, really, but because of how she listened.

"I'd been in Morocco reading diaries, reading André Gide, Flaubert's travels in Egypt, Gide's journal, Delacroix's journal," said Leanse, who is now a poet. The two undergraduates enjoyed discussing these diaries, as well as Tina's passion for recording her life in her own journal. "And I remember thinking how splendid her enthusiasm was. She resonated very much when others brought ideas to her." He never recalled her coming up with her own ideas. Instead: "I used to feed her conversational morsels, as though she were some sort of queen—the essence of my mind. I did find her incredibly cold. There was a surface sparkle. But I felt her steely absence of emotional accessibility underneath. It seemed to be a performance, a dependable reliable performance. But underscoring it was a kind of enthusiasm that had no responsibility. It was a substitute for real exploration. I sort of felt there was something I could do to break down this veneer of implacable self-possession, of never losing control.

"I suppose," Leanse concluded, "in that way, she was a very enthusiastic receiver."

But a number of her new Oxford acquaintances saw Tina in the more active role of pursuer, someone with a private directory of amatory targets, men with connections or careers who might eventually prove useful to her. In the Britain of the seventies, that kind of tactical cunning was considered fairly unappealing in young women. And yet, almost none of her targets, if such they were, appeared unaware of her motives; they simply drew the distinction between cunning and contrivance. "There was nothing conniving about it," protested one of her ex-lovers. "I think she just liked sex." Tina's earliest successes were based not on concealing her goals and desires but on flaunting them.

"I was seized by this avalanche of excitement," was how the movie and television director Tony Palmer later described his first encounter with Tina, a date that is recorded in his diary entry of February 22, 1972. She was still in her first year at Oxford when she met Palmer during an intermission at the National Theatre production of Eugene O'Neill's *Long Day's Journey into Night*. Then twenty-seven, Palmer was already well launched into his career. He had started off as an assistant to the extraordinary British film director Ken Russell, was about to launch his own seventeen-part television series on American popular music, and was a friend of the Beatles and the Rolling Stones. Later he would go on to make an eight-hour movie about the composer Richard Wagner, starring Richard Burton and Vanessa Redgrave, as well as films on Maria Callas, Handel, and Yehudi Menuhin.

"When I saw him across the Theatre, I remember thinking he had the face of a fanatic," the young Tina would later write in a fictional rendering of her romance with Palmer. "For the first time in my life I allowed myself to disintegrate and the relief was almost unbearable. I was in love with the disappointments of his mouth."

What particularly struck Palmer, he would later say, was not Tina's looks—he never thought her a beauty—but the realization, practically instantaneous, "that this was an extremely intelligent woman. Intellectual, not. She didn't have the intellectual discipline to organize her thoughts—they were sort of scattershot. But intelligent, and quite fiercely intelligent, in the sense that she was acquisitive for knowledge." He never felt Tina selected him to advance her future career; it was something else, Palmer decided. "I knew what she wanted from me. She thought I knew a bit about music. And most of the first times we went out consisted of her quizzing me about music and composers."

With Palmer the fateful night he met Tina was the British novelist Angela Huth, a shy, gentle woman fifteen years her senior, who was his wife at the time. The marriage, both partners would claim, was a short-lived disaster, with, Palmer recollected, a number of breakups and reconciliations. In its very brief midst, Tina and Palmer embarked on a passionate relationship. There were many frantic phone calls from Palmer. During one of these conversations, Huth specifically recalled her husband thrusting the receiver at her and demanding she talk to Tina.

"She sounded just a bit—a bit shaky, I think," Huth would recall. "Tony did tell me that he rang her up a lot. And he wrote her letters. Oh absolutely. He wanted to goad me a bit, I should think."

Palmer would deny thrusting the phone at his wife. But he did claim that Huth "was endlessly berating Tina as the source of all of our problems. It was rubbish. And I remember pointing out to Angela at the time that it is very rare in one's life that one finds someone with whom one has a fairly healthy sexual relationship. And yet actually what matters is that you're very good friends!

"Angela did say at one point, 'If you ever see that horrible woman again, I will leave you immediately!' " Palmer said. "Whereupon I went to the telephone and rang Tina immediately and said, 'Please help me! Today!' But I wouldn't want to give the impression that Tina was a marriage-wrecker, because as far as I was concerned, she wasn't."

Palmer was wholly aware of what he might offer the younger woman. "Although she was still a student, she had plans," he recalled. "I did push her in a certain direction. To be interested in other things than the things she already knew about." Specifically, she wanted to be a writer, Tina informed Palmer. When she was eight, she had actually written a play about Henry VIII and one of his wives, an achievement of which her father remained inordinately proud. "In one strange passing reference so long ago, she told me the person she would most like to have been like is Tom Wolfe," Palmer said, who had given her one of the author's early books. "And she could have been Tina Wolfe. You can see why. This energy. This excitement. The eccentricity. You could see why she wanted to emulate that. She wanted to be taken seriously."

It was this desire to be perceived as a woman of substance and high seriousness, Palmer believed, that drove Tina even then: "Certainly in the inverted snobbish world of London intellectual circles to appear that voluptuous, that sexy, that straightforwardly wanton— it's very hard to be taken seriously," Palmer said, but he was more than happy to help. Young as he was, he was not without influence.

"My one moment of glory was in the late sixties, because I was great friends with a lot of rock 'n' roll people," Palmer later explained. "I think I might have introduced her to George Harrison. I introduced her to John Lennon. Absolutely I introduced her to Dudley Moore. It's possible I introduced her to Tom Stoppard. I would hate to say I introduced her to the big time, but I did introduce her to an awful lot of people. That is true.

"But what endeared her to me—and I don't think it's ever left her—is that she just wants to know things. She has a kind of child-like lust, lust for experience, lust for sex, lust for knowledge. Lust for knowing how the world is!" What particularly delighted him was her particularly un-English boldness, her lack of subterfuge: "She grabbed. There's something aggressively, assertively lusty about her." Palmer was enchanted. "There was nothing she didn't want to do and want to try. Nothing. You can read your own interpretation into that. I won't tell you any more. You knew that the minute you met her."

Among the more conservative old guard, the titled scions of the British establishment, such behavior was viewed as irremediably peculiar. "Debs didn't want to *know* her," one old boyfriend, the son of a wealthy peer, remarked. Unmasked ambition has never received an especially warm reception in Britain. Allied as it was in Tina's case with sexual fervor, it sent a shiver through the less purposeful upper-crust undergraduates at Oxford. Word had reached a number of students, said Robin Leanse, that Tina had an early amatory encounter in a flat boat—called a punt—on the river Cherwell.

Few of her pursuits were especially private in those days. "Tina was obviously on the make, which was slightly offputting," one of the few men she desired in vain would later recall. He was aware of her flirtation, but thought he recognized from what it stemmed: "It was not as if she was in love with me. She was trying to mix." However, as a member of what one observer called "the fast upper-class set," his interest wasn't piqued. He thought "her drive overwhelming," and the young woman propelled by such ambition "quite nervous—nervous and overweight."

In his Oxford days, this man was a ferocious poker player, reckless, caustic, handsome. If he deflected Tina's attentions, it was because of what he considered the vast untidy sweep of her ardor. "She was out for the main chance, which was slightly offputting," he said. "She had an affair with Tony Palmer. He was older and quite ugly. While we were at Oxford, he was making a study of modern music. Tina was *always* on the phone with him her first year. You don't understand. Tina—she had multiple affairs." In later years he would dwell on her fondness for older men. "Now a lot of people would say she's really doing it for safety reasons. Looking for a mentor. That she's very insecure. That's why she can't relax. She's too nervous and thinks people see right through her."

One day, he recalled, he was driving with Tina through Oxford and spied a young peer, "a very rich Byronic character, dressed like a Dickensian figure with a frockcoat and a vest."

"Who is that man?" Tina asked.

"That's Lord Neidpath," she was told. Jamie Neidpath. Her friend found him "somewhat crazy."

"Within short order, Tina was having a relationship with him."

Lord Neidpath himself recollected his three-month romance with Tina with a distinct lack of fervor. "I liked Tina. But she was *far* too ambitious. Let's say it was clear the career was going to come before anything. If one wasn't going to fit in with her career, one wasn't going to remain popular with her for very long. Probably she did have another boyfriend as well." It was Tina who ended the romance, Lord Neidpath recalled. And then along came Martin Amis: "Obviously, *he* was going places."

Sweeping through certain circles at Oxford at the time was yet another impediment to Tina's swift social climb: the notion that she was Jewish. Nothing Tina herself mentioned to most of her new friends might have led them to this conclusion. Indeed, she was largely mute on the subject—perhaps for good reason, given the currents of casual, unrepentant anti-Semitism that still flow through upper-crust British discourse. This certainty about her origins, said a member of the group to which she aspired, arose strictly from what was divined from her behavior. How could anyone so driven be anything other than Jewish? She was so very eager.

"She's a tough, ambitious girl, clearly very ambitious—she's Jewish and quite like her mother." That was how one of their number explained his instant realization that he was dealing with an outsider. To this day, the alien status of Tina Brown, her place outside their charmed circle, is a cherished theme among those she once called her friends.

"But you know she was so much on the outside," said another old friend, this one titled. "It is such a joke—there are all these stories going about now about how she went to boarding schools and was the daughter of the rural gentry, as though she'd grown up with a paddock and a lot of horses right outside her country house!" A bitter laugh. "She just could not stand it. She was a Jewish girl who wants to come to England and conquer the world! A total outsider. Someone with her nose pressed against the windowpane. She is to journalism what Barbra Streisand is to movies."

As is so often the case, these insiders, their sensibilities grown morbidly acute and sharpened by fear of invasion, were onto something. Tina's dark, beautiful mother, Bettina Kohr Brown, indeed had a German Jewish father: John Kohr, who owned gas stations. On Bettina's mother's side, the background was Irish: "a terrible combination," she used to say. For the longest time Bettina was known as "Tina" as well—until her daughter Cristina matured and began her romantic pursuits. "I started getting *her* phone calls and she began getting mine," Bettina once explained to a friend. "Hers were more exciting." From then on, the mother retreated into her given name and allowed her plump, fair daughter center stage. Although, given Bettina's nature—open, witty, inquisitive, forward—"retreated" might be the wrong word to use. She was thin and glamorous, her skin, however bleak the weather, invariably nut-colored. Cats were her special passion—she collected all sorts of strays—but this tenderheartedness was by no means her ruling force. There was, as well, a quite determined aspect to Bettina. "The mother would get on with whoever she felt was useful to her," it was noticed.

When she met George Brown at Denham Studios outside London, he was just a casting director, but still married to Maureen O'Hara. Unlike her red-haired predecessor, Bettina appeared to have had no reservations about George Brown ("Today something terrible happened," she wrote in her diary the day World War II broke in Europe. "George didn't phone"). Nonetheless, it took her four years to get him to marry her. "Even using all the tips in the women's magazines," she plaintively declared, "like putting scent on my pulse points." On August 12, 1948, the scent apparently overwhelmed Brown and he caved in. Bettina was twenty-five, George ten years her senior.

The couple took up residence in the small, pretty town of Little Marlow, not far from an assortment of British film studios. There they bought a modest cottage with a bay window and twin gables. George and Bettina had a large garden packed with rosebushes out in the back, a small potting shed—and a host of movie colony neighbors whom they entertained assiduously, along with the occasional rich prospective backer. Evenings were jolly but disciplined and well-regulated affairs, devoted, without apology, to the furtherance of the family's ambitions. "Who shall we have to dinner to massage the Iranian/Swiss/Belgian money?" George Brown would ask, whenever a new film needed backers. "Everyone," Bettina would reply. "And if he's anything like the Indian twenty percent, it better be a buffet." These social occasions were not necessarily foolproof methods of attracting financing. The prospective backer, as young Tina noted, "usually disappeared the next week anyway. When the roof blew off his tax shelter." Nonetheless, Bettina persevered. She possessed sharply defined social aspirations, and these, too, she put in the service of her husband's career.

"Tina's mother was a sensationally upwardly mobile lady," the London gossip columnist Richard Compton Miller would say in later years. In his young days, he had attended Bettina's famous dinner parties with an actress who was then his girlfriend. There, guests found "all the right people" assembled: the actors Jack Hawkins and Stanley Baker were much in evidence, as well as Joan Collins, Sean Connery, Sophia Loren, and Peter Sellers. And young Tina: she, too, was "absolutely at these dinner parties," an alert and parched presence, drinking in every syllable uttered. Even as a small child she had been quietly, studiously part of the proceedings, "sitting on the lap of the most important man in the room," as a family friend once observed.

"I was brought up to regard everything as 'copy,' " Tina would later say. "I always felt that I was there as the observer, and I used to scuttle off to my room and write my diary for hours and hours. Very irreverent, very satirical."

Tina's father, although "delightful," was not especially interested in high-flown guests, but he soldiered on. He was jovial company, got along with just about anybody, and was a good source of gossip about the stars with whom he worked. Knowing the value of these connections went far beyond a juicy anecdote, however, Bettina worked tirelessly at them. Her husband was essentially a B-movie producer and required her assistance. Despite the smallness of their house, her parties were "beautifully arranged, everything was absolutely pristine," said Compton Miller. "Not shabby-chic at all. Everything rather pukkah and nice. But you know—very nouveau. And why not? Very Hollywood-ish."

In her younger days, Bettina had been a secretary to the famous film director Alexander Korda, and had subsequently done publicity for Laurence Olivier, but she seemed to have been designed for a less auxiliary sort of life, one that would have permitted her to give full expression to her dashing personality and take center stage. She was extremely tall and slender, her straight black hair swept back to reveal a high forehead and prominent cheekbones that framed a thin, delicate nose. Inky black brows, thick as wings, swooped above deep-set eyes fringed with startlingly long lashes. "Gypsyish, a bit," was the verdict of Tony Palmer, who appeared to have been the only person to

20

whom Tina confided that her mother was partly Jewish (and then only after he had told her *his* mother was Jewish as well). He found Bettina "spiky, sharp-tongued. But it was never offensive. There was a kind of acidity to her—which in Tina's best writing there is too."

What there was not, a friend recalled with surprise, was any emphasis on a deeper culture within the family. One summer, when he visited the elder Browns in retirement (by the mid-seventies they were living in Spain, in a large house in San Pedro de Alcantara, near Marbella), he was astonished to discover what they didn't have. "No books. There were simply no books at all."

Unlike her daughter, Bettina was happy to discuss her Jewish antecedents. "Bettina Brown was an absolutely stunning woman," was the first impression of Valerie Grove, now a columnist for *The Times* (London), who met both Bettina and George in the early seventies. She thought Bettina "exuded glamour," indeed, looked like a flamenco dancer in her gold-hooped earrings and vibrantly colored dresses. "How could Tina ever compete with such a mother as this?" Grove, along with other family friends, often wondered.

In fact, Bettina spotted in her favorite child the same extraordinary destiny that Tina privately foresaw for herself. "The mother lived through Tina," one acquaintance decided. Both parents worshipped her. "Right from the start she was a rather exceptional girl," George Brown would say in his old age. "Everything she set her mind to, she did with intense application. She was extraordinarily resolute."

Of her older brother, Christopher, friends of the family remembered little. "A tall, quiet, nice guy," said a resident of Little Marlow. "But the only one in the family with get-up-and-go about her was Cristina." It was as if, presentable and good-looking though he was, Chris Brown vanished, evaporated almost, inside the tiny house in Little Marlow. Palmer tried mightily to summon him up from the past. "If I say he made no impression on me, that sounds very cruel. But I think that's about it! I mean, I am even struggling to remember what he looked like."

It was on their daughter that the Browns' hopes rested. Tina took up with just the sort of men who added spice to their lives. "Tina was absolutely, deeply in love with an actor called Nicky Henson," recalled Compton Miller. "But he was very much a Jack-the-Lad sixties-type actor, riding a motorcycle, wearing black leather. Very glamorous. It was quite unusual for a girl that age, going to Oxford, to be with a quite well known B-movie actor."

The elder Browns' own lives, by the time their daughter matured, were ones of bemused reflection rather than serious accomplishment. "Her father had film aspirations way beyond what he actually achieved," Palmer said. "Look, I don't wish to diminish her father in any way whatsoever, but the heyday of British films—we are never quite sure when this heyday was. They were good English chaps. But Harvey Weinstein, Steven Spielberg, they were not."

Thus, in young Cristina, her parents vested a fair portion of their own ambitions, still shiny with disuse. It would be a considerable burden to her at the start, but one she shouldered without resentment. "I remember her talking about how there was such pressure on people to make them succeed very early," recalled Robin Leanse, who was informed by Tina after some months of acquaintance in Oxford that she was busy writing a play. It was not a task she had set for herself, apparently. She explained to Leanse that she and her best female friend, a dark-haired classmate named Sally Emerson, who was also at St. Anne's College, were both feeling very competitive about making their mark, without really knowing what it was they were trying to do.

"One could tell this was not a natural thing for her to do, but was sort of forced on her. I think she felt she had to do it," was Leanse's impression. He had the feeling her father was behind the idea of playwriting. There was no resistance to such parental prodding, however. "She was really in some ways going with the current and doing the things she could do." It was only in later years that Tina was fully capable of examining the effects of such an upbringing: George Brown alone was not responsible for the woman she had become. The origins of her ambitions, the striving that seemed to have taken hold of her personality, had their roots in Bettina, said the daughter. "It was almost too much sometimes," a friend recalled. Bettina, for her part, put a lighter gloss on her projected ambitions. "I always said that all I wanted from Tina was a cable saying: *Married on his yacht this morning!*" she told a friend.

By the end of her first year at Oxford, Tina had reason to feel profoundly dissatisfied with herself. Clearly, whatever parental coaching had come her way had left her unprepared for certain aspects of life. She had fallen pathetically short of her goal of insinuating herself into the best social circles. She had enjoyed her English literature courses, but had not brought to her studies the intensity she applied to other areas of her life. "She was intelligent, very intelligent, but wasn't a great scholar," Tina's tutor, Dorothy Bednarowska, recalled. "Very lively, though, very lively indeed. You can make of that remark what you will."

"Lewd,"and "vainglorious," as Tina referred to herself, she had committed obvious blunders. She had amassed probably too many boyfriends and involved herself in the disintegrating marriage of one of them. She had become the source of gossip and envy among suspicious students. She hadn't accomplished what needed to be done.

"I think it was soon after that that Tina sort of thought, 'Well, this isn't very productive, this isn't a productive line of operation. I'm going to be more serious,'" said one female classmate who had watched her carefully. There was certainly a resolve to change. By her second year, Tina had stopped drinking even the occasional glass of wine. It wasn't fear of addiction that brought her to this decision; previously she had drunk socially, but not much. She simply found, she told her boyfriend Simon Carr, that she had developed an allergy to alcohol. It made her feel sick. Very likely there were other reasons why she abstained as well.

"I am now doomed to perpetual vigilance," Tina said. However melodramatic the pronouncement, it was obvious she relished such a destiny. No one would ever see her drink again.

Amused observers concluded that Tina was falling under the salutary influence of Sally Emerson, her best friend. "Sally's always been quite focused," recalled an Oxford graduate, "and she wanted to be a writer."

As it happened, Emerson—small, pretty, more muted than her friend Tina—did indeed eventually become a novelist and married Peter Stothard, another Oxford student of the era, who is now the editor of *The Times*. Like Tina, she kept a diary; it was this that initially cemented their friendship. In their second year together, Emerson became even more vitally important to Tina, and the two were inseparable. Emerson had landed a prize: she was editor of *Isis,* the university's magazine. Tina became its features editor.

It was in this capacity that a young man named Stephen Glover first met her in the spring of 1973. "I had an idea to interview Bron Waugh and some poet called Grey Gowrie, who later became a Tory minister," Glover explained. "Bron," as Auberon Waugh was known to his literary friends, was not merely the son of Evelyn Waugh, who wrote *Brideshead Revisited* and other memorable novels. He was until his death at sixty-one a famously witty columnist, celebrated in

England for the relentless malice of his prose. At regular intervals, he produced a poisonous "Diary" for the British satirical magazine *Private Eye,* much of it total invention. His privileged youth had left him with a bitter hatred of private schools. "Why spend good money you could spend on wine and antiques and pictures on placing your children in the care of pederasts and sadists?" he used to wonder. At the time of Glover's brainstorm, Waugh had been poking particular fun at the Earl of Gowrie's poetry and his taste in women ("Appalling man, unbelievably thick—he went to Balliol because it was the only place where Wogs would be accepted," he explained).

When Glover arrived at the *Isis* office with his great idea, he found, as expected, Sally Emerson. Also there was "Tina Brown, standing opposite, looking at me suspiciously." He had no idea who she was. Glover told the women what he wanted to do. It was to be his maiden voyage in journalism. He had already persuaded Waugh, also an Oxford alumnus, to agree to the interview.

"What a brilliant idea!" the voluptuous blond woman, suddenly friendly, exclaimed when Glover finished his pitch. "Can I come with you?"

Stunned, Glover acceded, and called his subject. Waugh, too, had never heard of Tina Brown. "Well, you *said* you were coming by yourself," he remarked grumpily. "But if you want to bring somebody—fine."

Glover and Tina drove down together to Combe Florey, Waugh's house in Somerset, which had once belonged to his father. "It was not love at first sight, no, not at all," Glover thought. "Bron's wife was there for a start. And cooked his lunch. Cooked mine, too."

"Shall I write it up?" Tina asked her new friend after the interview was over. "Of course we'll have a joint byline."

"Fine," Glover agreed. He hated interviews, especially the bother of rerunning the tape for good quotations.

But although the Gowrie piece carried Glover's byline, the Waugh interview in *Isis,* interestingly enough, was under Tina Brown's byline alone. A very flattering piece it was, too. Combe Florey she described as a "palatial seventeenth century retreat," where Waugh was "safe from the repercussions of his scathing pen." The professional misanthrope possessed, beneath his venom, a "shyness," along with "a genuine affection for the English novel, which is almost touching in its conviction." Waugh liked the piece a whole lot.

Glover, very gallantly under the circumstances, never mentioned the omission of his name to Tina. "I thought it far too petty to raise," he would later say.

Asked if his reaction would have been as mild had Tina Brown been a man, he replied, "Good question. Um, no. Possibly not."

Seven years later, he would be written out of the script entirely. Just as she was about to become the most-talked-about new editor in London, Tina would recall for the benefit of an interviewer how she came to meet Waugh, the most important man of her life—at that time. "I asked him for an interview and set off to Somerset with a beating heart," she said.

The interview with Waugh was not without other, more permanent consequences. It proved invaluable to Tina Brown, both at Oxford and afterwards. It opened doors and brought her, at age twenty—much to the agony of some of her student peers—serious journalistic assignments from important publications. It propelled her far outside the relatively puny student world which had until then confined her.

Actually, it wasn't the interview, workmanlike and admiring though it was, that accomplished all this. It was Auberon Waugh himself. He was so totally besotted with Tina Brown, so amazed by her wit and her writing, so delighted by "a certain sort of readiness one sensed in her, nothing ever shocked her," that he begged all his important friends to hire her, and raged at the few who did not. Like his rivals, he was under few illusions about Tina's motives; unclad ambition was simply part of her allure, as foreign and delectable to certain Englishmen as an odalisque.

"Part of her friendship for me was consciously getting to know The Real Thing," Waugh would explain shortly before his death, by which he meant the world of real literary celebrity that he then dominated. "One doesn't hold that against her. She left a profoundly good impression."

It was Tina's determination to leave a round of profoundly good impressions, ones that lingered in various literary minds long after her Oxford years. Her contributions to *Isis* were cluttered with kindly adjectives, adornments of the famous. "She somehow used the magazine to get to know a list of people she wanted to get to know," as Dufort put it. There was an interview with the actor Stanley Baker; a more revelatory one with her thirty-eight-year-old flame, Dudley Moore ("Fear preserved his virginity for three years, but the moment of truth came at last in an Oxford hotel. . . ."); and a genial tribute to Alan

Coren, then deputy editor at the humorous magazine *Punch,* whose imagination Tina found "eclectic." And a second homage to Waugh, present on this go-round at a luncheon thrown by *Private Eye.* Some of these literary ventures would be signed "Cristina Brown." Others merely "Tina Brown."

The final project Tina decided to embark on was finished by the end of her busy second Oxford year: completing the play her parents wished her to write. It was a mere twenty-five pages long; the cover showed a drawing of a man, his expression wild, limbs frantically clasped around a tree. He is flanked by two women, both pulling at him. The play was called *Under the Bamboo Tree,* a phrase lifted from T. S. Eliot, and as several interested patrons at its various performances in Oxford, Edinburgh, and London had reason to discover, it was about a classic romantic triangle in which (to quote a *Sunday Times* article of the day) "an errant husband is demolished by truth." This particular errant husband seemed to be closely based on the real-life writer and director Tony Palmer. In fact, Tina told him as much, after sending him a copy of her work. A second character in the play appeared patterned on his unhappy wife, Angela Huth. And the third side of the triangle—the eighteen-year-old mistress of the husband—bore a significant resemblance to the ambitious new playwright, Tina Brown. "A vivacious young student" is how she described "Sara," her alter ego.

In some ways, the play betrayed all the hallmarks of youth: energy, passion, generous splashes of wit, often highly successful. There were also heavy doses of Noël Coward thrown in at critical moments, mainly, one feels, to mask the blushes of the author. But the play has a very mature and surprisingly cool harshness of tone, providing an unsparing glimpse of the young university girl who caused such a ruckus in a marriage with her obvious methods: ". . . when he told me six weeks later he was having an affair, I had no idea it was the same girl, the one of eighteen, the girl at the Theatre with the big tits and adulation," the distraught wife informs the audience. And the fictional Tina is equally disparaging about her own methods of attracting talented men: "I heard myself saying how I'd always been an admirer of his work and thought the play the best thing he'd done," Sara says. It was a favorite tactic of the author then. It would remain so. Only one thing was certain. At nineteen, there was no critic more cutting about the youthful Tina

Brown than Tina herself. She was a woman with a capacity for ruthless self-examination, a person of uncommon, early talents.

"I saw the play at the Bush Theatre in London," Huth recalled years later. "And I don't remember very much about it. Except it seemed to me that quite a lot of my best lines had got into the play."

And, in fact, it is to the wronged wife that much of the play's sympathies and all its choicest bon mots are devoted. It is also the offended older woman who somehow understands the essence of a sound and sensible marriage: "Staying around when it's boring." As for Tina's character, she is variously described as "fatty" and "about as sophisticated as a tin tack." By the play's end, both women join forces and excoriate the man they love. "Oh God, I thought he was vulnerable and needed my love and attention," cries young Sara. "Now I realize he's just a man who can't cope with his wife." For his part, the husband is reduced, literally, to nothingness: a pile of empty clothes in a chair.

Perhaps because of this sisterly denouement, Huth grew amazingly friendly with her former rival, which was typical of Brown's long-established pattern of recycling acquaintances and erasing the most ingrained resentments. Besides, Huth would later say, she preferred not to raise the subject of her former husband: "I wouldn't have *dreamt* of asking Tina about what went on. To this day, I don't really know." The last time Huth flew to New York from London, in 1998, it was at Tina's personal invitation. Tina was then a woman who, as editor of *The New Yorker*, commanded far more recognition on both sides of the Atlantic than Huth.

"Have you ever written for us?" Tina inquired.

"I must have sent ten or twelve stories," the older woman replied. "And they always write back saying, 'You're nearly there. Try again.'"

"Oh do try again," Tina begged her.

"And I was just finishing a collection of short stories, so I sent one in," Huth said. "And behold! They took it!" Nor was that a solitary gesture of warmth and affection. Tina put the writer up at her own expense at her club, and beside her bed Huth found a bouquet of flowers and a personal note of welcome from the editor, alongside a stack of the latest novels, each individually wrapped by Tina's assistant.

The final night of her stay, Tina threw a lavish party in the novelist's honor at her apartment: Norman Mailer, Tom Wolfe, and Dominick Dunne were among the invited. Huth knew only Dunne and the millionairess Drue Heinz, who accompanied her to the party because

Tina had particularly asked to meet her. Three butlers served the guests at six round tables. Huth found it "heavenly. . . . It was so beautifully done."

But years ago, when she was just starting out, the youthful Tina effected one last change in her life with that promising play, as the British columnist Philip Oakes himself noted in an interview he conducted with her over a quarter of a century ago. The story about her ran in the *Sunday Times* just as *Under the Bamboo Tree* was about to open at the tiny Bush Theatre. "Should [she] re-dub herself Tina Brown?" wrote Oakes—a bit late, considering the decision had already been made by Tina herself. She had clearly been undergoing a certain amount of anguish about her identity. Contemporaneous as well as later stories on her insert an "h" into Cristina. Even her birth certificate carried the extra "h," although George, her father, claimed she had been born without it. There always appeared to be a certain degree of fluidity about her.

"Tomorrow night, whatever the billing says, is the last time she will be calling herself Christina," wrote Oakes.

As was indeed the case. The very last time. From then on, she was something else.

Chapter 2
The First Rung

In late August 1973, just as she was about to start her last year at Oxford, Tina Brown turned up the heat. Whatever presumptuous ambitions student chums thought they had detected in her previously were suddenly thrown into the shade by the glare and dazzle of the new Tina.

"My name is Tina Brown, I'm putting on a play and I'd like you to be in it," she told the young actor Robert Benton in a Scottish pub, shoving the manuscript of *Under the Bamboo Tree* into his hands. Benton told her any such production was absolutely out of the question. He was a busy man, putting on three shows for the Cambridge University Theatre, which he headed. She had simply come to him too late, he told her, and she would never get a director.

"I've already got a director," she replied.

The two were in Edinburgh, site of Britain's biggest annual arts festival. Benton was amazed at the audacity of this undergraduate. Amazed and defeated, ultimately, by this "simply irresistible force." One thing was certain, he thought at the time. "She was a well-connected girl."

With Tina at the festival, he observed, was the famous writer Auberon Waugh, there for "support," the actor supposed; and a young but established actress, Jenny Agutter, who had very likely, Tony Palmer would recall, been introduced to Tina by him. There were hopes, never materialized, that Agutter might play the role of the "vivacious young student." Benton read the manuscript and found it "really quite good." The young actress

Mary Hamilton, who played the part of the wife, decided that "it was actually one of the best plays I've ever read." Years later, she would be, briefly, the chief executive of the Royal Opera House (by which time she had reverted to her real name, Mary Allen), but the memory of what Tina could have become never left her: "I think she is an extremely accomplished magazine journalist. I also think she gave up what could have been a successful career as a serious writer—she could have been an outstanding playwright."

Even more impressive, Benton decided, was that the day the show opened—and indeed it did open at the Edinburgh Festival, to good reviews—"We had every critic from London known to man up to see the play. Benedict Nightingale from the *Financial Times*. Michael Billington from *The Guardian*. I never knew how she did it."

Others found themselves quickly figuring it out. Ann Barr, whose London desk as features editor at *Harper's & Queen*, Britain's leading society magazine, used to be next to that of its arts editor, Jane Stockwood, received an odd call one day when she picked up the phone of her absent colleague. It was the era of fashionable clubs—Zanzibar, Annabel's, Morton's on Berkeley Square—and the lanky, impenetrable women, later dubbed "Sloane Rangers," who frequented these spots in Mummy's pearls. In her heyday, Barr was famous for recording the activities of this new social category. She was a majestic force, astounded and dismayed by what she heard in 1974 from a perfect stranger. The caller was evidently young and female—and completely ignorant about the ways of society magazines.

"The voice says, 'This is Tina Brown calling from Oxford,' " Barr recalled. " 'I want to know what Jane Stockwood will *do* about *my play*.' She wanted us to review it. Well, we didn't review plays by *girls* at Oxford." There was an audible sniff of displeasure. "That's just what Tina was like. A pushy, pushy personality. I suppose she would know better now than to ask such a thing."

A bit later in 1974, the British humorist Miles Kington, arriving to speak before the Oxford Union debating society, received similar treatment. Out of a crowd, a young woman "came dancing up to me." She wore dark glasses and had "a thrusting bosom." He had no idea who she was, an ignorance the stranger immediately dispelled.

"You don't know me, my name is Tina Brown and I am going to be very, very famous some day," were her first words to Kington. She claimed to be a playwright, with something or other about to open that "you *must* go see." Kington was vividly aware, even then, of why he was selected. He was an established writer at *Punch*, the satirical magazine, a useful sort of connection, he realized, for a hungry undergraduate. "I remember thinking, 'Put those dark glasses on your bosom, darling.' "

Undeterred, Tina gathered around her an eclectic group of the famous, the well known, the potentially successful, and a few odds-and-ends people who ended up drifting, going nowhere, and achieving little. These, however, were in the minority. Dudley Moore, dressed in yellow velvet trousers, escorted her to Oxford parties, seemingly oblivious to the gapes of startled students. Then at a party in December 1973, Tina met the handsome young Martin Amis, the son of Kingsley Amis, and she fell instantly in love. Amis was already a freelancer of some renown.

"I fell in love with her, too," Amis would later concede. "I was writing a column about sex under the pseudonym 'Bruno Holbrook.' " Strip joints and girlie magazines were his themes. At the party, he revealed he was not only Martin Amis, he was the author of sex pieces in the intellectual left-wing magazine the *New Statesman* that had acquired a certain cachet.

"Oh, you're *Bruno,*" the blond undergraduate said admiringly. She would call him "Bruno" forever after. Amis immediately understood the undercurrent of her tone and the reason behind it. "That seemed to be the key attraction," he said. After he was checked out by Tina's parents, the couple launched a passionate affair in an assortment of venues—among them the Browns' home in Little Marlow. Despite the remoteness of the village, word got around.

"My mum found her in bed, in her mother's bed with that Amis fella, Martin Amis," David Glennerster, son of the family housekeeper, would recall. "Amis—among others," he emphasized. "She would tell my mum, 'Oh please, Minnie, do tidy up the bed, my mum will be so cross. *Please,* Minnie.' She was a bit of a messy girl, that Cristina. More brainylike."

Continuing by Tina's side her final year at Oxford was Auberon Waugh, then thirty-four. He made it his business to champion his young protégée in every corner of the literary world. Many of his friends were importuned to find jobs for Tina, among them Anthony Howard, who was then the editor of the *New Statesman* and always looking to promote new talent.

"I know a very smart undergraduate," Waugh told Howard.

Howard was aware of why this "very smart undergraduate" had been singled out by Waugh for his attention. "Bron Waugh had fallen for her and always was besotted by her," he said. Nonetheless, he was willing enough to give her a try. "We met, she then wrote three pieces for me. I remember one piece was called 'Eights Week'—that's a rowing week at Oxford when all the crews from various colleges race each other. It was a very good piece." Another was about taking finals at Oxford; and a third described the eccentric, frantically paced existence of British expatriates living out a peculiar retirement along coastal Spain—the very life, in other words, Tina's own parents were then leading.

Entitled "On the Beach," this short piece was set at the Marbella Club, and possessed all the brittleness and charm of its author: the clever outsider in the thick of things. On the surface, the unimpeachable joy of the huntress taking perfect aim; but the prey itself (ersatz countesses and princes, impressionable tourists) was clearly fairly small time. Running beneath the mockery and mild venom was the dismal undercurrent of failure. It was the best piece of the three:

> Gone are the days when the brush salesman with the heavy tan and a card signed Lord Snowdon could be assured of a cordial reception at the door. Sly interlopers trying to gate crash by swimming in from the boats are quickly weeded out by Count Rudi, the lantern-jawed manager who polices the swimming, while at thrilling intervals, the club owner, Prince Alfonso, a suave bumblebee in yellow and black boxer shorts, descends to make a lightning check that all goes superbly well in his kingdom by the sea. . . .

Among Tina's fellow students, this sort of literary triumph in the great world outside Oxford met with mixed reactions. "Everyone was very sniffy about it," her old boyfriend Simon Carr saw right away. "They would say, 'Why is the New Statesman employing a middle-class Oxford girl to write about Marbella?' " Among the sniffiest, as it happened, was Carr himself. In 1973, he ended their relationship. "Because I was jealous of her, I was jealous of her appearing in the New Statesman. I couldn't bear it!" he said. He wasn't envious of her success, he claimed. He was "jealous of her talent. She was clearly so much better than I was."

In Martin Amis, however, no such awkward career competitiveness or jealousy raged. Indeed, now the shoe fit snugly on the other foot. If Tina was a talented newcomer, Amis was perceived, then especially, as having the more certain and glamorous future. "He writes wonderfully, which made me terribly insecure at the time," Tina would later say, and then went on to describe, in literary dimensions only, the mastery and control with which Amis directed her young tastes. "He taught me to sneer at Rupert Brooke and Shelley."

Any number of Amis's likes and dislikes were, in Tina's eyes, worthy of adoption; he seemed so much her superior. "Tina Brown pointing to a lacuna in my emotional repertoire, would later say that I had never had my heart broken," Amis wrote later. "And I can now recognize that I somewhere harbored an unconscious distrust of love." This distrust, masked as invulnerability, made him all the more desirable in Tina's eyes. Amis had landed a job on the *Times Literary Supplement*. He was twenty-four to her nineteen when they met, not merely an amusing writer about sex and other matters, but a man of the world and victor of many a romantic skirmish. Moreover, unlike Tina, he had true pedigree. His father in his field was, for all his well-documented caddishness toward women ("A promiscuous man in the days when it took a lot of energy to be a promiscuous man," was how Martin would describe him), a far more respected artist and celebrity than gentlemanly George Brown. Any serious analysis of Amis's parents, Hilary and Kingsley, and their complicated relationship might have given Tina pause about her chances for happiness with the son.

It was easy enough for young Amis to find women. Despite his small stature, Amis was more beautiful than Tina, his body thin and compact, his light hair worn long and brushed back, emphasizing pale eyes and an unyielding jawline. The young couple were seen necking at *New Statesman* parties, "snogging on the stairs," as one disgusted observer put it, "behaving like adolescents." They visited each other in Spain, where both Martin's mother, Hilary (divorced from his father by then), and Tina's parents had homes. The pair even shared, friends noted, their own peculiar language. "Both he and she had a hand in reinventing the language—*yob*, for instance," said Carr, referring to the current British term for lower-class boor. "Tina claimed credit for this. She said she gave it to Martin." She would also say, "I must leave. I'm going back to my *sock*," which was her word for flat, its provenance the dank, redolent bachelor pads with which she had become acquainted.

"All I know is I regarded them as an absolutely perfect couple," said Valerie Grove, the journalist who became fast friends with Tina during that time. "Because they had the same sense of humor. They talked in the same way. They both had a sort of mid-Atlantic twang, the way they pronounced things. '*Wa-a-all*,' they'd say." Or, as an alternative, cryptic references to the hip satirical magazine *Private Eye* were mixed by the couple with drawled-out Americanisms. "Tina and Martin could have these conversations using references like this. But of course they're useless to anybody who doesn't get the reference," Grove concluded. "It was cool. They were cool."

That was entirely the point. One night, in a Marbella nightclub, Tina found herself being importuned to dance by a stranger, a stubborn young man, demanding, persistent. Grove was there, watchful: "He was pathetic—a nothing little guy. He just wouldn't take no for an answer." Nonetheless, she was astonished at the vehemence of Tina's disdain. "As we went, Tina just said, '*Cock*sucker.' It was amazing because it was 1973. People didn't use language like that. It was so Martin Amis to say that really, the way she was just coolly able to dismiss him."

Oxford friends thought they detected in Tina a tough new shell of glazed impermeability. It shocked them, because the university environment at that time was, as one friend recalled, "very hedonistic." There was a softness to the general student mood, a negligent feeling that was almost frivolous. Gone were the days of intense ideologies and angry demonstrations. By the mid-seventies, "There wasn't much to demonstrate *about*," said one of the graduates. Virtually alone among them, Tina seemed to have a purpose her last year; even at parties, she appeared in vague pursuit of some aim or other. Sometimes this involved sloughing off the less motivated.

"By that time I was still sort of nursing some feelings for Tina, but she seemed like a girl who was surrounded with bodyguards," recalled Robin Leanse, who eventually went on to achieve his ambition of becoming a prize-winning poet. It was, he felt, the last sort of goal that would appeal to Tina in her newest phase. "There was a clique of men around her all the time, they looked very louche and very sinister," he said. "Tina was just hanging out with them like some moll. So I went up to her and said, 'You think you can do better for yourself than go out with a poet like me?'

"And she said, 'Yes. Yes, I do.' "

She was, after all, a relatively well known personage, despite her youth, and the focus of considerable media attention. For several reasons, not merely her romance with Amis, it was a heady period of her life. She went on to win a *Sunday Times* award for her play, for which she had compelled the notice of established theater critics, the vaster and more discriminating world outside Oxford.

And why not? Nothing seemed beyond the realm of possibility. Her smiling face and impressive cleavage sprouted from a printed satin dress in the British version of *Cosmopolitan* magazine, where in March 1974 she was hailed as "the stunning twenty-year-old playwright." Just opposite was a picture of the bright Cambridge graduate Arianna Stassinopoulos ("the gorgeous Greek"), then as now a celebrity and the focus of considerable interest. It was, however, Tina who got top billing.

She was swiftly learning how to use the press. To the gossip columnists she imparted the delightful news of her affair with Amis. Thus, her early fans learned of this "story-book" romance between two promising writers, as well as the "warm glow between them."

The glow went out, and Amis dumped her. ("As he always so chivalrously put it. He had all these terrible expressions," said one old acquaintance.) It was right before her final exams, an Oxford graduate recalled. Tina found herself saddled with an unremarkable but respectable enough degree, a "second," as it is known at Oxford, and—for the first time in her life—a broken heart. Amis was fully aware of the agony his decision provoked. "Well, yes, it was very painful," he conceded. "You know I was twenty-four. And also, this I believe, if you're the child of a broken home, as nearly all of us are these days, it makes you distrust love. Because you know it's not an absolute value. The child like Tina whose parents were and remained happily married had more trust."

If so, the demolition of her affair with Amis, and with it her hopes for the perfect alliance of promise with talent, writing with writing, put an end to all such trust. "I suppose that after Martin I became very wary of young men who snatch one's affections and then move on," Tina would later explain to a friend. True to form, she never wholly broke with Amis. Throughout succeeding years he would be, like so many others, recycled in various incarnations. He was a guest at her parties, often in the company of his famous father; a contributor to her magazines; occasionally a recipient of her confidences. In the spring of 2000, she would publish Amis's autobiography, which, completing the cycle of courtship to friendship to business, contained references to their early love affair. But in her last semester at Oxford, Amis was her signal failure. Like her inability to gain a toehold among the social elite, he represented humiliating defeat, the prize just beyond her grasp.

With her friend Sally Emerson, Tina threw herself a memorable graduation party in mid-June at the Cherwell Boathouse on the river. Here she had more luck. It was, said one guest, "a blissfully sunny day." There was gin mixed with fruit, punting along the river, and most telling of all, a sizable crowd gathered on a steamer, composed of the reigning London literary and journalistic establishment of the day: Anthony Howard, Auberon Waugh, Martin Amis, Fleet Street editors, important critics, a photographer from *Cosmopolitan,* even Wyche Fowler, who would one day become a U.S. senator. Tina made a speech that Fowler considered "very pretty and accomplished." Others found her frighteningly self-possessed, as though she'd lived a thousand lives and recalled them all. "I've never seen such a knowing, seen-it-all look in the eyes of one so young," remarked one woman to her husband.

It was by no means Tina's first party; she had thrown a number of them by then for other undergraduates. But it had the basics: a charming setting, a guest list of relative celebrities, a mild amount of drink. "Tina always had a very deep instinct of what celebrities were for," recalled her old boyfriend Carr. They were, ultimately, for her.

In this sense, the last festivity at Oxford was her Ur-party, the ancestor of future social contrivances that both soothed and fueled her in times of triumph as well as of despair. These events were often shrewdly thought out, a fine combination of exclusivity (the guest list) and informality (the setting and, often, the food). Through them, she would mold and stretch her career, in much the same way that her mother, Bettina, had deployed social occasions to further George Brown's career.

Tina had given long and serious thought to what she would do after Oxford. True, she had won a major award for *Under the Bamboo Tree,* but how likely was it, she worried, that she could earn a substantial living as a playwright? "You must understand Tina at Oxford. She loved literature, really loved it," said her friend Stephen Glover. "And she wanted to be a writer." On the other hand, he added, "she certainly had a fear of being poor—she told me that. She had a fear of being poor in her old age. She said she wanted to make money. Now of course you usually don't make money as a writer. . . ."

Tina knew that much. But she was so awfully good in that line of work, it seemed a shame to waste the talent. Besides, she had a flat, a walk-up near the British Museum, that was subsidized, she told a friend, by her parents. And so she began to write in earnest—freelancing for the *Sunday Times,* the *Sunday Telegraph Magazine,* and *Punch.* Her fears of poverty were staunched by meager fees and, as usual, by the help of concerned male friends.

The British newspaper columnist Alan Watkins recalled lunching with Auberon Waugh during this early phase of her career. When the check came, Watkins said, Waugh appealed to him, with a special favor in mind. "Do you want that receipt?" Waugh asked him. "Can I have it? I want to give it to Tina." The receipt was apparently designated to boost Tina's expense account with whatever publication happened to be buying her latest piece. "I was perfectly amenable," Watkins said. After all, "She was starting on her career." He never did find out if Waugh actually handed the receipt over to Tina.

So everyone in London who counted was helping her in one way or another. Everyone was beginning to know her. Or would soon enough.

In the fall of 1974, Ian Jack, who was then the head of the lifestyle section of the *Sunday Times* in London, was intrigued when his boss, the universally admired editor Harry Evans, who ran the paper, came to see him. By Evans's side was a pretty young woman with short blond hair. "A bright young person," said Evans, who wanted Jack to give her some work. It was not an unusual request from him. Jack asked the woman, whose name was Tina Brown, to take out a male escort from an escort service and then write about the experience, which she did. She wrote a few other pieces as well. They were all fine.

"Unknown to me, she was given a sum of money by Harry," Jack recalled, "to go to America." Unknown to just about everyone, she had been even more enterprising. A trip to the United States was by no means Tina's only goal. "She said she liked to hang around the corridor outside Harry's office, chatting him up a bit," recalled the gossip columnist Nigel Dempster, an early confidant.

"Harry was the sexy editor of all time, amazing in action," Tina instantly decided. "Whoosh, whoosh, whoosh. Writing headlines, cropping pictures, throwing things out." The young woman watched him awhile in perfect silence, cooling her heels outside his office. Harry kept her waiting, unremarkable for him, but an irresistible maneuver, as it turned out. "And I was gone, completely gone," Tina would declare years later. "He had these piercing blue eyes and when he turned around and looked at me, I was toast. And that was the end. It was love at first sight."

It was not wholly that for Harry. Nonetheless, with money from the *Sunday Times* and $500 she had received after winning a journalism award, Tina bought a plane ticket to New York. There she rented an apartment from a death therapist. It was an unusually limited and melancholy period in her life: her roommates were two Pan Am stewardesses. Christmas Eve found her watching television in the apartment in total solitude, police sirens howling out on the street and her only invitation "Cocktails at the Death 'n' Dying Center" from her landlady. From across the Atlantic, she pelted Harry with letters. "A love correspondence, really," her recipient would later describe it. "The letters were so marvelous, I fell in love." A few months later, he too found himself in New York, and they met for a drink. It was at this point, Tina decided, "He sort of looked at me in a different way."

Some of her articles from that period were also love letters of sorts, the best among them a charming sketch of the novelist and screenwriter Anita Loos. Inevitably entitled "Loos Talk," the article about the author of the classic stream-of-consciousness novel *Gentlemen Prefer Blondes,* then eighty-three and unstoppably voluble, was as bright and polished as the young woman who crafted it. Loos's "enormous gold spectacles" were "like the eyes of a praying mantis," Tina wrote. And yet she clearly loved her subject. The piece is a homage, in a way, not only to Loos but to the bygone spunky collectivism of a film industry from which both the old lady and Tina's father had sprung:

> *"Bylines don't matter a damn. They are all froth, honey," says Loos. "It's the work that matters. When I was writing for Irving Thalberg, I'd slave for three months on a script and find I'd been billed as a collaborator with three no-talent punks I'd never clapped eyes on. And so what?" she beamed. "We all had fun."*

For Tina, fun itself—the suppressed giggle—became the subject of many of her pieces. Indeed, it was inserted into each phrase, edging every judgment, italicizing each point of view. She wrote the obligatory sketches common to many new female writers: the Playboy Bunny ("The Bunny Recreation Room seems to be under a permanent pall of pre-menstrual tension. . . . To my right, Bunny Elaine, a strapping brunette with haunches like panniers, is eating a cheese sandwich"); the gossip columnists, the sexual/social climber.

There was so much she wished to say, and New York City, with its gratifying quickness and instant rewards for a certain directness of approach, willingly offered its unveiled face to the boldness of her gaze. After some pleading from Tina and the intervention of *New Yorker* critic Brendan Gill, who had befriended her, her path was smoothed. "Tina wants to know, who are these New York feminists? Talk to her," Gill begged the writer Nancy Friday. "I can do better than that," promised Friday. "I can give a party."

So the young Englishwoman was invited to a feminist gathering. Friday, involved even then in her literary sexual explorations, spent all day cooking for the assembled women, who unloaded their grievances until ten in the evening. "We all convened. Gabbed. Marvelous drinking and laughing," Friday said. Then the men arrived, and everyone ate. Tina took it all in. And that's how Harry and Harry's newspaper were ultimately rewarded with a long article by his favorite writer.

Headlined TOUGH AND LIBERATED, Tina's description of the feminist gathering proved less than flattering to the participants. "There's only one thing a man can do better than a woman and that's piss in the wind," boomed one guest, whom the writer described as a "roguish looking, six-foot brunette" with a "dark brown voice" and a remarkable capacity for tequila.

Incensed, Friday contacted Pat Kavanaugh, her London literary agent, who, it turned out, also represented Tina. "Pat wrote, 'Tina didn't mean it to sound the way it did. Harry made her do it,'" Friday would recollect. "I found it bitterly amusing. I thought, 'Well, that's feminism for you.'"

Indeed, after a while, many of Tina's observations, her references, appeared to be directed not so much at the reader as at the author herself. There were fewer and fewer collaborations with the nominal subjects of her pieces—Bianca Jagger, Jerry Hall, Erica Jong, Brigitte Bardot. Ultimately, Tina became the star of her own articles, either subversively or out in the open. In New Jersey, she got a job as a go-go dancer, which led to all sorts of revelations in print concerning her body and the uses she might put it to. "Big Ed says bring your bikini," Tina was warned before her audition. But that was the least of it. All sorts of provocative remarks about her physique ballooned from the mouths of the critical businessmen who owned the go-go club. It seems likely these were intended by the writer to penetrate other, more distant targets.

> *"You've got a great ass," he added kindly. "No really—we like our Show Go girls to be a little full." He turned on the radio. "Now let's see you move. . . .*
>
> *"Frankly, we could book you topless," said Angelo. "But your crotch swivel needs a lot of practice."*

In London, on assignment from *Punch,* Tina's tentative offer (unfulfilled) to pose as a nude model led to similar results. "There is of course the problem of your nose," murmurs one prospective employer, not wholly deterred. This was followed by further revelations.

> *"Well, well, well," marvelled the lupine Roger, massaging his left armpit and ruminatively plucking at the occasional tuft that constituted his beard. "This really is a turn-up for the book. We're always putting in ads for models but they rarely come in off the streets—aren't you a bit heavy in the stomach though?" He kneaded my midriff.*

In the autumn of 1975, practically a year to the day after Tina had turned up at the *Sunday Times,* Harry Evans offered another suggestion for "the bright young person" to the editor Ian Jack. "Perhaps you can put her on a contract." Jack agreed to the request. He was not completely astonished by Evans's interest in the young woman. Earlier, the great man had amazingly enough actually taken out his own pen and deleted some editing changes he considered superfluous that had altered (and—Evans believed—seriously damaged) Tina's copy. As the piece dealt, among other things, with a famous shirtmaker named Herbie Frogg, everyone thought it astonishing that Harry Evans, famous for wearing hideous black glasses and dull suits, would give a damn.

It wasn't only Harry who was impressed with Tina. She startled other editors as well—and not only with her work. Ian Jack's reaction on being asked to attend Tina's twenty-first birthday party at a wine bar in Notting Hill was initially one of weary reluctance: "Oh, who'd want to go to this snip of a thing's twenty-first birthday party?" Arriving late, he found the wine bar packed; among the guests were the journalist and future television broadcaster Clive James; Martin and Kingsley Amis; Tina's best friend, Sally Emerson; and her parents, George and Bettina. Subsequent parties that same year yielded the theater critic Kenneth Tynan, the actress Patricia Hodge, and, interestingly, the famous editor Harry Evans.

"Let's go to lunch," proposed Hunter Davies, who at the time was editing the woman's section of the *Sunday Times.* He had some story ideas for Tina.

"No," Tina parried. "You come to *my* place."

"It was totally professional, a lunch in her flat," Davies recalled. The table was set when he walked in, cutlery neatly framing the two plates. "But such a strange thing for a young woman to do. Such a strange thing for any freelancer to do."

Quite a number of top-ranking professionals found their way to Tina's flat her first year as a real journalist. When Alexander Chancellor was made editor of *The Spectator,* Auberon Waugh immediately importuned him: "You have to hire Tina Brown!"

"I really doubt it," Chancellor replied with some asperity. The two men were in the middle of what Chancellor described as "a long rather boozy lunch on Charlotte Street."

"Why don't we go see Tina now? We're right by her flat," Waugh persisted.

Tina wasn't there. Nonetheless, as Chancellor observed without surprise, "We got in somehow." The men climbed to the top floor of the small house and let themselves in. The flat was oddly decorated, infantilism against a backdrop of sexuality. "With rather unsophisticated bullfighting posters on the wall," Chancellor remembered. "A Teddy bear on the bed. A really sort of enormous expanse of mirror in the bedroom. On the side."

Eventually, Tina came to *The Spectator* to see Chancellor, who was not entirely impervious to her youthful freshness. "She was, you know, terribly, terribly keen and wanted to do anything, make tea, you know. She did, yes. She looked rather attractive, a blond Monica Lewinsky. I mean plump, buxom, and flirtatious in a perfectly nice sort of way. She behaved with total propriety. Sort of vital and attractive. And you know, she's intelligent, too. And quite fun to talk to. But I was sort of wary—such a wimp! I was sort of nervous about doing this job, anyway. I wanted to ease myself into this job gently. I don't know why I didn't hire her. She was just too much of a goer. I needed something a bit gentle. I wasn't ready for all this enthusiasm."

The next thing he knew, Chancellor got a letter from Waugh.

"Dear Alexander, you fool! You bloody fool! You've lost her!!" it read.

"And I *had,*" Chancellor said. "So that was it in a way."

Around this time, Tina popped up one weekend at King's College, Cambridge, which had recently gone co-ed—after 530 years without women. It was once again the *Sunday Times* that sent her, possibly because, as an alumna of an all-girls college, she would find the experience an exhilarating novelty. Apparently she did.

A day after her arrival, a pretty undergraduate named Sarah Papineau found Tina in the King's College kitchen making tea, and invited her to her room. It was a Saturday night and both women were dateless. Barely twenty at the time, Papineau didn't think of Tina as a journalist on assignment, but rather as the friend of a mutual friend—which she also was. She imagined that a few pictures would be taken of the new breed of college students for the *Sunday Times*. But she never thought she would be quoted by Tina. "She never told me she was writing a story," Papineau later said flatly (although at least one of her university friends said he was told by Tina that she was reporting). "I honestly thought I was entertaining *her*."

Besides, Papineau had other reasons for desiring company that night. She was feeling very low. Her beautiful boyfriend at the time, known for his compact rear end, was, after the first big rush, no longer overwhelming her with attention.

"Well, he's nice," Tina offered. She had already met the fellow in question earlier in the course of her research.

"I don't know," Papineau demurred pointedly.

"Well, where is he tonight?"

"I don't know," Papineau repeated miserably. "Off somewhere." Worse, she added, her inattentive boyfriend actually lived, as did she, in the newly co-ed college; she had absolutely no way of avoiding him. When he went out without her, she met him on the staircase. It was this series of grievances that the lovesick student poured out to Tina.

"Oh, I can't *believe* he behaves like this. How terrible," Tina said sympathetically.

A few weeks later—it was March 21, 1976—Papineau's mother, living in London, opened the *Sunday Times* and read a passage that distressed her. She brought it to her daughter's immediate attention that very morning. The passage seemed to be based on a depressing reality familiar to both women.

> There's the sad saga of—let's call her Jane—a second year brunette, and Julian, a third year economist whose honed buttocks are permanently encased in denim knickerbockers. Jane was a freshwoman when Julian swooped. She discovered Cambridge through his eyes and for a year they were joined at the hip. . . . "It's impossible to break up; I meet him everywhere," said Jane, following him out into the night.

"I think my mother was more humiliated than I was," Papineau said. Nonetheless, the experience had a lasting effect. Papineau never got over the fact that Tina "took advantage of my being upset." She has, she said, "never sat down with a journalist since then. I think Tina was just trying to impress Harry Evans with all that."

If so, there was every reason to believe she succeeded. Despite Evans's intervention, Tina never did get a permanent contract with the *Sunday Times*. Ian Jack was more than happy to write one up for her. But intricate newspaper union problems cropped up, thwarting the deal. Just a week before she was due to appear at her desk, Jack phoned Tina to tell her not to bother to show up for work.

The next thing he knew, Harry Evans requested his company for lunch at the Garrick Club. "I'm the editor of this bloody paper. You're to listen to me and to no one else," Evans warned his subordinate.

Astonished, Jack promised to hire Tina. "Harry, we'll correct all that," he hastily assured his boss. He was completely taken aback by his companion's mood, disconcerted by the prickly figure across the lunch table. This was not the Harry he knew. Harry was usually so genial. The editor of the *Sunday Times*, revered by his minions, admired even by his rivals, never talked this way.

"It's too late," Evans snapped. "She's going to do something else." His tone was desolate.

Chapter 3
Harry's Dilemma

When Tina quietly took up with Harold Matthew Evans—forty-six at the time and married, with three children—she was selecting for herself one of the most remarkable, successful, and attractive men in all of Britain, and very likely one of the most vulnerable as well. Evans in his days at the *Sunday Times* was quite simply the best, bravest newspaper editor that country had ever known. There was, and is, admittedly not much competition for that title. Britain is a nation unshielded by a First Amendment and its newspapers and book publishers are famously cowed by the faintest hint of a libel suit from the most culpable, hypocritical, and venal of plaintiffs, rendered mute by government officials armed with injunctions, mauled by the writs of the mighty and the rich. With its scattershot contempt citations, its myriad statutes and irascible judges restricting press disclosures, the country is a living example of what might easily have happened to freedom of speech in the United States had the founding fathers never amended the American Constitution.

Unarmed and unaided, Harry Evans repeatedly fought and challenged the prevailing powers of his time. In 1972, he led a daring press crusade against Distillers Ltd., the newspaper's single largest advertiser and the marketer of the drug thalidomide, a sedative once widely prescribed which was subsequently found to cause hideous birth defects among the newborn children of mothers who had taken the drug. What the newspaper wanted, as it made clear from the start when it interviewed dozens of the afflicted families all over Britain, was a decent amount of money for the young victims. OUR THALIDOMIDE CHILDREN: A CAUSE FOR NATIONAL SHAME, read the headline. The OUR that modified the subject was Evans's own inspiration; he wanted the reading public to feel a shared sense of responsibility for the tragedy. This banner headline was spread across the top of the opening shot in a *Sunday Times* series on the damaged children. "In a future article the *Sunday Times* will trace how the tragedy occurred." The newspaper, in other words, was announcing it wasn't content with merely publishing stories of afflicted children; it wished to reconstruct the history of the drug.

As might have been expected, however, this promised investigative article was stopped dead—and Distillers withdrew £600,000 worth of advertising from the newspaper. "In the case of the thalidomide tragedy, the British laws of contempt said that as soon as the parents sued the makers of the drug, an automatic silence on public discussion about who was to blame went into effect," Evans would later recall with considerable disgust. "We discovered we were hitting a brick wall. And the brick wall was the legal system in England, which had no constitutional provisions for a free press." Evans was fond of calling the British institution "a half-free press." He was overcome with envy of the American judicial system, where "a prior restraint is unthinkable"—and for good reason. The thalidomide marketer immediately appealed to Britain's attorney general and an injunction was issued, successfully stopping the newspaper from publishing any articles detailing how the dangerous drug came to be made and then widely distributed to expectant mothers. Indeed, before publishing the first heartbreaking article on thalidomide, Evans wondered if he would be arrested, a fate he half welcomed. "I'll go to jail, that's what I'll do," he confided to a reporter. "Bloody hell, it'd be worth it."

The thalidomide case wound its way to the House of Lords (where the newspaper lost its case), then moved on, at Evans's urging, to the European Commission of Human Rights, and then all the way up to the European Court in Strasbourg. A draft of the banned *Sunday Times* exposé on the crippling drug was attached to the commission's decision, which upheld the right of the newspaper "to clarify matters of great importance. . . ." Thus, the investigative piece became at long last publishable. In 1977, five years after that first article appeared, the campaigning newspaper did in fact tell its readers in detail how thalidomide had ruined some of their lives. After a lot of pressure from the American press, a total of £32 million—£27 million from Distillers and £5 million from the British government—was ultimately distributed to the young victims. It wasn't nearly enough, but it was ten times what the children had first been offered.

However unequal the powers of the drug manufacturer and the government that had tried to prevent him from publishing, Evans was more than a match for them both. Behind the scenes, he had scurried around to members of Parliament, politicians who might push his crusade forward, even when it seemed to be at its weakest. Evans was mildly left wing in those days, a parvenu from the impoverished North of England with a large chip on his shoulder and a grudge against the upper crust; but that didn't stop him from currying favor with the reigning Conservatives. One of those he approached was Dr. Thomas Stuttaford, a Tory politician and a physician, who found the moral circumstances of the crusade compelling. He immediately buttonholed his party's prime minister, Ted Heath. Stuttaford's arguments to Heath were chosen selectively: purely political, and therefore much more persuasive.

"This has caught the public's imagination," he warned the prime minister. "We are rapidly losing our appeal to the general public."

Heath, the doctor observed, wasn't in the least interested. "This is just a problem between the drug company and the *Sunday Times,*" he retorted. "And I don't care to be particularly involved."

But here Heath underestimated the moral fervor of some of his own supporters. The British public, Stuttaford insisted, "had taken to their hearts these little stumpy disabled children." If the prime minister wasn't going to give them government backing, Stuttaford would tell his colleagues "to vote everything down until we got what we needed." After Heath capitulated and a financial victory for the thalidomide families was announced, Stuttaford sent the prime minister a letter: "Dear Prime Minister," it read, "I hope you noted, it was the lead item on the evening news."

The *Sunday Times* of the 1970s, in other words, became under Evans an exciting force for social and political change, much like *The Washington Post* of that same era under Benjamin Bradlee. The *Sunday Times* belonged to the talented elite, not the social elite, like its boring adopted brother, *The Times,* which was the demure and sober paper of record. The *Sunday Times* was simply the paper everyone wanted to work for. Lord Snowdon himself, onetime husband of Princess Margaret, had been commissioned to refurbish an old building for the *Sunday Times,* and he fashioned a semicircular wrought-iron well around the central balcony of the building.

Both papers were owned by Lord Thomson, a genial Canadian in

Coke-bottle glasses. He was the most docile and pliant of proprietors, never meddling in editorial content, having been nudged by Denis Hamilton, editor in chief of the two publications, into what Harry described as "the right relationship." Thomson's two papers were actually rivals, always separate, each disapproving and disdainful of the other. They were even housed in adjoining buildings on Gray's Inn Road with a bridge connecting the two. Crossing the bridge into *The Times* was a disturbing experience for reporters from the rival newspaper. "You really thought you were going into East Berlin," recalled one old *Sunday Times* man.

The two newspapers were also widely divergent in popularity and profit-making ability. *The Times* was a decided money loser. The *Sunday Times* could have made a huge profit—but somehow didn't. By 1976, its circulation reached 1.5 million. The *Sunday Times Magazine,* always a pampered and brilliant section of the paper, became famous for its extravagances as well as its literary coups. "We had our pick of the world's writers and the world's photographers," one of its editors recalled. "You know we could get Gore Vidal. Get Karsh out of Ottawa, do an interview with Indira Gandhi. Get Norman Mailer. V. S. Naipaul. They could do wonderful things. I liked that. Harry thought this was out of control."

Evans preferred pouring money into major purchases of books by famous people, which would then be serialized—an idea other British newspapers soon copied—and into investigative reporting. "Whatever story was in the works, we could do it bigger and better than anyone else," a *Sunday Times* newspaper executive would later recall. "It was true. We were the top paper in the world. This created terrific espirit de corps."

Unlike the patrician Bostonian Bradlee, however, whose reporters Carl Bernstein and Bob Woodward more or less stumbled into the devastating presidential scandal that would be called Watergate, exposing iniquities was what Evans set out to do from the start. He had been born far enough outside the establishment to see its moral limitations as well as its strategic weaknesses. When he first arrived at the *Sunday Times* in 1966, it was, for all its strengths, a stuffy place—so stuffy that people addressed each other in the newsroom by the military titles they had held while doing national service. It was not uncommon to send copy over to Major Murphy or Captain Dow or Chief Petty Officer Darker. The top editor was called Brigadier Hamilton.

Under Evans, those military titles evaporated along with so much else. In fact, he was something most big-city reporters had never seen: a true provincial. "Evans arrived wearing a slug gray raincoat and what looked like an army suit," Murray Sayle, a longtime journalist, recalled of his first day at the *Sunday Times*. Soon, a lot of lower-middle-class reporters with funny accents and inexpensive educations from Britain's industrial North found their way into the newsroom, many of them his former colleagues from small-town newspapers. They had a different agenda. There was nothing accidental about his newspaper's targets, nothing happenstance about its aims. Big companies, unnecessary tragedy, big government, big scandal—those were Evans's prey. He had limited weapons and unlimited ambition, and he would stand Britain, the old Britain of official secrets and immutable classes, on its head. For a time.

Evans built up and reorganized the newspaper's investigative team, which was called "Insight." There were core groups, four people in each group on Insight; but at any given moment, five to eighteen journalists might be working on the same story. These stories could easily take from four to six months to complete, sometimes even longer, and they were free from interference by the well-schooled proprietor, Thomson, or indeed anyone outside the investigative team itself. Evans boasted of having carte blanche, almost. "One thing [was] made clear to me when I took over," he said. " 'You're going to be free to write, investigate what you like. But you're never going to be free to attack the royal family.' " Harry didn't need the royal family. He was already in paradise, attacking everyone else, unhindered, untouchable.

Under Evans's aegis, the *Sunday Times* launched a famous series on the mole Kim Philby, a high-level operative in the British Secret Intelligence Service MI6 who, as it would eventually be revealed, secretly worked for the Soviet Union. (Philby also happened to be, to the eternal sorrow of the United States, the British liaison officer with the CIA.) Evans's journalists even followed the spy to Moscow after Philby defected and interviewed him there. These coups were not universally well received. In the British government, there were those who suggested that in tracing the trajectory of Philby's treacherous career among credulous associates, the newspaper had "aided the enemy." Among those most incensed was George Brown, no relation to Tina but at one point Prime Minister Harold Wilson's foreign secretary. Tipsy one night at a party (or so word around the *Sunday Times* had it), the foreign secretary had actually gone up to the proprietor of the *Sunday Times* and "grabbed him by the collar."

"You've got to stop these young Commies at *The Sunday Times* from destroying the secret service," Brown informed Thomson, "or I will have your peerage taken away!"

"Can he really do that?" wondered Thomson the next day. On being assured Brown could not, Thomson said, "Well, that's okay, then." The Philby series continued: eighteen journalists resumed their work.

Most clever of all, the *Sunday Times* managed to recoup a lot of the costs of its investigations by turning Insight's more compelling stories into quickie best-sellers. This would become a fairly diplomatic move since, it was observed, "Harry threw lots and lots of money at those stories. Oh, untold millions of pounds." So it made sense for Evans to give reporters plenty of time off to write best-selling books, whose authors shared handsomely in the profits along with the paper. "It got to the point," a veteran Insight journalist would later say, "that no one was particularly interested in pursuing an investigation *unless* there was a book deal attached." The *Sunday Times* Insight team, for example, produced a major investigation of the DC-10 aircraft that crashed near Paris in 1974. Subsequently, a number of the journalists involved produced a book that analyzed the plane's design defects.

Of course, there were penalties to be paid for such daring. The newspaper braved a total of 250 libel suits (and won 249 of them). The annual profits of the *Sunday Times* were sometimes nonexistent, depleted, in part, by the money invested in Insight, serialized memoirs, and other sections of the paper; in even greater measure, by recalcitrant unions. One editor who was about to take over the *Sunday Times Magazine* was informed by his predecessor, "There is quite a lot of overmatter"—by which he meant articles paid for but unlikely to be published. As it turned out, the cost of the "overmatter" amounted to £70,000, a sizable sum in those days.

From time to time, Evans would tell his personal assistant George Darby, "I don't know how long Roy Thomson will keep this going, you know. We lost three hundred thousand pounds last year." Here Evans was referring to various costly industrial disputes which, year after year, were causing no end of havoc. And yet the possibility that the newspaper might be shut down because of wildly profligate union intransigence never alarmed him enough, apparently, to impose a strict cost-cutting regime on his end of the paper. "No one at the top ever asked him to do so, so why would he?" explained a friend. The journalism was all that counted in Harry's eyes. "You could say it's

JUDY BACHRACH

the Boy Scout in me," he said years ago. "I'm told I regard truth as a religion. That's right."

That was in some measure accurate. Evans possessed a degree of innocence that was strange and even unsettling in a middle-aged editor of one of the best and biggest newspapers in the world. "It was a combination of intellectual ferment with Harry's almost naïveté—'naive' is the word I would use," his old friend and subordinate Magnus Linklater would later recall. Oxford-educated journalists watched, startled, as Evans inquired of the ladies who pushed tea carts through the building about certain stories and whether or not they offended the sensibilities of the average reader. A reader like, say, Harry Evans himself. Evans, the Eton-educated Linklater decided, was "genuinely the man in the street." All about him were chatty, beautifully educated journalists, "who used to talk at an intellectual level which was sometimes quite formidable. And which Harry, frankly, very often didn't take part in. But he had the ability to cut through it and bring it all down to earth."

And yet this, his subordinates decided, was part of what made Evans a truly brilliant editor—the conviction that the opinions of ordinary people were vital to the direction of a newspaper; that the newspaper, in fact, had a duty to appeal to the powerless.

Even after disposing of the slug gray raincoat, Evans dressed lower middle class, his small, spare body packed inside dull, unassuming gray suits and white shirts, his delicate face blocked by duck black glasses as heavy and square as those sported by Michael Caine in *The Ipcress File*. *"Très ordinaire"* was the verdict of his longtime subordinate George Darby. Evans played Ping-Pong with such proficiency that guests at his "big bourgeois house in Highgate" were often led to the table tennis room specially built to accommodate this passion. There Evans, armed only with a pair of dinner plates instead of a paddle (at least on the evenings when he felt charitably inclined toward the less expert among his guests), would nonetheless manage to trounce them. Ping-Pong, however, was deemed a lower-class sport.

With his wife, Enid, a schoolteacher of some distinction, Evans lived in the Holly Lodge Estates, an enormous Victorian collection of neo-Tudor houses built in the 1900s. They had married in August 1953, just months before Tina Brown was born. Harry's three children, Ruth, Kate, and Michael, went to local schools. "A perfectly nice woman," was the general verdict on Enid, "natural and unpretentious," intelligent and willful. She was a devout believer in the much flawed but free National Health Service. Harry, more mal-

50

leable, practical, and easier to sway, was of a decidedly less ideological bent.

Nonetheless, he clearly enjoyed the way Enid's brain worked. "Enid found that piece of yours every interesting," was a frequent compliment paid by the boss to his staffers. He told intimates he had stayed in the provinces largely because Enid was pursuing a career in education—and indeed, his wife loved discussing the subject with friends. She was earnest and high-minded, although these qualities were frequently undervalued by her husband's crowd. "While a woman of sterling worth, no Gina Lollobrigida, or even Germaine Greer on a good day," was how she was characterized by one friend. "I seem to recall glasses and severe straight hair."

Within this domestic setting, there was clearly some impatience on Harry's part—an itchiness that appeared tied, oddly, to his naïveté. "Harry was I believe building up in those years a lust for the high life, which eventually had to burst out in some Tina or other," remarked a friend. Evans spoke wistfully about younger women and seemed to entertain the almost magical belief that in a big-time city newspaper he would find swift resolution to a lot of his personal problems. This was evident from the start, even before he arrived at the *Sunday Times*. When the writer Hunter Davies, an old friend from the industrial North of England, asked Evans why he had decided to leave the area and try his luck on a newspaper in the capital—Davies thought the move would be a disaster—a sudden silence descended on the conversation. Evans, he recalled, said nothing, but simply wrote with his finger on the dusty hood of a car parked nearby. When Davies looked down, he saw scrawled just one word—a joke very likely, he decided:

"SEX."

Once ensconced at the *Sunday Times*, the columnist Philip Oakes recalled, Evans was renowned for "being frightfully envious of other people's sex lives. He always thought they had a far, far more wonderful time than he did—which was true, I'm afraid." Oakes himself was one of those enjoying himself. "I was then involved with a gorgeous girl," he said. "Harry was absolutely beside himself, tremendously admiring, quite sort of covetous." In fact, Evans couldn't seem to shake the notion that everything revolved around sex. A particularly obtuse Harold Pinter play, he insisted to a friend, "is all about sex! All about sex! Isn't it?" Didn't it contain a reference to a London street on which stood the Post Office Tower? And wasn't the Post Office Tower a "penile" building?

With an elderly woman present in his corner office, Evans was once observed gazing out the window, transfixed by the vision down below of an enormous pile driver pounding away at a heap of rocks. "C'mon over, c'mon! Look at this!" he called to some luckless subordinate, who also happened to be present along with the old lady. "Doesn't that remind you of something?" He pointed to the pile driver.

Encountering a totally blank expression, Evans snapped impatiently: "Sex!"

To the great relief of the subordinate, it turned out that the old lady was stone-deaf.

Mixed in with Evans's innocence, however, was a high degree of cunning, which he usually kept under wraps. He worked often and best on two levels: the journalistic level, big splashes on contentious subjects that brought down the wrath of the establishment; and the political/social level, which allowed him to mix with the cream of the very establishment his newspaper was ostensibly attacking. He was equally comfortable with both the front row and backstage, the sunlight and the shadows. Physically, he was unprepossessing, which was useful. He was a small, pale man, about five feet seven inches (although, true to his nature, in his autobiography he would unblushingly add an inch more), with dark hair slicked back in uncompromising severity; light, deep-set eyes fringed by improbably long lashes; and a fine thin nose that skewed slightly to the right. In photographs, this face was frankly open, secure in its tranquil virility. Up close, Evans was almost feminine in the delicate molding of his features, as jittery and deceptively frail in appearance as a doomed Puccini heroine—and every bit as impassioned. Women found him devastating.

"It's that damned intensity that makes you want to take him to bed," one woman declared. "That, and the longing to educate him."

Even in his early days, Evans possessed lethal charm and the wit to use it unsparingly. Tea cart ladies and the man on the street were by no means his only targets: two Labour chancellors of the exchequer, Roy Jenkins and Denis Healey; the American secretary of state Henry Kissinger (whose memoirs Harry bought, edited, and according to two former staffers for the *Sunday Times,* heavily rewrote for serialization); the actor Richard Attenborough, who bent his ear; a celebrated big-city American newspaper editor—they were all Evans's allies, his confidants, and occasionally his backers. Because of him, the word "glamour" was transmuted into a verb in the newsroom.

"Oh my God, Harry's being glamoured again!" reporters would tell each other every time Evans fell for another celebrity. This began to occur with increasing frequency. When Evans invited Kissinger to lunch at the newspaper, a waggish editor posted on the bulletin board a projected menu for the two friends, which included the dish *Foie de Paysan Mekong.*

"Harry's face," one of his journalists was overheard to remark, "always bears the imprint of the last bum he kissed."

Of course, there were some who fully understood why this socialist-bred boy from Manchester felt the pull, the whirl of the center. "He loved power. He loved cocktail parties and all that," Evans's old friend and colleague Don Berry observed. "It was another thrilling bit of life that opened up to him. He wanted to know how government worked." He wanted, in fact, thought Berry and others on the staff, to be a bit *too* close to power to suit his friends. "Harry helped Henry Kissinger with his book," Berry said. "I thought he was wrong about that. I didn't think he should get that close to somebody like that. I thought he should have kept at arm's length from people like that."

Sometimes, as in the thalidomide crusade, where ethical issues were paramount, Evans's dual approach to personal and professional success was applauded because it promoted publication of a vital piece of journalism. But there were those who would later be mildly critical of some aspects of a few investigations. It was observed, for example, by the former *Sunday Times* reporter Phillip Knightley, who had worked on the story of Kim Philby, that although the British intelligence service claimed to be shocked and horrified by the *Sunday Times* exposé of the notorious defector and how he succeeded in conning his fellow spies on two continents, the highest echelons of the newspaper had, in fact, made a secret deal with the British government.

Indeed, far from being disgusted by the revelations of the *Sunday Times,* the Secret Intelligence Service (SIS) knew beforehand what to expect in its pages every week, according to Knightley; in fact, the reporters' telephones were bugged. Evans himself was ordered to meet with a go-between, who reported back, as Harry would discover only years later, to the British spy agency. There was some fear on the part of Evans's boss, editor in chief Denis Hamilton, that publication of the story would help the Russians. In vain did Harry argue that Moscow already knew the Philby story, thanks to the traitor himself. So by that time did British intelligence sources. There had been a "terrific cover-up," Evans told his superior.

Afraid of imperiling the lives of intelligence officers, Hamilton met with the Labour prime minister, Harold Wilson. A Foreign Office bigwig, Sir Denis Greenhill, was deputized to act as liaison between the newspaper and the spy agency. Violently opposed though he was to allowing a huge newspaper inquiry into Philby's life, Greenhill reluctantly consented to negotiate secretly with its scrappy editor, Harold Evans. "Will you let them see a draft to make sure we don't put anyone at risk? All I've said is that you will consider representations," Hamilton told Evans. Harry agreed. "None of us wanted to risk anyone's life by some unwitting reference," he later wrote in his memoirs. He was ordered to "say nothing to anyone."

Moreover, the *Sunday Times*'s famous thalidomide crusade contained within it at least one element that might give serious pause to a number of newspaper journalists in the United States: "the inconvenient fact that we had come to thalidomide scandal via what critics of the press call checkbook journalism," as Knightley wrote in his newspaper memoirs. With some reluctance, Harry agreed to the demands of two sources, a leading lawyer and a pharmacologist who wanted to be paid for their help. The pharmacologist, who had access to a lot of important internal documents on thalidomide and ostensibly the ability to interpret them, received £8,000 (about $20,000 in those days). "Nothing improper about it, it was not stuff you could get any other way," Insight deputy editor Bruce Page would later insist, and in this he was seconded by Knightley, who called it "a logical and defensible position . . . some information can only be had for cash." In Britain, payment of valuable sources is pretty much rampant; and the newspaper felt it could justify its position because how, without help, could it possibly hope to understand thousands of complex scientific documents? But it was not an easy area. And to make matters worse, Page would later recall, the article had to be reworked because "the expert got it wrong . . . it was complete bullshit."

The sort of journalism that Evans was part of then was, for all its virtues, its breadth of coverage and its dazzle, in certain ways different from the kind encountered on some better American newspapers. It was troubling to Knightley that he, for one, didn't learn of his newspaper's quiet accommodation with the British government on the Philby exposé until fifteen years after its publication when he read Evans's memoirs. "And what about our readers?" the investigative journalist wrote. "Shouldn't we have told them at the time?" Years later, Harry himself would say of the Philby investigation, "A lot of things were going on in the background between the Service and others I'm still not entirely clear about. But it was a brilliant success." In Evans himself, there appears to have been an impatience with the constraints imposed on him by his own rigidly corseted society. "The U.S. has always been a magnet; in my case, for the freedom," he once said.

But at that moment, in the nervous and uncertain Britain of the late sixties and seventies, Evans was pursuing perhaps the only kind of journalism that was practicable. And he produced, after all, what even former friends called "the best newspaper in England," a newspaper with "editorial integrity, with a real sense of its independence." He managed to do this despite his limitations, which were sizable. As one old *Sunday Times* staffer observed, "He didn't read, you know. He wasn't educated. He hadn't read Proust, say. He wouldn't know the books. Books on politics, yes, he would read that. But not Updike."

However, he was surrounded by admirers, people who understood their boss hadn't had the advantages of many of his subordinates. And he was a quick study. It was an era when everything and everyone—the dashing little *Sunday Times* editor in his bad suits included—was on the cusp of change. Harold Evans was way ahead of his time and his country, but he was also a prisoner of both. He was mordantly suspicious of and yet enthralled by power and the people who had claimed it. He was captivated, as those born luckier and wealthier generally are not, by celebrity. "We're a very elitist and aristocratic society," he once said. "My father used to say that knowledge is something you have to wrest from the ruling classes."

Which Evans did.

Born in a depressed area of Manchester on June 28, 1928, Harold was the eldest of four sons of Frederick Albert Evans and his wife, Mary Hannah Haselum Evans. Early on, he received the nickname "Posh" from his schoolmates, largely, he believed, because of the combined steady incomes of his parents, which were lofty enough (compared, at least, to those of their neighbors) to allow for the purchase of a family car. Frederick Evans was a train driver who had left school at thirteen to work in a foundry. He was used to getting up at two or three in the morning, used to working for long stretches at a time away from home, and yet, as his eldest son swiftly realized, "He exulted in his work." Nonetheless, he wasn't about to allow his sons to follow in his footsteps, and all the family's efforts were devoted to this particular goal. Harry's mother, who had left school at an even younger age to work in a cotton mill, eventually set up a small grocery store, which began by selling sweets and ice cream out of the front room of their terraced house.

In fact, the elder Evanses may be said to have come up in the world, especially when compared to their own antecedents, some of whom, Tina would later indicate to a friend, may have been Jewish. Harry's parents at least could read and write. Harry's paternal grandfather, a railway plate layer, was capable of writing only his own name. After he became famous, Harry was made vividly aware of the irony in all this by his thoughtful father, whom he admired without reservation. "A damn sight better man than I am," he would recall shortly after Frederick's death, perhaps with a twinge of guilt, because certain traumatic domestic changes had altered his own life.

By the time he was fifteen, Harry had finished high school. He had failed the all-important eleven-plus exam, an arbitrary test which in its day pushed promising students along a superior academic fast track into what were called grammar schools ("for real snobs," Harry would insist, although two of his younger brothers vanquished the exams), and was supposed to weed out inferior minds. However, he did pass another exam, allowing him to enter St. Mary's central school in Manchester, which overlooked the very railway sheds where his father worked. But he was an indifferent student. "Academically," a friend once wrote, "he still regarded himself as a loser."

Nonetheless, he loved school. He got to wear a regulation blazer—"the important part," he felt back then. And just as delightful: he learned Shakespeare, thanks to an excellent headmaster—specifically, *As You Like It* and *Midsummer Night's Dream*. And so he received, despite his early failings and those of the British educational system, the very gifts that had eluded his father and grandfather.

He was determined to become a writer, even going so far as to enter business school for a year to learn shorthand because he had heard, somewhere or other, that's what you needed to "get on" as a reporter. It was, in fact, this skill that allowed Harry at sixteen to join the staff of the *Ashton-under-Lyne Reporter,* housed at the time in a sooty redbrick building on a pleasant cobblestone square in the center of town. Opposite the newspaper building was the town hall, and behind it was a coroner's office. Each day, Harry went up the stairs in the back to the clanky noise of linotype machines and the smell of damp paper and ink. There he sat in the reporter's room; it had a telephone box in the middle. He covered inquests, council meetings, the courts, and earned exactly £1 a week, writing up to eleven columns for the paper.

Called up at eighteen to perform his national service in the Royal Air Force, he became even more enterprising. He founded a newspaper—the *Flying School Review,* it was called—and rushed out to sell the first copies, which boasted a cover with a lot of aircraft on it.

"Bugger off," he was told by annoyed servicemen. "Christ almighty, we're looking at fucking airplanes all the fucking time—and you put them on your fucking cover."

Harry's second issue of the *Flying School Review* also featured a lot of aircraft—next to the spectacularly lush and bosomy figure of the film star Diana Dors, naked except for a strategically placed fur muff. It was a complete sellout.

But it was in the RAF, too, that he learned what his next step in life would be. For the first time, he was among men who had gone to university. Without a degree, he decided, he could go nowhere. He enrolled in a brief course on "The Rights of Man." It was the beginning, he felt, of his true calling: journalism with a purpose.

He would be twenty-one before he entered Durham University, for him an inspired choice. The town of Durham itself had been a center of learning in Saxon times; it boasted a calm, beautiful cathedral, which Harry loved, and its university was renowned for its medieval buildings, long spiral staircases, an Oxford-style collegiate system, and a staunchly middle-class student body—composed largely of prosperous students who had failed to get into Oxford or Cambridge. But what the institution lacked in cachet, it more than made up for in other ways. Harry received his degree in politics and economics. "It was the turning point of my life," he would later recollect.

Durham was also where Harry met Enid, then a young biology student from Liverpool, whom he married while still in college. She was a small, plain girl of some ambition, very intelligent and down-to-earth. The two took long walks along the moors during the early days. "I used to chase Enid up the stairs," was how Harry described their courtship to friends, and it always seemed to these fellow northerners—the journalists and their wives who got to know the couple in the grim industrial towns of Manchester and then Darlington— that the two were, all things considered, pretty well suited. Enid was, almost everyone who knew her agreed, a kind woman, who invariably made younger newspaper staffers feel welcome. At their apartment in an old suburban house, the couple threw a strawberries-and-champagne party. It was during the course of this gala that

Harry revealed his interesting method for refueling his astonishingly high level of energy. "I take a cold bath every morning," he would explain.

On the other hand, despite the amusement value of such irrepressible confidences, Harry was "slightly mysterious really," his old friend John Tisdall noted. Like Evans, Tisdall's first big job was on the *Manchester Evening News,* only Harry was of the two the more senior. He was an assistant to the editor and the editorial writer, with an office right next to the editor himself. It was observed that he didn't mill around with most people, but kept himself always slightly aloof. Harry did, however, make time for television, which was auditioning a lot of northern journalists and allowing them basically as much time as they wished on the air.

Evans took to television effortlessly and instantly. He could talk on anything at all, practically without drawing breath, and so it came as no surprise that he was invited by Granada Television to discuss the problems of the city of Liverpool. "This really consisted of talking endlessly for an hour and a half, in a very limited range," it was drily noted. "Harry Evans talks endlessly."

In 1963, he was made editor in chief of the *Northern Echo,* published in the depressingly small and unappealing Quaker market town of Darlington (pop. 80,000), which the skimpy publication itself very much resembled. The morning newspaper was filled with dark cramped copy, dull news, indifferent photography, and its bored and listless staffers numbered around fifty. Darlington had clusters of fine old buildings from the Victorian era, a malodorous river called the Tees, and not much else.

The *Northern Echo* considered it "the main hub of the northeast region" because of its position on the main railway line, but this was a dismal boast. Everything was dying in the Northeast of England in the sixties: heavy industry, steel, shipbuilding, coal mining. Harry Evans, on the other hand, was thirty-five years old and in a hurry. "He instantly became the best-known newspaper editor outside London," as it transpired. Amused staffers watched as their editor drove "to Newcastle and Middlesborough to appear on some rinky-dink late night show watched by ten people. Tyne-Tees Television. That sort of stuff."

Evans hired a young woman named Mary Redcliffe as a weekly columnist, and she promptly disrupted the equanimity of local Anglican bishops and other moral arbiters by writing about abortion and contraception, as well as the interesting divorce of the Duchess of Argyll, who had had oral sex with one of her partners—as a famous photograph introduced at her trial purported to show. "I'd better ask Enid about that—hang on," Harry ordered Redcliffe when she phoned in her copy. A few minutes later, he came back to the phone. "Enid says you're right to write about it."

"One of Harry's aims was sort of to put new life into this region, make it dynamic, all that kind of thing. He thought a newspaper could do that, absolutely," Don Berry, Evans's colleague on two successive newspapers, would later recall. Almost instantly Evans began a campaign. The horrible odor on the Tees River emanated, it turned out, from a group of chemical factories along its banks. It became known, thanks to Evans and his inventive headlines, as the "Tees-Side Smell." As his subordinates looked on amazed, their new editor announced his intention to make the factory owner, Imperial Chemical Industries (ICI), one of Britain's mightiest corporations and a major local employer, responsible for cleaning up the fumes.

"George," Evans ordered a bewildered middle-aged photographer on his staff, "I want you to take a picture of the Tees-Side Smell."

"That's done it. I knew he was a funny bird. Now he wants me to take a picture of a *smell*," muttered the photographer. As it happened, however, capturing that odor was entirely feasible. The terrible smell was accompanied by a thick haze, visible from just one locale, a village green Evans had recently discovered. "That picture became part of the campaign, and we used to run these stories all the time with a little logo, 'TEES-SIDE SMELL,' " Berry would later explain.

Everything began to change at the *Northern Echo* under Evans. There was a complete redesign of the paper; the headline faces, entirely Gothic when Harry arrived, abruptly dropped their Teutonic masks. A new newspaper logo of an arrow appeared ("a thrusting urgent logo," as one journalist described it), its point hitting home. Circulation rose to over 100,000. "He was the first person to make me think that working on a newspaper was exciting—I mean, everyone who worked on the *Northern Echo* just felt they were part of this wonderful elite," said the writer Philip Norman, describing his early years working for Evans.

One thing particularly struck the young reporter. In 1966, Norman was assigned to review some local theater production, and apparently his criticisms landed too close to the mark. Evans received a bitter diatribe from the theater about the new reviewer.

"I see nothing wrong with our critic complaining that you are too expensive and your audience too noisy," Evans wrote back. Norman, a recent refugee from a "knocked-out rubbishy little newspaper" in the same small town, was stunned to receive a copy of that letter, dazed even more by the stalwart defense it contained from his hero. "It was amazing to think that your editor who was so big time was behind you in this, that he would defend you."

Moreover, this champion of the underdog was by no means done with crusading. In a burst of inspiration, he decided to take up the cause of one Timothy Evans, no relation, but a Londoner who had been convicted of murder and hanged in the early fifties—wrongly, as it turned out from the *Northern Echo* stories. Although the Timothy Evans case was to become one of the most famous British miscarriages of justice of all time, reporters were puzzled but amused by the impassioned series exonerating a long-dead man in another city. "This all happened in West London and whatever the hell it had to do with a Quaker town in the Northeast, nobody could fathom, you know," one *Northern Echo* colleague would later remark.

Nonetheless, the series on the martyred Londoner was an instant success, not least in London itself. And perhaps after all, this was the real bull's-eye Evans had been trying to hit when he launched his crusade. In 1966, he received a welcome call from a deeply impressed Denis Hamilton (or "Brigadier Hamilton," as he was known at the *Sunday Times* since that was the rank held under Field Marshal Montgomery during World War II). Born a northerner, the newspaper's editor in chief was more likely than anyone else on the venerable *Sunday Times* to read a publication as small and relatively inconsequential as the *Northern Echo*. He was a tall, handsome man, mustachioed, quiet, very low-key. "Hamilton used to go home on Friday night and read the paper Sunday morning, if he read it at all," one old hand remembered.

"Harry was hired by Denis to sort off kick the shit out of it basically, and take it somewhere else—Denis knew not where," one of Harry's allies said of his appointment. "But obviously Denis was not the sort of man who was comfortable with the sixties. He could see the sixties happening all around him—and there he was with his toothbrush mustache and his restrained manner and military bearing."

One year later, Hamilton appointed Evans editor of the *Sunday Times,* much to the surprise of older men with far more experience on upscale London newspapers who considered the new hire "a pushy provincial journalist." Nor were they alone in their reservations. Hamilton himself eventually came to entertain serious doubts about his choice. "Harold," as the older man called him, was in Hamilton's view a needy character, "emotional and highly strung." He was someone who required "constant counsel and comfort," an editor who had to be backed by "a stronger figure to see that his talents were not wrecked by his misjudgments." He was also, the older man decided, "the world's worst recruiter." Equally appalling, Hamilton wrote in his memoirs, was Harry's shameless flamboyance and relentless self-promotion. "I shunned publicity, never having liked it. . . . Harold Evans by contrast revelled in it and it got to the point where, without my permission, he started appearing on television chat shows, which I had to stop because I thought it totally improper for the editor of the *Sunday Times* to be seen there or on quiz programmes. This great weakness of his for self-projection continued. . . ." Still, Hamilton conceded, "When all was said and done, Harold proved himself an editor with immense flair . . . Harold's strength was his brilliance as a journalist. . . ."

And there was certainly a lot to admire about Evans. Among other things, he did precisely what he was supposed to do. He kicked the shit out of the newspaper—out of staid old British journalism in general, for that matter. He had what his former friend Magnus Linklater called "a quicksilver mind." Like Evans himself, it was never still. With a group of subordinates he wrote a book on his newest love, skiing, which was subsequently turned into a television series. He also produced a style book for newspapers, *Editing and Design,* which, although by no means as good (or, alas, as concise) as E. B. White's tract on writing, became a classic—and ultimately the first of a five-part Evans series on all aspects of journalism, including layout. In the office, he worked ceaselessly, helping to rewrite a reporter's stories, always at the last minute. He was an impatient typist, who could never be bothered to hit the carriage return all the way, so stories came out, one old friend recalled, looking "like long waves of rats' tails."

"Harry is very much a hands-on editor. He would always be in the composing room in legendary shirtsleeves on Saturday nights, keeping a general eye on things, making constructive suggestions—like leave out a purple passage or cut down the photo," a former associate recalled. "Harry's own northern proletarian origins, obvious in his speech, easy manner, and the presence of many Australians, Irish, and Scottish persons etc., made his *Sunday Times.*" Invariably upbeat, he kept coming up with ideas, inspiring certain journalists, sending congratulatory notes to others—some so valued that their recipients hold on to them to this day. He was manic with energy, rarely to be found in his office.

"Getting face time with Harry was rather difficult," a longtime acquaintance recalled. "Harry got into his head that male urinary problems were caused by pissing too quickly. So it was his idea to have a really long slo-o-o-w piss and often he would do this while reading copy with one hand and pissing at the same time with other. If he saw someone taking a quick piss, he'd always tell them, 'You'll regret it later.' Because he thought for certain that all prostate problems came from pissing too quickly."

Many on the *Sunday Times*—at least the men (and the staff was predominantly male)—would wait for precisely this moment to confront their boss. Once in the bathroom, determined to slow down the emptying of his bladder, Evans had no choice but to face four or five anxious and frustrated employees, armed with their perennial question: "Harry, what do you really want us to *do*?"

And Evans would tell them, although never in a peremptory or dictatorial way. Many an ambitious journalist on the *Sunday Times* was under the impression that he and he alone was Evans's pet employee, specially destined by him for some pulsating future. But Evans had the ability to crown certified duds as well as potential stars with this ennobling certainty. "I used to think the Master had his eye on me, and would approve if I did good things," said Philip Norman, recalling his relationship with Harry. "So I was never as pushy or as ruthless as I should have been. Because I thought, 'Oh, I mustn't add to his burdens.' You know, he had the world on his shoulder. And if I showed appreciation and restraint and patience, he will appreciate it. And in the long run there will be a reward. Sheer stupidity."

One of the incidents that caused Norman to eventually sour on the boss he had previously worshipped and toward whom he felt profoundly grateful (with reason: after leaving Darlington, Evans had rescued him from the northern rigors and brought him to London and the *Sunday Times*) occurred around 1970. Norman wrote an article for the *Sunday Times Magazine* about Richard Attenborough, in which he detailed Attenborough's "sort of prancing absurdity" and "idiotic streams of consciousness about how wonderful everyone and everything was." The headline stripped across the top of the article was DICKIE DARLING, which the actor particularly resented. Attenborough was not yet at that point in his career a widely admired director with an Oscar nomination in his pocket (ultimately received for *Gandhi*).

The next thing Norman knew, he was called in by Evans for a severe tongue-lashing.

"Dickie is in tears this morning," he informed Norman.

"But all actors are in tears about everything all the time!" the reporter protested. He was astonished by the change in his erstwhile champion. After all, on the *Northern Echo*, this was the man who had mounted such a stalwart defense of Norman when he had come under attack from a local theater. That era, it now appeared, had ended.

The *Sunday Times* journalist Philip Oakes, who had encouraged Norman to write his critical profile, watched aghast as his friend's career seemed poised for a swan dive. He liked Attenborough, having spent time with him in Hollywood, but was vividly aware, as Harry himself must have been, of the star's foibles. "Philip told no more than the truth really," Oakes said about the piece. "Harry was terribly starstruck." Not that this was much comfort to Norman, with his job on the line. "Philip was absolutely convinced he was going to be fired. Harry was saying, 'How could you have done this to Dickie? It's dreadful.'"

Ultimately, Norman kept his job and Oakes eventually heard an interesting story. "Dickie begged Harry not to fire him," he said. But what struck Oakes most was this: "Harry wasn't so friendly with Attenborough. It was the prestige that interested him."

In fact, Evans detested firing anyone. As one old veteran of the *Sunday Times* concluded, "Harry's dominant characteristic is he likes being liked. And almost everything else is subservient to that." Reshuffles of his staff, which occurred periodically, were painfully chaotic and confusing affairs, leaving a lot of employees, long assured by Harry they were treasured assets, stunned by job swaps to positions they found distasteful. "He wanted to make changes to freshen things up—and he wanted to convince them it was some sort of promotion or a better use of their talents. And he also genuinely wanted to feel it was!" one editor said, describing Harry's reorganization plans. "In my view, none of it was cynical or manipulative. It was entirely instinctive—like he did a lot of things."

However keenly Evans may have empathized with the wounded feelings of his friends, his own sensibilities, as his fame grew and his ambitions flourished, were in a persistently delicate state of flux. The satirical British magazine *Private Eye* was a particular source of anguish to him, as it invariably referred to him as "Dame" Harold Evans. It was a silly play on the name of the famous actress Dame Edith Evans, but Harry took it very personally, going so far as to have his lawyer demand a letter of apology from Lord Arran, a newspaper columnist who had first deployed the title. Evans felt that to be dubbed "the Dame" was suggestive of an "imputation of effeminacy."

Evidently, this had absolutely no effect on rival critics, or at least not the effect Evans intended. The doings of "the Dame," occasionally described—much to Harry's horror—as "aging," were thereafter duly invoked week in, week out, in *Private Eye* in gossipy bits of ostensibly trivial importance. For instance, on August 9, 1974, *Private Eye* reported:

> *His* Sunday Times *colleagues grow still more disturbed by the conduct of the editor Dame Harold Evans.*
>
> *Not content with riding to work on a 900 cc BMW motorbike, frequently followed by his chauffeur-driven office car, the Dame has now purchased a black leather Hell's Angels style suit. On the back are inscribed in metal studs the words* "ROCK CITY."

On November 9 that same year, a fresh item appeared:

> *Dame Harold Evans has fallen off his motor-bike. The accident happened two weeks ago. When he limped into his offices three days later, he told the hacks, "This must NOT get into* Private Eye"*!*

"So you think that's funny, do you?" Evans barked at a boy of sixteen who had the temerity to approach him at the height of the skewering campaign and ask how he felt about the gossipy stories.

"Well, yes," the boy persisted bravely. "I think they *are* funny."

"*Private Eye* is an evil magazine," Evans retorted. He was appalled, he told the boy, that the magazine did not take him seriously. The boy had no idea what it was like to be the object of such a stream of ridicule.

Nor were temper tantrums in public Evans's only form of protest. Time and again, he threatened suit against *Private Eye*. Sometimes, he did more than threaten. In October 1975, at Evans's urging, the High

Court ordered the magazine to pay what newspapers at the time called "substantial" libel damages to him, after *Private Eye* admitted having published an untrue item about him. After a great deal of legal activity on his part, England's bold champion of free speech also wrested a groveling apology: "... *Private Eye* now acknowledges that over the past three years they have continued to make untrue and unfair statements on a number of occasions about him." However, Richard Ingrams, the magazine's feisty editor, made sure to hail Harry loudly and cheerfully at every party where they were both present with the salutation, "Hullo Dame!" Well after Evans left British journalism, Ingrams was still writing, "I have to be careful what I say about Harold Evans as the fellow has a nasty habit of suing for libel, an aspect of the great crusader for press freedom not often noted by his admirers."

And the plain fact of the matter was, as *Sunday Times* staffers noted, *Private Eye* had gotten quite a lot of its stories right. Harry *was* behaving differently. He *was* riding a motorcycle—much to Enid's dismay. "I know Harry shouldn't drive so fast, but he just loves it," she confided to friends, struck "by how un-angry and how tolerant she was." There were other changes as well, just as intriguing. Evans's thick black glasses came off, replaced by contact lenses that brought home the startling blue of his eyes. His shirts were colorful and hip, not white. His hair was no longer slicked straight back, but shaped and cut into a bold dark pouch that swept across the nape of his neck. His interest in the bright young freelance writer Tina Brown—perhaps there *was* something more to it than an impersonal admiration for her journalistic skills.

For example, in June 1975, *Private Eye* reported seeing Evans, quite unaccountably, at a poetry festival. "The Dame was accompanied by his beautiful and talented young discovery Miss Tina Brown." And still later that same year:

> *Why does Dame Harold Evans spend so much time furtively pacing up and down in Bloomsbury?*
> *Is he trying to find the British Museum reading room? For apparently he is writing a book—about Uganda.*

"Uganda," as delighted readers knew full well, was *Private Eye*'s insider code word for "screwing." In Bloomsbury, hard by the British Museum, was the very walk-up flat, with its vast expanse of mirror along the bedroom wall and the Teddy bear strategically placed on the bed, where the captivating young Tina Brown resided. Evans was by no means her only male visitor. But he was decidedly the most alluring, if least available, prospect.

So all in all, it was a confusing time for Evans. In the summer of 1975, the year their affair became common knowledge in certain literary quarters, Tina was just twenty-one.

They had first met at the newspaper two years earlier when Tina was down from Oxford promoting her play, but the general feeling at the time was that this early encounter had resulted in no lasting consequences. Not for Harry anyway, and not at that point. She was by no means Evans's first interesting flirtation. But Tina was a different, more purposeful entry into his life. She had boyfriends, whose names and qualities she was not apparently shy about disclosing to an increasingly distraught Harry. Well, he was married, wasn't he?

In fact, one of her boyfriends learned he had been the subject of a discussion between Harry and Tina. "I'm afraid I got involved with a toff," she informed Harry—in reference to the wellborn young man she had acquired as a lover. "Harry said nothing. Just sighed heavily; that's what she told me," recalled the suitor.

Everything about Tina seemed young and maddeningly forthright: her choices, her possibilities, all of them endless. She could write plays and articles, she could inveigle and repel, attract and deflect, depending on her mood. The directness of her gaze had been likened to "the last thing a cobra sees" before it is confronted by a mongoose.

Harry was out of his league, no question about it.

Tina gave Valentine parties at her walk-up flat in Bloomsbury for two successive years. These were catered, free of charge, by her old Oxford pal Alex Dufort, who was then personal chef to Elliot Richardson, at that time the American ambassador to the Court of St. James's. During one of these affairs, the young man snapped a picture of Harry and Tina together; but he discovered, to his surprise, that Evans was by no means at ease. Not because Harry was estranged from Enid and attending the party of his girlfriend, but because he was worried about Alex. In fact, Harry then turned the tables, taking a picture of Dufort and Tina together—"and he deliberately took it out of focus, as if to say, *Leave my girlfriend alone!*"

And yet, she had made eyes at *him*. She had stood patiently in the hall outside Harry's office at the newspaper until he noticed her. She had sent him delightful letters from America after he packed her off there on a retainer he kept secret from his own editors. He thought her "a bluestocking," intensely "cerebral." She thought him "very wonderful" and "the Nijinsky" of sexually attractive editors.

And as her birthright, Tina possessed all sorts of exotic assets and accomplishments that a man from the North could never expect to acquire. Indulgent movie colony parents, a glamorous upbringing with movie stars for neighbors and friends, private schools. An Oxford education. And she had written an amusing play about Evans's favorite subject—a sexual liaison—which had received quite a bit of acclaim from people who counted and then won the *Sunday Times* drama award for student playwrights.

If Evans had any apprehensions about Tina's more upscale family, however, Bettina and George Brown set his mind at rest. They took to him immediately, being used to their daughter's taste in men of advanced age. As Tina's mother used to remark, "Some of Tina's boyfriends were so old, George used to wonder whether to call them 'Sir.' "

On the other hand, there were obstacles not so easily overcome. Evans had children, one of whom, the son, was having enormous difficulties at school, where he was the target of particularly cruel classmates. Harry was very much torn between Tina and his family. Enid was, after all, a sound, good woman; he genuinely liked her. Among his friends there was a general conviction that he was behaving like a fool. It was said that within his circle the Labour chancellor of the exchequer, Denis Healey, a frequent guest at the Evanses' dinner table, took the wayward husband to task, as did another Holly Lodges neighbor, an Indian diplomat.

And Tina herself—she was a worry. She was so very young, chronologically at least. And out there. And bold. In fact, perhaps the word "young" didn't quite do her justice. As one of Tina's old boyfriends remarked, Harry was basically a very *young* middle-aged man, but Tina was "very old" for her age. She knew people: not the politicians and rough-hewn journalists who formed Harry's circle, but film stars and glamorous young things and the sons of useless aristocrats, with whom Tina had sophisticated and complicated ways of interacting. She would meet, say, a houseguest of some Scottish aristocrat, and describe him— in print—as an "aging Hooray Henry with a huge glistening chin and severe indigestion." She would then explain, another evidence of her unsettling precocity, her knowing ways, that "it is too evident that the two men are at the end of a lost weekend." None of Evans's contemporaries, veterans of escapades with less exhilarating and provoking women, faced such problems. He didn't know what to do.

"Tina and I are going to give a party at Langan's. Do you want to come along?" Evans demanded on the phone one New Year's Eve, inviting a subordinate to one of London's more fashionable restaurants, partly owned by the actor Michael Caine. Evans, his friend noticed, was really pleading, as though at wit's end.

"Harry! It's eleven o'clock!" objected the staffer, who was home with his wife on a night so bitingly cold that all the locks on the family car had frozen solid. He was not in the mood to thaw them out just then. "I can't come now."

But Evans was insistent. There were evidently sixty people invited by the hot new couple—by Tina, really—to the stylish restaurant, among them Jack Nicholson, assorted dress designers, and the novelist Pat Booth, who had originally begun her career as a model. But most of the people there were young, the same age as Tina.

Evans was beside himself. "I can't talk to them! I don't know *what* they're talking about. I don't know their names," he begged over the phone. "You'll have to come here and help me."

When the compliant employee finally relented and made his way across town, he was met by Evans awash in a sea of camaraderie and gratitude. "I'm paying for you," he whispered. "Don't worry, I'm paying for you."

"Harry, you're giving a party," warned his friend. "You're paying for everybody! Tina's not going to ask her friends to pay for their meals."

"But I don't want to pay for all these people," Evans protested. This drain on his resources, imminent and unavoidable, had somehow never occurred to him, and he couldn't think how to get out of it. "What can I do?"

"Harry, don't think about it, is my advice," his friend said.

Evans refused to be talked down, however. At eleven-fifty he called over Peter Langan, the restaurateur. "Have you got a side of ham and some cheese?" he asked, suggesting that was what the guests would prefer for their New Year's repast.

"Not here, you're not!" Langan retorted. "Look at this fucking menu. You're not going to sit here and eat slices of ham."

But the thing was, that was what Evans was most comfortable doing. Then.

Chapter 4
Playing for the Big Time

As for Tina, her affair with one of the most powerful and talented men in Britain worried her to distraction, almost. She was sure it would end in a broken heart: hers. There were calls to Harry. During editorial meetings at the *Sunday Times,* participants would be distracted by a ringing phone, and then a series of tense, urgent whispers from their boss. "I can't talk to you now, I'm in a meeting," Harry would hiss into the receiver. "*Yes, I love you.*"

She poured out her troubles to, among others, Tony Palmer, who was by then accustomed to his role of confidant, having proffered Tina a shoulder to cry on during previous emotional crises. He had the wherewithal to judge the trajectory of Tina's liaison with the celebrated editor since he knew everyone involved: Tina of course, but also Harry, whom he admired, and even Enid to a lesser degree. Enid, Palmer felt, was important to Harry's life, although there was, to be sure, little glory attached to her role. She was as functional and unadorned as a desk set. "She was the one who was organized. She knew what day of the week it was," Palmer said. "If I say she was sort of a supersecretary, that would be unfair, but she had that kind of aspect."

But perhaps such an individual was more necessary to Harry's life than some glamour girl just out of school who wrote plays about her failed romances. This particular romance, Tina sensed, bore within it the hallmarks of almost certain defeat. Harry had three children he loved. More to the point, Harry was, as Palmer noted, "already extremely successful and very eminent and much older." Would Harry, too, leave her? "She was extremely concerned about that," said Palmer. "Extremely concerned."

It was Harry's status that most troubled Tina. So worried was she about the disparity between their respective professional achievements—and how others would view her swift ascent on the newspaper—that she stopped writing for the *Sunday Times* altogether. "Terrific for my personal life but rather a disaster for my work," she said back then. That was what accounted for Harry's bad humor when he informed a subordinate that it was "too late" for the *Sunday Times* to reconsider hiring Tina Brown. She was gone. Gone to the *Sunday Telegraph,* as well as other publications for which she freelanced.

Her self-imposed exile did little to restore Tina's confidence, however. To Martin Amis she confided other aspects of her reservations about Harry. She felt guilty about Enid and the children. She was miserable that she and Harry couldn't be seen in public together. All sorts of humiliating postures had to be adopted to hide the very catch Tina had worked so assiduously to hook. Worse, some of these subterfuges, as subterfuges so often do, made them even more conspicuous as a couple. Reporters would spy Harry emerging from a restaurant with his collar up and Tina by his side. Equally terrible, Tina confided to Amis, she "found herself in a kind of cliché position. She was very aware of that. . . . So there was much to talk about."

There were, in fact, any number of people available to listen, most of them, as it happened, men in whom Tina felt an especially tender interest. "She was far more sophisticated than me. I was just the bit on the side, a toyboy, a distraction," one of her lovers at the time would later remark. "She was officially seeing Harold Evans. Among others. I can understand why these things happen. It was not a concern of mine."

One thing about Tina troubled this man, however. "It used to horrify me, just make my blood run cold, the way she talked about some of the men in her life to me when those men weren't around. Oh, she talked about Bron Waugh. And she made some very cutting remarks on Harry's size. He was so short, she said. She could be frighteningly dismissive of these figures. She has a cartoonist's eye."

She was, in fact, nervous and uncertain enough about Harry to take out more than one insurance policy. This occasionally took the form of socializing with other men—at least one of whom Harry himself would soon learn about. These new conquests Tina flattered shamelessly. Her legs, she informed one, turned to "elegant avocado" whenever they kissed. Or, alternatively, "You are the apple of my eye, the cherry of my cake. . . ." Some of these men were younger even than Tina herself and just starting out.

"Oh, she was clever and delicious. I was learning a lot from her—you can say that," Nicholas Monson, a steady escort at the time, would later explain. The feeling was for some time mutual: Tina called Monson "Captain Wonderful." He was two years her junior, but decades younger in worldliness and professional attainment. Doubtless, this was a major part of his appeal. Monson had no wife, no responsibilities, no children, no power over anyone. Tina tried to readjust this discrepancy by introducing him to people on the *Sunday Telegraph* who might help him. And indeed that is where Monson flourished for a time. He was grateful.

It might be argued, however, that theirs was a very fair exchange. On the one hand, Monson would recollect, Tina "inspired me to get up off my ass. My articles began appearing in the *Sunday Telegraph Magazine*. And a big epic poem I wrote also appeared." On the other, Monson had something of value to offer Tina. They met when she included him in an article she was writing, entitled "Debs and their Delights," about which she knew little. Monson's family was endowed with "a Queen Anne house on 1600 acres, 11 bedrooms, in Lincolnshire," as well as an especially interesting lineage. John Monson, a direct ancestor, was quartermaster at the battle of Agincourt. The family received its first knighthood from Henry VIII; in 1611, the Monsons got a baronetcy, then a peerage in 1728, which made them, Monson explained with considerable pride, "among the oldest ten percent of aristocracy."

All of this could be of particular interest to Britain's reading public, Monson felt, but perhaps a source of antagonism as well. At twenty-two, he wrote a heartfelt piece on inverted snobbery for the *Telegraph Magazine*—the manner in which the sons and daughters of earls and dukes and such were, in his opinion, callously treated in the new Britain of meritocracy and achievement, the Britain of the upstart Harry Evans, in other words. Tina showed the article to the great Evans himself.

"Harold cannot believe you did that by yourself. He thinks you're a *wunderkind*," she assured him kindly.

She herself was far busier. Besides writing for the *Sunday Telegraph*, she also worked for the magazine *Punch*. It was the deputy editor Alan Coren himself, whose "eclectic imagination" young Tina had found so praiseworthy in an Oxford profile, who in 1975 returned the favor by giving her work. "Quite a lot of well-known writers worked for *Punch,*" Miles Kington, who was one of them, would later recollect. He was mildly interested in what the new girl was up to. She wore, he observed, dark glasses, even when it was raining, and was extremely flirtatious. "She used to turn up at *Punch* with a what-should-I do-next? kind of attitude," he said.

On learning Tina lived near the British Museum, Kington informed her they were neighbors. At her behest, he showed up for a drink and the two chatted away aimlessly until evening fell. Kington glanced at his watch. "I had better get home to my wife," he apologized, at which point he saw a look of anguish cross Tina's face.

"Oh God! You're married! You'd better go," she said. If she was looking for an alternative to Harry Evans—and given her packed social life, there was every reason to believe she was—another married journalist clearly wasn't it.

Kington came away with a wry thought: "I believe she saw me as a wasted opportunity."

Tina was in no mood, as fellow writers remarked at the time, to waste anything, least of all opportunities. "The most sought-after journalist on Fleet Street" was how British *Vogue* described Tina, a journalist who could snare the most recherché of subjects. Bianca Jagger ("a girl with more cachet than cash," in Tina's view, since the beautiful Nicaraguan was then in the midst of divorcing the tight-fisted Mick Jagger) was provoked enough by her meager circumstances to confess to Tina in an interview: "If I'd been around Cocteau I might have smoked opium. To be around Keith [Richards] and Anita [Pallenburg] and have my teeth fall out from shooting smack is not, I think, the same thing." Brigitte Bardot unveiled her own sorrows. "I have a special *tendresse* for Marilyn Monroe. Such big, sad eyes. . . ." Tina was particularly proud of that profile. She herself, she claimed, had a particular *tendresse* for women. Of a certain type.

"I love meeting well-known women," she said. "I'm interested in what makes them a success and then I prefer them, as a race, to men. Not sexually of course, but I like working with women and for women."

If true, this was news to any number of her acquaintances, especially those members of the feminist sisterhood Tina had briefly embraced across the Atlantic during the lonely months she spent there. Unburdened by the constraints and imposed bonhomie of contemporary feminism, Tina was aware of her impact on other women, especially those who had received less of the attention and publicity she so assiduously courted. In its own way, their hostility validated and even added spice to her efforts, arising as she was sure it did from pure envy. It is usual in Britain for reporters to spend what is known as "three years in the provinces"—places every bit as grim as Darlington or Manchester—before being permitted to ascend to the top and write for lofty London publications. That fate, Tina had managed to avoid. "The trouble is I've done all my learning in the national press and there's no doubt excited a bit of envy from people who've done it in other ways," she said.

What other explanation could there possibly be for the bitterness she aroused? Tina was by no means alone in ascribing it to mean jealousy. Angela Huth, who subsequently befriended the woman who had bewitched her husband, Tony Palmer, rushed to her defense. "Inevitably a person so young who does so well is the subject of a certain amount of envy and gossip. And of course she was," she recalled. "I would hear a lot of people being bitchy about her fast rise on the *Sunday Times,* which seemed to me to be entirely unjustified. Because she did extremely good work."

Her fellow writers, Tina loudly complained, were especially anxious for her to fail. "Not the stars," she explained hastily. "They have always been lovely to me. But there has been quite a lot of hostility from other journalists when one was out on a job. You know— 'Here's the smarty-pants out of Oxford, who thinks she knows everything.' "

On the other hand, was it Tina's fault that virtually everything she did ended up in the papers? That she was praised to the skies by gossip columnists and critics alike? She was astute enough to recognize that she had come along at precisely the right moment, that her gifts alone were not what accounted for so much adulation and bright copy. Being a woman, a blond woman, a woman with a brain, did not exactly impede her ascent. "I should think discrimination works in our favour at the moment," she admitted at the time. "They're so desperate for women writers that we're probably going to get unfair publicity and be rather spoilt. When some luckless man who's been grinding away at fifteen plays a year doesn't get a chance."

As it happened, Tina wrote another play in 1977, called *Happy Yellow.* It was set in a New York apartment inhabited by three young women afflicted with man trouble, and following its performance at the Bush Theatre, it was widely and well reviewed. An amazing accomplishment, considering it was a rather awkward piece of work, especially when compared to the self-knowledge and sophistication displayed in Tina's first play.

Based in a fairly loose fashion on the four miserable months she had spent in New York, the script possessed all the flaws of life unedited: insight, pathos, and humor, in very short supply, uneasily cohabitating. One of the play's main characters, an unintelligent figure of fun, interestingly enough, is depicted as being hopelessly in love with a rapacious married man, although nothing about the relationship is in any way comprehensible. Once again, the playwright was ruthless in the dissection of her own shortcomings, her judgment in selecting a married, much older man. "When a guy has grey hair tangled up in his medallion time isn't exactly on his side. . . . Are you sure you can't do better than a bullshitting married man with five bloodsucking kids?" inquires one of the characters. This time, however, there was a surprising lack of authenticity about Tina's work. Such lines as "Hi! Welcome to Fun City," or "No way, Larry. I'm in a different scene now. There are four more like you pleading for it," or, even worse, "Weird . . . I'm late for my masturbation workshop," appear to be included only as the playwright's way of assuring her audience that she had indeed absorbed the culture and parlance of New York.

And it worked, too. "One mark of its assurance is that the dialogue offers no clue to the author's British nationality," wrote Irving Wardle of *The Times*. "Miss Brown has a malicious ear for verbal giveaways and she trains it impartially on Americans and English." In any event, Tina was more than pleased. "The onus was always on me not to disappoint," she said.

In Harry Evans she found, among other characteristics, an outsider of similar, unswerving ambition, careful not to disappoint. But Harry was also someone who, unlike his young girlfriend, frankly identified with those he led. Eleven o'clock Saturday nights, a subordinate recalled, found Harry in his office with "the chief printer and compositor and the people who had labored over some of the bigger stories," breaking out a bottle of Scotch while the presses rolled.

"Often we hadn't slept for the previous two or three nights," recalled one *Sunday Times* reporter—which didn't prevent his colleagues from sticking around the place, long after they should have been home with wives and children, congratulating each other "after the weekly battle for excellence." Saturday nights would also find Harry in the composing room in shirtsleeves consulting with compositors on stories about to appear. So tightly woven was this group that years later one reporter, a woman, was overheard to remark of that golden era, "The *Sunday Times* wasn't a job. It was family."

In many ways, such an existence, erratic, late night, arduous, precluded life with any real family. "I allowed work to destroy my family life, I didn't spend enough time with my wife and children," Harry himself would later concede. "At the end of the day you have to ask yourself if professional happiness can compensate for personal failings and errors."

In Britain, all sorts of movements and revolutions appear a decade later than in the United States. It was the seventies, therefore, before the sexual revolution visited the *Sunday Times*. "There were several women actually who had it off with everybody," journalist Philip Norman would later recall. That did not sit well at home. Many of the male journalists were married to stunned and deeply offended women with lots of children and few jobs, who had not yet discovered feminism. Their weapons were meager: "Wives tipping all their husbands' suits out the window," was one of them. Another wounded wife stormed the doughty old Gray's Inn Road building, barged into its offices, and tossed the contents of her husband's desk out the window and onto the pavement.

Nor were the women at the newspaper itself much better off than their unappreciated married sisters sorting through piles of dirty laundry. The female journalist was simply typecast in a different, although equally utilitarian, way. "Women were supposed to be Dollybirds and sit with their legs drawn up and their stockinged feet on typist stools, shaking their long hair over their shoulders," said Philip Norman. "That was what they were like. There was no real route to getting on with your job."

Tina was all of these things, and yet somehow none of them. Of course she possessed much of the ammunition of the Dollybirds. "She flashed her boobs," was how her friend the *Daily Mail* gossip columnist Nigel Dempster described Tina's direct methods. But not always. "She told me I had the loveliest eyelashes of any editor she'd ever seen," recalled Alexander Chancellor, who used to invite Tina and other journalists to weekly lunches at *The Spectator*. He found the young woman's flattery amazingly incisive. "It's quite a small category of people. But it was quite a good compliment because the only thing I have *ever* been proud of is my eyelashes. So I thought it was clever of her to notice."

And yet, at the same time, Tina was beginning to acquire—indeed, was anxious to acquire—some of the armature and homely talents of a housewife. Around the *Sunday Times,* people were given to understand that Tina and Harry now shared a flat near the paper on Gray's Inn Road; not that this was ever announced publicly, and not that Harry even bothered to inform some of his co-workers of this change of address. Editors who phoned Harry at his old home in Highgate, the one he had shared with Enid and the children, were simply given to understand by Mrs. Evans, in muted fashion, that her husband's phone number had changed. "I'm afraid he is no longer here. You can find him at—" and she rattled off the new number of her absent husband.

In 1978, Harry and Tina moved again, taking up residence in a rented Regency house, shaped like a wedding cake, near the House of Commons. Its garden was surrounded by a brick wall covered in wisteria and ivy. Her old lover Tony Palmer, dropping by, was astonished at the change in her, "this fantastic pride with which she told me how they moved there, what they put where." Cushions, colors, fabrics, furniture, all had abruptly acquired for Tina a kind of talismanic appeal; they became her prizes, hard-won, for working overtime, and acquired a magic of which she spoke with peculiar reverence. Indeed, she began to view her work as a means of settling in even deeper with Harry.

"I can say, 'I am writing for that sofa, that chair,' " she told another journalist. These items became temporary household gods, anchors of her relationship.

What amused Palmer most, however, was that none of these newly purchased objects in which Tina took such fierce delight was arranged by his old girlfriend with any deftness or natural harmony. Tina, despite being "motherly" and "enveloping," had no real bent for domesticity: it was as alien to her as the ironing board. The house, he found, "was a bit of a mess, to be honest."

Enid, who remained in the Tudor house with the large abandoned Ping-Pong room, the older curtains, and the more established furniture, was distraught but outwardly stoic. To friends, she reported simply that the breakup of her marriage had been very hard on the children. Tina, victorious yet penitent, guilty about Harry's children yet incapable of restoring their father to them, underwent certain privations. One by one, she dropped her boyfriends. "Go away! I shall miss you. I love you very much," one of these was commanded after a lovemaking session he found "so mechanical, so cold." Later, an explanatory call came: She was, she insisted, going to marry Harry

Evans. And then yet another explanation, this one fond and almost plaintive: "Now it's too late. I have made my choices."

To Palmer, she was equally direct. "I've got to behave myself now, otherwise this has no chance of working," she told him. He understood her forbearance. Harry was a catch; the sacrifice was, relatively speaking, small. It was simply an offering, a gesture of goodwill. "It was a purely behavioral thing for her," Palmer said. She was "extremely conscious that if the relationship was going to work, she'd better mind her p's and q's."

And why not? Harry was a remarkable man. "It was no coincidence she grabbed him," Palmer felt. "She was completely smitten by him." Harry's working-class antecedents, his stretched and oozing northern vowels were no barrier, in Tina's eyes, to a permanent relationship.

That generous attitude did not extend to a number of her better-born friends, however. It was generally assumed, for instance, that Auberon Waugh's dislike of Harry, given full expression on the pages of *Private Eye* (the number of references to "Dame Harold" grew geometrically), was intensified not only by jealousy but also by his disgust with Harry's background. The idea that Tina preferred the grandson of an illiterate from the impoverished North to the wealthy and talented son of a brilliant writer seemed preposterous. "Bron was frightfully angry about her becoming Harry's mistress, really that launched a great hatred," the *New Statesman* editor Anthony Howard would recall. When Harry bought the memoirs of Mohammed Heikal, an aide who was very close to the murdered Egyptian president Anwar Sadat, *Private Eye* dubbed him "The Aswan Dame." Waugh was cheerfully unrepentant. "Oh, of course I called him Dame Harold. He took *enormous* offense in those days. So he became Dame Harold for the rest of his life! I never called him anything else!" The epithet referred to his rival's physical deficiencies, Waugh insisted, the ones Tina had remarked on to one lover. "We always assumed he was conscious of his height."

But such prejudice was by no means universal. After all, Tina had fallen for Harry at a time when Britain was packed with heroes from the North. The Beatles and the Stones had genealogies and accents every bit as unexalted as Harry's. "I adore regional accents, be they Manchester or Belgravia," Tina told an upper-crust lover, thus neatly equating the two—and simultaneously soothing two sets of competing egos. Besides, Harry during their first years together was a resounding professional success. With him beside her, she could go anywhere. Almost.

For even with such an escort, it was virtually impossible for Tina to please certain of the elite. Tina's own background was a puzzle. Her hasty delivery, unplaceable pronunciations, and the odd flatness of her vowels reflected in a certain way the character and goals of their owner: "aspirational" is how Tony Palmer described Tina's accent. Her ruthless exclusion from the upper class—Britain's answer to the guillotine—began to rankle. Although Tina wrote for the *Sunday Telegraph,* for example, Lady Pamela Hartwell, that newspaper's imperious and very social proprietess, snubbed her royally one night at a party.

"She dismissed me as *no one,*" an outraged Tina complained to a boyfriend. She was in considerable pain over the slight. "She absolutely could not stand it," recalled her friend. "She absolutely could not stand going to a party and being snubbed by the wife of the owner of a newspaper. She was a Jewish girl with parents living in Marbella who comes to England and wants to conquer the world."

It would be a mere matter of months before she got her revenge.

In May 1979, Tina, vacationing near Marbella with her parents, received a letter from a strange character named Johnny Elliott, imploring her to take a perfectly terrible job for which she seemed ill-suited.

A handsome, big-shouldered former cavalry officer in velvet-collared coats, Elliott had vivid black hair, high color, and a large fleshy nose, and would ultimately end up serving a three-year jail sentence for fraud ("... quite nice of him," he remarked of the judge, "since my brief had warned me I was going to get four"). But at the time of his business relationship with Tina, he was simply—along with an Australian businessman named Gary Bogard—part-owner of a soggy old society magazine, *Tatler.* Its offices were then on 15 Berkeley Street, which was the only remotely chic thing about it. It was, as Tina's friend Simon Carr observed, "the poodle of the upper classes." The magazine featured a lot of dowagers in badly cut evening gowns and quite a few earls on horseback. It sold perhaps eleven thousand copies.

And yet, *Tatler* had a long and amusing history. Founded in 1709 by the essayist and wag Richard Steele, its first issue, a broadsheet, was distributed free in the fashionable coffeehouses of London. Significantly, it went out of business two years later, but the name was used sporadically throughout two centuries by one clever journal after another and never died out—although the definite article in the publication's title did, and it eventually became known as *Tatler*. Steele, who was said to have invented gossip, was inordinately proud of his creation. "I have resolved to have something which may be of interest to the fair sex," he promised.

By 1979, that promise seemed to have totally faded. *Tatler* was then edited by an American woman, Leslie Field, who had written a book on the diamonds owned by the Queen. Its predictable covers, previously crawling with ads for wines and luxury raincoats, now boasted, much to the annoyance of Johnny Elliott, a new look: a peculiar collage in which Tio Pepe sherry and Aquascutum sat alongside photographs of society's darlings. Clearly, the owners felt, the entire cover should boast some gorgeous young thing, preferably wellborn. A change was necessary.

Elliott and Bogard, recalling that a certain Tina Brown had written an article on debutantes in the *Telegraph,* thought she just might be the answer to their prayers. Wasn't a perky girl with those upper-class preoccupations and connections just what the fading magazine needed? She had been recommended by the gossip columnist Dempster, who had been offered the job of *Tatler* editor himself by Elliott, but turned it down flat. "It was a terrible magazine," Dempster realized. "Just the worst."

Tina herself was inclined to agree. "I hated all those pictures of balls and race meetings," she said. "They drove me crazy—people having a quick stroke on the stairs at a hunt ball." Nothing about the magazine appealed to her: "As seen through the old *Tatler* most English parties seemed to be thrown at Madame Tussaud's," she decided. "Each photograph featured some fresh tableau of the stiff upper crust coming to terms with a glass of warm Amontillado." Moreover, she was certain the owners had been mistaken in her credentials. She was no large-boned Sloane Ranger in twinsets who spent weekends in country houses. "All I had done was write a piece in the *Telegraph Magazine* about debs. I mean I might just as well have been writing about strippers, but it happened to be debs."

On receiving the offer, however, Tina dashed home from Spain and took a quick poll of all her friends. To one of them, an old admirer from her Oxford days, she confided her fears. "Tina was very, very concerned about how it might affect her reputation. She felt awkward about it," said this old confidant. "She is much more high-brow than most people realize, that's why she thought she would be selling out by editing *Tatler.*" To Tony Palmer, she unloaded similar misgivings. She was fearful, she said, after the success of her small plays and clever articles, of ending up the editor of a bad joke. "*Tatler* sort of meant rubbish, if you see what I mean," recalled Palmer. "It also had a fearful snobbish attitude." The Tina he knew "disapproved of those things—*at that time, at that time.* Well, because there was a kind of inverted snobbery about her. She was like a lot of people of that generation. She sort of had a grudge against the world."

Palmer told her to take the job. It was a fine opportunity to show off her skills. In fact, Tina didn't need all that much convincing. By 1979, although well known and certainly widely envied, she was in some danger of growing stale. Her articles no longer appeared in the *Sunday Times.* Her two plays, although well reviewed, never went farther than the small London theaters. Her stories on debs and go-go dancing auditions, Bardot and Playboy Bunnies, were taking on an achingly familiar cast. No matter what or who the subject, these were basically mini-series, mini-tempests, with Tina at the eye of the teapot. "I'm-attractive-and-men-can't-leave-me-alone kind of pieces," was how one writer summed up her work.

"Whatever happened to Tina Brown? She was quite the up-and-coming figure," an old friend and boss inquired of another journalist one evening at a party. "And we've never heard of her since."

They were about to do so again. In mid-May, Tina "plunged," as she phrased it at the time, and took the job of editor of *Tatler* for £12,000 a year (roughly $30,000 back then and a 50 percent increase in her average salary). She was probably aware of gossip suggesting her imminent professional demise and alert to the notion that landing the editorship of a failing publication at a modest salary was not likely to enhance her cachet. At least she went to great pains to counter the prevailing rumors by offering herself up for a press interview. It would be written by her aristocrat friend Nicholas Monson, who dutifully took her to Langan's Brasserie and fired questions at her. Her responses, however, were terrible and, worse, boring, he decided. Tina, he was coming to realize, was not a spontaneous wit.

"Hang on!" Monson protested. "Let's start over." But it still didn't work.

He made a third stab. "I'll give you twenty questions and you answer them in writing at home."

"Who have become your friends in journalism and who your enemies?" read the Q&A article.

"I think the two are interchangeable in journalism," Tina wrote back. "In weak moments I think, 'Right! Enough is enough! I am off to America where people really want you to succeed.' Then after two weeks of dumb indiscriminate New York enthusiasm I start pining for the malice of my London friends."

"Why did you decide to be an editor?" Monson asked.

"Because I was asked to be—and I'm too young, which always seems the best age to do something," was Tina's written reply.

"Well, that was better," Monson concluded. And indeed it was. Tina's much touted youth in the article became even more youthful. She had asked Auberon Waugh, she said, for an interview "when I was eighteen" during "my second year at Oxford." In fact, she had been a year older at the time, and her friend Stephen Glover had requested the interview.

Langan's Brasserie, the site of their original failed interview, was no accident. Tina was entitled, said her new bosses, to free expense account lunches and dinners at that restaurant and at the Ritz Hotel, as well as any number of cab rides she wished to take. *Tatler*'s luxury-loving part-owner, John Elliott, was famous for making deals with BMW, Sabena, Air France, and many of the fashionable restaurants— much to the shock and dismay of his partner, Gary Bogard.

"Why isn't this person being charged for this ad?" Bogard would demand to know after lunching at the Ivy.

"Because when we last had lunch there, Gary, you didn't see any money change hands, did you?" Elliott would reply tartly.

Elliott had an answer for a lot of things in those days, but he didn't have an explanation for Tina Brown. She drove him crazy. For starters, she spent a lot of money, which was the one commodity—un-like lavish lunches and cab rides—that was always in very short sup-ply at the magazine. And yet, as one old *Tatler* hand remembered, "She had to have new photographers, professional photographers— and the kind of people she hired didn't even know the names of the people they were taking pictures of. She was spending money like water. She just went through the money!" Worse, she didn't appear to have any sort of appreciation for the class of people they were writing about—and for. She admitted as much herself.

"I wanted to do them with a bit of irreverence, tongue in cheek. It *couldn't* just be a service magazine for the rich," Tina would protest. "English people have far too much sense of humor, and none of them have any money anyway."

To her old friend Simon Carr, she was even franker about her exalted subjects. "I will never make the mistake of believing I am one of *them*."

There were those on the magazine who were horrified by such an attitude. A lot of the old guard were, too. A Scottish aristocrat who had shown Tina around his vast acres was so taken aback by the upstart's reflections ("the fact that he looks as if he's climbed out of a sock is no reflection on his pedigree," Tina had written) that he described her piece as "the worst act of betrayal since the massacre of Glencoe." Even those who approved her changes at the magazine had to concede that "every issue had booby traps in it. There were so many wild people writing for the magazine that it was always stabbing people in the back, sort of as if it were messing its own cage in the copy."

"She was taking the piss out of people," one old *Tatler* observer recalled, "writing the kind of acerbic stuff about the social strata. If there were two photographs of the same socialite, she'd put in the bad photograph. There was a thunderous dip in circulation. Then it picked up again."

And the odd thing was that—as just about everyone noticed—Gary Bogard, *Tatler*'s richer proprietor, who owned three quarters of the magazine, absolutely adored her. Yet "she never consulted with Gary. She *told* him what she was doing," one acquaintance said. In vain did her detractors run to Bogard and complain about her shocking expenditures and her insolent attitude toward the upper classes. "The fact is that Gary Bogard thought that everything Tina did was correct."

Far from ending, *Tatler*'s circulation, after its initial dip, actually tripled. Even one of Tina's most obdurate critics was forced to conclude that mocking the upper classes seemed to have a remarkably salutary effect on its victims: "They did love it in a way, those people." Readers began to study the magazine spines for some of the editor's peculiar but revelatory mottoes: "The magazine that bites the hand that reads it," read one. "The magazine that *shall* go to the ball," promised another. And still a third, one particularly optimistic Christmas: "Deeper, crisper and breaking even." Tina, even her enemies had to admit, did do the most amazing things for the old magazine. In fact, she saved it.

To get to *Tatler* in Tina's earliest days—she took office the same year, 1979, as Margaret Thatcher—you had to take the elevator to the sixth floor of the Berkeley Street building, then pass by a money-lender.

"Appropriately enough, some would say," observed Nicholas Coleridge, one of the people Tina hired. "Moneylender, *Tatler* side by side. And it rather set the tone."

Young journalists dashing in each morning to the magazine would overhear, through the barely open door of the neighboring office, a male Cockney voice talking on the phone: "Oim sorreh. But unless yew get that eight hundred pounds in moy hands by four o'cluck, weah fawclowsing."

Tatler, for all its snobbery, was equally beleaguered, its credit as dubious as any one of its neighbor's clients. But it did boast slightly more numerous and glamorous employees, all of them young, eager, some pretty—and many destined to spend much of their careers, in one incarnation or another, with Tina or Harry. Tina herself was omnipresent and very much in control. "Invariably being interviewed on the six o'clock news on how she was going to turn *Tatler* around," one friend mentioned. Close by was a stringy young fellow, Miles Chapman, who rewrote the headlines and vaguely muttered under his breath about Tina ("They had a volatile relationship," it was recalled). Then there was the classified advertising manager, Gabé Doppelt, "stirring the gossip around a bit"; the magazine photographer, a thin and talented black Englishman, Michael Roberts, best remembered "in his camp period, interviewing models wearing raccoon hats"; and Harry's quiet daughter, Kate, who became the *Tatler* switchboard girl. Deputy editor Georgina Howell was perpetually dismayed when her articles for *Tatler* on cultural events were killed by an ungrateful Tina at the last second because more exciting copy had come in, practically gratis, from such august names as Auberon Waugh (the magazine's wine critic, who wrote under the pseudonym "Crispin de St Crispian"), the travel writer Jan Morris, the novelist Julian Barnes (*Tatler*'s restaurant critic), or Martin Amis. Either that, or because there was simply no more space: "Tina had interviewed another dictator's wife."

For £4,000 a year, Coleridge found himself writing seven different articles a month, some under pseudonyms. Like everyone else at the magazine, he felt vulnerable, as though he might be fired at any minute by the volatile Tina. On the other hand, Coleridge was useful to the struggling magazine. It was he who would phone publishers and inform them that "the magazine was putting together a major review of the new illustrated books." Then he would make his pitch. "Could you please bike them round to us as fast as you can?"

Motorcyclists bearing expensive books from compliant publishers arrived all week long at *Tatler;* they were assembled in several huge boxes—books worth "maybe eight hundred pounds," Coleridge thought.

Then it was up to him to hail a taxi and take the books to a secondhand bookdealer. "D. Levin of Grape Street," Coleridge said, recalling the name of the bookshop. "Well, I'd sell them for cash. We might get two hundred and fifty quid. I would hand it to Tina. She would hand it to Julian Barnes, because he was the restaurant critic. He would then go out with the cash—because at this point it was difficult to get checks from the company—and pay cash to have dinner somewhere like the Connaught. Then he would write a corruscating review saying it wasn't quite up to the standards of *Tatler* readers. And that was kind of how the magazine kept afloat."

But it was by no means the only way. Although reactionary, the Thatcher era had its points. It had, for one thing, character—often bad character, but character nonetheless. "The upper classes," Tina noted, "were in an optimistic mood." A restless one as well. "In 1979," Lord Hesketh, a thirty-three-year-old squire, informed Tina, "the way to tell an English gentleman is by the quality of his drugs." Gone from its pages, *Tatler'*s readers noted with relief, were members of the horsey set along with photographs of well-fed *grandes dames* clad in yards of pink satin. In their place were notorious nouveaux, the odd newspaper editor (often pictures of Harold Evans), the ridiculous royal (Princess Michael of Kent), and rich Yanks—among them Betsy Bloomingdale and Nancy Reagan. Cartier lighters gave way to cigarette butts; socialites were shown amorously entwined with lovers. And many of their nightly doings were chronicled in a regular society column by that notorious divorcée Margaret, Duchess of Argyll, whose interest in oral sex had become a matter of interest to Harry and the rest of the nation years earlier. She was rarely seen at *Tatler* headquarters without her poodle, which she cradled in her arms while complaining bitterly about her gossipy rivals. "Marg of Arg," Tina and her subordinates called the scandalous duchess behind her aging back, invariably sheathed in a thirty-year-old Chanel suit. She had, like her young blond boss, decided views and a way about her.

There are certain fields in which I really do wonder whether I am quite up to par: modern art is one of them. I find it difficult to understand what one is supposed to say or how to react

84

when faced with a seemingly blank canvas or an enormous mass.

And off went the duchess, reviewing not the art, of course, but the guest lists at the exhibitions. Subsequent *Tatler* articles became much more daring: there were crafty assaults on the yet-unmarried Prince Charles, whose "romantic record . . . would make Giovanni Casanova blush." One of Waugh's wine columns was headed: CRISPIN DE ST CRISPIAN GETS HIS TONGUE AROUND SOMETHING SPANISH. Among the bright, poorly paid staff, there was a remarkable feeling of being somehow launched into a defiant, indescribably amusing venture, one closed to the rest of the world. "We all used to have dinner together a lot, mostly I think because we were too afraid to see other journalists," said one. "But there was a tremendous esprit."

On the new *Tatler* covers were pretty young women devoid of even a smidgeon of title: Marissa Berenson, Margaux Hemingway. Or, alternatively, pretty young women with neon titles. "Stars, stars" were what Tina craved, even at that early stage. "Money isn't necessary for the *Tatler,*" observed Miles Chapman. "If you want to get Princess Caroline of Monaco for your cover, you slip a note into the gold sandals that Manolo Blahnik just sent round to her, saying, *Here we are! We want you to be on our cover!* Yeah, that's what Tina did. That's what you do."

"Full ashtrays, empty bottles of Perrier and creased copies of the 'Golden Bowl,' " Tina, who wrote the story on Caroline, noted, surveying the debris of the princess's new life. She was careful to give her subject, fresh from her divorce from the foolish playboy Philippe Junot, exactly what she was seeking: a more solid and even dignified appeal, the image of a born-again beauty regally sweeping up the remains of a youthful fiasco. "Here, the Caroline we found was a low-key, serious young woman isolated near the palace in a bluish-pink house scattered with brainy books and expensive shoes."

There was an acute sense of timing associated with such pieces that horrified the more left wing. "What it did, it caught the Thatcher Zeitgeist. It caught the new snobbism, it caught the horrible renaissance of the upper-class twit," Philip Norman thought. "The upper-class accent returned."

He also couldn't help noticing, since he then worked for the *Sunday Times,* that Tina appeared to benefit from her close proximity to power. "The connection with Harry might not have been totally unhelpful. I seem to recall that not long after Tina took over the *Tatler,* a lot of *Sunday Times* editorials referred to *Tatler* magazine as a sort of weighty source for some pronouncement that same week: 'As *Tatler* magazine so rightly put it in its current issue. . . .' "

And indeed it was astonishing how fascinated the London media suddenly seemed to be with the doings and articles of a tiny magazine read by almost no one in all of England. It wasn't only the *Sunday Times,* led by the fairly partial Harry Evans, that wrote approvingly of Tina's publication. Nigel Dempster of the *Daily Mail* plugged the magazine every chance he got—and publicly scolded those who mocked it. On the occasion of *Tatler*'s 270th birthday party, which was held at the Ritz a mere year into Tina's reign, the *Daily Mail* breathlessly revealed the guest list: David Frost escorting Lady Rothermere, the wife of a newspaper proprietor; Joan Collins, who had known the new *Tatler* editor as a dull, quiet child; Sabrina Guinness, who was then in love with Prince Charles; the playwright John Mortimer—and of course the lofty Harold Evans, approvingly referred to as "a fine Prince Consort if ever there was one." Everyone agreed that even at that early stage there was much for the relaunched little magazine to celebrate.

"I wheedled and begged all the big writing names I knew," Tina would later recall of her attempts to marshal both excitement and respectability on behalf of her new venture. Those big writing names—some of them discarded lovers—she recycled again and again: as columnists, as adored subjects, and occasionally as victims of her own venom, depending on her mood and the needs of the magazine. Nor were these old boyfriends her only contributors. Every month Tina herself contributed to *Tatler* its most popular column, written in a style that was described as "not always madly accurate." It had a well-defined field of interest: rich and eligible young men who were not likely to sue *Tatler* after being smeared by its editor in print. "Rosie Boot's Guide to London Bachelors," it was called. It was amazing how many of Tina's old flames found their way into that particular column and how swiftly she seemed to forget that she had ever been fond of them.

"If he wasn't such a notorious tightwad, Neidpath could be a wonderful catch for someone who was sound on Bismarck's foreign policy and didn't mind him leading a double life. . . ," Tina wrote of the Lord Neidpath she had once pursued at Oxford. ". . . His career has been almost as richly diverse as his sex life," she observed of poor aristocratic Nicholas Monson, whom she had dumped.

And "Yes girls, he's back." That was how she launched her profile of the same Martin Amis who had wounded her so deeply just six years earlier during her final exams. Tina's actual name and personal experiences with Amis were omitted from the column. Instead, the mythical Rosie Boot described in general terms the handsome writer's caddish bent. He had, after all, parted from a gorgeous young thing named Gully Wells (the stepdaughter of A. J. Ayer, she told readers) during Oxford finals. For her part, Rosie Boot wasn't in the least surprised by his behavior. ". . . Do remember girls, all his relationships end badly after six months," she warned.

"There was no particular system in place for weeding those things out," Coleridge would later explain. "Fact-checkers, there were none."

"This is a hoot," Tina would announce when an especially malicious article arrived on her desk. Gamely, she fielded phone calls from those she referred to as "ratty-voiced debs" with hot tips for the editor: "Look, I'd like to remain anonymous but I know this frightful shit you really ought to send Rosie Boot to interview." She complained bitterly that all the dullest bachelors she had to interview invariably ordered soufflés for dessert, forcing her to spend an extra half hour listening to their prattle before racing back to her desk.

She was great fun, that Tina, her office mates conceded. But at the same time they were frightened of her. She was, they thought, "tricky, changeable." And acerbic. But "very powerful" and "very quixotic." There was a big staff turnover right from the start. "If you weren't a Tina person, she took a dim view," one *Tatler* hand recalled. "She wouldn't consider taking on any of the old staff. We had poor old Peter Townend, the social editor. He was sort of pushed to one side. Georgina Howell—that exploded." No one felt secure under her reign, least of all, to do her justice, Tina herself.

"I feel I have missed out," she complained during this period. "Because I have always thought I have never worked hard enough. I never behaved really badly, never have been really irresponsible. Maybe now it's too late."

And for what? she couldn't help wondering. Maybe it was too late for a lot of things. In the autumn of 1980, word went around the office that despite all the editorial improvements and the huge rise in circulation (it had, at that point, more than doubled), Gary Bogard, now the magazine's sole owner, was unwilling to lose any more of his money for the sake of *Tatler*. Or even for Tina, of whom he was extremely fond. The magazine, rumor had it, was losing an estimated £7,000 a month. Two years into her reign, intimations of impending doom increased. Bogard, it was whispered, was within "five minutes of pulling the money out."

Then those rumors stopped, to be replaced by others. Those who had nursed their own suspicions (suspicions Bogard himself would later dismiss) found the July 17, 1981, issue of *Private Eye* enlightening:

> *A peaceful fishing weekend at Bideford, Devon, is disturbed by some vulgar guests from London who arrive at my hotel in a silver BMW.*
>
> *The brassy blonde in dark glasses who doesn't sign the register turns out to be called Tina Brown, editor of the snobby* Tatler *magazine. Her companion is the paper's proprietor, Australian tycoon Mr Gary Bogard.*

No one at *Tatler* knew whether the rumors were true. But they hoped they were.

"Jolly good of her!" was the verdict of a grateful subordinate. "Because the magazine had been going since 1709; it would have been a shame if it had ended in 1981."

It didn't end, of course. But financially, *Tatler* never truly flourished under Tina, although she was so remarkable at what she did that the few years she spent at its helm—just three and a half in all—became legendary. She worked nights as a matter of course, shuffled and reshuffled staff. And Tina's wheedling worked at least as well as her imperiousness. Harry wrote for her, as did the actor Robert Morley and the writer Christopher Hitchens. Brooke Shields appeared on a *Tatler* cover and Lord Snowdon offered her his photographs of the young and pretty Princess of Wales.

Late one night, Taki Theodoracopulos, a rich Greek playboy and the youngest son of an industrialist shipbuilder, heard the doorbell ring. He was a well-known columnist, a wicked chronicler of high society for *The Spectator,* who was occupying at the time a very large and "grand" house in London. The interruption made him nervous because there was an eccentric sort of party going on, the kind of party Taki would later describe as "to be imagined, not talked about." He told the butler to stand aside, and answered the door himself. Just in case.

"I thought it was the fuzz," he recalled.

It wasn't, he saw at once. It was a very short couple. Harry Evans he recognized right away because he was famous. The blond girl beside him he'd never laid eyes on.

"I'm Tina Brown," she said, sticking out her hand. "I've been named editor of *Tatler*. I'd like you to be our travel writer."

Flattered, Taki accepted on the spot. He would have loved to demonstrate his hospitality by inviting Tina and Harry into the house, "but in view of what was going on, I thought I'd better not."

It didn't matter. For some time, Tina and Taki had an excellent relationship. Taki, ever irrepressible, did indeed write about travel, although not in a wholly traditional way. Athens, he claimed in *Tatler*'s pages, was an ideal travel destination for the ultrachic because "there are a few Greek ship-owners who can speak without using their hands, and they all have yachts." Rich Greek denizens, he promised readers, will never renege on invitations to freeloading foreigners, "even if they've extended them when drunk."

Tina couldn't have been nicer, he decided. Everything he wrote, however louche, mean-spirited, or offbeat, she loved, although she paid him hardly anything. She even took him to lunch—at Langan's, of course—and, true to her passion for conserving and recycling all assets, wrote about *him,* deploying his quotations at no cost to the magazine. "I know journalists are whores but pushing the keys of a typewriter is better than pushing a pocket calculator," she quoted the shipbuilder's son as saying. "I hate businessmen."

"We were fun until I wrote a piece about how Princess Margaret had actually gone to bed with Basil, this enormous black man—he's famous, serviced all these Englishwomen and has a bar called Basil's [on the Caribbean island of Mustique]," Taki would later recall. "So I wrote how he had pretty much done it with Princess Margaret. And then added a little bit about how people were nervous that when the Queen was visiting Mustique, maybe she'd sleep with him." As it happened, Basil himself would eventually admit to having once been "a bit of a rogue." But when asked about rumors concerning "how far his service to Princess Margaret extended," he swore he only danced with her. These revelations were published, interestingly enough, by Tina Brown herself—some two decades later, in America, by which time Princess Margaret's goodwill was of no practical importance to her.

That early piece, Taki soon discovered to his annoyance, was spiked. It wasn't as though Tina had any special affection for Princess

Margaret, she told him when he called to complain. Her objections were more basic and pragmatic than that. "You did a wonderful job on the old porker but we simply can't run it in England," she said.

A week later, Taki thought he had learned the true reason behind Tina's reluctance. "She was staying with Princess Margaret in Mustique. Ergo, the spike." He quit.

In fact, Tina was flying to Mustique to write a profile for the magazine on Princess Margaret's close friend and benefactor, Colin Tennant (the second Baron Glenconner), who owned the little island, had given a plot of it to the princess as a wedding present, and lived, as Tina wrote in an adoring article, "in a sort of mini Taj Mahal on the beach." There was evidently no end to Tennant's fine qualities. "I do have," he told Tina, "an affinity with black people." A large and attractive picture of *Tatler*'s editor, her face shielded from the sun by a lovely wide-brimmed straw hat, accompanied this piece. It showed Tina lunching on the grass across from Princess Margaret, and Tennant himself awash in what Tina described as "his usual elegance."

Of course, Taki understood his former boss's resistance to publishing his piece. "I would have killed that column too," he admitted. "In 1979, you didn't talk about the Queen getting laid by some black stud." However, he felt Tina should have been franker about her motives.

But what were Tina's motives exactly? True to her promise to Simon Carr, she never put on upper-class airs. In fact, she was a good mimic. Princess Diana was her office specialty, and any number of the mannerisms and accents of those she interviewed would on succeeding days be mercilessly diced and sliced at the office. On the other hand, as one of her editors remarked, "She was quite ambivalent, that was noticeable, about the society she was writing about. Tina was very impressed by that kind of big rich handsome person—she loved all that!"

The egalitarian Lord Glenconner, who took pride in getting along nicely with people of color, was by no means confined to her article about that Mustique *déjeuner sur l'herbe*. Many a *Tatler* piece was studded with the Glenconner/Tennant name for no good reason that Tina's staffers could see. The actual dialogue of that famous picnic with Princess Margaret—"What, no mustard?" Her Highness yelled at the onset of the meal. "How am I expected to eat sausages without mustard?"—somehow never made the pages of *Tatler*, although its editor found the incident amusing enough to confide it to a fellow journalist years later, once she had resigned from the magazine.

At times Tina would receive, after a certain amount of wickedness from her pen, what she called "flak." But on close examination, it was impossible to see what wounds she had inflicted. Perhaps this was what truly lay behind the refusal of the upper classes, on reading what she wrote, to take offense: there was none, or at least very little. She was basically writing in invisible ink, the kind that fades after a minute or so. Discarded boyfriends, low-level socialites, gate-crashers: their crimes and misdemeanors made fine, amusing copy. But the big game went unbagged. "There was a side to her that was enormously star-struck," it was noted.

At the same time, an old *Tatler* hand felt, "there was a side to her that sometimes absolutely didn't love all that. I think she kind of came to hate some things about *Tatler*. It's underpinned by society. There was a slightly sort of Becky Sharp air about *Tatler* in those days." There was, for that matter, a slightly Becky Sharp air about Tina herself. That was not the whole portrait, though, not then and not ever. But it was certainly part of it.

The question was, which Tina would win—the Tina who secretly despised those she wrote about; or the Tina who quietly yearned to make her way among them? Really, there was no one she could go to for advice on that question. Harry, torn by the very same conflicts and confusions, could be of little help to her there. Without doubt, he enjoyed those late nights he spent at the *Sunday Times* with the printers, the pressmen, and the men who reminded him of his father and grandfather. But he also worshipped the stars, who reminded him of who he had become. "He was so tremendously impressed by fame, do you see?" said the *Sunday Times* columnist Philip Oakes. "He was constitutionally incapable of not being impressed by fame."

Anyway, Harry had his own problems. Other ones. Bigger ones.

Chapter 5
The End of an Era

"Look!" Harry was told by Denis Hamilton, his proud predecessor, the day he was appointed editor of the *Sunday Times*, "I'm handing you a Rolls-Royce!"

And it was true, Harry was later to reflect. There were few strictures on his independence and judgment. Aside from the royal family, he was free "to write, investigate what you like." For twelve years that Rolls had skimmed along the roughest terrain, its driver unchecked.

By late November 1978, however, that gleaming machine was in the process of being junked. Pickets suddenly appeared on Gray's Inn Road outside the offices of *The Times* and the *Sunday Times*. Harry's faithful employees were not on strike. They were being locked out—by management, which suffered roughly an $80 million loss as a result. Journalists, still paid full wages, suddenly found themselves with plenty of time on their hands—a whole year's worth, as it turned out. The indulgent Thomson family of Canada, which owned the papers and had tolerated for years the losses, crusades, and union eccentricities of one or both its properties, was fed up to the teeth. *The Times* was used to hemorrhaging money; the *Sunday Times,* although an occasional moneymaker, nonetheless never probably realized its potential. Above all, the owners were disgusted with the quirky blue-collar unions, their members as ornery and self-destructive as any marauding band of teenagers. "Industrial disputes had driven *The Times* Newspapers board to the point of despair," Denis Hamilton, the onetime editor in chief of both newspapers, later wrote, comparing the last, doomed fracas to "the Battle of the Somme."

It was no exaggeration. Tens of millions of newspaper copies— 3.5 million in one *month,* Harry complained—had simply never been printed because of some hopeless industrial dispute or other. Harry found himself wallowing in admiration for the tough methods deployed across the Atlantic by *Washington Post* owner Katharine Graham: she flew in newsprint by helicopter in order to vanquish a pressmen's strike at her paper. Gone were the poor northern boy's socialist instincts, his unswerving devotion to the workingman. In 1979, he ended up voting for Margaret Thatcher for prime minister, an amazing turning point since, as one old *Sunday Times* hand pointed out, "In the seventies, we took a poll and we could find only one person on the staff who voted Conservative." Indeed, on the very day in July 1977 when Harry's labor of love, his long-delayed thalidomide investigation, was at last allowed to be printed in full without fear of jail sentences, contempt charges, or fines, one third of the copies— 540,000—simply never appeared. The print unions, it turned out, were involved in yet another dispute with management. In vain did Harry plead at midnight with the printers union committee. When the run began, only eight of the nine presses were operated—depriving whole areas of the country of Harry's paper and the dénouement of his famous thalidomide campaign.

Like his subordinates, he found himself during the lockout with a depressing number of leisure hours at his disposal, some of which he clearly put to good use—on Tina's behalf. Among those he invited to lunch was Ann Barr, who in her capacity as deputy editor of the society magazine *Harper's & Queen* (*Tatler's* more widely read and wealthier rival) would obviously be a useful sort of acquaintance to cultivate.

"What do you pay at *Harper's* for articles? What do you pay your people?" Harry asked innocently of his lunch partner. At that point, Harry had lived more than half a century without betraying the smallest interest in the budgets of society editors, but somehow a new mood had overtaken him and now that was all he could think of.

"I couldn't possibly answer that, Harry," Barr replied smartly, "as your girlfriend is editor of the competition."

"Oh, she's only a *lit-tle* girl," he assured Barr.

Barr was amused, impressed. What a splendid turnabout this was in the long and challenging history of the sexes. "Tina used Harry in the beginning," she observed. And not only in the matter of pay-scale inquiries. "She used a lot of Harry's *Sunday Times* writers in *Tatler*." These professional ties and connections between the couple gradually multiplied. Harry's former deputy, for example, was a wellborn journalist named Frank Giles whose wife, Lady Kitty, was the daughter of a peer. Lady Kitty's pretty daughter, Sarah, became features editor of *Tatler* in 1981, where she was known as a gossipy addition to the staff. "Radio Giles," one of their number called her. From then on, she lived in Tina's professional shadow and sometimes moved where she did.

Thus began between Harry and Tina the devilishly intricate and celebrated dance of mutual dependence that in later years would be cloaked in the peculiar language of the nineties. "Synergy," it was called, a word that didn't do justice to the urges and needs met, the services encompassed. It was a dependence that was, as Barr guessed, of particular value to Tina at the outset. But not exclusively. Like so many of his subordinates, Harry was pretty despondent during the year of the newspaper lockout. "It was a very miserable period," one of them noted. "It's not fun being paid to do nothing."

Worse, Harry was practically alone, separated from employees, friends he had been used to seeing daily, as well as from family, children. "He was absolutely wracked with guilt," another friend recalled. "On the one hand, he had Enid, with whom he had three children and a life together. And on the other, he had Tina, with whom he could share his love of journalism. Tina had what I think of as a co-dependent relationship with Harry. He needed her and she needed him. She was enormously attached to her father and this relationship with Harry recreated her earlier relationship with her father. It was one of those touching older men, younger women relationships. Very touching."

Tina's father, as it happened, very much approved of Harry, and vice versa, perhaps because their personalities were completely different and yet not in conflict. George Brown was, even in retirement, an amiable but tense man, with a quick temper, unlike Harry, whose preferred mode of reacting to threatening situations was flight, although when cornered, he seemed able to indulge and mollify the most impossible and tempestuous staffers, rarely losing his composure. At leisure for the first time in his hurried and hugely successful life, Harry was glad to talk about theater, film, literature with George Brown, who was by then living with Bettina for most of the year in Spain and in declining health. From his earliest youth, Harry would recall, he had loved those Hollywood movies "in which heroic journalists slew dragons." Movies that had totally disappeared by the time Tina was born. Indeed, he was closer in age to Tina's father than to Tina.

Bettina, also having married an older man herself, was very pleased for her daughter. Harry was, she informed those who asked, "a delightful man." She wasn't worried about the single status of her daughter. "As long as they stay as cozy together and as happy together as they are at the moment, I would be very pleased for them."

From time to time, Tina and Harry visited the Browns in their white stucco house in San Pedro de Alcantara, where they had lived since 1973. There the floors were orange tile and the garden studded with aloe plants, geraniums growing in large pots, comfortable wicker chairs, and bowls filled with olives. Prowling around the house were Bettina's nine cats and a three-legged dog named Percy with only one eye. There was a tennis club in the neighborhood. And in the nearby town of Ronda was a house inhabited by Hilary Amis, Kingsley's former wife, and, often enough, their son Martin.

One thing a good friend of the Browns noticed was how rarely the subject of their only son came up. Tall, blond Christopher Hambley Brown (reduced to "Chris Brown" in his movie credits) would follow in his father's footsteps and become a producer, living in a small house in London's middle-class West Dulwich suburb. Nonetheless, "Christopher was someone the parents rarely referred to," a family confidant remarked. "Compared to Tina, the boy was never the focus of the family."

In fact, it was her daughter's pursuits, if not her sharply focused ambitions, that particularly inspired Bettina, and in the oddest way. Still raven-haired, she was launching a new career for herself in the expatriate community around Marbella as, of all things, a journalist. In 1979, on the very day her daughter was offered *Tatler,* Bettina was appointed editor of *Spanish Home,* a magazine described by the British press as being "for those who take pride in their haciendas." Four years later, at sixty-one, she had a local radio program called *What's New, Pussycat?*

Nor did she stop at that. Within short order, she was writing for other glossies on a wide range of subjects. They included not simply the aging British movie stars, shady fugitives from justice, and saggy, down-at-the-heels Eurotrash who were her neighbors and eventually her specialties (Tina used to call her mother "the Hedda Hopper of the Costa del Sol"), but other topics even more exciting. There was an eagerness about her literary ventures, as though she were fighting to stretch each minute into a life—and not her own life either, but one of a younger, freer woman with unlimited reserves of time, energy, and good fortune.

Bettina ran with the bulls at dawn, covered a horse fair at Jerez, and went on a wild boar shoot at the Count of Cordoba's hunting lodge in the Sierra Nevada, which she would later depict to her friend Valerie Grove as "a squalid little place full of high-born Spanish grandees dressed as Mexican bandits, eating baked beans out of tins." When the new Marbella water chute opened, she was among the first to slide down the contraption. Sometimes George accompanied his frenetic wife on these jaunts, dutifully snapping pictures. "A sort of journalistic Bonnie and Clyde," was how Bettina described their adventures together, delicately neglecting to mention that Clyde was by that time seventy, paunchy, and white-haired.

"It's ridiculous," she declared after hot-air ballooning for a story in an English-language magazine based in Spain. "I'm doing the sort of thing Tina did . . . at eighteen." But she said it without a trace of remorse. In fact, it was with pointed self-mockery that she spoke of her life in exile, the heat, the leisure, the expats giving "parties all the time," and the "ten widows to every seventy-five-year-old man." She really did not miss London at all, she insisted; it transformed her, she told her friend Grove (who wrote a profile on Bettina for the *Standard* of London) into an old-age pensioner, "growing rheumaticky and discontented, my coat wrapped around me and fumbling for my bus pass and my purse."

She had fled such a fate among other expatriates in San Pedro, who did not ask her perpetually, as did her British friends, "What if you become ill in Spain?" Bettina, like her daughter, who dreaded poverty in old age, could well imagine a life governed by fear. Like Tina, she possessed a sharp sense of the absurd—a sense that she might even *be* absurd. She had learned to use humor in a studied, protective way to mask and give license to her desperate flights of rejuvenation.

This, then, was Harry's new family. Not his only one, of course, but his relief family, the backup, composed in equal measure of eccentricity and glamour. That glamour was by then a bit faded: George Brown was in retirement, and his lively wife was seeking to pursue, now that their daughter was launched on a buoyant career, certain job opportunities that had previously eluded her.

But then a lot in Harry's life was beginning to fade: the cachet of his non-operational newspaper, the pull of his marriage, his guilt about Enid, whose pain was pronounced but cloaked in dignity. "The divorce was very bitter and the process of long duration," recalled an old friend.

Harry was not idle during the lockout. He was meeting with close business friends, among them the expansive TV personality Melvyn Bragg, whom he knew because, said Bragg, "Harry made it his business to know everybody." Another was Bernard Donoughue, who was a senior policy adviser to two successive prime ministers, Harold Wilson and James Callaghan, and whom Harry admired above all because Donoughue, the son of a metal polisher in a car factory, had graduated from Oxford and now worked as did Evans himself, among powerful establishment men.

Bragg, Evans, and Donoughue were particularly interested in a potentially remunerative venture: they would bid for a television station in Harry's old stomping ground, the Northeast—Tyne-Tees Television, where Harry got his start as an on-air personality. Then they would "take it over and set up a huge information center there," Bragg claimed. All three friends were very anxious to make money, Harry not least because he was involved in a costly divorce from Enid. "To end their 25-year marriage he had to give her the matrimonial home in North London as well as pay maintenance for her and the younger children equal to some 35 percent of his income," *Private Eye* informed its readers. Harry, it added, "has long been moaning that he is broke." Certainly the venture, aside from being a wonderful career opportunity, could have solved such problems. Bragg just knew, "We would have made a fortune."

Nonetheless, Harry turned down that delightful prospect and, with little ceremony, pulled out. His friends tried to argue him out of it, to no avail. Harry, Bragg realized with a sinking heart, was "an honorable man." So honorable that "he didn't want to be bidding for another business when his troops were suffering from the lockout, he didn't feel he should be doing it when his friends were in trouble." With that decision, the television venture collapsed.

In fact, everything was collapsing around Harry. In November 1979, the newspaper lockout ended and people went back to work, but there wasn't a lot of merrymaking when the presses resumed their roll. The losses were staggering. The newspaper Harry had called "the adventure playground for journalists" was losing some of its passion for daring and great feats of valor. Within nine months, the journalists of *The Times* went on strike, demanding a 21 percent pay increase; it was, as everyone knew, "just a fantastic slap in the face for Thomson. He'd paid all these guys for a year to come back to work. And what does he get? A journalists' strike!"

By the end of 1980, Harry calculated, press room squabbles had resulted in lost copies on twenty occasions; a total of 4 million homes had been deprived of his paper. "Nobody," he realized, "seemed to care anymore."

Least of all the owners. Shortly after the journalists' foolhardy strike, staffers were summarily informed that the two newspapers were up for sale, preferably as a duo. No one doubted there would be bidders for the *Sunday Times,* which despite the devastating financial pounding it had endured was chock-full of ads and likely to make a profit. But its homely stepbrother, *The Times,* was in deplorable financial condition. The question was, who would buy such a troublesome pair? Who would even buy the *Sunday Times,* with its large circulation and impossible unions? Who would buy both?

Harry decided *he* would lead the charge. He would head a consortium that would raise large sums of money, buy out the owners, and save the *Sunday Times* and maybe even *The Times.* What he envisaged was raising money from a small group of investors, offering stock to the staff, and creating an editorial trust. "Easier said than done . . ." he recalled.

Much easier. Katharine Graham, when Evans flew to Washington to ask her for cash and counsel in this venture, turned him down flat, informing him the consortium was an insane idea. On the other hand, plenty of others, mostly Harry's loyal staffers, would have followed him out a penthouse window.

"All the journalists on the *Sunday Times* wanted this independent consortium—two to three hundred of them, I should think," recalled Magnus Linklater, who was once that newspaper's magazine editor. And who better than Harry to organize and speak for them? Even as top editor of the paper, Harry used to pick up ringing phones should no one else be around, and say as casually as you please, as though answering phones were his *job,* "Hello, news desk." He was a natural leader. A born newspaperman. An extraordinary fellow. "It was actually rather puerile of us—*Daddy will save us,*" Don Berry, a top editor and one of the most devoted Harry admirers, would later concede.

And yet, that's exactly what Daddy was telling the troops. Daddy would save them. And who could have doubted such a claim?

.   .   .

Of all the suitors desperate for the hand of the *Sunday Times,* Rupert Murdoch was, in the eyes of the sellers, the richest and most desirable. True, aside from Harry, the competition for the prize wasn't especially choice. The newspaper owner and scoundrel Robert Maxwell was among those burning to possess the *Sunday Times,* as was Lord Rothermere, another millionaire newspaper owner. But there were other factors to consider. Murdoch was willing to buy *both* newspapers, the success as well as the financial flop.

Harry and his hardy band of followers found out about their ruthless rival soon enough. Harry had known Murdoch in a slight but ongoing and intriguing way for years. He had invited him to his home in Highgate, with a dutiful Enid presiding, when Murdoch, heir to an Australian newspaper dynasty, had already substantially expanded operations. He was known in England as the vulgar ruffian who had bought *The Sun,* which ended up promoting a daily diet of tits-and-ass (thus earning Murdoch the sobriquets "Dirty Digger" and "Thanks for the Mammary Murdoch"). Because of the uproar he caused, the magazine of Harry's own newspaper had even done a profile of Murdoch, although not without a lot of difficulty.

Outraged by the impertinence of the *Sunday Times,* Murdoch adamantly refused to talk to its reporter and warned off his subordinates. "An odd posture for a newspaperman," Harry thought. In his memoirs, Evans wrote with some asperity about that Murdoch profile and certain appalling errors of judgment that surrounded its publication. Apparently, Murdoch knew well ahead of time what was going to be written about him in the *Sunday Times*—thanks to a person Harry referred to only as "someone": ". . . someone made a mistake and sent this first draft [of the magazine profile] to Murdoch. The magazine's idea was that their manifest readiness to receive corrections at an early stage might encourage Murdoch and others to give their versions of events. . . ."

Subsequently, Harry sent Murdoch yet another version he was ready to publish, on which the newspaper was "ready to consider corrections."

Certainly Murdoch was, even then, powerful and frightening enough to try to placate. By the time the *Sunday Times* was up for sale, he owned eighty-four newspapers, and not just in Britain and Australia. He had established himself in America with two San Antonio papers on which he'd spent $19 million, the tabloid *Star,* into which he'd poured $12 million, and above all, the *New York Post*. In London, he owned the tell-all *News of the World* (also known as *The News of the Screws*) and the racy *Sun*'s circulation had surpassed 3 million. These were not, however, the rags with which Murdoch could ever hope to polish up his image. To accomplish that goal, he certainly needed a far better class of newspaper. Harry's, for instance. And the staid old *Times* as well.

Naturally, Harry was extremely worried. He would soon receive word from a high-ranking newspaper executive that Murdoch wanted Harry to leave his enviable top post at the *Sunday Times* and possibly become editor of the financially troubled *Times*. How comforting was that? Harry had read his own newspaper's profile of Murdoch, which noted that he had the disconcerting habit of firing his editors. Besides, Harry was the leader of a rival consortium anxious to buy the newspapers as well—"and did a tremendous amount of work in doing so," according to a former friend.

Nevertheless, around the time he learned that Murdoch was both his rival and his secret admirer ("He thinks the world of you," said a mutual acquaintance), Harry allowed himself to be courted by the tycoon—twice—at Murdoch's home on Eaton Place, Belgravia. On the second occasion, which was a dinner that took place on the evening of January 17, 1981, Harry was accompanied by Tina. Her influence on her live-in companion—and her ability to dip beneath the surface of power and charm and draw certain vital conclusions—may be deduced from this beautifully written but essentially frivolous passage from her diary. In it Murdoch is portrayed against the backdrop of a bright and merry landscape straight out of Disney, the scene dominated by an imp rather than an ogre:

> *I had to admit I liked him hugely. He was in an American country gentleman's three-piece suit and heavy shoes, and was by turns urbane and shady. His face seems to have been made for the cartoonist's distortion—the gargoyle lips, deep furrows in the brow, the hint of five o'clock shadow that gives him such an underworld air when he's sunk in thought. But when he was standing by the fire with one foot on the fender laughing uproariously he seemed robust and refreshing. There's no doubt he lives newspapers . . .*
>
> *The truth is that, although he'll be trouble, he'll also be enormous fun and H. has had so many years of Thomson greyness this vivid rascal could bring back some of the jokes.*

That seductive dinner suggested that, at the very least, Harry was quite anxious to further his own ambitions at Eaton Place—at a time when he was urging trusting friends to stand fast against Murdoch and all other unworthy prospective buyers. "That sounds suspiciously as if the takeover was already being regarded as a *fait accompli*," his former friend and colleague Magnus Linklater would later write. True, on a previous visit to Murdoch, Harry had uttered a defiant, "The *Sunday Times* isn't yours yet. We want to succeed with our consortium," to his gracious host. But how terrifying a threat was that supposed to be, flung as it was across Murdoch's own lunch table? Especially since Murdoch had just uttered the tantalizing, irresistible question: "Would you like to edit *The Times?*"

In other words, at some point or other Harry appeared to be distancing himself from the very idea of the consortium he had so ardently peddled. That, Linklater later concluded, "would open him to a charge of bad faith not only towards those who worked on the consortium but towards the journalists on the *Sunday Times* who gave it their whole-hearted backing."

What was Harry doing? it would later be asked. Why was he leading a pack of noble, independent souls intent on buying the papers in order to save them (and save, by extension, the exemplary traditions of journalism Harry himself had espoused) while simultaneously flirting with the "vivid rascal" who intended to gobble them up himself? Harry, who had always believed that "the most crucial feature in journalism is: What freedom does the editor have?" Yet he was quietly dealing with a multimillionaire who believed that freedom of the press belongs to the man who owns the newspaper. Murdoch had never made any bones about that. He was—and is—a proprietor who considered newspapers to be, immutably, an extension of himself and his beliefs.

"It is quite clear in retrospect that at a significant point Harry had switched sides," said Linklater. "Or a better way of putting it: he recognized that the reality was that Murdoch was the preferred purchaser as far as the owners were concerned, and whatever he did was irrelevant, because they wanted to sell both papers together, and Murdoch was the only possible purchaser."

Denis Hamilton, who had hired Harry and been his boss for years, put it even more bluntly in his memoirs: "Harold Evans, though he made a great show of leading a cavalry charge of *Sunday Times* journalists intent on buying out the owners, soon threw his hat in with the Murdoch camp." Very likely, no amount of bellyaching was going to change the decision of the owners to sell to Murdoch. Moreover, Harry would later explain, he had learned the owners would never sell the paper to the consortium under any circumstances.

But the problem was, said Linklater, that he for one never knew about Harry's evolving change of heart, or about his temptation to switch jobs. In retrospect, Linklater felt, "Evans had made at least a mental commitment to Murdoch" earlier than he had realized. On the other hand, there were others who did receive such intimations from Harry himself. "It became clearer and clearer that Harry didn't have the stomach to fight," said Bruce Page. "I'd be amazed if anyone was totally astonished." Page had left the *Sunday Times* by then, but when he talked to his former boss during this difficult period, Harry suggested to him that Murdoch was someone who couldn't be dismissed out of hand. "He didn't conceal it . . . I think he was hoping until the last minute for alternatives. Harry didn't make a complete and firm decision until late in the day."

Besides, one by one, the alternatives to Murdoch disappeared. And the newspaper baron himself could be very engaging and persuasive. "Murdoch charmed him," said another colleague. "Suddenly Harry was saying, 'He's the best bloke of the bidders.' "

Certainly, had he been paying proper attention, Harry might have received an indication of the fate that awaited him, even before the sale to Murdoch was formally approved by the government. One Saturday in the composing room, Murdoch turned up, much to the astonishment of many. Harry had written an editorial about the newspaper magnate's bid for the *Sunday Times* and *The Times*. Staffers were horrified to see Murdoch in the flesh, examining a page proof of the editorial on their premises. Worse, Murdoch was calmly inking a notation on some minor point onto the proof, and handing it over to the managing editor, who in turn gave it to Harry. Just as though he owned the place, one might have been tempted to say. Except that those who owned the place would never have committed such an infraction.

"Rupert had spotted a factual inaccuracy," recalled Don Berry, the news features editor, who witnessed the scene, aghast. "I was actually appalled by this. Here was this man—he didn't even officially own the paper yet—and he's making marks. That's what was so frightening. This was an outsider who had promised no interference. . . . Rupert was saying, 'You can be independent.'

"Harry told me it was a factual inaccuracy which he consciously didn't correct for the first edition. But for later editions he did. I do remember protesting to Harry, 'This is really bad news.'" Harry wrote Murdoch an admonitory note, and reported the results: "Harry said Rupert had apologized profusely."

Don Berry wasn't fooled. "Everyone told Harry that. We said, 'You can't trust this man.'"

Thus, when *Private Eye* announced less than two weeks after Harry's private dinner with Murdoch that Evans, "regarded by the Digger as 'one of the world's greatest editors' . . . is now said to have his eye on *The Times* since he has become bored after 13 years editing the world's greatest Sunday paper," there was considerable consternation.

Even the satirical magazine professed to be genuinely puzzled by Murdoch's career plans for Harry (or "the Dame," as it still persisted in calling him). "The question is being asked whether the Digger would hold such a high opinion of the Dame if he knew the lengths to which Evans has gone in recent weeks to stop him getting the papers. . . . Now the Dame has no choice but to oil up the Digger, which he seems to be doing nicely."

Harry's response to *Private Eye*'s suggestion that he was switching sides was classic Harry. The man who had boldly proclaimed, "A democracy that does not have a free press is not a true democracy," and deplored the use of Britain's stringent libel laws as well as a "ragbag" of other restrictions to muzzle that true democracy, issued a libel writ, for the third time, as *Private Eye* made sure to inform its readers. Some weeks later, Harry made the announcement himself to his staff: he was leaving the *Sunday Times* and was going to be editing *The Times,* Britain's paper of record. And then Harry burst into tears.

In theory, Murdoch, who paid $28 million for the two properties, was obliged to go before Britain's Monopolies Commission in order to acquire them (a final authority that might have impeded the bid), but this was obviated when reams of figures were presented to Parliament which indicated that both *The Times* and the *Sunday Times* were in desperate need of salvation by Murdoch since they were financial basket cases. Harry, listening to such drivel from the press gallery—the *Sunday Times* had made a £700,000-pound profit in 1980—felt he knew better than anyone that this was not the case with the *Sunday Times.* "It was for me sitting gagged and bound . . . perhaps the most bitter and frustrating moment of the whole affair," he wrote in his memoirs. And still he joined Murdoch.

"I went to *The Times* because, quite simply, I couldn't resist it," he explained to his old colleague Philip Oakes, and it was the truest statement he would ever make about the gnawing episode that has haunted him ever since. In later years, Harry would offer all sorts of sincere regrets and interpretations about his behavior in the face of crisis, as well as the motives behind it. These representations often showed him in the strangely passive and novel position of victim: victim of Murdoch, victim of his own frailties, it hardly mattered which. Harry had been afflicted. He was propelled by "ambition and conceit." He had "a lot to answer for." He was duped. As for Murdoch's character, it kept mutating like an Ebola virus with each telling. Harry would, for instance, claim to have been seduced by Murdoch: "Every editor and many a politician who deals with Murdoch thinks that they're the one who is really going to change him," he said, rather revealingly in retrospect. "They're like a woman who goes out with a womanizer. She thinks, 'This time, this time he really means it. He really loves me. He'll really marry me.' Well, Murdoch's like a womanizer in that sense. He has this fatal capacity to instill the confidence in you that you and he have a special, exclusive relationship." At other moments, Murdoch was portrayed as worse, far worse than any tyrant or mere womanizer. "It's like Milton's *Paradise Lost*," Harry later complained. "The most interesting character is Lucifer."

But Murdoch represented something else for Harry, which went completely unmentioned: a handy capitalist tool, a means of laying to rest his origins, along with the socialism, poverty, anger, and rebellion that had informed them. "All Harry's best pieces, the *Sunday Times'* best pieces, were attacks on state functions. Thalidomide was one," recalled an old associate. "It was a radical office." Weary of that radicalism, of destructive unions, of being a perpetual outsider, Harry joined up with a man intent on destroying the first two, and who, as a brash Australian, reveled in being an outsider. Murdoch was now offering him, in February 1981, the editorship of the most entrenched establishment newspaper in the country. That was the real, the only seduction; Lucifer came running only when Harry whistled.

And yet, in relinquishing the "radical" *Sunday Times* with its gallant crusades, its investigative bent, and impertinent commentary, Harry was giving up, without realizing it, something vital he had always taken for granted: his own security. Those nasty class struggles that he had hoped to bury with his move to a more upscale publication were bound to be resurrected. At the establishment paper, said an ally, "they didn't like him or the *Sunday Times*. They regarded the *Sunday Times* as a blight on *The Times* and its traditions."

For his part, Harry remained determinedly oblivious to such palpable animosity. He seemed to forget that on the *Sunday Times,* as a former colleague put it, "people would protect Harry. We would speak for him. I always thought of it in Roman terms. Harry was in the circle of people who were all looking out for him. And if anybody tried to knife him, they had to go through the rest. Now on *The Times* he was in the middle of a circle of people who were all looking in. And stabbing him."

Without a doubt, those fatally seductive powers Harry attributed to Murdoch were working their will, and he harbored, initially at least, the fond notion that theirs was indeed "a special, exclusive relationship." His first instinct on switching over to editing *The Times* was to refer to himself and his new boss in especially jocular and intimate ways, as if they were just two wild and crazy spiritual twins. "Murdoch and I are two relatively impulsive people restraining each other," he said. *The Times,* he added, was "a great challenge, the greatest of my life." And he was intent on "attracting a younger readership."

Murdoch's goals were very precise: expand circulation and cut expenses. Harry's talents did not encompass both possibilities simultaneously. He named new editors (some of them receiving salaries much higher, old staffers discovered to their annoyance, than theirs), redesigned the sports and business sections, and thereby managed to increase circulation by 13,000—to 294,000 readers. He also deferred to his boss on a number of occasions. In his biography of Murdoch, William Shawcross quoted the newspaper magnate's recollections of acts of obeisance:

> "Harry used to come to me and say"—(he mimicked a fast and mouse-like whisper)—" 'I'll do anything you like. Just tell me what you'd like.' And I'd say, 'Harry, nothing. Please get on with it. But please be consistent.' " Evans, he claimed, was forever switching the paper's policy on big issues.

The men did have one or two things in common. They were close in age; Harry was fifty-two at the time, Murdoch his junior by two years. They nursed a fondness for younger women, whom they married. They were ambitious, tireless workers. And they were iconoclasts who despised the British establishment. But after some months such similarities appeared to count for little.

Not much seemed to go right at *The Times* once Harry got there. Even the Queen Mother, it was widely rumored, stopped reading the paper. Harry tried with the same forced jocularity he had cultivated in describing his closeness to Murdoch to endear himself to the lifers at the paper. "It's called the editing theory of maximum irritation," he said. "I intend to be involved in all parts of the paper at all times." This did not go down well in the newsroom.

"He never established any loyalty among the old *Times* people," reflected one of them. Old hands used to calmer, more pacific seas were especially disturbed at all the noise and fuss that erupted on the day Egyptian president Anwar Sadat was murdered. Harry made over the entire paper at 4:00 A.M. when the news came in. "Yet there were senior people asking if we could wait a day and reflect before we rushed into print," said one staffer.

And so Harry failed, as his old friends always predicted he would, at setting up a new power base in this alien territory.

True to his promise, said one old *Times* editor, Harry set about the difficult business of initiating job cuts. "Rupert gave Harry substantial sums of money to fire people [who received] big checks in their pockets. The figures are roughly that fifty-four people had been fired by Harry. And then Rupert came back one weekend to find he had hired fifty-seven new ones!"

The precariousness of his new position wasn't lost on Harry, but he took unfortunate and futile steps to try to anchor it. There were more observations of alarming deference on his part, which had never before been evident in his remarkable career. Within a year, Alexander Chancellor, who was then editor of *The Spectator,* witnessed it himself. Over lunch in the penthouse executive dining room at *The Times,* Harry asked Chancellor to take the position of *Times* literary editor. Chancellor considered the job offer absurd.

"Come on, Harry, I don't read any books," he protested. Then he looked up, amazed. Murdoch himself had materialized at their table, asking if he might join them. Chancellor wasn't fooled by the owner's sudden attention. It had nothing to do with him, he thought, even though he'd known Murdoch as a child; his father had been the top executive at Reuters, then owned by Keith Murdoch, who was Rupert's father.

"He was obviously getting bored with a bunch of advertisers in another dining room. He's a restless man," said Chancellor. "And Rupert was sort of drumming his fingers impatiently on the table all the time. Terrified of being bored, while we were terrified of boring him."

"Does Algy interfere with you a lot?" Murdoch abruptly asked Chancellor. It was a reference to Algernon Cluff, the rich and firmly conservative proprietor of *The Spectator* at that time.

"Well, not so far, certainly," replied Chancellor.

"I'd never dare interfere with Harry. Would I, Harry?" said Murdoch. Embarrassed, Chancellor stole a quick glance at Harry. "Harry had a sort of pathetic grateful look on his face. At this being said in front of a third party."

And yet, beyond a doubt Murdoch was interfering. The proprietor sent him right-wing pieces marked "Worth reading." He thought Margaret Thatcher beyond reproach and Harry wrongheaded in allowing his newspaper to question what she did. "You're always getting at her!" he said. He had an aversion, Harry felt, to "balance" and insisted the newspaper needed more "conviction," which Harry interpreted as toadying to the Tory government.

To a number of outsiders, it appeared that Harry's position at the helm was being quietly shredded, and not only by Murdoch but by Harry's own subordinates. Like the new owner, certain journalists were disgusted with another facet of Harry's. "He never seemed to be able to make up his mind about anything," one said. There were those among Harry's old followers who attributed his difficulties at *The Times* to the class war he had been so keen to circumvent—without success, evidently. And there was something to this theory. But it was by no means the whole story. Even Harry's old boss and former champion, Denis Hamilton, had tried to argue Murdoch out of appointing his protégé. "I told Murdoch it would turn out disastrously and it did," Hamilton wrote, not long before his death. Harry, he noticed, was "constantly (as he had done with me) overspending or temporarily disguising expenditure."

On the night of March 30, 1981, just hours after Ronald Reagan was shot, Harry was found celebrating the launch of a book on the Beatles over dinner at Langan's. Like the rest of the guests, he was left for quite a while in total ignorance of the catastrophe that had taken place in Washington.

Philip Norman, the author of the Beatles book, observed that considering the terrible urgency of that event, Harry "seemed to be called back to the office awfully late. It always struck me as odd, because they must have gotten the news of this at the paper pretty early in the evening. Harry didn't get the call at my party until after ten o'clock at night."

Later, Norman dissected this delay in detail. His old boss, he felt, had been ill served by his own newspaper staff. "They weren't telling him what they should tell him. They were deliberately not doing what they should."

Nonetheless, Harry sustained, outwardly at least, an impermeable optimism. Rupert had given his word: *The Times* was to be an independent publication. Apparently certain of his future, Harry put in a buoyant phone call to the United States where his friend Anthony Holden, the biographer of Prince Charles, was working as a correspondent for the rival English Sunday newspaper, the *Observer*. Holden wanted to stay put in Washington for the rest of his life, he said. But Harry was insistent. Holden should come back to London immediately, where he would be made features editor and assistant editor of *The Times*. In fact, he would be Harry's heir in due course.

"How old are you, laddie?" asked Harry.

"I'm thirty-two," Holden replied.

"Well, I'm fifty-two. I've told Rupert I'll do this job for eight years. Think of it, lad, editor of *The Times* at *forty!* I'll groom you."

So Holden came back to London, jaunty, full of hope for the future. Within a few months he was one of the few invited to Harry's wedding.

Tina very much wanted to get married. This was not exactly what she told the gossip columns. "When you have been together for as long as we have, unless you want nippers you don't marry," she said. But that was just verbal salve for blistered pride. Harry was for a long time quite resistant to such a denouement. "He was going through great agonies about Enid," a friend recollected. "He had a big conscience about that. He's a very decent man and he was very fond of his first wife." But what about his girlfriend? Tina needed status, the kind not easily supplied to a woman by merely landing a good job. There had been snide assaults on her in the press. One of her former boyfriends had actually revealed an oblique tidbit on the nature of Tina's undergarments, flimsy apparently, and somehow or other this shameful confidence had made it into *Private Eye*. She was enraged at being turned into a figure of fun; what she needed was a large fortress, preferably Harry's. Unfortunately, she rarely saw Harry. He was spending most of his time on his new job; dinners together were infrequent.

"He comes back late, and all we talk about is *The Times*," she complained. She had been with Harry for six years, and was weary of their unregularized life in the terraced house. And the thing of it was, she wanted nippers and always had. "Why hasn't he proposed to me?" she asked a friend, who would later explain, "I know she was getting to the point that unless he proposed to her," the relationship might come to an end.

In August 1982, Harry and Tina flew to America for an ostensible vacation. There they visited Grey Gardens, the East Hampton, Long Island, retreat of journalist Sally Quinn and Ben Bradlee—a perfect choice of hosts under the circumstances, since their own courtship and professional experiences very much paralleled Harry and Tina's. Bradlee was of course the central hero of the Watergate scandal, a venerable and dashing editor in his day, and a fast friend of John F. Kennedy in earlier times. It was Bradlee who had molded *The Washington Post* from a dull backwater daily into the warrior newspaper that first exposed the iniquities of President Richard Nixon. He was the Harry Evans of the New World.

Quinn, pretty and blond, was a talented journalist for the Style section of *The Washington Post*. She had launched her affair with Bradlee back in the early seventies by writing him a series of unsigned notes indicating, as their recipient observed, "a crush that was getting harder and harder to handle." Bradlee, twenty years her senior, was swept away by his star writer, whose social cachet received even more of a boost as the liaison developed. Six years later, by then divorced from his second wife, he made Quinn his third.

Inside Harry's suitcase, unknown to Tina, was a beautiful pearl choker, her wedding gift, which he had secretly purchased. On some ridiculous health pretext, he had even pushed Tina into getting a blood test. He too felt it was time to marry. Tina herself only received his proposal twenty-four hours before the wedding he had planned to take place in East Hampton. Harry was "a bag of nerves," it was noticed, alternately anxious and excitable, and above all, feeling a fair degree of guilt—still.

Acquaintances, if they were the adult offspring of divorced parents, found themselves buttonholed by Harry shortly before his wedding. He wanted to know how they felt decades later about their parents' split. Journalists who had separated from their spouses were treated to earnest lectures from Harry "about wives and families and children and responsibility." Families shouldn't be partitioned, he chided them.

"It's disgusting, Harry, but the world is full of it!" one of his victims snapped back. Harry nodded wearily. The world was indeed full of men who left their wives.

Bradlee, as it turned out, was to be the best man, and Anthony Holden was to give away the bride. "I'm in charge of him, you're in charge of her. Make sure none of them runs out of this thing," Bradlee told Holden. "C'mon, let's go out. I need a drink."

The two men sat sipping their drinks in John F. Kennedy's rocking chairs, which were placed on the porch on either side of the front door. It was noon when they spied Harry running out the door, headed straight toward town. He was sprinting, actually, it was observed, "at the rate of knots." He was a regular jogger, in excellent shape for his age, but this dash didn't bear much resemblance to his usual exercise.

"Was that Harry?" Bradlee was stunned.

"Yes!" said Holden.

For an hour the two sat, wondering if Harry had run out on his own wedding, terrified of telling Tina of their suspicions. In any event, Tina had other things on her mind: the October issue of *Tatler* was a mess. "I'm trying to get the right photo spread," she wailed to her friend the American writer Marie Brenner. "And I'm trying to get the right photographer!"

When Harry finally came back from town, it was with a big grin on his face directed at the worried Bradlee, and a freshly dry-cleaned suit over his arms.

Eventually, the guests arrived: Lauren Bacall; the novelist and future film writer/director Nora Ephron; and the real estate magnate Mortimer Zuckerman, who published *Atlantic Monthly* magazine. Tina wore a white dress for the occasion. There were tears in her eyes, and in Harry's. The ceremony took place in the Bradlees' Italianate garden, on the edge of the Atlantic, and as Tina was walking down the steps to the garden, about to take her place next to the groom, she whispered: *Who is that guy?*

She was staring at a stranger. He had on a very loud pair of yellow plaid golf socks and a suit of silvery hue into which a complicated pattern was woven; it gave off eager glints in the bright sunlight.

"That's the judge," Tina was told. "The Honorable Sheppard Frood." From a tape inside a ghetto blaster, which Harry had deftly purchased and hidden in the bushes, boomed the strains of Mendelssohn's *Wedding March*.

At lunch after the ceremony, served poolside at Grey Gardens, Lauren Bacall was informed of the newlyweds' plans for that evening: Harry had bought tickets for *The Pirates of Penzance* in Central Park. Harry was very fond of Gilbert and Sullivan. It was just another little surprise he had in store for Tina.

"No, he's not taking her to see that!" Bacall announced. "I'm making a promise." She disappeared a minute, came back, and said, "You tell Harry for me that they are *not* going to Central Park. They are going to see Miss Lena Horne's one-person show, and they are dining with Miss Horne after the show."

They went there by limousine.

Some evenings later, the groom found himself dining once again in company, but not Miss Lena Horne's, and certainly not Tina's. Within very short order, the bride had flown home to London, where, apparently, *Tatler* and its messy photo layout needed her even more than Harry. That night, he dined with an old friend, Murray Sayle, who had worked for the *Sunday Times* in its golden era, and had courted and married a woman much younger than he.

At the Algonquin Hotel in New York, Harry ate snow peas and, for dessert, profiteroles. He was in a reflective mood. Once he had wanted nothing more than a younger woman. He had even made discreet inquiries of Sayle about the breed: Was there a future in such relationships? Was it a good idea or not? Now he had married one.

"See, when he first had talked about younger women, it was with apprehension," Sayle said. For good reason, really. "It passed through his mind that the beginning of Tina was the end of Enid."

Harry and Enid "had come a long way together," Sayle said. He had, as Harry knew, spent evenings with Enid and found her not only intelligent but a good source of story ideas. Her particular interest was education, especially the education of children with learning disabilities. She was, in Sayle's words, "the sort of woman you'd expect a serious editor to have as a wife."

Harry appeared thoughtful. His wife, the new and glamorous one, was off editing her society magazine across the Atlantic. "He perceived he was leaving something behind which he understood and entering into uncharted waters," Sayle said. "Because Harry was paying his dues to become a revered figure. . . . He was on that path and Enid would have been the perfect consort."

Harry was not feeling proud of himself, that much was certain. "I deserted one family," he often said. And he had good and sufficient reason to reflect on the likelihood and repercussions of abandonment. Rupert Murdoch, after all, was his new boss. How likely was it that this tough new employer would stay wedded to him? At that point in his life, Harry had grown acutely aware of unions, all sorts of unions, and their potential for dissolution.

On the other hand, said Sayle, "Well, you know Harry. Once he had attained eminence, he felt he *deserved* Tina."

And so he did, very likely.

Chapter 6
Moving Day

Nothing went right at *The Times* after Harry's marriage to Tina. Had he been a believer in omens and portents, he might have been better off. In fact, he would have saved himself much humiliation by quitting his first day. Within seconds of arriving at his new job, Harry had thrown his jacket over his chair and manfully rolled up his sleeves. A half hour later, his wallet was swiped. This, it was later decided, set the tone for Harry's destiny at the paper, and in Britain too for that matter.

There were, of course, those who still admired and regarded with bemused affection practically everything about Harry, but they tended to be the new recruits. "He was particularly good at plonking himself down next to an attractive woman reporter, and murmuring in his North Country accent, 'No, *no*, that's not the way to start this story,' and then commandeering her typewriter and hammering out a new intro," recalled Bevis Hillier, whom Harry had handpicked for *The Times*. "I am not implying he was an old lecher. It did just happen to be a pretty reporter quite often."

Murdoch, less charmed, had ideas about how to widen the appeal of the stuffy old *Times*, and none of them included rewriting intros for beautiful women. Still, they weren't all bad ideas, even Harry could see that. No longer, Murdoch decided, was the paper intended for "men in pinstriped suits and bowler hats." There simply weren't enough bowler hats left to sustain such an effort. "Rupert took the view that this was a mad strategy," recalled a close associate. "By the early eighties, there was still a

British establishment, but it was very different from the one that had gone before. The ad industry, the media, new entrepreneurial classes, the self-made were the top people." The Ruperts of the world or the would-be Ruperts were Murdoch's target readers. They would buy *The Times*: 700,000 of them, he hoped.

The problem was, Harry Evans was no Rupert. He was neither ideologically inclined nor especially impressed by the Darwinian nature of the new Thatcher mood sweeping the nation, which precluded most forms of passion, save the central one of making money. As a self-made man, Harry had no aversion to wealth. But as a self-educated one, he had restless, ranging loves: Bach's *St. Matthew Passion,* skiing and healthy diets (he was particularly fierce on this subject), jazz, swimming, and Ralph Ellison's *The Invisible Man.* He was not an intellectual; he did not have the discipline for it. He was simply curious in a freewheeling, idiosyncratic fashion, his imagination impaled wherever his twitchy mind happened to alight. Murdoch, more stolid, brought to the venture certain skills and beliefs. Flatten the unions, swell the coffers. It was his conviction that the best way to make *The Times* accessible to the Rupert readers was, as a former friend put it, "by dumbing it down."

Thus, months after Harry's first inauspicious day, as Bevis Hillier observed, "Evans was having rows with Murdoch, who had decided to get rid of him." The main reason was money: the paper was losing about $30 million a year. In any event, it was clear that Murdoch blamed Harry for practically everything that went wrong.

Such an eventuality was not entirely unexpected, thought Hillier, nor was Murdoch solely at fault. "Staff were divided—some thought Evans hopeless. What I felt was that he was a great journalist but an indifferent administrator." Evans was by no means Murdoch's only failure, however. On the *Sunday Times,* newly vacated by Harry, Murdoch had appointed as editor the courtly Frank Giles, an establishment figure who didn't quite have Harry's work ethic. "Giles used to go home promptly," recalled Magnus Linklater. He, too, had a difficult reign: after much pressure from Murdoch, the *Sunday Times* acquired "The Hitler Diaries." These had been examined by the famous historian Hugh Trevor-Roper, Lord Dacre of Glanton, who subsequently had second thoughts on the matter. "Fuck Dacre," said Murdoch. "Publish." It was not an inspired directive: the diaries turned out to be fraudulent.

Meanwhile, on *The Times,* there was no shortage of hungry, ambitious contenders craving the job that Harry still held by the skin of his teeth; among them, Harry's wellborn deputy, Charles Douglas-Home, a nephew of the Tory prime minister, who, Harry was warned (to no avail—he disbelieved the warnings), was secretly plotting against him. Moreover, Harry was clearly wearying of Murdoch, who simply couldn't help meddling in the newspaper.

Harry made no secret of his gradual disaffection, grumbling to staffers about the tyranny under which he languished, and these confidants promptly fed his grievances to their proprietor. This mounting disaffection, however, did not prevent Evans from urgently attempting to curry favor with his boss, sometimes in the most extraordinary fashion, as William Shawcross noted in his biography of Murdoch. In barbed communications Harry would smooth a somewhat combative memo with, "Yours loyally, Harold"; ask the proprietor for his notions on how the newspaper might cover the budget; or alternatively, drop a famous name, flashing it in the direction of Murdoch much as a starlet might dangle her hotel room key at a producer.

> By the way, Henry Kissinger offered to write pieces (for paying his fare or something like that). He is president of the US [soccer] league and knows a lot about the game. If you like the idea I'll take it further, or you can meet him when he comes here in April. . . .

Murdoch's prejudices, his resentful attitude toward the entrenched "effete" classes who had snubbed him—these too were gladly shared by Harry, or at least he made a great show of doing so, even at the expense of those he had tried to lure to *The Times*. "I did talk to Alexander Chancellor," he wrote Murdoch of the man he had courted as book editor, "but came to the conclusion he represents part of the effete old tired England." Meantime, he assured his boss that his battles with the unions were admirable. "We are all 100 percent behind you. . . . Thank you again for the opportunity and the ideas."

But Murdoch proved nowhere near as seducible as, say, Harry himself. "Murdoch wanted the paper to provide intellectual weight, newspaper support for the Thatcher revolution," according to a *Times* associate who happened to share those Conservative sentiments. "And although Harry was no mad left-winger by any means, he did follow the anti-Thatcher consensus of the early eighties." Harry, it was decided by this friend of Murdoch, "came from a sixties and seventies collectivist, center-left environment."

How could the two men possibly stay hitched? that particular editor wondered. "I think if Rupert Murdoch really thinks very power-fully about something, you've got to let him play with his toy train. So, take the combination of somebody who's not ideologically on the same wavelength as the proprietor—and who's also spending a lot of money on a loss-making paper that is causing Rupert real financial problems—these two combinations were fatal. Together, they sealed the fate of Harry Evans. He certainly would have lasted *longer* if he'd been more careful with the budget, even if he was ideologically on the other side. He still would have been gone, but not as quickly."

That exit, as Murdoch made sure, was heralded long before the protracted and widely publicized event. In the winter of 1982, the columnist Andrew Alexander, who worked for a rival paper, the *Daily Telegraph,* was asked by Murdoch, much to his surprise, to come to his office and discuss *The Times.*

Alexander arrived at Murdoch's office at the appointed hour, but reluctantly. "I'd rather not say what I think of *The Times*," he told Murdoch. He didn't especially want to undermine Harry, but he did think the editorials—known in Britain as "leaders"—were flawed.

"Right," said Murdoch. "You're going to tell me the leaders are intellectually inconsistent. And they are!"

"Well, they run along fine, but then the thread is always broken by a 'But' or a 'Nevertheless' or 'On the other hand. . . .' And it ends with an opinion that is quite the opposite of what was originally stated in the first few paragraphs."

"That's because of Harry," Murdoch explained dismissively. "Harry always agrees with the last person he's spoken to. He'll put the stamp of approval on a leader someone wrote, and then the next person he lunches with will have a totally different opinion and then Harry will go back and fiddle with the leader and make those changes. That's why."

In mid-February 1982, Harry was anointed "Editor of the Year" by Granada Television at the Savoy Hotel in London for his "remark-able achievement" of changing *The Times* "almost out of all recogni-tion." The event got gratifying coverage. Basking in the festive warmth of Harry's newest honor was Rupert Murdoch. From time to time, he trained a gentle smile on the man he had called "the world's greatest editor."

"Uh-oh," thought Andrew Alexander, watching these awards. "Harry's gone in two months."

Actually, it was one month. On March 9, Murdoch asked for Harry's resignation; only to hear, "You cannot have it. I refuse." The

Editor of the Year couldn't believe it—neither the outrageously impertinent demand itself, nor the total insensitivity of it. His beloved father, Frederick, the train driver and devoted family man who had prodded all his sons to get an education, had died just eight days earlier. Mary, Harry's mother, had been too ill even to appear at the graveside and would die soon after.

Just after Frederick's death, Murdoch had written Harry a particularly eloquent note of condolence, full of thoughtful touches and the promise of generous leave. "You must take any time you need to attend to the necessary family arrangements."

Evidently, Murdoch had meant every word of it. His disappointment when, shortly after the funeral, Harry reappeared at the paper was considerable. Murdoch had already conferred privately with Charles Douglas-Home, Harry's deputy, and been assured of his eagerness to take Harry's job. All that remained, Murdoch felt, was to deliver a few well-chosen words to dismiss Harry.

"The place is in chaos," Murdoch told him. "You can't see the wood from the trees. . . . Your senior staff is up in arms."

If Harry refused to leave as bidden it was because he felt—with some justification—that his boss had no *right* to fire him. To appease the government monopoly watchdogs when he first bought the paper, Murdoch had agreed to the appointment of several "national directors," specifically charged with approving the appointment of editors, and their feelings on the matter of firing Harry had not been canvassed. Meanwhile, *Times* journalists were moaning to anyone who called that the atmosphere at the newspaper was "just horrid," that the place had erupted in fact into "open warfare." Harry was camped inside his office. A successor was waiting in the wings impatiently drumming his fingers. And Murdoch was defiantly unrepentant.

For days, the TV news shows overflowed with Harry. He was their hero, Rupert the villain. Would Harry vanquish the cruel giant? And if not, what would it take to make the great man go? In his strolls outside his house and his office, he would encounter TV crews and photographers. This appeared to have its effect. There were huge dark bags under Harry's eyes, but his lips were curled with determination. He had adopted a tone of self-sufficient if hastily cobbled optimism in his responses. "I have no idea what's going to be the outcome of this turmoil," he confided to a friend who met him on one of these occasions. "But I tell you one thing, and that is, at the end of it I will still be around. I will still be there."

And Tina? She was very much there during this time, although not front and center necessarily. She was an extraordinary amalgam: a shy virago. Her words were chosen with specific and crass bellicosity. "I'm going to whip some life into a flagging product," was how she referred to her mission at *Tatler*. But in her private life, there were still demurrals, shroudings, a rejection of center stage. From the narrow Regency house close by Parliament, she emerged, her square-shouldered woolly coat flapping open to reveal strands of lusterless pearls drooping past a thin white Peter Pan collar above a dark cardigan. In those days she was, if not oblivious to her looks, at least unequal to effecting their enhancement; uninterested, too. She wore her short blond hair indifferently cut and clipped back by a barrette. It gave her face a more open expression, but at the same time there was a tentative, puzzled aspect, and her lids and neck were often lowered as though in submission.

Tina seemed to function as Harry's lighter backdrop in that moment, against which the more powerful but embattled editor was offset. With the camera crews and newspaper photographers constantly arrayed in their front yard, she placed herself a few steps behind her husband, a look of smiling, tender concern sweeping her own sharp features. In one hand she held an open umbrella, her imperfect shelter from the stormy March skies. Whatever Murdoch had proven to be, he was not, she was now forced to admit (as was Harry), "enormous fun."

"What do you do about Murdoch?" one acquaintance asked Harry during that terrible time.

"Bernard Donoughue and I thought the only way out is to have him killed," Evans replied, referring to his close friend and erstwhile business partner who wrote editorials for *The Times*. "It wasn't a serious suggestion," his listener decided. He was quite certain Harry wasn't about to go off and hire a hit man. It was simply, he thought, "a demonstration of his desperation and hatred of Murdoch."

On March 15, a Monday, after much wrestling over egos and financial packages, Harry caved in and consented to leave. Anthony Holden, his features editor and chosen successor, also left *The Times*, but under his own steam, without a penny from the newspaper, and far more resolute. "Mr. Murdoch wants a poodle as editor," he told those who inquired. "If Harold Evans goes, I go too and so will *The Times'* proud tradition of independence."

Harry had been with the company sixteen years, with *The Times* just a little over a year, although how independent he had been at that last paper—and how proud—are both open to question. He certainly had his hand outstretched at the very end. But that hand had once run the best newspaper in the country. In a financial and strategic sense, he was right to wait, to force everyone, especially Murdoch, to cool their heels while he pondered the most beneficial moment to depart. Such tactics were rewarded when he received a parachute that was considered platinum at the time, especially for a journalist: £270,000—more than half of it in cash, along with the company car and a year's extension of an interest-free mortgage. Rupert won, but Rupert paid.

"Of all the people involved in that squalid episode, you were the one who emerged with most dignity," Murdoch would tell Holden some two years after the debacle.

"What you mean is I didn't take any of your money with me," said Holden.

"Yah, that does have something to do with my judgment!" Murdoch laughed, then added thoughtfully, "It was the best thing that ever happened to you, I should think."

But it was not for Harry. Naturally, he talked big, regaling a friend with details of encountering, on a visit to the States, a rattler in the Grand Canyon. "I took it on—I worked out my tactics very carefully. Then I beat it to death." But this sort of allegory fooled no one. He had been bitten publicly, without dignity, rejected not just by Murdoch but by his troops, who had always offered him in previous wars and conflicts their undying allegiance. The trouble was, quite a number of people no longer appeared to be receptive to what Evans had to give. From this signal lack of desire, Harry would never wholly recover. Really, he was through with England, although it would take a while before this became apparent.

Tina threw him a party the first night of his exile. That was her way, whenever things went wrong. Or right. Holden was there and Donoughue, along with Tom Stoppard and John Mortimer. One by one they all filed into the small terraced house, each performing acts of obeisance to the greatest editor Britain would ever know. The next morning, according to one old friend, Harry received a flattering job offer: his own imprint at a British publishing company. He rejected it out of hand, deciding instead to write a book on his experiences, a rather evasive and discursive one, as it turned out. Slowly the truth was dawning on a number of people; there was no place for him anymore.

Tina's old lover Tony Palmer recognized it at once. "This is how English society works," he said. "If a relatively small number of people turns against you, you are unemployable. It's not that you can't get a job, of course you can. But it percolates down through the system. You can't do the things you want to do. This is a very, very English thing."

And so, quite abruptly (who could have imagined such an up-heaval just months earlier?), established roles within the Harry-and-Tina relationship were reversed. The couple mutated, at first almost imperceptibly. Tina, after all, still held her well-publicized job as the glamorous editor. Unlike Harry, she had actually saved an ailing pub-lication from perdition. "The old Dowager," as she dubbed *Tatler*, had been transformed into at least minor nobility, circulation expand-ing from 10,000 to 35,000. It had, unlike Harry's *Times*, a clearly defined mission. "At *Tatler*, life was a party, but the party wasn't just *any* party," recalled Miles Chapman. "It was a party where you met and wanted to meet interesting people. . . . New people, stimulating people."

Because of these ceaseless exertions, there was, as another of her staffers would later admit, "a quite disproportionate feeling about it, being very successful. It was so small it didn't even show up on the sales monitors. And yet she managed to leverage this thing into a much bigger league." And Tina had done it all without money, with-out a lot of staff, and without Murdoch.

Such a blow to Harry's ego was softened in those days by Tina's maternal sensibilities, which were remarkably developed in a woman so young, childless, and emphatically modern. Tina was twenty-eight when her husband was fired by Murdoch, but she knew exactly how to soothe him. "Harry's helping me so *much*," she would tell their mutual acquaintances. "Harry's helping me to lay out the pages." Her listeners were intrigued, but on the whole not surprised by this able demonstration of devotion.

"Tina took care of him," Palmer recalled. "That's Mother Earth-come-to-me-and-be-comforted." He had seen that quality in her long before when, as her boyfriend, he had visited her at her parents' house in Spain. She was quite unlike her own more brittle mother, Palmer felt, very enveloping and fussy when it came to the well-being of her men. "The Mother Earth figure: there was a very powerful element of that in Tina."

Nor was Harry insensible to the comforting resolution of his wife. "Tina," he would later concede, "had the worst of it. I left *The Times* completely shattered and she held me together."

Of course, there was more than loyalty at work here, her friends instantly recognized, although that was a strong component in the durability of their relationship. As it happened, Harry *was* helping her lay out pages, was interested in the spacing and the headlines, and was proving vital and instructive, then and forever after. He was then and would always remain her gifted professor, reading articles long before they went to press, criticizing the typeface, the photos, promoting the ambitions of certain writers. Sometimes this was done subtly, sometimes not. Journalists employed by Tina would be told by Harry before an issue appeared how much he appreciated their work. In any event, his wife owed him at least as much as she was letting on. She was simply, for the first time, raising the volume of her debt to him on every possible occasion. One of their friends from that era was struck by the insistence with which she dwelled on the subject:

"She wanted to give support. She was extraordinarily loyal. But more than that, I think she genuinely felt this guy was a teacher and she was bloody well going to learn."

Tina had to learn quickly. Less than a month after Harry left *The Times* she found herself saddled with a new boss. His name was Samuel I. Newhouse, Jr., known as Si, and he was a reserved American billionaire with a passion for magazines and modern art—one of the richest men in the country, in fact—who liked to spring out of bed at 4:00 A.M. With his brother, Donald, Newhouse owned the vast Condé Nast publishing empire, its worth estimated, within a few years, at $7.5 billion. It included *Vogue* magazine, *GQ, Mademoiselle, Glamour,* and—in the spring of 1982—the ridiculously small but witty and influential British society magazine called *Tatler.* Newhouse, however, didn't discover Tina. And she was by no means thrilled to be working for him, or his large American organization.

It was Bernard Leser, president of Condé Nast, who closed the *Tatler* deal on April 2, 1982 ("I refused to do it on April 1 because I am superstitious," he would later say). Leser had spotted *Tatler*'s owner, Gary Bogard, one night in London at Harry's Bar—and put the idea of selling *Tatler* in his head. He was ready to buy at any time, he said. "Love what you and Tina are doing with the magazine. We share the same vision," he told Bogard. He was aware, as was Daniel Salem, then the chairman of Condé Nast Europe, who also wanted the deal, that Tina had been romantically linked with Bogard in the press. A little flattery couldn't hurt.

Bogard, however, didn't need the soft soap. He wanted the cash—*Tatler* was a financial drain, a matter that certainly didn't seem to concern Tina very much. "It started to run out of money incredibly quickly," recalled one old employee. "To the owners, it was shocking to see how much the costs went up." Nonetheless, Tina had leveraged the shabby old Dowager into a luscious and desirable property. Word was that Condé Nast paid more than $1 million for *Tatler*, which considering the limited circulation it then enjoyed was a price predicated largely on hope. But Leser took the plunge, he said, because "there was a buzz in London." The buzz was Tina.

"We would never have bought the *Tatler* had it not been for Tina," said Leser. "I professionally fell in love with Tina, I was absolutely convinced that she was potentially one of the greatest editors one could have. There was a touch about her, a flair, an irreverence, a charm." He introduced her to Si Newhouse, who "immediately shared my conviction."

Within five months of the magazine's purchase, however, serious trouble began. The golden Tina, the hot young property, was suddenly—everyone noticed it—deeply unhappy with her job, her life. "Tina found it very hard, after working in a tiny tight company, to accommodate herself to the way Condé Nast worked. She found it uncomfortable," recalled Leser. "We had a tough time of it."

"Tina was just pissed off," explained a former staffer. "She'd done *Tatler* long enough. I think she wanted to not work so hard."

But these were merely the avowed reasons for her new remoteness from work. Like her husband, Tina was not at all sure what to do with herself. She had made efforts other than writing a year earlier when a friend induced her to try television, an on-camera stint on an awards program, but the results apparently were truly awful. "She didn't quite fire on television," the friend said. "Curiously enough, there's a nervousness about Tina. A public nervousness." Everyone noticed this edginess; it was simply her nature. Alternately forward and retiring, she was still the girl of her homely and undistinguished childhood. The public Tina, the one outside home, office, and marriage, seemed to want nothing so much as to vanish.

Harry, on the other hand, did not. After his public resignation, he was working in the English countryside on his memoirs. They would be called *Good Times, Bad Times,* and although the book certainly starred Harry, it was a rambling and discursive work. When the book was published, Harry would get considerable acclaim for skewering Murdoch in print—or in some instances, since he had after all taken

Murdoch's hefty payoff, a jab in the ribs for selling and then telling: "a pay-off which made the whole country whistle," as Auberon Waugh wrote.

The couple had rented a large place in Kent, a comfortable hilltop house with lots of lawns, galleries, and a big library. It was built around the 1920s and packed with cozy bedrooms. Friends rolled up the long gravelly driveway, among them George Darby. Darby was an editorial manager of proven efficacy. He had collaborated with Evans on a previous book, *Pictures on a Page,* which became a classic, and Darby was famous, as he said, for being "sort of a good mimic. So I can do you Harry's writing." This unique gift, he recalled, was put to good use in the house in Kent.

"I did write some of *Good Times, Bad Times,*" Darby would later say. "I drafted some chapters, I researched some chapters and wrote them. And then Harry rewrote them. . . . And then Harry pitches in and writes about what happened to him that I didn't know about or had forgotten about. So my basic role was to cover the ground." Harry's acknowledgment concedes that "passages of this book . . . owe a debt, as did the original adventures," to an assortment of people, "especially George Darby." No complaints," said Darby, referring to the acknowledgment.

The whole book was dedicated to Tina. But most of life was hard going. She was in a reflective mood, visiting friends noticed, strolling about the wide emerald lawn that circled a gazebo, and obviously pondering her future. "How do you combine working with having children?" she asked one of the guests, who was astonished by this choice of topic and was for the first time in their acquaintance "struck by how sort of soft she was." In fact, Tina seemed newly taken by all sorts of things having to do with children. A Japanese folding baby backpack absorbed her interest at a party she hosted for David Lean. How did it work? she wondered, marveling over the neatness of the contraption.

Tatler staffers also saw a new Tina: a distant, distracted one, whose odd mood worried them, especially during the late autumn, after she returned from a vacation in St. Petersburg, Florida, where Harry was a visiting professor for a brief period at the Poynter Institute for Media Studies. "In an instant I saw it happen," her deputy Miles Chapman would later recall. "She came back from holiday and I saw the light go out. The lightbulb of her interest. She had *done* Tatler. She had done it for three years. She needed to be stimulated."

Still, she busied herself with other concerns, a few agreeable. A compilation of her *Tatler* pieces appeared—the book was called, inevitably, *Life Is a Party*—and champagne and kedgeree were consumed by a crowd at a party at the famous Soho restaurant L'Escargot. But some close friends of the enchanted couple appeared to have drifted away—or were pushed. It was widely observed, for instance, that Peter Stothard, the husband of Sally Emerson, who happened to be one of Tina's few intimate female friends, had *not* quit *The Times* after Harry left. Indeed, despite having been recruited by Harry, Stothard eventually became editor of the paper. Tina found that deviation from blind loyalty unforgivable: "Sally very nearly didn't get that friendship with Tina back," recalled an old friend, adding that the rupture between the two women lasted almost a decade.

At that time, so many of Tina's feuds and friendships, desires and aversions were based on her husband's station. "Tina became restless because Harry was pushed out by Rupert," recalled Bernie Leser, who had brought her into the Condé Nast fold. He understood in a way. He was an old friend of Tina's parents, George and Bettina, and pretty sympathetic to the plight of their daughter.

Still, no one was prepared for what actually happened. On New Year's Day 1983, a note from Tina announcing her resignation suddenly appeared on the desk of Condé Nast's chairman, Daniel Salem. It was exactly eight months since he had purchased the magazine—and, he and Condé Nast had assumed at the time, Tina as well. Now with one stroke, half the assets of *Tatler* were gone.

"To be honest, she didn't give us much advance notice and I thought that was very wrong of her. Most editors give a lot of advance notice," Salem would later say. "What she put in that note to me was that she was resigning for 'personal reasons.' " Leser, his partner in the acquisition, figured she was leaving because of Harry's terrible job loss, which contributed to Tina's restlessness. But her abrupt exit deeply annoyed Salem.

Harry was performing an assortment of odd jobs, none of them wholly satisfactory. At the film company Goldcrest, he was given a mandate to set up a twenty-four-hour-a-day cable TV news service, for which he seemed to have small appetite. "Only an idiot would be so hooked on news," he told a journalist. "But I see it as a service, which is available when you want it. . . ." He was lecturing in Florida, had been asked to teach a course at Duke University in North Carolina, and made a television series in Switzerland on skiing. "Oh, this is okay, I can write, I can freelance," he told himself in the first weeks after being dismissed by Murdoch. But the costs—the surprisingly painful financial costs—of such a freelance existence were rapidly mounting.

No longer was he the beneficiary of a generous expense account. Suddenly, Harry discovered, "I'd go to lunch and I'd have to pay!" That came as a terrible shock. "Within a week, I was spending seventy to eighty pounds on *food*," he told a friend. "I realized this can't go on."

More than a decade later, he would detail the dreariness of that sunken time to an American magazine editor, Jim Fallows, who was himself about to be fired. One day, Harry recalled for Fallows, he had been the superpowerful editor of an important newspaper. Practically the next, he was "working on some underfunded documentary in Switzerland"—obliged to undertake all sorts of humble tasks from which he had previously been exempt. The TV crew had rented some props from a local shop, for which he had assumed responsibility. Harry found himself trudging back to the rental place laden with the paraphernalia.

"I used to be a great newspaper magnate and now I'm trying to get the refund on these props we brought back," he said. His message, his listener felt, was: "Life has its ups and downs. And he had been through the downs, he was trying to say. He had been down, and was scrambling to make a living."

So when Tina resigned from *Tatler*, it was because her view of things, she thought, had been fatally altered, compromised; Harry and Harry's fall had readjusted the filter through which she had traditionally received her impressions. One night, right after Condé Nast had bought her magazine, she returned to the new, improved *Tatler* office, moved now to Condé Nast's Vogue House, a professional building dotted with warrens of little offices. There she gazed at a mound of photographs—shots of the wealthy, the titled, the famous—and it struck her suddenly that she preferred those well-known faces she saw in the photograph on her desk to the ones she encountered in real life. A worrisome sign, she decided.

"In my three years of editing *Tatler*, I had been Alice Through the Lightbox," she wrote in *Life As a Party*, a collection of some of her early articles. "It was time to return to reality or find myself stranded on the other side."

Life, in other words, was no longer a party.

* * *

Si Newhouse was distraught over Tina's resignation. "Can't you use Tina and Harry in entirely separate roles working as editors, as a team?" he demanded of Leser. But Leser could find nothing among the various Condé Nast properties that would work. As a couple, the two were unusable on the same publication. "In England we couldn't. There was no slot open," Leser said later.

Nonetheless, Leser felt there was a much more important role for Tina in the company, specifically at a new magazine Condé Nast had brought forth in March 1983 under the hapless editorship of Richard Locke. The publication, a revival of a smooth and urbane magazine launched in 1913, was called *Vanity Fair,* and despite the tremendous fanfare that greeted its rebirth, it had a lot in common with the pre-Tina *Tatler.* It was old, it was revered, it had potential, and it was a mess.

Everyone hated *Vanity Fair*—the press most especially; the advertisers after the first issues when they read the attacks in the press; and Condé Nast's editorial director, Alexander Liberman, a powerful and talented man who never wanted the publication relaunched in the first place. And Newhouse. It was in those early days the kind of magazine that hired Gore Vidal as a film critic—and then "figured out he lived in Italy," an old hand recalled.

There was also the matter of the covers: an illustration of a centaur playing a flute, Philip Roth with his finger up his nose, the intellectual Susan Sontag flaunting her white-streaked mane, all captured in artistic black and white, the better to highlight the subject's every pore. They were not designed to seduce advertisers—and there was a flood of these initially—into a lifetime of fealty. Within three issues, one of which included a novella by Gabriel García Márquez, Locke was gone, unmourned.

He was replaced by Leo Lerman, sixty-nine, a man with deteriorating eyesight at the time, who had truly loved the original *Vanity Fair.* That version had died in 1936 and never made a nickel. D. H. Lawrence, F. Scott Fitzgerald, Walter Lippmann, Gertrude Stein, e. e. cummings, André Gide, Dorothy Parker: these were the early magazine's contributors, its golden nuggets, and Lerman had always yearned to sit atop such a treasure. He was not, he insisted to everyone, an interim editor. He was there to stay. In his new station, he had a lot invested: pride, stature in the artistic community. "You know, Leo was the kind of guy, every opening night on Broadway, he'd send telegrams to everyone he knew," it would later be remembered. But employees noticed that a special bathroom was being built for him in his office, so he wouldn't have to make his way down the long halls. His health was rapidly declining.

"Si, I think Tina is very hot property," Leser told his boss. "I think she's absolutely right for *Vanity Fair.*" He did not wish to pursue the matter to its inevitable conclusion because Lerman happened to be one of his oldest and closest friends. But the penny dropped.

In the summer of 1983, a youngish woman with a dreary flat British accent who, it was observed, "dressed very kind of English"— which meant she wore twinsets—appeared in the offices of *Vanity Fair* on the fourth floor of 350 Madison Avenue in New York. She was not at all glamorous or even pretty. She wore red-tinted sunglasses, vision-corrected, and when the weather turned cooler, little tweed coats of indefinable shape and brand. She was very quiet at first, very much in the background. She was obviously not there, everyone noted thankfully, to rock the leaky boat of *Vanity Fair* yet again, or to challenge anyone's position, or even to discuss things at great length. She would simply sit on Leo Lerman's desk and gaze quite fixedly through those thick tinted glasses at the board in his office where future articles were posted. In fact, she walked quite freely into that office.

But there was nothing threatening or even prepossessing about her. Her needs were modest; a little windowless office in the back was her temporary headquarters. Of course, everyone wondered who "that woman" was. The name *"Tatler"* meant nothing to the Americans. It was some little English magazine of no account. "No one thought of her as a danger," it would later be recollected with considerable mirth. Leser, the quiet Englishwoman's champion, knew better: "She was the lady in waiting. It was uncomfortable for her."

And from time to time, she even made herself mildly useful. For instance, when the film writer Steven Schiff was profiling the British actress Patricia Hodge for a tiny article, he was told there was someone on staff who might help and Lerman urged him to call "one of Hodge's best friends, Tina Brown"—which he did. As it happened, Hodge had once starred in Tina's play *Happy Yellow,* so she could be of help. But that was it, more or less. After a few months, the newcomer seemed to have outlived her usefulness; or perhaps she never discovered it. She drifted off, by and large unremarked, and returned to England.

Alone among his staff Lerman was watchful, wary. Tina made him nervous. *Vanity Fair*'s culture writer James Wolcott, newly hired, was asked to review a forthcoming book by some former big-wheel

British editor named Harry Evans, now down on his luck, concerning his famous losing battle with Rupert Murdoch. And it was remarkable, Wolcott found, the interest that Lerman took in this book. He kept prodding Wolcott about it, as if it were some guaranteed bestseller.

"And I thought, 'Well, wait a minute, why do we care about Harry Evans?' " Wolcott would later recall. Lerman was clearly anxious for a major pan of Harry's work. "Don't hold back. Say what you feel," he ordered Wolcott, praying for the worst.

In fact, Harry's book received a fairly mild review, but within short order Wolcott came to realize that unlike the rest of his staff, "Leo must have known something." On New Year's Day 1984, a year to the day after Tina had quit *Tatler*, she was reassigned by the very company she once thought she had left. She had been vacationing in Barbados when she was called to appear at a lunch in New York. Bernie Leser was by this time no longer her only champion in the company. Si Newhouse wanted her there, as did Alexander Liberman. The two men had something of importance to tell her. She didn't have to guess what it was. She arrived in the midst of one of the worst winters the city had ever known. Packed in her bag were cheesecloth skirts, some T-shirts, and a bikini. "The first thing I did," she said, "was go out and buy a new wardrobe." She would receive a salary of $100,000 and a clothing allowance with which to do so.

Thus, she became the new editor in chief of *Vanity Fair* (its third in ten months), queen of a magazine that had already cost the company more than $20 million. She was in that moment Si's girl, Liberman's girl, and Harry's girl, too. For the rest, she was the figure at the center of a bull's-eye.

Tina Brown was then thirty years old, with the matchless survival instincts of a jungle animal, but she had clearly made a rash and very possibly unwise decision in accepting Newhouse's offer. Ad pages at *Vanity Fair* were way down. Of course, she had good reason to jump at the notion of moving to America; it was not merely career enhancement that propelled her. Harry, guilt-ridden as ever, would have to leave his family behind in England when he joined her. That was not entirely a bad thing, in Tina's view. Indeed, she acknowledged as much a year later: ". . . I always felt his first family were very important. When we came to America it was like a new start. He and I were finally on the same footing in a foreign place, having to start a new life."

On the other hand, just two months before her fateful trip to New

York, *Vanity Fair*'s publisher, Joseph Corr, Jr., had been replaced by the candid David O'Brasky. And what was O'Brasky telling the press, now that Tina had accepted the position of editor in chief? "We'll be scrapping for pages," he said. "A lot of people have already made their budget decisions for 1984." *Newsweek* magazine reported the general media assumptions: ". . . *Vanity Fair* has squandered its initial good will."

Inside the publication itself, goodwill—all will, in fact—had evaporated. Lerman, everyone saw, was truly shocked by Newhouse's decision to push him aside and kick him upstairs. His new job was "editorial adviser," a title that was invariably framed by quotation marks in articles about the move. Lerman wasn't fooled. "Bob, I've been . . . uh . . . *promoted* to the fourteenth floor," he drily informed Bob Colacello, a writer who, like much of the staff, thought such a move extremely bad news. In fact, Lerman despised his replacement to such a degree that, frail as he was, he would avoid entering any office in which Tina happened to find herself.

"Tell me about *that woman* you work for," he would command those remaining employees when they came to visit him. His intellectual friends were outraged by the treatment he had received. "*Yours* was the *Vanity Fair* I wanted to work for," a departing editor assured him. The remaining staff quickly learned how far-reaching the changes at the magazine would be. Exiled from the covers were the grainy portraits of admired thinkers and writers. "Intellectuals should be read and not seen," Tina declared, but she was by no means feeling as resolute and unconcerned as she sounded. Her friend the British television personality Melvyn Bragg came to see her in New York, and discovered that she was in despair over the atmosphere that reigned.

"She was deeply down in the dumps," Bragg said. "People were stabbing her in the back and she wasn't used to that. She was used to a culture, London, where she was admired, rightly, liked, rightly, supported, rightly. And she had her own pals, who were wittier than anybody else." And there she was, Bragg recalled, in alien territory, virtually friendless, and "very black about what was being done to her. They were trying to get her out!" Of course, Tina knew all about "London bitchiness and London snideness and all of that." But the degree of venom at *Vanity Fair* was truly startling. "At that early stage, she was hurt."

In fact, much of New York, without knowing Tina in the slightest, seemed to view her professional demise—and that of the infant magazine she was baby-sitting—as a foregone and on the whole cheerful conclusion. And quite often they shared those opinions with her in public, as she later recalled: "At the beginning my wan face was seen at a few cocktail parties and people would come up and say, 'I hear you're going *right* down the toilet.' " She had been totally unprepared for such a reception. She wasn't even sure she wanted to spend all these years as an editor. It was writing that intrigued her more. "I was and am a writer," she insisted. "As paranoid, insecure, neurotic as any other. When I am writing, I bite my nails and crumble if I don't get reassurance."

What was she doing in New York? Evenings, she would return to her tiny rented apartment, studded with furniture covered in leopard skin, and brood about the injustice, the pain, and the slights. In London, put-downs and insults were masked behind thin veils of irony or silence. No one ever talked in such a blunt, forthright way—except perhaps Tina herself, from time to time. New York, on the other hand, seemed to be filled with all sorts of Tinas, people who had arrived there long before she had and knew the score. She hadn't counted on quite that number of mirror images in the New World. "It is like Vietnam out there," she complained bitterly. "When you first arrive everyone's gunning for you. You don't make friends here, you make contacts."

In response, Tina grew withdrawn and fearful, even ill: "I dreaded going out and I dreaded going home to the tacky apartment I had rented . . . I developed some strange fantasy virus like an emotional collapse."

It was around this time that Tina's old friend Alexander Chancellor, the editor of *The Spectator* in London—the same "tired, effete" Chancellor who had turned down Harry's job offer at *The Times* and then been (unknown to him) excoriated by Harry in a note to Murdoch—came through New York. He called Tina. "Come around," she said, "we'll have dinner."

Chancellor was astonished at the hivelike atmosphere that prevailed at *Vanity Fair*. Tina, when he arrived, was still in her office, "busy-busy-busy," and he found himself talking to a bunch of flushed and overwrought subordinates, all of them complaining about the brutal schedules they were forced to endure. "We just produced an issue, and now we have to produce yet another one next month!" they cried.

Chancellor did his best to console these hectic creatures. "We at *The Spectator* produce an issue every *week*," he told them gently. "And then we all go around to the pub."

The lights were just coming up over Madison Avenue when Tina emerged from her office and greeted Chancellor with a hug. It was not simple affection that prompted such a gesture. He felt her lips against his ear and a whispered rush of fear issuing forth: "Don't say anything until we're out of the building."

Once in the elevator, when they were alone, he tried again to form a sentence. But Tina pressed a warning finger against her mouth. "Shhhhhh. Wait till we're out of the building!" They rode down in silence.

The two friends took a cab uptown. It was only when they were out of earshot of everyone at *Vanity Fair,* Chancellor noticed, that Tina "became very sweet" and started to relax. At last he was allowed to speak. He had a wonderful idea for her magazine, he explained over dinner. He'd recently been to lunch at Buckingham Palace, with Queen Elizabeth and Prince Philip seated across the table, and had discovered, as he told Tina, that "when you arrive at Buckingham Palace there's some buffoon in fancy clothes who says, 'Would you like to visit the bathroom?' You say, 'No.'

" 'Plenty of time, I promise you,' says the buffoon.

"Well apparently the reason is people go mad, and on the fine Aubusson carpet there's sort of Lady So-and-So or someone—and immediately her bladder fails. There are puddles all over. Very odd. Anyway I tried to give an amusing account of that lunch."

It was a very amusing account, declared Tina in her relaxed postprandial mood. Very amusing indeed. Exactly the kind of story she wanted for her *Vanity Fair.* "Great—write about it," she commanded.

And Chancellor did so. In fact, he titled it "Closet Queen."

In the end, Tina didn't run the piece on the Buckingham Palace lunch. But then that, as people would gradually come to realize, was her *Vanity Fair,* too. Lots of ideas, lots of commissions, lots of amusement, lots of buzz, lots of killed articles, lots of wounded feelings, lots of expectations raised and squelched. Lots and lots of money.

Chapter 7
Of Myth and Money

All sorts of interesting tales accompanied Tina to her exalted perch in New York, some of them true. That she had in her bachelor days been the lover of the acerbic, married writer Auberon Waugh (to the question "How could you fuck a man so ugly?" a new employee learned, she was said to have replied, "I'd fuck anyone who wrote that well"). That she had had a relationship with Dudley Moore, only to discover that "one of his legs was shorter than the other." That almost two years had been mysteriously peeled from her actual age—thirty—so that she was now supposedly a precocious sixteen when first at Oxford.

Pressed on this subject by an interviewer armed with contradictory recollections from Oxford contemporaries, Tina amended her history only slightly: "I might have been just seventeen," she said. In fact, she had been just some weeks shy of eighteen.

It also emerged, somehow or other, and eventually became part of accepted lore, that the *Vanity Fair* editorship had been plunked in her lap by the beneficent Si Newhouse when she was still in full swing at *Tatler*. "And that was not true," Daniel Salem, who had bought the magazine for Newhouse, would later say, incensed.

And yet, wasn't that an entirely appropriate way to begin anew?

Just months earlier, she had considered, seriously too, writing a novel, but now the idea repelled her. "Sitting on my own, tormented by introspection. Yuk." Times and circumstances had certainly changed, along with her venue. "The era of the power suit, that was the era I was editor in chief of Vanity Fair," she would say years later in a radio interview. "I look at those photographs of me now, in my red suit with my red nails, my high-heel shoes, and I think what an incredibly vibrant, over-the-top, wildly razzle-dazzle time it was."

It was, in short, her time. No stranger to the getting and dispensing of publicity, as she had amply demonstrated at age twenty when she was a mere student with a play to peddle, Tina knew the value of "buzz," as she would later come to call it. It was the modern-day cousin of myth. If buzz wasn't a true reflection of the real thing—of fame or impressive attainment or acclaim—it was so often the precursor of these qualities that it could easily pass for genuine. So the stories that swirled around her in the United States were rarely dispelled.

Like its latest editor, Vanity Fair was arrayed in myth, pretense, possibilities. Old-timers could remember its glorious predecessor, killed by the Great Depression. Like Tina, the magazine was about to be reborn, although at the time no one was giving either mother or child odds on survival. "This is a disaster," Si Newhouse kept saying. The magazine's circulation stood at 274,000 when Tina arrived; its advertising pages had dropped from 150 in its first issue to a bare 15. "I'm in Sweeney Todd's chair," Tina said at the time. Nor was she exaggerating by much. In June 1984, one of Tina's top editors became the second to discover from "a dear friend" that Vanity Fair would no longer be accepting advertising past a certain date.

"My source says he heard it from Leo Lerman," insisted the friend. From this, people at the magazine concluded that Lerman was anxious, now that he had been removed from its helm, to see the magazine die. There he was, they told each other, sitting high above them in the Condé Nast Building, trying "to actively damage it." Tina took careful note. A writer who had been hired under Lerman's tenure found that Tina "indicated in many ways" that any friendship with the former editor should cease. "So I decided I better stop running up and down to Leo's office," this journalist recalled. "I liked Leo, but I needed that paycheck."

Bad enough that the non–Condé Nast media were anxious to see Vanity Fair tumble into its grave. Ed Kosner, the editor of prosperous New York magazine, was so outraged by the high fees and salaries Tina was offering, the competition she might generate, that he forbade one of his freelancers on a six-month trial contract to write for Vanity Fair. There were many such double-edged swords in Tina's armory. "The fact that Tina was plucked from a society magazine like *Tatler* and came from England and was a young attractive woman," said an early ally, "this both frightened and tantalized the press."

Who could honestly blame her, then, for using whatever was at her disposal: truth, omission, exaggeration, buzz, her husband's labor, old colleagues from *Tatler* whom she cajoled and imported by the handful to come work at the magazine where she was so isolated? One by one, these bewildered British émigrés landed in New York: Miles Chapman, the magazine's new assistant editor, whose specialty was "heads and decks"—bold, amusing headlines and, beneath them, a stark précis of what the ensuing story was actually about (it was a novel idea at the time, saving the reader considerable exertion); Chris Garrett, who ultimately became managing editor; Michael Roberts, the new style editor; Sarah Giles, listed as an editor at large, whose function at the magazine, detractors said, seemed to consist of acting as Tina's subject-wrangler, guard dog, ambassador, and partygoer.

"I was a producer, and worked very hard," was how Giles herself would sum up her job. "And I only went to parties after hours. I came up with subjects, ideas: Madame 'Baby Doc' Duvalier, Salvador Dalí, Liz Taylor, David Bowie, Fidel Castro, the entire Redgrave family, among many others." The perceptions of some of her peers distressed her. It was noted by them, for instance, that she sometimes accompanied Tina to parties. "I was not Tina's maid," she said. "Tina wanted all sorts of people around her when she went to parties."

On all these Brits, Tina lavished money—Si Newhouse's money, which seemed inexhaustible in those days. Enormous bouquets of flowers crammed their small apartments whenever they seemed tempted to return to England. They were all she had. Aside from Si Newhouse. Although who knew about Si? "I can honestly say that I've made no new friends since I've been here and if it hadn't been for my husband, I'd probably have been very lonely," she said.

The most significant element Tina set about changing was not really the intellectual bent of the publication. She was always, as her husband pointed out, "more of a bluestocking than people give her credit for being," so the depth of content would give way only gradually. But the *Vanity Fair* covers underwent a great deal of plastic surgery. No more Irving Penn shots of dank middle-aged intellectuals looking inward, she resolved. "Intellectuals should be read and not seen," was Tina's motto. The magazine needed a sexiness, an energy, and as its identifiable image, a succession of beautiful stars from her own father's fabled line of work. But the sheer number and caliber of these lovely creatures would easily surpass those George Brown had managed to assemble in his more modest career. Indeed, her earliest chosen cover icons reflected a few of Tina's own characteristics—those that she chose to emphasize, anyway.

BLONDE AMBITION read the cover cutline of the April 1984 issue, Tina's first. The cover girl (over Harry's protests) was Daryl Hannah, blindfolded and holding Oscars in both hands.

"And that was another thing with Tina. GO BLONDE—when in doubt, GO BLONDE," recalled James Wolcott, who had started writing for the new publication under Lerman. When Lerman was deposed, Wolcott instantly saw a pattern develop under Tina, her own traits somehow transforming the nature—and certainly the packaging—of American journalism. "Ever since they used that cover line, *Blonde Ambition*, everybody is using it," Wolcott said.

Within short order, George Brown's former star Joan Collins—not a blonde but certainly a dramatic symbol of British success in America—was contacted by Tina. The actress, then at the height of her fame, was in California on the set of the hit television show *Dynasty* when her telephone rang. On the other end, calling from New York, was the plain little nobody Collins "didn't particularly remember as a teenager." She identified herself instantly as the child of the gentlemanly producer for whom Collins had always had a soft spot. George had been such "a nice old boy," Collins thought. Always a twinkle in his eye, and very polite. More than you could say about most producers.

"Oh Joan, please, please, *please* do the cover of *Vanity Fair*," begged Tina, now all grown-up and, despite her early dullness, obviously someone of importance.

The actress considered the offer indulgently. "Well, in two weeks I'll be off the set. We can do the cover shoot then."

"It's got to be in the next couple of *days!*" Tina protested, clearly panicked. "Oh please, Joan, please. You were my father's friend. Please do it as a favor to me."

"Within two days I'm in a studio," Collins would recall, still amazed years later at her easy acquiescence. On the whole, she decided, it had been a good idea to appear on the December 1984 cover. Draped around her wrists and neck were platinum bands, yards and yards of gems procured specially for the magazine shoot. "Zillions of dollars' worth of diamonds" on loan. Even Collins was impressed. "And the cutline on the cover is SHE RHYMES WITH RICH. Very subtle, I must say."

Exactly a year later, an even more celebrated British-born star was induced to appear on the magazine's cover. QUEEN ELIZABETH read the cutline of *Vanity Fair*'s Christmas issue, and there, sure enough, was a brightly wrapped present from photographer Helmut Newton. Dripping with diamonds, breasts bunched together and bursting perilously from her velvet Santa-red décolletage, Elizabeth Taylor stared provocatively at the reader, her ruby pout alone an assurance of subscription renewal.

Within Tina there still simmered a few cauldrons of the old British mischief that had made *Tatler* such glittering fun. An Annie Leibovitz photograph of the comedian Pee-Wee Herman sporting a pair of jockey shorts on his head, found shoved inside a drawer, was briefly considered cover material by Tina—until the aging Condé Nast deputy chairman Alexander Liberman, Russian-born and more sedate by temperament, got wind of her plans.

"Tina, my dear, that photograph of the comedian wearing the underpants? Do you really think so? I question it." And Tina, mulling over the warning of Si Newhouse's powerful friend, the potentially dangerous man she called "czar of all the Russias," weighing it against possible consequences, dropped the idea. "Tina knew how to handle Liberman," her friend Miles Chapman explained. "He knew he was dealing with someone with a bit of spark. And he thought she was his baby in some ways."

But the baby possessed amazing precocity in matters of self-preservation. The picture of Herman ran inside the magazine, under the inevitable headline "Jockeying for Position." A certain caution prevailed and the cauldrons of mischief cooled.

There was ample reason for that. Hollywood stars were merely window-dressing for the publication. "Women run New York," Tina gravely informed a British reporter. "A successful woman is not a novelty here; she's the norm." She meant not merely the growing group of female executives but another, more traditional kind of successful woman, the ones who, like her, had married well—but infinitely richer, ruling society from their husbands' roosts. The 1980s were the decade of the Reagans, of highly stratified ladies in size 6 suits who lunched with each other and a few of their gay escorts at Le Cirque or Morton's: Nancy Reagan, Pat Buckley, Betsy Bloomingdale, Nan Kempner, the social gadfly Jeremy Zipkin perpetually dancing attendance. Tina examined these women and came to the conclusion that "there are a lot of homosexual men in New York because the men are so frightened of the females that they turn to each other."

In fact, it was Tina who was "frightened of the females." Frightened but beholden. She needed them, their pictures and their parties, their corporate husbands and wealthy friends, to provide tattle and access for her new magazine, much as their titled British counterparts had once provided material for *Tatler.* The problem was, she didn't know them and she hated parties, her own excepted. "She always wanted to go with a protector when she went to these parties, with a man especially," explained the Venezuelan Reinaldo Herrera, who, being socially well connected, was tapped frequently to perform this function when he joined the magazine. It was not an unflattering role. "This had the added attraction of making you feel incredibly protective and powerful. As though she were just a little girl in terrible need of protection, funnily enough. Strange for so powerful a woman." Of course, he noticed, Tina was never entirely defenseless, even when at her most seemingly shy. "She always knew everything. Who was the most important person in the room. Everything."

In order to cultivate the prickly society women, Tina turned to Bob Colacello, a Republican writer with ties to Nancy Reagan, foreign businessmen, and a fondness for the rich, about whom he could be unerringly protective. Colacello had once worked for Andy Warhol's *Interview* magazine (he would describe its staff affectionately as "a dysfunctional family" with everyone speculating on how loaded someone or other had been the previous night), in which capacity he had learned a considerable amount. Among other things: always stay at the Ritz. He was worried about Tina, even though he liked her. She had a history of mocking the very people she covered, especially the wealthy. In her new job that was no longer acceptable.

Colacello's biggest fear was Tina's nationality, the culture from which she had emerged. He'd met a number of British aristocrats when he traveled with Andy Warhol, and found their level of snobbishness disheartening. He was worried, too, about the nature of the British press: so much of it was yellow, tacky, full of devastating gossip about those who ruled society. None of this could be safely transported to America.

"Tina, this isn't London," he warned his boss. "In England, the rich all call up Nigel Dempster and tattle on each other. But not here. Rich American people, if someone talks about them to the columnists and that person is caught tattling, then the door never opens again."

And another thing, he told her: "The rich don't have a sense of humor about where they came from or who they really are. So you really have to do a lot of writing and editing between the lines."

"I appreciate the advice," Tina said.

And certainly she put such counsel to good use. Within two years—and despite all her obligations as editor and wife—she herself crafted a lengthy *Vanity Fair* ode to the grand hostess Gayfryd Steinberg, who, along with her husband Saul, then a brazen greenmailer, ruled Park Avenue. It was there that society's newest parvenus occupied a thirty-four-room apartment that once belonged to John D. Rockefeller, complete with a red-and-gold living room and a multi-million-dollar commode in gilded bronze.

The article was an extraordinary compilation of cunning prose and empty spaces, the author's observations applied in light, feathery strokes with special attention paid to each subject's point of pride. Gayfryd was, Tina noted, "Greyhound-slim with a postmodern haircut and reckless shoulders." Her husband, the voracious conqueror of Wall Street, was actually "passionate about art," especially Rubens, Rodin, Hepworth—staid old standbys, with excellent resale value, which Tina blandly assured readers "have an audacity that reflects a wayward intellect." And yet, Gayfryd Steinberg was not happy with the piece: she hadn't wanted an earlier husband who had committed suicide after she married Saul mentioned. She should probably have been more supple in her rush to judgment. "In a future episode of my script, Gayfryd Steinberg, literary lion, hallowed benefactress, *grande dame,* receives excellent notices as the year 2025's Brooke Astor," wrote Tina. Those were her last lines. The last lines on the Steinbergs have not yet been written. But fourteen years after Tina's article, when their fortunes declined, Gayfryd and her husband hawked their penthouse triplex, sixty-one old masters, and the gilded furnishings.

Tina knew, as always, exactly what she was doing. As she pointed out to a fellow writer in a moment of staggering candor, "One's betrayals here have to be rather more subtle. One has to be a little more careful. Here it takes three years for a beer-can millionaire to become the equivalent of the Astors. It's something that would take four generations in England. That makes New Yorkers insecure. . . . I can't be nearly as iconoclastic as I was at home. Also the money here is very heavy. . . ."

This touchingly insecure, heavily moneyed place in which she found herself was, in Tina's view, clamoring to be conquered. Indeed, compared to Britain with its immovable class distinctions and rigid expectations, it was barely barricaded. An accomplished wall-scaler could do almost anything, once inside, and extract the kind of seemingly revealing details from the lives of the more fortunate that readers invariably appreciated. Tina even coined a word for this sort of intimate social writing. "Insiderly" she called it.

That did not mean that she herself wanted to party with Gayfryd or Nancy, Betsy or Pat. No. She had no time for such things, and besides she was shy and somewhat unwieldy socially. "That was the reason for Sarah Giles," Chapman would later say of Tina's other British import, Sarah Giles, who was wellborn, very pretty, and gossipy. "Giles was there because there's another Englishwoman of a certain age, a certain hair color, who can go to parties for her." That was why Tina hired journalists of all sorts: to retrieve those "insiderly" touches in a kind of proprietary fashion, as if they themselves mixed nightly with their rarefied subjects, or wished to, or might once the finished piece was read. It was precisely the kind of reporting most respectable American journalists deplored and campaigned against. Until then.

Still, she had her standards. No charity events, please, Tina told her subordinates, but the private, recherché parties to which most reporters were never invited. There was even a column called "Vanities" devoted to such "insiderly" chronicles. Alas, top-flight material was hard to come by.

In the fall of 1985, the young writer Michael Shnayerson, an eager refugee from *Avenue* magazine, also devoted to chronicling the rich and powerful, was hired at $65,000 a year to bring social élan and elite connections to *Vanity Fair*. That he was totally lacking in such assets became perfectly apparent only after he arrived. "Very quickly, Tina realized that Michael was just a guy who had a job—and went home every day to his little apartment in the Village, and did not socialize with Pat Buckley or Nan Kempner," it was observed.

Worse, the new recruit, in trying to liven up "Vanities," attempted what his friends called "a Truman Capote thing." He wrote a letter to Pat Buckley, the wife of the conservative columnist and a top New York hostess, with a request: "Would you mind if someone came to your dinner party?" Meaning another reporter.

The letter was poorly received by the Manhattan hostess. "Pat Buckley called and just complained in Tina's ear about the rudeness and cheek of this editor of hers." She also complained to Colacello about the suggestion. Within three months of his arrival, Shnayerson was removed from his position, made a contributing editor, and re-placed by the smoother and more socially savvy Colacello.

Colacello became part of a small group of Tina advisers, all men, put together in the early days of her ascension. She would dine with them periodically, soliciting information and ideas, a regular human vacuum cleaner, some thought, sucking up the contents of the brains grouped around the table, her wide blue eyes gazing at each speaker fixedly, absorbing every point. "I try to produce a kind of club atmo-sphere," she explained. Interestingly, she considered leadership, her ability to "motivate a group of people, have the idea and the tenacity and drive," among her most estimable qualities. "I got that ability from my father," she said, although there were those who might have disputed such a claim.

In fact, a number of editors were aghast at the evolution of the magazine. All sorts of high-flown subjects, tenderly cradled in the old *Vanity Fair,* quietly disappeared under the new regime: an emphasis on art, for instance. Another dispute concerned literature. After a few issues, Tina didn't want it in *Vanity Fair.* The trouble was that *Vanity Fair,* conceived originally as a high-minded literary magazine, had under her predecessors paid huge sums for fiction—"something like thirty thousand dollars for a Saul Bellow novella," was the recollec-tion of one old-timer, and a sizable amount for a Deborah Eisenberg short story, which was sent back to the author, at Tina's insistence, where it underwent a lot of cutting.

"How can she call it a *short* story?" Tina demanded, fuming. "It's five thousand fucking words long!" She was equally irreverent about Isaac Bashevis Singer. In 1985, she had asked John Heilpern, then her arts editor, for a special short story for the Christmas issue, and he persuaded Singer to write one. *"BEEF IT UP, SINGER,"* Tina scrawled in red on the manuscript. Heilpern, as he made clear to his uncompre-hending boss, was quite sure that Singer might have difficulty pursu-ing such a course. "I had to gently explain to Tina," he would later tell a journalist, "that Beef It Up Singer was a recipient of the Nobel Prize for literature."

All in all, these were terrible times for Tina. To Miles Chapman, who was helping her in her hour of need, she confided her feelings of isolation, a sense of imminent and inescapable peril. He felt very sorry for her. "She just didn't know from which particular shrub someone was going to jump out and start shooting at you." Worse, as Chap-man pointed out, "*Vanity Fair* was publicly failing, which was deeply embarrassing to Si and the company. It took us a while. I reckon there was a two-year lag between what we were doing and the general public *realizing* what we were doing."

The trouble was, *Vanity Fair* didn't have two years to prove itself. By the end of May 1985, in fact, it might not have had two days. Despite all of Tina's pleading ("I begged," she would later recall. "Oh, I begged"), Newhouse had decided to fold it. He'd been having reservations about the publication for some time; since its inception, it had drained almost $44 million from his coffers. And to what end?

"I think we have a problem with *Vanity Fair*," Newhouse told Richard Shortway, a top executive whose job it was to oversee *Vanity Fair*, among other publications.

"Yes, Si, we do," said Shortway. "The rumor is its publisher is no good."

The reference was to David O'Brasky, a tough executive. "His nickname is David O'Brasive," Shortway had warned from the outset.

"I'm convinced he's going to be good. He's a Yale man," Si had insisted.

Now it seemed even that asset was not enough. On Memorial Day, Shortway received a phone call from Tina. She was on the West Coast, vacationing—but not quite. "Dick, what is going on?" she demanded. "I'm quite sure Si is closing my magazine." She had ample reason for concern. Pam Van Zandt, Condé Nast's head of human resources, had told her she couldn't hire anyone new for the magazine; Douglas Johnston, her ad director, was being interviewed for a job at *The New Yorker*.

"What does that say to you?" she asked.

"It worries me very much, Tina," Shortway conceded. "I'll be in Si's office at six A.M." This was a perfectly normal time to meet with the boss, as all Condé Nast executives knew; in fact, the best time to get his ear.

"You want to make the stupidest mistake ever? *End* it," he told Newhouse early the next day. Shortway was one of the few at Condé Nast who could talk to his boss that way; they had socialized together. Like Newhouse, he was very fond of Tina ("Instinct," he would later explain. "Thirty years of instinct made me know she was a great editor"). To Newhouse, he said, "You've got the right editor. Now make Doug Johnston your publisher."

"Give me an hour," Newhouse said. He wanted to deliberate.

An hour later, the phone rang. Six more months—that was what Newhouse promised. That and a new publisher, Doug Johnston.

Tina never did thank Shortway for his prompt intervention, nor was he much distressed by her neglect. On the other hand, she had by no means relied on his tactics alone to win the battle. She too had entree into Newhouse's office; she too knew how to make use of it.

"She burst into tears in Si's presence," Bernie Leser would later recall. "Her passion and strength of conviction, Si told us, made an enormous impression. He admits to having been very moved by her."

How artless Tina's display of grief before her boss had been was open to question. Perhaps it was just what it seemed. But like most great generals, Tina would make a study of certain winning gestures and moves. A *Vanity Fair* staffer heard she had given advice on the subject to another Condé Nast editor. "You know when you want something from Si—and you're not getting it—burst into tears," Tina said. "He doesn't know how to handle it."

In any event, she had won her battle. True, it wasn't the war. For months afterward, she assumed every time Newhouse summoned her it was to break the news that it was all over. Eventually, she told people, she and Newhouse actually developed a routine, a fairly mirthless one.

"No, you're *not*. No, I'm *not*," he would assure her whenever they met. "No, you're not fired. No, I'm not closing the magazine."

If anyone could make the most out of a few months' reprieve, she could. "Tina was like on a mission," one of her writers would remember.

And she was a resolute warrior, too, with an uncanny knack for peering into the future. A profile of Benazir Bhutto, commissioned months before her triumphant return to Pakistan, appeared almost magically just days after she came home to the country she would rule. A piece on the Duchess of Windsor, by the time it was published, coincided neatly with her death. At Tina's disposal were all the weapons necessary for battle: unpredictability, ambush, compromise, and zeal.

Of course, no one in the office wholly loved her.

There were two Tinas, her employees would say. "Basically, she's a very cold person," one of them observed. "I mean, she's a little bit like a being from another planet. And yet she is capable of flashes of this enormous charm."

Certainly, the men were charmed. There was, for instance, the matter of her frailties, which her male acquaintances often found endearing, especially the writers. Tina was extremely nearsighted. Sometimes she wore hard lenses, but when these gave her trouble, she removed them. Staffers would wave to her in passing, completely unobserved. "The thing about Tina is she has no peripheral vision," it was decided. "So you could come right up behind her and she didn't know. It's as if she had tunnel vision."

She also, it was noticed, was afflicted with an imperfect sense of direction. A food vendor on Madison and 43rd Street would be approached by a confused Tina, requesting directions to West 44th Street. She was often oblivious, lost in thought, impenetrable. "She would go into the ladies' room—she had her own—and not close the door," recalled a writer. "Because she is in her way a little spacey. She's thinking about what she's thinking about. She's not all that comfortable socially."

Then there was the matter of Tina's chic. She had none. "She would also put on raincoats inside out," a *Vanity Fair* staffer said. She had no idea what constituted New York executive attire; it was an area so far outside her normal pursuits that some of those she hired found themselves duty-bound to give her instructions.

Valiantly, she would try to rectify such defects. "They have a saying in New York, 'When the going gets tough, the tough go shopping,' " she preached to a British journalist. "And it isn't as flippant as it sounds. Everyone notices whether you are wearing a designer label or not, and if you are scruffy, nobody listens to you."

But the thing was, even when Tina bothered with such matters, even when she capitulated to the advice of the stylish editors who advised her and spent her $20,000 wardrobe allowance on what became known as her "pink Chanel period," nothing looked quite right. Invariably, some detail went awry. In Bel-Air she appeared, shortly after attending a lunch and before going to the Academy Awards, in the uniform pink Chanel suit with very high heels. "Tina, you still have foil on your buttons from the dry cleaners," one of her writers pointed out.

"Why did no one tell me? Why didn't they tell me?" she cried, glaring at the offending buttons and ripping off the foil.

So there was in general, and not only among the men, a fairly widespread feeling of protectiveness toward this shy, remote Englishwoman, a tenderness and a goodwill that overrode certain less touching aspects of her personality. "If you don't like my identity you won't like the magazine," Tina promised upon her arrival in New York. But what exactly was her identity?

There was her daunting chilliness, all agreed, the self-sufficient air she had of never being fully on anyone's side. When Tina's old friend Taki, then writing a column for *Vanity Fair,* got busted for cocaine possession in 1984 (a gram was found in his pocket), he quickly discovered how dispensable he was. "My column was immediately dropped. She never told me I was fired," he would remember in later years. That call came from a staffer, clearly under orders. "*They* dropped your column," he said.

However, while in prison, he did hear from Tina: "My dear Taki, I was in the South—I had no idea what happened." Just the nicest letter in the world, thought Taki, perusing the note in his cell. "Well, it was nice receiving it. I don't know how much of it was true. And she did rehire me after I got out. And then afterwards, it didn't work. It just didn't work out." Taki, in her view, was mocking the powerful, the wealthy—the very figures she needed. "I don't like to kick midgets, go after people who can't defend themselves," he said. "She didn't like the people I went after."

Once, said a recruit, Miles Chapman took him aside in his first days at the magazine, and told about the Tina he had worked beside ever since her lively London days. "My only piece of advice?" he said. "Don't try to be her friend."

But after all, there was much to be grateful for. How could she have time to make friends, learn directions, choose good clothes? She was so absorbed in her work, so removed from the ordinary concerns of daily life, wholly immersed in her new, still feeble creation, plunged into the common good, as most of them thought, for all their sakes.

And by June 1985, one month after Newhouse's attempt to pull the plug, there was reason for celebration, Tina believed. On the cover of that month's *Vanity Fair*—THE REAGAN STOMP, read the cutline—was an exclusive picture, a laughing president in a tuxedo, his wife in a pearl choker and a long shiny gown, literally kicking up a heel. It was Bob Colacello, the Republican friend to the rich, as well as the Venezuelan socialite Reinaldo Herrera, also with *Vanity Fair,* who pulled the strings to get the magazine into the White House. In pursuit of the Reagans, Herrera had called first Jeremy Zipkin, the first lady's close friend, and subsequently Nancy Reagan herself. This issue was considered so crucial to the survival of the magazine that Tina appeared at the shoot, along with Harry Benson, the photographer, and a *Vanity Fair* assistant equipped with a tape recorder that played exclusively Frank Sinatra songs, favorites of the first lady, who had a well-known crush on the singer.

Inside the magazine was a long, devotional piece on the Reagans by the conservative columnist William F. Buckley, Jr., terminating in a rather peculiar analogy. He compared the first couple to the Greek mythological characters Philemon and Baucis, a husband and wife so determined never to be separated, even by death, that they were turned by Hermes into intertwining trees. The ensuing fuss—the buzz swarming around this example of slavish idolatry—was practically guaranteed. The entire issue, wrote the left-wing columnist Alexander Cockburn, was "repulsive." In fact, he added presciently, the new magazine "is what *The New Yorker* would look like if it were edited in Los Angeles."

That was precisely the point. Had *The New Yorker* been edited in Los Angeles, for example, it would inevitably have attracted writers like the onetime Hollywood film producer Dominick Dunne and the present-day screenwriter Stephen Schiff, two early Tina recruits who regularly cinematized their subjects in print: Claus von Bülow, accused of trying to murder his wife; and the California socialite Wallis Annenberg, daughter of the billionaire philanthropist. And so many others. "When this issue comes out next week, every magazine in New York is going to want you to write for them. But you're mine, and I want you to sign up," Tina informed Dunne, after he had written about the trial of the man who had killed Dunne's daughter.

The idea of a father's writing about such a delicate subject was Tina's own, suggested in 1983. Dunne dutifully kept a journal throughout the trial ("If I hadn't kept that journal, as Tina suggested, I would have gone mad," he later wrote), and it subsequently provided him with something quite permanent, aside from sanity. From then on he received a substantial income, courtesy of *Vanity Fair.* Unlike his brother, John Gregory Dunne, he was no literary stylist, having begun writing at age fifty. But really, no one cared about such a relatively inconsequential drawback at the magazine. He had assets far more invigorating and vital to offer to Tina: his little black book, his memory bank.

The rich, the potent, the murdered; these were Dunne's characters, and by extension, ultimately *Vanity Fair*'s. In fact, singly or as a group, they would people all subsequent issues. As Dunne told Tina on their first meeting at a dinner party when she appeared to be at pretty loose ends, he *knew*—in however convoluted a fashion—so many of the vivid and dramatic denizens of the world that was dear to her heart: Elizabeth Taylor, who had appeared years earlier in Dunne's movie *Ash Wednesday;* the beautiful actress Sharon Tate, who "was the girlfriend of my barber, Jay Sebring," and, with him, was ultimately murdered by the Manson gang.

How extremely insiderly! Tina couldn't believe her luck. She began her pitch to Dunne over lunch at La Goulue, a Manhattan restaurant swarming with wealthy Europeans. She was about to take over *Vanity Fair,* she said, but that was a big secret, just between them. Her lunch companion had just what she needed, she candidly explained. "She said it would take her years to train someone to have the kind of contacts I had," Dunne wrote.

But by far the most significant and high-impact Hollywood movie star issue of those early days came in October 1985, its degree of importance instantly signaled by the byline: Tina Brown. The fact that her subject was not of Hollywood but from Britain, not a film star but actually Princess Diana, was of absolutely no consequence. It was Hollywood to the core: the wealth, the misery, the approaching scandal, the love-gone-wrong. The cover picture, it was widely recognized, bore a certain physical resemblance to the author of the piece. Perhaps Tina herself had noticed that?

Called "The Mouse That Roared," the article described the sullen, brooding rites of an emotionally unstable princess, who spent "hours cut off in her Sony Walkman," dancing on her own or "studying her press clippings." Much of this information, word had it, came to Tina via Anthony Holden, Harry's close friend and protégé from London, and a biographer of Prince Charles. Diana's husband couldn't have been overly pleased with Tina's conclusion, which received a fair amount of worldwide attention and enduring repetition. "The debonair Prince is pussy-whipped from here to eternity," she wrote.

It was an inspired choice of phrase, not merely the clattering vulgarity of it, but the unstoppable and thrilling resonance of the implicit suggestion that Tina was actually describing her own husband, her own marriage, her own self. "A curious reversal has taken place in the marriage: Diana the shy introvert, unable to cope with public life, has emerged as the star of the world's stage," Tina had written.

Naturally, the newspapers had a fine time dissecting this passage, especially in Britain, where Harry Evans just three years earlier had been a towering figure and his wife a shy arriviste who hadn't fully arrived. "He was the glittering star," wrote the *Evening Stan-*

dard, in a bath of crocodile tears. "Then he found himself out on the street."

Of course, British views on gender equality were slightly behind the times. Harry was, by nature, the more considerate host, "so sweet and ungrand," it would be remembered. In later years, a friend invited to their Quogue country house—a compact and relatively modest retreat—noticed it was empty, "except for what was obviously a washerwoman walking around with this huge, huge bundle of sheets and dirty towels, so high this person was obscured." Only when the wash was put into the machine did the visitor observe that the busy little servant was, in fact, Harry.

And as for Tina, by November 1985 she was exhausted, overworked, and quite pregnant. It was exactly six months after Si Newhouse's decree of a half-year reprieve, and she was in her glory, jubilantly telling people that the magazine had sold 400,000 copies that year. Ad pages were up 33 percent. Unmentioned was the fact that *Vanity Fair* was $10 million in the red that year (in any event, a $4 million improvement on the year before). Tina was, she insisted, "euphoric" about both her "babies."

"Nothing is sweeter than being in the second phase in New York where you have shown you can stand it," she said.

The difficulty here was that Harry hadn't yet tasted any of that sweetness. For some of each week, he wasn't even in New York with his powerful wife. "He spends two days a week in Washington overseeing something called the *U.S. News & World Report,*" explained a London gossip columnist.

As it happened, Harry was working for Mortimer Zuckerman, the real estate magnate and the new owner and editor in chief of *U.S. News,* whose own credentials as a newsmagazine proprietor were at the time very much debated. Zuckerman had achieved success, the East Coast elite had decided, in an infinitely less lofty realm. Known for many years as an ambitious, tough, money-hungry man, he finally gathered a measure of currency in some circles for being at one point the lover of the feminist leader Gloria Steinem, although she seemed as astonished as anyone to find herself by his side. As one of his employees put it, "Mort got terrible press. He was known as 'the lisping demi-billionaire.' There was this real psychodrama between Mort and Harry."

This psychodrama was even more complicated than most. Harry had been hired by Zuckerman, as best anyone could tell, to throw the mantle of his reputation as a brilliant crusading editor across the shoulders of his new boss. But however valuable that protection, there were always limits on Zuckerman's gratitude.

His functions, too, were bewildering and ill-defined. Zuckerman wanted to sell his recent acquisition, the Atlantic Monthly Press publishing house, and he had designated Harry as salesman. "Harry found this buyer for him, the Mondadoris of Italy," a friend of that era said. "And the Mondadoris were going to make Harry editor in chief." This deal, however, never materialized; Zuckerman sold the publishing company elsewhere. "Harry told me that he didn't even know Mort was making the deal, while we were trying to sell it," said James Glassman, who was president at the time of the Atlantic Monthly Company.

It did not escape Zuckerman's reporters at *U.S. News* that their boss was "the butt of all jokes," or that if Harry and Tina broke rank from the rest of the media and embraced Zuckerman, they must have had their reasons. Some of these reasons went unexpressed; others fell into the lap of astonished listeners.

"I'm here to keep Mort honest," Harry said one night in the fall of 1985, picking at his food across the table from a female journalist he barely knew. He spoke of Zuckerman in measured, mostly kindhearted terms (that one quotation excepted), and appeared truly grateful to have found a niche. The two were seated alone in a Washington restaurant. Tina was, as usual, in New York.

Abruptly the conversation swerved from the business at hand, which was to describe Zuckerman and analyze his character for a piece the journalist was considering writing. "You know you're a very attractive woman, very, very attractive woman," Harry said, leaning forward and gazing with some significance across the table.

"Thanks," said the reporter. "It's certainly good to hear that when you're a month-and-a-half pregnant, as I am."

Harry didn't turn a hair. "My wife is pregnant too, you know," he continued smoothly. "Silly girl didn't even *know* she was pregnant. One night in bed, she turns to me, says, 'Darling, my nipples are hurting.'

"I said, 'Darling, you sure you're not pregnant then? Nipples do hurt when you're pregnant.'

" 'No, don't be stupid,' she said. 'Of course I'm not pregnant.' But she was. Didn't even realize she was pregnant."

It was a striking conversation, and not merely for what it revealed about Harry as a husband, thought the reporter, but for the darting, streaky course of it: Harry's swift glides into intimacy and suggestion, the smooth turnaround, and his casual plunge into the subject of his wife's nipples to an acquaintance he had met but a few weeks previously.

And quite probably Tina was not unaware of her husband's vagrant flirtatiousness, and made uneasy by it even at that early date. "The first time I met Tina, she said, 'I hope you're looking out for Harry,'" said a remarkably pretty and prosperous Washington woman who was friendly with Harry during that period. "The next time I saw her, she was cold as ice. The subtext was that I was having an affair with Harry. Which I wasn't."

It was the general supposition in October 1984, when his friend Mort Zuckerman made him editorial director of *U.S. News & World Report,* that Harry would in very short order become its editor, with a lot of glory restored to him after a career blown to bits by Rupert Murdoch. Alas, certain ghosts from that shattered past followed him to his new country. "Zuckerman better be warned that Harry Evans spends other people's money like a drunken sailor," declared a former (London) *Times* man—for publication.

In any event, Harry always denied wanting to scale the ladder at *U.S. News,* which had a circulation of 2.2 million, about half that of *Time* magazine. But James Glassman, who was named executive vice president of the weekly magazine, saw at once the jaunty spirit with which "Harry took on the role of editor in almost everything but name. For instance, Harry brought in an art director he had worked with in redoing *The Times* of London, who was very good and did a very good redesign. Harry was in charge of the covers." He was also "good at conceptualizing, thinking up ideas for stories."

As it turned out, much of his frenetic activity went for nothing. "I'm very wary of having Evans, who's British, become editor of this most American of magazines," Zuckerman, who was Canadian, confided to Glassman. A facile explanation, Glassman believed, and perhaps somewhat disingenuous. "I think there was a germ of truth to that. But probably more important was that Mort was afraid of Harry."

Afraid, thought Glassman, that Harry "would take the magazine out of Mort's control in a way Mort would probably have found frightening." And Harry with all his talent would have done just that, Glassman knew; the magazine would inevitably bear the imprint of this gifted, experienced editor.

Thus, the more youthful and relatively untried Shelby Coffey III, formerly the Style section editor of *The Washington Post,* was made editor of *U.S. News* in Harry's stead. And then, when Coffey failed to satisfy, came David Gergen, a dull establishment figure who had been a White House communications director under Ronald Reagan. Always Harry would say that he hadn't much wanted the job anyway, was happiest where he was.

But where was he?

"Mort never really defined Harry's role," Glassman decided. It was nothing personal, really, no reflection on Harry. It was simply Zuckerman's way with most people. "Mort used to have this phrase, 'Get you involved. We want to get you involved with *U.S. News!*' It was never clear what that exactly meant." Privately, Harry vented his frustrations to Glassman: "He did say there was no clarity to his role." He never said he wanted to be editor of *U.S. News,* not even to Glassman. "That was the interesting thing. Harry didn't want to let on that he was disappointed."

And so for two years, Harry drifted. Doing well, of course, but essentially anchorless, bobbing along on a fierce current that might at any moment dash him against the rocks. When he had tired of his poorly defined job with Zuckerman, he reduced his time there and joined as an executive the freshly formed New York outpost of Weidenfeld & Nicolson, which then united the cachet of the British publisher Lord Weidenfeld with the considerable fortune of Ann Getty. The company had some serious authors: Anthony Burgess (his two-volume autobiography) and Eileen Simpson, among others.

In this job, at least, Evans occupied a large New York office, complete with a secretary and appurtenances that reflected his hero's status across the Atlantic. But here too, few seemed entirely certain what he was meant to be doing. George Weidenfeld would murmur, sotto voce, awestruck, "Harry Evans"—implying he couldn't believe his good fortune in having the fabled ex–newspaper editor on board. But his listeners, Americans, would in essence shrug their shoulders. What was Harry Evans to them? What, in fact, was the thalidomide story? "There was this sense of having to tolerate him," recalled one old acquaintance.

"The big carrot of Harry's working for that company was that he was always going to deliver a new book by Kissinger. It became a kind

150

Tina (then Cristina) Brown at Oxford, where she attracted attention for her contributions to the student publication *Isis* and her succession of well-connected boyfriends. "A plump little pudding" as a girl, she was on her way to becoming a dish.

Tina (far right) threw a party for herself to celebrate her 1974 Oxford graduation. From the left: Bettina Brown, her glamorous, irrepressible mother; Auberon Waugh, son of novelist Evelyn Waugh and a writer himself, who was her lover and most ardent champion.

Tina in 1977. Already at 23 a successful playwright and journalist, eking out a living on 8,000 pounds a year ($21,000). Within two years, she would become editor of *Tatler,* a society magazine that she transformed into a witty, acerbic—and popular—publication by skewering the upper classes.

Tina with Martin Amis, son of the novelist Kingsley Amis and a former lover, in whom she confided when she began her affair with Harry Evans, the famous, crusading editor of *The Sunday Times*—and a married man 25 years her senior.

Harry Evans had arrived in London in 1966 with a thick northern accent and a drab provincial wardrobe. Hired by *The Sunday Times,* he was soon appointed, to the surprise of the British establishment, its editor.

Harry quickly shed his provincial ways to become something of a dandy, took to riding a motorbike to work, and earned a well-deserved reputation as a shrewd and fearless editor. He also left his wife, the mother of his three children, and started living with Tina Brown.

Harry was at the peak of his profession when media mogul Rupert Murdoch bought both *The Sunday Times* and *The Times* and persuaded him to take over at *The Times*. Strong-willed and perpetual outsiders, the two men inevitably ran afoul of each other.

Harry fought hard to keep his job at *The Times* but was finally forced to resign, and received a hefty severance. Married to Harry now, Tina was content—at this time in her life—to stay in the background as the consort of a hero.

Shy, reclusive Si Newhouse, owner of the vast Condé Nast publishing empire, bought *Tatler,* was dazzled by Tina, and made her the editor of another moribund magazine, *Vanity Fair.* The Browns moved to New York, where Tina (shown here with Barbara Walters at a society wedding) stepped into the spotlight and Harry found himself in her shadow.

Tina Brown, now the new editor of the struggling magazine *Vanity Fair,* was poised, everyone assumed back then, for a swan dive when she posed for this 1984 picture with her father, George. By then retired as a movie producer, he was enormously proud of his daughter, certain of her cunning and her ability to create something out of nothing. "Those wide eyes and that brow. You never quite know what's going on behind it," he said. His daughter, just 30 at the time, wasn't nearly as confident about her prospects as George, which might account for her wary and apprehensive expression in this shot.

Tina and her great rival, *Vogue* editor Anna Wintour, another English import and Newhouse favorite, co-hosted a boisterous book party in 1989. Tina's fabulous parties—with Newhouse footing the bills—were the hallmark of her reign at *Vanity Fair.*

Though hardly a fashion plate herself, Tina was a triumph at *Vanity Fair,* rescuing the magazine with provocative celebrity covers, laudatory profiles of those she needed among the rich and famous, and a wide variety of thoughtful pieces—a style of magazine journalism that was entirely new.

Harry training a polite but cautious gaze on Rupert Murdoch, the man who had sent him packing at *The Times.* Harry was now editor of *Condé Nast Traveler,* yet another Newhouse magazine, a job that some of his old friends thought was beneath him.

Fire on Ice: Sheri de Borchgrave, a flirtatious fact-checker (and a baroness) had been working for Harry Evans for some months by the time this picture was taken in late 1988 at a *Condé Nast Traveler* skating party, after which a close friendship ensued.

Tina with Mort Zuckerman, multimillionaire real estate developer and proprietor of *U.S. News & World Report* and the New York *Daily News*, who was embraced by both Tina and Harry from the very start of their New York careers. In return, Zuckerman proved an invaluable patron, furthering Harry's ambitions through good times and bad.

©Marina Garnier

Tina in 1993, a year after being anointed by Si Newhouse as editor of *The New Yorker,* an appointment that shocked and outraged many. Her brand of journalism and *The New Yorker*'s hidebound and hallowed traditions would make for an uneasy combination.

By 1994, Tina and Harry ruled supreme in the New York publishing world, she at *The New Yorker* and he as the president of Random House, another arm of the Newhouse empire. Not coincidentally, the same writers were often published by both.

Tina's fascination with Hollywood celebrities grew, if possible, even more intense at *The New Yorker*. Here she poses with Michael Ovitz, then president of the Creative Artists Agency, one of the most powerful men on the West Coast.

Once again playing in the big leagues, Harry could party with the likes of Dick Snyder (center), his rival at Simon & Schuster, and Barry Diller (right).

Tina and Harry flanked by actor Harrison Ford at *The New Yorker*'s lavish 70th anniversary party in 1995, where writers were greatly outnumbered by stars and socialites.

Also present were Si Newhouse, Tina's ever-generous and doting patron, and Tom Florio, publisher of *The New Yorker*, on whom Tina would eventually sour.

An ardent admirer of women, Harry eagerly awaits a kiss from Madonna, whose book he wanted desperately to publish. It went to another house.

Harry, who loved almost everything about America, including dude ranches, riding, and cowboy outfits, quietly became an American citizen in 1993, much to the astonishment of his British friends.

By late 1997, the wattage of New York publishing's power couple was clearly beginning to dim. Harry was in his last, most agonizing days at Random House—hammered by accusations of extravagance and poor judgment—while Newhouse, who had never before denied Tina anything, was growing surprisingly resistant to her demands at *The New Yorker*.

Harry cradling his love letter to his adopted country, *The American Century*, which took him thirteen years to write. He was working again for his old friend and consistent benefactor, Mort Zuckerman, as the editorial director of *U.S. News* and the *Daily News*—a job he held for three years.

Tina continued to hobnob with Hollywood celebrities. She is shown here at a party with actor James Woods (left) and the all-powerful Michael Eisner (right), chairman of the Walt Disney Company.

As relations between Tina and Condé Nast executives grew increasingly testy, Tina left *The New Yorker* in July 1998 and joined forces with Harvey Weinstein of Miramax films (whose parent company is Disney) to found a new magazine, *Talk*. Her Hollywood connections finally paid off.

Tina chats with actress Demi Moore at the unforgettable launch party for *Talk*, held at the base of the Statue of Liberty in August 1999. The party was "a defining moment" for Tina—and for her career. If *Talk* was a success, her record would be unbroken. If *Talk* went under, she would go down with it.

Even as *Talk* was languishing, Tina co-hosted yet another party with Elisabeth Murdoch (the daughter of Rupert Murdoch), shown here with Ian Schrager in London in April 2000.

Tina Brown receives a CBE (Commander of the British Empire) award, courtesy of the Queen, on her 47th birthday, November 21, 2000. Harry, who was writing books, was the more likely candidate for such an honor, but it was not forthcoming.

By January 2001, when Tina found herself beside actor Hugh Grant at a Golden Globe awards ceremony, *Talk* had become essentially a movie magazine, a vehicle for the stars, many of them beholden to Mirimax or Disney.

Harry and Tina could look back on triumphant parallel careers in publishing—on careers that had taken them to the very top. For a time. "This is definitely my last big roll of the dice," said Tina. Like Harry, she was keenly aware of the perils of lingering too long at the gambling tables—and yet she couldn't manage to tear herself away.

of standing joke," explained a colleague. "We'd be at an editorial meeting and Harry would look at his watch, and say, 'Ooo, have a lunch with Kissinger, must go.' And no one dared say no. We'd think, 'Maybe *this* time he's going to come back with a contract with Kissinger.' "

To keep in shape, Harry jogged. To keep up his spirits, he liked to watch women, and confide to friends their most appealing or provocative aspects. "Oooo, she's very fuckable," Harry would inform a male acquaintance who, being American, was duly taken aback and indeed made uneasy by the frankness of the confidence. Moreover, as he had never before heard the word used, the connotations of it, as applied to a charming woman, confounded him. "Was she eligible to be screwed?" he wondered. "Or did it mean he was open to that? Or did it mean he would like really to do it? I think it was the latter." Boy, thought the acquaintance whenever the adjective popped up, "this guy must be doing a lot on the side."

On the other hand, there was no evidence Harry was doing anything more than indulging in fantasy. Still, the subject would emerge and reemerge, unbidden. "He talked about it all the time, just women, his interest in women."

Even the birth of his first child by Tina—a boy they named George Frederick, who arrived in January 1986, six weeks prematurely—couldn't dampen some of this talk. Harry was fifty-seven, the father of a newborn, with three grown children.

"Hey, Harry, congratulations," said a friend after the child's birth.

"Yes, on the first try, too!" replied Evans.

Privately, things were quite different. The little boy's premature birth was a cause of considerable fear and worry to the couple. The ambulance had arrived late: "a botched job," a family friend would later say. George Frederick weighed only 4 pounds 8½ ounces when he was born by cesarean section and would have to spend three weeks in an incubator, a London newspaper reported at the time. Outwardly, Harry remained resolutely upbeat and optimistic. "Tina will probably be back at work in two weeks, and when she was being wheeled into the operating theatre her thoughts were about the cover of the April issue of *Vanity Fair*," Harry told a London journalist. The child would look a lot like young Tina, blond curls, almost angelic.

But between shepherding *Vanity Fair* and going through that extremely difficult birth, Tina was exhausted. Nothing had been easy for the longest time. "I remember her talking about how awful it was being pregnant, how she blew up like a whale and was just a blimp," recalled one confidante. It was a source, interestingly, of considerable reassurance to the women who worked alongside her.

This comfort which she managed to impart was, however, something novel and of fairly recent vintage. "Get that goddamn child out of here!" Tina had once shrieked to a contributing editor who had brought a screaming baby to the office. Those days were evidently over. No longer did women have to fear the impact of pregnancy on their careers, as they might under a male boss, distant from the terrors and distractions of working mothers. "Don't worry," one literary agent assured a client who wanted children, "you have no idea how different it's going to be working for a woman." Tina had been pregnant. It was a relief, other women felt, and a form of license as well.

"Thank you for the delicious outfit for Prince George," Tina wrote her British friend Valerie Grove in a cheery style, words misspelled, on the back of the card bearing a pretty sketch of New York in the spring. Tina loved the children's book Grove had sent, she loved motherhood, she loved everything. Baby George refused to be still for the camera, but what can you do? She enclosed a slightly blurry photograph of the baby she called "HRH" and promised Grove that the child "looks very like Edward VIII. Snub nose, crinkly hair and a dimple." "Having a baby is the best fun I've ever had," she concluded. "My only regret is not doing it earlier. I intend to have one every two years until I have to stop."

How could Harry not adore such a brave and resolute woman? Some time after she had settled into motherhood and returned to work, Tina appeared on network television. In his spacious Manhattan office behind his big desk, Harry steadfastly watched the screen. He was smiling expansively.

"*Did* you see her?" he inquired of anyone who happened to walk in about then. "*Isn't* she the most beautiful person you've ever seen? Ah, don't you think she looks *gorgeous,* the pink she's wearing? Did you see the way her eyes moved?"

You couldn't ask for a more devoted husband, a bigger fan. Whenever Harry talked, it was generally noticed, he wouldn't miss a chance to say how wonderful Tina was.

152

Chapter 8
Courtesy of Tina

Impossible to discuss *Vanity Fair,* Tina's *Vanity Fair,* which now exists only in altered form, without discussing money. It became the single most important lubricant of the publication, and its inspiration as well. In fact (this was after all the eighties), money became in most instances not merely fuel for *Vanity Fair,* the exuberant source of its glamour and its fluorescent appeal among celebrities, famous photographers, and eloquent writers with social contacts, but its substance. Most of the magazine's articles were, in one way or another, basically about money, even if they ostensibly concerned themselves with, say, the strapping but ultimately dissatisfied wife of Sylvester Stallone, or with the scentless rogue Claus von Bülow, snug in black leather, or with Ronald Reagan, who pursued an inclusive career of embracing the prosperous all the way to the White House.

All of this Tina absorbed in the same instinctive, reflexive way that she had once embraced the intricacies of British society. A watch manufacturer who was deliberating whether or not to place ads in such a questionable venue as the revived magazine asked her, "What's the difference between *Vanity Fair* and *Town & Country?*" Tina had a quick answer for that: "*Vanity Fair* is for the thinking rich. And *Town and Country* is for the stinking rich."

In every respect, Tina proved a quick study. The editor Sharon Delano, who came to *Vanity Fair* within months of Tina's arrival, would say, years after she had been fired: "More than almost any other editor I ever worked with, Tina had the ability to see the potential in a manuscript that a lot of other people would have thrown away. She was really gifted about knowing how a story works and how it could be made to work." Another early editor perceived: "When she took over the magazine, I saw leadership right away. She was very decisive." Tina herself realized from the start that "American magazines appear to be nervous of having a voice; they tend to be packaged—Muzak. So I am trying to bring a loud and idiosyncratic voice to *Vanity Fair* to break through the Muzak."

Naturally, there were quibblers about the nature and timbre of this voice. In fact, it seemed to be not so much a voice as an entire dissonant chorus. Back home in London, Tina's compatriots, the Brits she had left behind, professed puzzlement over the laborious composition of each issue, what Tina called "The Mix." There it was: a piece on the ditzy actress Shirley MacLaine contemplating her own parents' marriage; another by Norman Mailer reflecting grandly and at awful length on the sadism within the novel *American Psycho;* an autobiographical article on serving time on drug charges by the bon vivant Taki—*and all within the same issue,* as if they were strangers bunched together in an elevator stuck between floors, manned by Jean-Paul Sartre. What were they doing in the same place anyway? Where was the thread?

The brighter readers figured it out pretty quickly: ". . . the magazine revealed throughout an acute ambivalence as to whether it is satirizing morbid sex, the worthless rich and the spiritually disgusting Eighties, or selling them to its readers," one journalist noted.

It usually wasn't satirizing. With few exceptions (Donald Trump was one, and he threatened to sue), the rich were far too valuable to *Vanity Fair* for that. They were the elite who composed Tina's new aristocracy, the substitutes for the upmarket British dukes and Sloane Ranger heiresses who had appeared in her old *Tatler.* They were as integral to the magazine as Hollywood, or even Tina herself, eagerly cultivated and regularly applied to for access to their soirées and their equally wealthy friends; the German princess Gloria von Thurn und Taxis especially (whom Tina called "the Princess TNT"), because she gave vulgar and lavish splashes with indiscriminate guest lists.

There were even—and this was certainly a novelty in the sober world of upmarket American journalism—people hired by *Vanity Fair* not to write, but expressly to serve as conduits to money, stars, and status. Reinaldo Herrera, for example, whose wife, Carolina, was a New York clothing designer, served this function to perfection. It was he who got the magazine the cooperation of Gianni Agnelli and even Imelda Marcos, using the methodology with which he was familiar: "I got a call from Imelda's assistant, and I said, 'Imelda, *darling,* how are you?' And of course it wasn't Imelda, but that made her think I knew Imelda. Perfect! She put Imelda on the phone right away. The rest is history."

The British-born Sarah Giles, who had known and worked for Tina since her *Tatler* days, remained an office fixture on Madison Avenue. There the discussion of her intensive romantic pursuits (an impressive trajectory ranging from an early fondness for Martin Amis to the international negotiator Richard Holbrooke to a later fling with Harry's old boss Mort Zuckerman, by whom she became briefly pregnant) vastly overshadowed, in the opinion of some office enemies, her more utilitarian and valuable qualities to the magazine. Her output, after all, was prodigious. "But my closeness to Tina, that was always resentable," Giles felt. And here, perhaps, she was not wrong.

"A terribly insecure, spoiled little girl, a troublemaker, a loose mouth," one editor remarked of Giles. "Tina would send her off with various writers to work the phones and get Imelda Marcos or whoever . . . I don't know how effective her part was and how much these people just wanted to get done by *Vanity Fair.*" The feeling was, as one of the staffers put it, that Sarah "was the one who'd go with Tina and say to Tina, 'Here's So-and-So,' and find all these people. She had a horrible job, because people would go in and do these pieces, and Tina would still want to remain acquaintances. And it was Sarah's job to smooth it all out. I mean, it was such an eighties thing."

Nonetheless, this was what Tina expected, and not only from Giles or Herrera. At *Vanity Fair,* almost everyone was an ambassador. "Go out, go out and bring something back, even if it's only a cold!" Tina would exhort the troops time and again, by which she meant that their prescribed activities should include after-hours mixing, partygoing, and the ceaseless extension of prized social contacts, as much as writing. She was an extraordinary leader, forever tinkering with "the Mix" until the last possible moment, anticipating the buzz, the hot story with a kind of second sight her subordinates found eerie in its precision.

She was heedless about throwing out a cover story for the sake of something newer, hipper. Mikhail Baryshnikov triumphed over duller stuff in one instance, Gorbachev over the Hollywood star Ellen Barkin just as the eighties were winding down and a certain gravity set in (not for Barkin, however; she threatened to sue over her displacement, claiming she had been promised the cover in exchange for an interview). All this cost money, but it earned *Vanity Fair* the reputation of being, unlike any other magazine—including *Time* and *Newsweek*—on top of the news. "She may have been torn for a second about taking Ellen Barkin off the cover and putting Gorbachev on—and it didn't sell, P.S," a friend recalled. "And Barkin would have sold. You know, Tina occasionally did things for journalistic reasons."

And occasionally, these journalistic pursuits were festooned with certain details one might not easily find anywhere outside the supermarket checkout line. Thus, an article on General Noriega included references to buggery; a story on the fall of General Stroessner of Paraguay contained a passage on the military abduction of schoolgirls. A crime story on the murder of young women happened to mention that the killer "had removed a set of breasts."

There were compensations for such frenzy, of course, plenty of them. The most low-level assistant (and Tina was by no means famous for being kind to the lowly) received a chit entitling her to a Dial-a-cab that would see her safely home from *Vanity Fair*'s celebrated parties. The submission of expense accounts, far from being the agonizing affair it was at other companies, took on a wholly different cast at *Vanity Fair*. There such documents were scrutinized by the managing editor, Pamela McCarthy, as though they were diaries ripe with social secrets, tales to tell. Which they were.

"Mmmm . . . I'm looking at your expense account and you seem to be going out a lot. And I'm really pleased, Christa, that's great," McCarthy informed a new young British recruit, Christa D'Souza, one day, eyeing the itemized breakdown of the $300–$400 a week she regularly spent on such outings. Fresh from Condé Nast in Milan ("Where, I mean, bloody hell, they hardly paid you!"), the girl marveled at the sudden exaltation of her station. There she was, a pretty English flower, an assistant editor who occasionally wrote snippets on hot new restaurants and peculiar fads, and the first day at her desk, a messenger made off with her Chanel bag. Within hours a new one, shaped like a sausage, arrived on her desk—courtesy of Tina. It was an extraordinary moment. That this "amazing person, very powerful . . . the most remarkable person I have ever met in my life," should have concerned herself, and so swiftly, with an underling's problem, struck her forcibly. D'Souza marveled at such largesse, such generosity. Later she would describe those years as "a race to see how much money you could spend. I really felt that about the magazine."

And the salaries! In the early eighties, *Playboy* magazine paid $1 a word, a munificent sum for a writer in those days. By the end of the decade, *Vanity Fair* was forking out $25,000 for longer articles and $100,000-a-year contracts to favored writers. No longer did they have to scrounge for pieces, palms outstretched. Now they received steady, predictable incomes. Courtesy of Tina.

And with the income came the satisfaction of knowing the boss was worthy of the job—by no means a given in the world of journalism. Tina had a formidable, directed intelligence, as terrifying and on course as a targeted missile, but also in its way gratifying. There was little occasion for small talk. She wanted to know everything. "Many successful people, particularly men who have big egos, they basically want to hear themselves talk," one of Tina's female writers would later remember. "Tina was the opposite of anyone I ever worked for. She wanted to know what you knew. It was like having someone vacuum-clean your brain while you're sitting there. And it was very scary because you were on the spot every second, having to prove how smart you were. How plugged in you were. I felt this tremendous pressure to be very, very smart."

In the late eighties, a writer with a few social graces, a pleasing style, and an easy manner of earning the confidence of celebrities and tycoons might earn, say, $35,000 at rival magazines. One phone call from Tina, with her fascinating mixture of flash and cash, and nothing would ever again be the same: over lunch, the names of major stars were dangled, prospective cover stories were projected, and the writer's literary skills luxuriantly and at some length admired. Agents were summoned to negotiate the terms of the contract. By the end of it all, that same journalist would have more than doubled his salary.

"There she is, offering too much money again! I'll have to call Si to get this stopped," complained *New York* magazine's editor Ed Kosner. He was made seriously miserable by the bulging purse of his competitor. One by one, his better people—James Wolcott, Jesse Kornbluth, Marie Brenner—were being inveigled away from his shop by the blue-eyed British magician, brandishing wads of money, parties, perks. Every new arrival received some special gift. Brenner, whom Tina had known for years back in her London days, was permitted, once she arrived at *Vanity Fair,* to travel business class. The Harvard-educated Kornbluth—this was in 1989—asked his editor if he and his society wife, Annette Tapert, might fly to Aspen that Christmas to attend a party hosted by producers Don Simpson and Jerry Bruckheimer and the actor Don Johnson. No other journalists were invited, he informed Tina. Did she want him to go?

"Yes, go," she urged. And in a shot, both husband and wife were flown to Aspen courtesy of Tina. Tina understood, it was felt, what might be harvested from a party hosted by such amazing people. That Christmas Eve, Kornbluth watched George Hamilton in action. He saw Melanie Griffith, the fleshy, baby-voiced actress, and also Don Johnson, her husband at the time, and realized instantly that Griffith was a story, a cover. His wife went skiing with Bruckheimer.

So this was the kind of place *Vanity Fair* was. One month an important and much admired piece on AIDS and how it was decimating the fashion and art communities. The next, an article in which Priscilla Presley admitted she had had a "fling"—unconsummated—with the singer Julio Iglesias. Three weeks, all expenses paid at the Beverly Wilshire, for a writer working "on a story that wasn't even a cover story." Within a few years, salaries rose to $150,000, which was what Lynn Hirschberg was earning by the time she left—more than double what she had previously drawn writing at *Rolling Stone*.

And with this kind of money, all else followed. Everything in the writers' lives changed when *Vanity Fair* took over New York. They became upper-middle-class, the object of envious scrutiny among their less fortunate peers. Their children went to private schools. Their clothes improved, along with their newly discriminating palates. Their statures rose within the little media community that knew them—and then far beyond. The more exalted among them appeared often on television to promote *Vanity Fair* stories. Small wonder that a newspaper profile of their boss began with a quotation from strictly anonymous sources: "You won't get dirt on Tina Brown. . . . Oh sure I've got gossip on Tina. But *Vanity Fair* is paying for my new car, and I want to keep working for it. . . . Everybody wants to write for *Vanity Fair*."

Tina was very gracious with Si Newhouse's enormous wealth, very conscious of its beneficence and importance in a world of inflated egos and meager salaries. Could anyone honestly be surprised that her press was generally excellent? In a 1989 *Newsweek* article by the longtime staffer Tom Mathews, Tina was boldly described as "a beauty" in "a scarlet dress, two loops of pearls at her throat, her nails polished tooth-and-claw red, her ankles sculpted into drop-dead stiletto heels, her silvery voice rippling with London elegance." There was no end to the admiration she compelled. Moreover, Tina was wise enough not to horde her stardom, but to pass the crown around to her subjects for brief fittings. Why shouldn't they receive some of the enchantment bestowed by money? "She had writers go to London to parties, to the Academy Awards," Hirschberg would remember.

"They were stars, not writers, not editors. Other people make you a great writer. Tina makes people famous."

For such privilege, however, there were certain exactions. The *Vanity Fair* writer could easily find himself on a flight to Barcelona just to dine with Diandra Douglas, a lonely, beautiful woman then married to Michael Douglas. But the piece on her, after five drafts, never appeared. So many stories assigned by Tina, championed by her, paid for in full, were not published, and disappointment though there was, the reasonable *Vanity Fair* author understood—in a way. There was nothing personal in such rejections, and there was always substantial compensation. "I wrote two pieces for Tina for *Vanity Fair*, one on Brian De Palma which was cut by seventy-five percent," recalled Martin Amis, shrugging. "And one on Hugh Hefner, which was cut by one hundred percent. Both are collected in my book, *The Moronic Inferno*. We didn't fall out over that. It's not my way. And I also knew that this was the early days of her editorship—and I think it's universal—that you over-commission, chop and change. Then it steadies down. . . ."

Really, though, it never steadied down. "My ambition is to get the best," Tina informed *The New York Times* by the end of the gilded decade, after salaries had soared even further, along with circulation (up 63 percent in four years), and advertising (which had tripled to 1,193 pages). Then she threw down the gauntlet. She was Harry's wife, after all. She believed in discomfiting her rivals whenever possible. She delighted in spending other people's money to get what she wanted, and also in taking from the rich and giving to the more deserving among her strivers. The struggling writer she once had been, eking out a living on £8,000 a year (about $20,000)—that memory had not left her yet. It was still vivid when she began her first day at *Vanity Fair*. "We are still not paying enough," she warned *The New York Times*. And then set about stealing one of its livelier reporters.

So there was small sympathy for those who griped about their treatment and the way she clamored at the last possible minute for impossible results. At 11:00 p.m. on a Saturday in 1988, a phone rang. "That piece you're doing for the April issue? Can you do it for March?" Tina asked. "If I can get you tickets tomorrow, can you leave tomorrow? Can you get it in to me by Thursday?" And, as the writer found out, she could: "You would do the impossible for her because she would demand it."

"You know she applied a kind of business strategy to writers that other people apply to athletes," said Tom Florio, who ultimately became *Vanity Fair*'s ad manager in those years. "If you're going to push this athlete and have a star athlete, you gotta pay them their great wage. And I think that writers shouldn't really moan about the way she would change everything at the last minute. Because in her world, she's the All-Star coach. She *is* going to take it down to the last minute."

Tina's world, her gradually accumulating crowd of admiring subordinates came to realize—especially the hardscrabble Americans among them—was something brilliant, dazzling, and yet troubling as well. Its parties, for instance. They were not exactly social events, but riotous symbols of what the magazine was meant to represent, inclusion and exclusion, fun and terror, warmth and ice. On its fifth anniversary, *Vanity Fair* threw itself a bash at the old Billy Rose Diamond Horseshoe, a West 46th Street nightclub in the basement of what would come to be called the Paramount Hotel. At the time it was yet unnamed and being remodeled to the tune of $25 million by the entrepreneurs Steve Rubell and Ian Schrager. The hoteliers were Tina's new best friends and it wasn't hard to see why.

Hovering over pitch-black floors were enormous plaster palm trees, which hugged the freshly painted shimmering gold walls; against them, the florist Robert Isabell had placed real giant palms, their leaves sheltering yards of beautifully arranged flowers. Leading down to the party along the staircase walls was a long array of *Vanity Fair* covers from the pre-Tina years, while the back wall of the tiny temporary stage erected for the evening was lined with Tina's covers. And front and center on this stage were Calvin Klein's loveliest models, slender as a fading hope, in dresses the size of postage stamps.

Beside those models was Tina herself, not quite as slender, but fit certainly. It was a Monday night, February 29, 1988. In two years flat, with the aid of assiduous exercise, she had dropped the seventy pounds acquired during her pregnancy. She stood onstage in a clinging Patrick Kelly black lace top and furrowed black silk skirt, split just enough to display rows of black ruffles ("Very *Vanity Fair*-ish," as the society columnist Suzy was to report), rattling off the names of those to whom her magazine was indebted. That night, the deejay was a woman and the band an all-girl combo of black musicians, wearing platinum-blond wigs and mammoth diamond bracelets. The conga line was composed of wild Carmen Miranda types, heavy-breasted, swinging ropes of beads. The music was from the thirties.

Leading the festivities was Tina, flanked by the Carmen Mirandas, jiggling her heart out (to the surprise of friends) as the crowd bobbed and grinded its way through the room. Initially, spouses had been pointedly excluded from the event, but when it was signaled to Tina that this was bad form, she eventually repented. The more impressive part of the guest list—Barbara Walters and Mick Jagger, Henry Kissinger and Calvin Klein, Donald and Ivana Trump, Donald and Sue Newhouse, Mike Wallace and Norman Mailer, Larry and Billie Tisch, Beverly Sills and Abe Rosenthal, Gay Talese, Oscar de la Renta, and Gloria and Johannes von Thurn und Taxis, Liza Minnelli and Joan and Jackie Collins—reflected every particle of the magazine: its yearnings and funding, its more sober stories and stars, it sources and subjects, its covers and advertisers. Sometimes it was hard to tell them apart.

In the case of Calvin and Kelly Klein, gleaming early icons of the magazine, *Vanity Fair*'s big advertisers *were* its covers, their pretty faces plastered on the front of the May 1987 issue, and then, on the inside pages, ardently examined in an accompanying story. "Both of them had to be persuaded to do it," Tina blandly explained to a reporter who marveled at Klein's appearance on the cover. "I mean," she continued, "it was a scoop in Calvin's case, because he'd just got married to Kelly and everyone wanted to know what she looked like." The scarlet mouth of jewelry designer Paloma Picasso, about to launch her first perfume, also blazed from the cover of a September 1984 issue. A neighboring atomizer, however, was ultimately erased from the Picasso cover in what was assumed to be a spasm of shame, although, an editor confided, "It was an advertisement anyway." Certainly these instances had to be yet further examples of pioneer moments in American journalism, which had until then attempted to segregate advertisers from news subjects.

But if this state of ethical confusion wasn't amply scrutinized by the press—and it usually wasn't; Tina and her magazine got a largely free ride in those years—there were many reasons for such forbearance. And it wasn't simply because everyone in the media who wasn't bought wished to be. As *Vanity Fair* was quite different from any other journalistic enterprise, really foreign in its way with troves of indulgence for excesses, personal and financial, it was only natural that outsiders perceived it as a fairy-tale kingdom where other rules prevailed. Condé Nast, after all, was a private empire, shrouded in protective thickets of secrecy, impervious to the scrutiny of nosy stock-holders. It had a lot in common with the MGM of the thirties. Certain goals were accomplished, certain stars rewarded in an old-time Holly-wood studio way. At *Vanity Fair,* writers on the verge of nervous exhaustion got treated to a restful stay, all expenses paid, at a luxury spa. Birthdays brought the least cherished among them a hundred dollars' worth of exotic flowers. Chanel handbags and stereos were popular Christmas presents. "So, to spend one thousand dollars on a gift for an employee was not unusual," one Condé Nast executive would later say. "We don't have any checks here, as in checks and balances. We don't have any administrative process to flag that and send it to someone in authority to say, 'Stop it!' "

In the face of such largesse, who wouldn't be loyal? "She put trust in you—because you identified with her totally; my well-being and hers were congruent," one writer felt. "And my pride in working for her was total. She was the manager. She sent the baseball players out and they became stars. She could do this, knowing their salaries would go up, because she had Si behind her."

Who was going to argue about Calvin Klein and Paloma Picasso, or quibble about this new kind of reportage, which seemed so close to selling out, so near to compromising traditional principles of journalism? Anyway, where all this change seemed to be heading, no one knew. Although Tina did.

In 1988, for example, the same year as her fifth anniversary party, she wrote Mike Ovitz, the much feared founder and president of the Creative Artists Agency and very likely the most powerful man in Hollywood at that time, an astonishing letter, begging him for an exclusive interview with a writer she proposed: Jesse Kornbluth. In it, she compared Ovitz to the revered studio executive Irving Thalberg, a Hollywood genius long dead, and praised his "gifted sense of talent, material, timing and taste, plus, of course, extraordinary business acumen." It was not the apple-polishing that dismayed more conventional journalists when the purloined letter was published in *Spy* magazine. That was certainly par for anyone in the business. As one *Vanity Fair* staff member remarked back then, "Thank God they didn't see the letter we sent the Ceaușescus."

No, it was what Tina seemed to be promising Ovitz that worried many. A piece that could have been written, word for word, by his own mother. ". . . I would be watching over it *and shaping it every step of the way,*" Tina wrote Ovitz. "Jesse not only has the writing talent to do this piece, he is sophisticated, interested and *knowledgeably well disposed toward CAA.* He is also a person of the highest integrity" (my italics).

Very quickly under Tina's reign, a number of the carefully trained, the brilliant, the cautious had to alter their expectations. Indeed, once on board, certain parts of themselves were to be refashioned. Reporters with closets full of jeans and sweatshirts wandered onto the fourth floor of the Condé Nast Building wholly disoriented, perceiving, as one of them remarked, that "everyone there was wildly more sophisticated than I was. One felt weird to be an American, for one thing."

Certainly, the air was thick with upper-crust accents pouring from their alternately triumphant and aggrieved owners: Anthony Haden-Guest, on whom the novelist Tom Wolfe based his freeloading, hard-drinking British hack in *Bonfire of the Vanities* (indeed, in honor of the filming of the novel, Tina assigned an amused Haden-Guest to interview Bruce Willis, who played him in the movie version); Reinaldo Herrera wheedling Stavros Niarchos, the shipping magnate, to make himself available to the magazine; Sarah Giles asking a female friend to phone the home of Giles's boyfriend with the question "Has Mr. Zuckerman returned?" it would be recalled, or threatening, as another observer reported, to "tell Tina" about any perceived act of wrongdoing. Giles would later deny vehemently that she had ever suggested anyone phone Zuckerman to discover his whereabouts.

"People are so envious," Giles declared in disgust. "Mort went off everywhere, to Russia, to China. I might have just told people when they asked, 'Well, Mort's in Russia. Or Israel.' He was always traveling. He was simply one of a number of boyfriends."

"It really did have the atmosphere of a cocktail party and an exclusive cocktail party; you got the feeling people there knew they were at the best party in town—and that other people were *not* there," Fredric Dannen, a writer, decided the instant he walked in, elevated, as he swiftly recognized, to the new elite. That was in January 1990, a year in which *Vanity Fair* raised its circulation to 769,000 but was still, despite a slightly profitable previous year, more than $1 million in the red, although no one outside the company knew the exact figures at the time, and very few inside. There was nothing in the deftly suggestive, almost imperial ambiance to suggest a loss of anything, least of all money. Well-known writers could always be found lining up outside Tina's office, patiently waiting their turn. "It was like Zabar's," one of them felt. "You went in for five minutes, did your business, went out."

163

In the midst of all this sat Dannen, dazed and a little over-whelmed. There was his brilliant new editor, Sharon Delano, on the phone with the lofty intellectual writer Susan Sontag, whose call had interrupted his very first meeting because apparently Sontag had something "urgent" on her mind that could not wait and that only Delano could resolve. Dannen could hear only his editor's responses.

"Won't. W-O-N-apostrophe-T," Delano kept saying into the re-ceiver. "*Of course* there's an apostrophe, otherwise it would be *wont*." A long pause followed this perplexing remark. Then, "Wait a minute—you're confusing me." She excused herself to Dannen and removed a dictionary from the shelf, shuffling through its pages until she found the right word. "W-O-N-apostrophe-T," she managed tri-umphantly.

"Sharon, I don't mean to pry. But did Sontag just call you in a panic about the contraction of *will not?*"

"Don't tell anybody."

But at the same time a cold fear seemed to blanket *Vanity Fair* (an extension of the impenetrable cool that reigned over the fourth floor offices on Madison Avenue, one might say), seeping in through cracks in confidence, through stories assigned and killed, through writers al-ternately deified and trashed, depending on the moment, on Tina's whim. "It was terrifying but it was wonderful; well, because Tina was very much divide and rule," Christa D'Souza said. "Most people would get sick in the loos. There were always people crying in the loos. It was a caricature of an eighties magazine."

For the first time in their lives, many staffers were in mortal fear of losing what they had. It was pathetically easy to do so: contracts gen-erally lasted only a year. "When they want to pay too much, there's usually a reason," the fashion diva Diana Vreeland had warned a *Vanity Fair* writer who eventually discovered what she meant. "I didn't say, 'Fuck you' to Tina," the writer would later explain. "You know Tina's salary was, like, huge to me. I was living way above my means. I had no idea what that was, what that *meant* until I worked for *Vanity Fair.* Because by the time I left *Vanity Fair,* I was making a hundred and fifty thousand a year."

"The Kornbluths live, high above their means, on Central Park West," the writer used to announce to friends who visited his apart-ment. He felt like a character out of "The Rocking Horse Winner," a short story by D. H. Lawrence about a little boy with the knack of picking winning racehorses, who is haunted by voices who tell him, *There must be more money! There must be more money!* So although

Kornbluth was proud of much of his work for the magazine, when Tina shelved a story he'd been working on for six months, during which he'd produced four or five versions—it was on Werner Erhard, the distasteful founder of the movement known as est—he felt there wasn't much for him to say. What ammunition did he possess in the face of her indifference? Tina had called him up from her car phone to tell him his story was being killed. The entire conversation took no longer than three minutes. She had just received a warning letter from Erhard's lawyer, promising the magazine that although his client was an incredibly devout believer in the First Amendment, he nonetheless was prepared to defend his reputation. She also knew the television program *60 Minutes* was on the story, and nothing Kornbluth said managed to convince her they could beat television.

From then on, Kornbluth offered only one new idea to the magazine; he sold his research on Erhard to *60 Minutes* for $1,500. At the magazine he became known as a writer of celebrity stories.

Journalists learned not to ask too many questions. Even had they done so, it wouldn't have profited them much. There was always a backbeat at *Vanity Fair,* a subtle rhythm behind the assignments that only one person could hear. The British writer Philip Norman, for example, was summoned by *Vanity Fair* in the mid-eighties to write about the filming of *Absolute Beginners,* which was based on a famous Colin MacInnes novel that presaged the Swinging Sixties, an odd choice for the magazine. David Bowie starred. Norman was certain that this was what accounted for Tina's enormous interest. But it wasn't.

"Her brother was actually one of the producers. Chris Brown," he would later recollect. Not that it was immediately apparent to him or anybody, except Tina. "I remember going and meeting this very-very-very-very low-key bloke called Chris Brown, who was so unassertive, so quiet. And he just did not drop he was Tina's brother and this was why we were doing this, why the magazine was doing this." As it happened, Chris often left Tina unmentioned. "I make it a point never to discuss my sister with the press," he later declared. Some of his colleagues in the entertainment business knew about the family relationship. A few of Tina's friends barely knew the brother existed, she mentioned him that rarely. "I think she felt he was an embarrassment," one would later say.

Of course the old Tina, the wicked *Tatler* émigrée, hadn't vanished entirely. Every so often, bits of her popped up. Just five years after Tina's wedding ceremony at Sally Quinn's summer house on

Loup Island, the humorist Christopher Buckley, famous until then mainly for being the son of William F. Buckley, gave Quinn's novel *Regrets Only* a disappointing review in *Vanity Fair*. The resulting firestorm brought him a measure of renown.

It came, the offended Quinn told the world, as something of a surprise that her latest work of fiction was referred to as "cliterature" in the magazine of her great new friend Tina, and that the book itself was called "a one-pound beach cutting board and suntan lotion-absorber." Even worse, her friend Tina had not thought to warn Quinn in advance so that she might brace herself for this unpleasant surprise. As the sixty-fifth birthday party for her husband, Ben Bradlee, approached, Quinn thought better of her impulsive manner of acquiring buddies and cabled the Evanses to say she would find it more "appropriate" if they didn't attend.

"Tina's young and desperate for success" was Quinn's verdict on the whole affair. "And nothing matters to her except the magazine."

Actually, many things mattered to Tina. And some other things did not. The two women eventually made up. But what Quinn, living as she did miles away from New York's money and power centers, failed to realize at the time of the bad review was that Tina didn't need her quite as much as some others closer to her universe. If *Vanity Fair* was a success—and within five years (profits aside) it was a wild, raging, runaway, implausible triumph, the pearl of the Condé Nast empire and the talk of two coasts—it was as much due to what Tina kept out of the magazine as to what it contained.

It was noticed that certain portions of pieces were removed from the magazine for reasons that seemed to be non-literary. An article about Brian McNally, who owned the restaurant 44 at the Royalton Hotel, where Tina lunched most days with writers and editors, received some trimming after the author of the piece noted certain flaws in the running of the place: Ian Schrager's hotel wasn't, she suggested, quite the success everyone in New York had expected. Aside from that, she had discovered a few decorative but dead goldfish floating about, belly-up. Those observations were never printed.

"I don't think we need to be mean to those guys," Tina said, striking out the offending passages. She was very friendly with Schrager, whose hotels were the sites of many of her parties, and fond of McNally, whose restaurants she patronized. "Oh, so she *does* pull her punches," the author concluded, when the offending passage was struck.

Similarly, a reference to Calvin Klein was deleted by Tina, after the writer, Ann Louise Bardach, mentioned in her piece on a murderer who was "a sexual chameleon" that the wealthy designer was one of his sexual obsessions.

"Do you know who Calvin Klein is?" Tina inquired thoughtfully. "Do you know he's one of the biggest advertisers in the magazine?"

Bardach knew, of course. As did others in the room.

"Well, do we really need this section?"

It was Bardach's first piece for the magazine; she did not want to create a fuss that early. In fact, as the business side of the publication knew well, fashion ads were (to borrow their word) "flying," accounting for some $2 million a year in revenue—up from an initial $38,000 at the beginning of Tina's tenure. The famous name evaporated from her article.

With her new job, a heavy weight seemed to have settled on Tina and the leavening influences of impertinence and ruffian humor drifted out of her life. Every story was examined for implications and possible repercussions. When, for example, Nancy Vreeland, the daughter-in-law of Diana Vreeland, received a certain amount of society coverage on the West Coast—she also had a fairly colorful family background, which was considered invaluable in a *Vanity Fair* story—she seemed a natural for a profile. Certainly, Margo Howard, the daughter of Ann Landers, thought so when she pitched the idea in Tina's office. Through impenetrable tinted glasses, Tina eyed Howard, her expression unreadable, and perhaps purposely so, Howard decided. Then she picked up the phone and punched Alexander Liberman's extension.

"What would Mrs. Vreeland say if we did a story on her daughter-in-law?" Tina asked the powerful Condé Nast executive. It was only after receiving his reassurances that she okayed the idea.

As often, however, the reasons for backing down from difficulties within a piece were social. In 1990, Michael Shnayerson was assigned a story on Norman Pearlstine, then the publisher of *The Wall Street Journal,* and Nancy Friday, the author of books on sexual fantasies, who were about to be married. What Shnayerson evidently did not understand was that Tina and Harry were new fast friends of the couple, despite Tina's betrayal of Friday's hospitality years earlier when she examined the idiosyncrasies of the feminist gathering at her New York apartment.

Within short order, Shnayerson soon began to hear that Friday, as her books indicated, tended to be fairly blunt and earthy about sex. He also couldn't help learning that her husband-to-be frankly adored that side of her, and he made a few inquiries into the nature of their relationship among her friends.

One night, the phone rang in his apartment. It was Tina, blazing with anger. A friend had evidently informed Friday that her *Vanity Fair* profiler was aware of certain laudatory remarks she had made about Pearlstine's sexual prowess. Apparently she didn't wish to see such praise, however richly deserved, included in *Vanity Fair*.

"Now, listen, let's not do any more of this kind of reporting," Tina warned Shnayerson.

"Okay, fine," he conceded. Still, he managed a feeble protest. "But that's kind of what the story is about."

The next night, the phone rang again. "I thought I *told* you to stop reporting on her sex life!"

Certain he was about to be fired, Shnayerson objected vigorously. He told Tina he had followed her instructions to the letter and refrained from further inquiries. He had completely stopped reporting on Friday's favorite subject.

"Well, Nancy Friday has heard more about your asking about their sex lives," Tina said.

"Tina, I promise you—"

"I've had it!" Tina interrupted. That was more or less the end of the conversation.

The story on the couple, composed that night in four hours flat because of Shnayerson's extreme panic and fear after the second call from Tina, ran 7,000 words. It contained, of course, little about the intimate lives of Nancy Friday and her groom-to-be, and was evidently acceptable to all parties concerned. A week later the wedding took place at the Rainbow Room, Harry and Tina in attendance.

Tina had insisted at the very onset of her American career, when she was searching for a new kind of life, that "I want to kiss goodbye to the social label I had to cultivate when I was editing *Tatler*. That means not pretending I've been to every party in town." But in fact such a straight-arrow course proved difficult. Pretending was everything at *Vanity Fair*. The magazine was, for instance, pretending it was grand and ubiquitous and recherché, pretending it was for the "thinking rich," pretending life was a party. And eventually, as is so often the case, pretense became reality.

· · · ·

Harry Evans was by no means a newcomer to the States. His first and most compelling stay had occurred many years earlier, albeit in a more modest mode. In 1956, he arrived in America as a journalist on a two-year Harkness Fellowship. Everything about the country astonished him. It was so rich, so welcoming to foreigners like him (even if, as he noticed, New York street vendors found his accent completely incomprehensible), and, at the same time, so crazy. It was the era of race riots and white supremacists in Tennessee, of town meetings in rural Illinois and supermarket shelves groaning with luxury food. He traveled to forty states, unable to shed his amazement in any of them.

"I came from a country where nobody had a washing machine, where no one had fresh orange juice," Harry would later recall. "The richness of the society was absolutely dazzling for me."

Thirty years later, on the Ides of March 1986, he found himself ensconced, with his young second wife, in an eight-room co-op apartment on the third floor of a 1929 building overlooking the plane trees of Sutton Place and the East River. It was four years to the day since Rupert Murdoch had fired him. In the interval, his fortunes had changed—or rather, most especially, Tina's had. There were large sash windows in the living room, beautifully high ceilings, and (once Tina got done talking to the decorator Chester Cleaver, whom she hired after a nudge from her star writer Dominick Dunne) a violet entrance hall, a peach kitchen pulsating with matching peach balloon shades, mustardy-yellow wallpaper, a blue floral chintz sofa, a tapestry-covered Turkish bed in the den flanked by a pair of brass lamps, a strip of alphabet pasted across one wall in little George's sky blue nursery, and, in the living room, glazed chintz curtains in oxblood. The fireplace was marbled by Cleaver's assistants into a shade Tina called "as green and veined as a ripe Stilton cheese." Such labor was rewarded with free publicity and Tina wrote up the whole experience for the general public to read. There were also pictures to gawk at. In the pale mint master bedroom, twin white lamps perched on a table covered in Laura Ashley lace. It was all somehow supposed to be very old English and comforting.

In achieving her "dream house," Tina claimed to have been inspired by an unconquerable yearning for her native land—the "authentic whiff of England," as she put it—as well as "Lord Lambton's house near Siena in Tuscany." Like *Vanity Fair*, she had acquired the verbiage and pretense of extravagant and luxurious disarray that be-

169

came the essence of refinement, defining taste, class, and discrimination among those of impeccable lineage.

The magazine was, however, far more deft than its editor at sustaining such illusions. Tina wore, unlike her refurbished co-op, a slightly worn air of perpetual distraction. People noticed the same dress two and three days in a row. In early *Vanity Fair* days, when every ad counted, she dropped by the offices of Andrew Smith, then the general manager of J. & F. Martell, makers of Cognac. She was there to make a pitch for his advertising—about $20,000 worth—which he was considering running in her magazine for its special issue featuring the Reagans on the cover. Smith, who was born in Britain, was favorably disposed to the idea of meeting with the wife of the great Harold Evans. Yet, he discovered to his surprise, Tina was by no means anxious to ingratiate herself during the meeting. Her skill at pitching to prospective advertisers would be honed with time and practice. But on that day Tina was, Smith decided, patently discomfited in her role of selling to a stranger.

Smith glanced at her legs. What he saw amazed him. "She had hair growing, she hadn't shaved her legs. You know, you expect somebody from *Vanity Fair* to be very sophisticated," he said. "And she was wearing stockings, which made it worse."

Nor was the mythologized apartment, for all its flowery chintz and expensive mustardy hues, without its own secret flaws. "Of course, the real thing was to go into their bedroom," reported one guest. "Because under their bed were stashed a million things. Tina can't boil an egg. They're like Mr. and Mrs. McGoo. Terribly disorganized. They need handlers."

But not in all instances. Inside the offices of the Condé Nast Building, certain movements were afoot, plans underway. It was Si Newhouse's conviction that a new and original travel magazine might be just the ticket for his empire. After all, other organizations were virtually coining money with travel magazines, which meant that making inroads there would be far from easy. American Express's *Travel and Leisure,* as Condé Nast's president, Bernard Leser, knew, "had a stranglehold on the market." Undaunted, Newhouse bought the unimpressive travel publication *Signature* ("the organ of its advertisers," as one editor huffily put it), mainly in an effort to get its well-heeled readers, and initially thought of basing the new magazine on Fodor travel guides. Leser was made the embryo venture's president. The only question was, who would be the editor? Tina apparently had certain ideas on the subject, after learning *Signature* magazine had been bought. A Condé Nast executive heard she had gone to New-house himself with a suggestion. "You should hear from Harry," she said. Then Harry made his pitch.

"Si was enchanted by Tina, as we all were," Leser would explain delicately, when asked about this critical decision. "The professional love affair with Tina was pretty instant. However, we became immensely fond of Harry when we got to know him. Whereas Harry might not have entered the organization had it not been for Tina, we considered it very lucky to know Harry."

Not that Newhouse need much persuading. Alexander Liberman, who adored Tina, approved the idea of having Harry made editor and, as Leser noted, "Si made no decision without consulting Alex. He always sought it, although he didn't always follow it." Moreover, said another executive, Si very much wanted to keep the golden girl contented and soothing her husband was one way of accomplishing that. "Si in his heart of hearts wants this to be a benevolent patriarchal organization, where he is everybody's father," he explained. "He's able to dole out his favors to create small families. . . . His heart was in the right place."

So Harry's second journey to the New World made him within short order a far wealthier and more comfortably settled man than his first. But perhaps that wasn't quite what Harry wanted—or rather, how he wanted it. Tina was valiant in her assurances of her husband's well-being. "He is absolutely not envious. He is delighted for me and is having a wonderful time himself," she insisted. "He loves being in America, where there seem to be so many more opportunities for him. He is so well and bouncy."

But America was not necessarily at its most hospitable during Harry's second time around. A guest at a party thrown by the wealthy Wall Street mogul Saul Steinberg in 1985 recalled "this almost pathetic guy, following his wife around, wearing a bow tie. There was a sense he was a lost soul. He was a charming fellow, sure, but he didn't have a big job. There was his wife with the Big Job, and at that point he was very much Mister Brown."

Even now that he had a proper job as an editor of the magazine that was called *Condé Nast Traveler,* and no longer in a holding pattern position with Mort Zuckerman at the controls or with a small publishing company, there was a feeling that Harry was, once again, being buffeted about by fate. "It seemed as if Si was giving this to Harry as a sop," said one old *Traveler* hand. "It was probably Harry's lowest point professionally. I mean, the great Harold Evans would

171

not have thought he'd find himself editing a travel magazine. And I think the funny thing is, Si had absolutely no idea what Harry was going to do with it. He was still in such a Medici mode. He was still so patronlike."

As for the couple who received this Medici patronage, they found themselves in an interesting state of reversal. "I did when I arrived here get referred to as Mr. Brown," Harry told the English journalist David Jenkins, "but that's a very good alibi—or alias. But I never felt that. I was really proud of Tina. Really am, fantastically proud." More commonly, "Harry-and-Tina," as they had been referred to in Britain, evolved in the United States into "Teenanarry," as one journalist called them. This was not, it should be noted, how either half of the couple viewed the relationship. "He taught me everything about journalism," Tina told an interviewer shortly after coming to America. In fact, she remained emphatically and unapologetically reliant in many instances on Harry. But Teenanarry was, for all that, how the couple was generally perceived in this country.

Word of this alteration leaked home to Britain. "People who five years ago wanted to know why he should marry her can now be heard to wonder why she should stay with him," wrote Georgina Howell, who had once worked with Tina on *Tatler.* That was in 1986, the year Tina had given birth. "Their friends believe that they are ideally suited and will stay together," she added. "And at the time of going to press, the baby's job is still safe."

And so, despite Harry's indisputable support of his wife's growing prominence, the enormity of her fame exerted "a very difficult effect on him," an executive with whom Evans worked would eventually decide. As time passed, said the executive, there would be a part of Harry that wanted to "stand up and say, 'I'm in control of my life.' "

Chapter 9

Courtesy of Harry

If Harry felt that to be the editor of an upstart American travel magazine with an iffy future was in any way a comedown from his glory days in Britain, he gave no outward sign of it at the office. The word around the magazine was that Newhouse was pouring roughly $40 million into its first years and certainly there was solace in that. Heaps of money were flung about: to the author William Styron, to the photographer Helmut Newton, to others less talented—and on occasion, to a few whose stories simply, for one reason or another, never ran.

"What happened was we were always making outrageous commissions that cost fortunes," said Maggie Simmons, the magazine's first features editor. "There was no accountability." Famous writers especially, whom a worshipful Harry often encountered at parties with his more celebrated wife, were particularly begged to contribute: the suave economist John Kenneth Galbraith, the novelist Edna O'Brien, and the renowned Watergate journalist Carl Bernstein, although he became a very sore subject because after receiving an advance he estimated at $10,000, he never handed in the article on dude ranches he was assigned. "I couldn't find a story there," Bernstein would later say. "And I thought maybe by doing this I would be exploiting my children."

Some of these people could write very well, only not on travel. "To be a good travel writer, you should really talk to people," one editor observed drily, "and novelists don't want to talk to people. So we would get a lot of literary write-ups that were completely solipsistic. But of course they'd be paid in full."

Dazzling people came and went on the tenth floor of 360 Madison Avenue, where the publication was located. One was the artist David Hockney, who "went through about fifteen cigarettes in twenty minutes," leaving Harry, normally the most ardent of health nuts, in a daze of smoke and exhilaration ("A grrrrand man," he insisted) because, as his news editor Graham Boynton observed, "Harry was totally reduced to jelly by famous people." A gorgeous blond reporter walked into Harry's spacious corner office, after which, it was noticed, the door closed. A witness to the occasion was certain that nothing untoward occurred between them. Even so, he noted, "when she walked out, she was working for us. God bless her. She had credentials. I don't think she ever did anything. She tried. She was all right."

At the same time, a determined and serious ethos informed the new magazine, a sense of purpose, unthawed from the cold bitter years following Harry's exile from Britain. TRUTH IN TRAVEL was its slogan, and although the concept initially wasn't Harry's (it was invented by Jack Nessel, an old *New York* magazine executive editor, who had been brought in to help midwife the magazine), he adopted it at once and gave it alliteration. This was one travel magazine, Harry vowed to both editors and advertisers alike, that was not going to be in the pockets of the hotels, luxury resorts, cruises, and airlines. In certain rival publications, these businesses so often funded the trips of travel reporters, or paid for expensive ads, and then received as their reward reviews of unalloyed praise: "The Tom Carvel School of Marketing—Buy One, Get One Free," was how Tom Florio, the first ad director, described his inferior competitors. What this meant in practice, as Nessel soon realized, was that "there was a lot of lavish expense account spending, but the reason for this, I insist, was honorable. We were anxious to identify the magazine as one that wasn't going to be on the take."

Indeed, practically the first thing that happened after *Condé Nast Traveler* was launched in 1987 was that Varig Airlines canceled its advertising because the magazine had listed Brazil as among the very worst polluted and insect-infested countries. Even the business side of the magazine grew fond of such bold truth-telling, a rarity in the world of ad salesmen. "The interesting thing about *Traveler* was like we'd do a piece on an island—like how somebody got raped on this island—and then their marketing people would be devastated," one ad executive recollected. "Our attitude was 'Fix your destination!' " Nothing was off base, no expense in pursuit of truth-in-travel spared. In part, such open-handed generosity was the culture of the company at the time. "Budgets are non-creative," employees at Condé Nast would say, quoting Alexander Liberman.

"Harry just wanted Big Lavish Ideas," Graham Boynton recalled. "I spent fifty grand on a story that ran four pages in the magazine." It was a piece on wines consumed in midair. At that time, certain airlines were using their wine lists as a marketing tool. The only problem, Boynton suspected from the outset, was that "wine on the ground doesn't quite taste the same as at thirty-five thousand feet." Why did arriving at such a conclusion cost the new magazine $50,000? Because, Boynton explained, he felt it necessary to prove his thesis by flying in "two top wine tasters from England, Robert Joseph and Oz Clark, both very famous."

And there was more. "We got all the airlines to submit their wines," Boynton said. "We had a blind tasting on the ground on a Thursday. On the Friday, we hired the front end of a Pan Am 747— the whole front end was *Condé Nast Traveler.* There was a party of twelve of us. I think six tasters, a couple of researchers, myself. We flew to Los Angeles with the same wines and repeated the tasting at thirty-five thousand feet." Fortune smiled on the hardy band of adventurers and all sorts of insights were gained into high-flying wines. "We managed to support our thesis," Boynton concluded. "Wines taste slightly different in the air."

One early spring when the magazine was about to launch its first issue, which would contain a foldout guide to Arizona ranches, Harry and Maggie Simmons arrived separately at a dude ranch outside Phoenix. Harry, who loved dude ranches, paid his own way. Simmons did too; she was on vacation. "Both of us, separately, got terrible food poisoning," Simmons recalled. "A lot of people would have left it out of the story. No one, believe me, at American Express would have touched that. We put it in the article. I was editing that whole section and made sure it got in."

Simmons was often by Harry's side in the very early days when he made his pitch to initially skeptical advertisers. He knew just what to load and just where to aim. "The Insiders' Guide to the Outside World" was how Harry would describe his magazine. He was not merely interested in highlighting the terrible side of travel, in muckraking, he explained, but also in emphasizing which among the various luxury options open to the moneyed classes were the very best.

"There's a whole class of traveler who is just happy with a Carnival Cruise and that's it," Harry would concede to his audiences, who of course weren't all that interested in readers of modest means on a tight travel budget. "But there's also a whole lot of people who would gladly spend *more* money if they could find out what's really savvy."

And the wonderful thing was, these pitches worked. The first year of its existence, *Condé Nast Traveler* received more than six hundred pages' worth of ads; eventually, it made a considerable profit. Ron Galotti, the magazine's young publisher, was, his subordinates thought, an inspired choice. Although there were plenty of advertisers who thought that the new publication was high-handed and arrogant, the men who headed up the venture considered that a compliment. "One of the first parties we threw, we made it black tie, invitation only," Tom Florio recalled. "And if a client showed up without black tie, we wouldn't let him in. It was actually at the Petroleum Club in Houston. So it was all about setting a new standard. Ron and I had so much fun with it. And we believed in it so passionately. Like we thought we were righteous."

There was a deep devotion to Harry in those days—as there was to Tina in her bustling fiefdom. After receiving provocative letters from the public about some article or other, "Harry used to sit there at night phoning readers," Boynton recalled. "He'd say, 'Thank you for your letter. This point you make about Machu Picchu, I agree with it.' He was that enthusiastic." Within a year, *Traveler* was winning national awards. Harry's very frailties inspired affection. One day, as he opened his briefcase to retrieve the meager bag of fruit that often served as his lunch, a mouse hopped out, to the unalloyed amusement of a staff member. Harry's passion for the famous ("No one in those early years who wasn't somebody important could get an article published," it was said) was deftly, lovingly excused. As his employees told each other, "That was Harry. He was a bad manager in the sense he was running up all these unused stories and inventory. And yet he had such energy! He would literally run up the hall. Sometimes he would run to the men's room, I mean he would oftentimes seem to *have* to run to the men's room. Literally."

At the same time there was a tentativeness about Harry, those around him noticed, a lack in some circumstances of the certainty and charm that were his usual trademarks. For all his bravery, eloquence, cunning, and resourcefulness with advertisers, writers, colleagues, and friends, those qualities seemed to disappear in the presence of power. During Si Newhouse's visits to the magazine, Jack Nessel noticed that "Harry was hovering over him. Introducing me in a way I'm just not accustomed to being introduced, 'Mr. Nessel, this is Mr. Newhouse.' No, I am not kidding."

The promotional movie Harry had created for the magazine was remarkable, thought Nessel when he saw it. "Introducing Harry in a jogging suit, running in Central Park," he said. "It was the first indication of several I had that he was obsessed with showing how vigorous he was. He was jogging, surfing, things like that. What was he?"

He was fifty-nine, and he had witnessed firsthand the fickleness, the arbitrary rule of rich bosses. Men like Murdoch, Zuckerman, and now Newhouse could dispose of him at their pleasure in an instant if they wished. He was no fan of aging, disliked being reminded of it. The passage of time and the vulnerability it brought had to be combated.

One year later, on his sixtieth birthday, someone at *Condé Nast Traveler* decided to throw a birthday party for Harry. A cake was brought out. "I think it was a green cake, an oblong cake, and they put it down," Boynton would later recall. "And Harry drove his hand into it. There was this great handprint. And you *knew* what it was. Rage, frustration, unable to express his complete embarrassment and disappointment at this terrible thing this loving staff had done for him. Reminded he was getting old. He hated, hated it. . . . It just blew him away."

And perhaps he also wasn't so keen on this business of running a travel magazine, however credibly. Harry couldn't have seen it as a logical extension of his years as editor of London's major newspapers. He didn't believe—despite all the drive and focus he invested—that it was a step up in the world. Privately, he confided as much to a friend, saying that he very much missed being the editor of a big newspaper. He did not like working on a monthly, did not think it exciting.

That opinion was shared among some of Harry's old friends. One afternoon, Nessel lunched with Harry and one of these friends from Britain. Harry's attention was at some moment distracted, which was when Nessel found himself suddenly assailed by an outburst from the British friend, a respected author. "You know, Harry doesn't belong doing this. He's a *newspaper* man—can't somebody find a newspaper for him to run?" the friend declared passionately.

"Well, no one I know," Nessel replied. He was very much taken aback. "It's an honorable and creative thing to do," he said.

That same year, late in 1987, an American woman, previously married to a Belgian baron, was taking a course in non-fiction writing at New York University. The teacher explained that to get into some of the top magazines, it sometimes helped to start out as a fact-checker. Sheri de Borchgrave was absorbing this tip, wondering if it applied to her. She was small and very slight, with dark eyes set in a thin, heart-shaped face framed by masses of black curls that spilled well past her shoulders. She wore short dresses and spiky heels. Her first marriage had been a miserable affair. The Belgian baron had been flagrantly unfaithful, had threatened to throw her down the stairs, and was sexually sadistic. She was writing a book about it, in fact, which would later be published: *A Dangerous Liaison,* she would call it.

"A new magazine has started called *Condé Nast Traveler,*" Borchgrave was told by her writing teacher. "The editor in chief is Harry Evans. I know him. He would *love* you."

In early 1988, Borchgrave began working at the magazine, and Harry was just as she imagined, dynamic, charming. As it happened, she had traveled herself, very extensively and not just during her ill-fated sojourn in Belgium—she was big on Club Meds, even ended up reviewing a number of them for *Traveler.* So every once in a while Harry would call her in for help with a particular story. He was very flirtatious, she thought. On the other hand, those observing her in Harry's office found her pretty provocative as well when she appeared in a leopard-skin-print dress that emphasized the smallness of her waist.

Borchgrave was the only one at the magazine who knew, for example, that the nearest hotel to the Taj Mahal was not really, as had been supposed, at its foot, although a photograph shot through a tele-photo lens made it seem that way. It was really interesting, she decided, being a baroness and a fact-checker simultaneously, even though the job was by no means (whatever her writing teacher may have thought) a normal precursor to a fabulous writing career.

Then Borchgrave moved offices—to *Vanity Fair,* where she also worked as a fact-checker. Still, her old boss kept in touch with her.

It is possible that Tina herself noticed some alteration in her husband's demeanor around this period. In mid-November 1989, she threw a party for over two hundred people. The guest of honor was Nigel Dempster, the London gossip columnist of long standing who had just written a scandalous biography of the unhappy billionairess Christina Onassis. The venue was 150 Wooster, a downtown New York café owned by Brian McNally. The guests were a cautious, carefully selected mixture of the media elite, the rich, the important, and the self-important from both sides of the Atlantic. "Class A talents and literary Masters of the Universe," was how gossip columnist Liz Smith would describe them: Amanda Burden, stepdaughter of William Paley, the founder of CBS; Mortimer Zuckerman and his companion, the designer Diane Von Furstenberg; Jann Wenner, the owner of *Rolling Stone;* the director Nora Ephron; Abe Rosenthal of *The New York Times* and his wife, Shirley Lord; British publisher Lord Weidenfeld.

Wearing a deeply cut dress of short, stiff black silk that flared at the hips, a string of pearls at her throat, Tina greeted friends and enemies alike: Reinaldo Herrera, whose social contacts were so important to her; Graydon Carter, then the editor of *Spy,* whom she loathed; Liz Smith, the columnist she found useful.

There were, however, certain edgy aspects of the evening, some entirely predictable, others not. Tina's co-host that night was the editor of *Vogue* magazine, Anna Wintour, her tiny frame sheathed in a bright Japanese print. She was also a favorite of Si Newhouse, also British, but slender and exquisitely boned. The two women had little use for each other. But as they both were friends of Dempster (and often beneficiaries of his goodwill), each bore the temporary imposition of the other into her evening with equanimity.

And then came the first unanticipated explosion. Pointing at one of the guests, Argentine playboy Luis Sosa Basualdo, Dempster informed the assembled celebrities that Basualdo had received $1.2 million of Christina Onassis's money when she died a year earlier. He then suggested Basualdo had "murdered" Christina Onassis. Some of the guests took this as a joke, among them Tina herself.

"It was hilarious and in the most appalling taste, just the worst taste possible. I was rolling about laughing," she recalled later, delighted. "And then gradually I became aware that there was a certain amount of laughter, but not a huge amount, and I looked around and saw that those who were laughing were Anthony Haden-Guest, Anna and her husband, me and Harry, all English. None of the Americans. They were all unamused and shocked. Nigel had been making fun of the rich. Listen, I'm not saying they were wrong, but it was very funny."

Basualdo, one of the "unamused," threatened suit. Unfazed, Dempster then pointed to Danny Marentette, who had inherited a Detroit automobile fortune, and introduced him as the man who had taken Onassis's virginity. Then he carefully repeated some of his previous remarks. "Slightly irreverent," was how Dempster subsequently characterized his speech in his London gossip column. One of the guests stalked out of the party and headed for the bar. Liz Smith was mystified. "The British are very different from us Americans," she explained in her column. "Yes they are."

As might be expected, all this scandalous talk simply boosted the level of noise and excitement at the party. Late in the evening, Juliet Nicolson, a pretty Englishwoman who worked in publishing, was deep in conversation with her old friend Harry Evans. The two had worked together previously in great harmony and were seated close together at a table. With her short cap of pale blond hair and vivid blue eyes, Nicolson looked a lot like Tina Brown, a resemblance that perhaps impressed Harry as well. Although sixty-one at the time of the party, he was a famously irrepressible flirt. Lots of women thought it meant nothing; others weren't so sure.

"What are you doing?" The original Tina Brown suddenly appeared over Nicolson's shoulder, hovering, livid. Her voice was icy.

"Nothing," Nicolson replied hastily.

"You were flirting with my husband," Tina persisted, each word clipped. "And I don't want you to."

"Don't be so silly, darling," Harry begged her.

"No," said Tina, ignoring Harry. "Not with *my* husband, you don't."

The cold wrath of a woman so hugely successful, untouchable, horrified Nicolson, she told confidants. She swore that Harry was simply a friend, and that having worked side by side some years earlier, they shared the affection of colleagues.

However erroneous her conclusions, Tina was not assuaged. She had, after all, realms to protect beyond *Vanity Fair*. It was the conviction of some of her friends that "Tina did not think a single woman ranked nearly as high in this society as a married woman. And that one of the reasons Tina would never leave Harry is that it was important to her to be a married woman. The fact that she is Mrs. Harry Evans—that is an important thing for her to have, signed, sealed, delivered, and out of the way." Single women simply didn't possess, in Tina's eyes, the social distinction of their married sisters. "That's a very British view. In the class world that still persists," said one *Vanity Fair* subordinate. She would fight for her marriage, among so many other things.

· · ·

That she was sometimes distraught and moody was, in any case, understandable. On February 22, 1989, the London papers were full of headlines fraught with a terrible significance for her. GROPED GIRLS ON TRAINS was one. Another read: CHANCE IN A MILLION TRAPS A SEX PEST FILM PRODUCER.

These were references to Chris Brown, married and the father of two—the tall, unprepossessing producer of the movie *Absolute Beginners,* who had been interviewed for *Vanity Fair,* and also happened to be Tina's brother. Only no syllable of the family connection appeared in any contemporaneous article of his arrest, this at a time when Tina Brown was, aside from Margaret Thatcher and Princess Diana, Britain's most famous woman.

Even Chris Brown's most forthcoming victim, a young woman from London who had identified him to police, was ignorant of the relationship until eleven years later, when a writer doing a book about Tina Brown and her husband phoned her with the very old news.

Chapter 10
Secrets and Subtexts

"Now I know, you *stupid* man. I know who you are! But what do I do in this situation?" Anne Orange-Bromehead was thinking the moment she met Tina's brother, although the word "met" seemed somehow inadequate.

The young theatrical agent's blood turned to ice when she saw the tall man in the dark trench coat walk into the London agency where she worked. It was not a reaction the genial producer-director usually inspired. His name—Orange-Bromehead glanced at the business card she had just been handed—was Chris Brown. She couldn't believe it. She knew that name. She knew that face, all too well. She had simply never put the two together.

Chris Brown was thirty-eight at the time; among his box-office hits was the Neil Jordan movie *Mona Lisa*. Orange-Bromehead was ten years his junior. "I just froze," she would later recall. "There is a degree of fear, but there are other things mixed in with that, and it's hard to name these emotions: shock, fear . . ." And he? Chris Brown hadn't a clue who she was. Of that she was certain. As far as her visitor was concerned, she could have been anybody.

Outwardly, it was the most mundane of meetings. Brown had come to discuss the possibility of hiring one of her agency's clients, a very good actor, for a situation comedy. Brown was managing director of Witzend Productions, then run by Allan McKeown, who was the husband of the comedienne Tracey Ullman. The company had been responsible for such hits as *Auf Wiedersehen Pet* and Ullman's show *Girls on Top*.

"Chris Brown was actually a bit of a name, the sort of name that would trip off the tongue," Orange-Bromehead would say years later. "And therefore I knew the name. In one part of my life." And in the other part, the awful part she tried not to think about—"There he is on the train." Should she reveal what she knew about him to her boss? And what would happen to her and her career if she did? Anyway, it was such a humiliating story, who would want to tell it? There were others in the room, everyone talking. But that day in her office, she couldn't concentrate on a syllable uttered.

Eight months earlier, in the spring of 1988, she had, as usual, taken the train from West Dulwich, the suburb where she lived, to Victoria Station in the center of London. A tall man entered her compartment and sat "flat right up against me on the train" in the seat directly facing hers. This was odd, she thought then; frightening even. There were plenty of available seats that day. But it was such a minor incident. Still, she couldn't forget the man.

He was perhaps six feet four inches, with "a very interesting shape to his skull—ovalish," with a thinning hedge of hair. He had narrow eyes behind light glasses, a straight nose, and, she observed at once, wore very peculiar thick-soled leopard-skin loafers. Why is that man wearing those leopard-skin shoes? the young woman wondered. She decided he wished to look younger than he was.

And then it happened again in May, only much, much worse this time. It was rush hour on the train to Victoria, and there were no empty seats, not an inch of space in which to move or escape, and Anne found herself standing smack against the man she had previously encountered. Now the danger was real. He was rubbing up against her in a really disgusting, purposeful way. It left her "dazed," paralyzed. All she could remember thinking was: "This can't be happening, I don't know what's going on here." Then she stumbled off the train, where a woman—a complete stranger but very kind— calmly waited for her on the platform.

"I saw what happened, you must go to the police," said the stranger, who had seen the tall man groping her backside. And with that, she marched Orange-Bromehead off to the police station. The police, as it turned out, knew something about her assailant, or at least his modus operandi. A sales manager named Tracey Thomas had reported a similar incident, in which a tall attacker had forced his legs between hers on the Underground. And a third victim had filed a complaint. Realizing there were other victims gave Orange-Bromehead a huge sense of relief. "I'm not a nut, I'm not a daft woman," she told herself.

And five months later, there he was, Chris Brown, of all people, right in her own office—and so laid-back, so self-possessed, Orange-Bromehead thought, eyeing him silently. He thrust only his business card at her this time around, looking like the product of an expensive early education, which indeed he was: the Dragon School in Oxford, then as now one of the finest British prep schools. And then, right after that, he attended St. Edward's.

Brown was chatting away, earnestly discussing the sitcom his company had in mind. Was this something her gifted client, the actor, would be interested in doing? When he left, she told her boss everything. Then, at his behest, she called the police and told them her tale of coincidence. "I know this sounds crazy," she said. "He visited me, this is his business card."

With charges of sexual assault on three different women against him, Brown pled guilty at Horseferry Road Court, and narrowly escaped jail. There were certain elements in his favor, it was decided; he had been married seventeen years, was the father of two children, and had by confessing his guilt spared two women a day of painful testimony in a courtroom. "Clearly normally a responsible person" of "previously good character" was the verdict of the magistrate, Charles Davidson.

But despite such good character, he never apologized to Orange-Bromehead. Had he done so, who knows how this story might have ended? His main victim was by no means anxious to lodge a formal complaint. "If he had said he was sorry, said, 'Do you realize what this could do to me?' I would easily, very easily have retracted it," she said years later. Because she felt she knew what was going to happen to Chris Brown. A few months later, she would even learn where he lived—close by her own home in a brownish three-story attached townhouse.

Out of this townhouse came his wife late one afternoon. "Quite little, dumpy, dark hair pulled back in a ponytail," Orange-Bromehead said. And she longed to tell him, to tell them both, "I haven't done this to wreck you. I *have* wrecked you, but that wasn't my intention."

After pleading guilty, Brown was fined £250 on each of the three charges and ordered to pay £150 to two victims. Brown's lawyer assured the magistrate that although his client "has been walking on a tightrope," nonetheless, "everything is being done to stop this quirk manifesting itself again." He had been "seeing a psychologist" voluntarily since the day of his assault on Orange-Bromehead and "getting a lot of benefit."

But not, apparently, enough to have told the truth about his "quirks" to those who needed to know. On the day Brown was to appear in court to receive his light sentence, he informed his boss, Allan McKeown, that he wanted to have the day off from his £35,000-a-year job.

"Grandma is sick," he said.

The next afternoon, McKeown picked up his paper and read the headline in the *Evening Standard*. The following day, February 22, 1989, there was a picture attached to another article: the familiar long, narrow, feline face, the small eyes, and thinning hair. It made McKeown sad because "Chris was our managing director, he was doing great. He had great enthusiasm, all the makings of someone who would be very effective in the business." But effective for how long? And how would it reflect on the company? Everything about McKeown's production company was detailed in the tabloids—connected with a guy who assaulted women.

"All my shows," McKeown recollected mournfully. "I got in, brokers were on the phone. We literally had gone public only three months before. Our share price fell! Plus, I work in the States, live in the States. I mainly employ women—because women are better. And he's the only guy in the company. So how could I keep him on?"

McKeown called Brown into his office. "There's nothing I can do," he said. "You have to leave the company immediately."

A group of Australian friends from the entertainment industry rallied round. "I hope you Poms haven't overreacted. A lot of the boys have their wangers dangling out over here," they assured him. Chris Brown went off to join the rest of "the boys" in Australia, where he again took up work as a producer.

At *Vanity Fair,* Brown's increasingly famous younger sister puzzled over these events. "We're all very worried about my brother," she told Reinaldo Herrera, without going into details. Nonetheless, somehow word of Chris Brown's transgressions got out, but it was strictly word of mouth. In London, Fleet Street gossip had it that "Tina was calling editors to keep it out of the columns."

Still her magazine became—as was so often its function before and subsequently—a vehicle for probing certain aspects of her life, agreeable or not. Thus, just a few years after the incidents involving Chris Brown became public, Ann Louise Bardach, ordered to write a piece about sexual addiction, complained bitterly to her editor that she "didn't understand the assignment." Why was she, a prominent investigative journalist, doing it at all? What did it have to do with *Vanity Fair,* its nature or its cachet? Then she handed the article in, and met with Tina.

"Well, you know my brother is one of these," she said.

So much of *Vanity Fair* was an extension of Tina Brown that where one left off and the other began was impossible to determine. From the start, the magazine was her laboratory, analyst's couch, the manifesto of her desires and the reflection of her ambitions. Occasionally, she even made its articles her articles—literally—writing them, despite her exhausting schedule, herself. "Ugh! This almost destroyed my marriage," she confided to a writer at the end of the eighties after scrambling to finish a piece on the movie executive David Puttnam, while running the magazine. "I'll never do it again."

But how could she stop? She was so much better than 90 percent of the expensive labor on which she depended that the impulse to go ahead and do it all overwhelmed her. As early as the summer of 1986, Tina booked the Concorde to London, while her friend and employee Sarah Giles went economy class. A young Oxford student named Olivia Channon, an heiress to the Guinness fortune and the child of a Tory cabinet minister, had just died of a drug overdose right after final exams at Oxford. A perfect *Vanity Fair* story, as far as Tina was concerned, combining as it did impenetrable class and privilege, despoiled youth and destruction—that rank whiff of the tabloids, highly perfumed by money. And who better to write it than an Oxford graduate?

Of course she couldn't do it alone, not with her brutal schedule. Through her friend the London-based American literary agent Ed Victor (one of her son's multiple godparents), Tina secured the services of yet another Oxford student, a contemporary of the tragic girl. Allegra Mostyn-Owen, startlingly pretty, with light straight hair and large clear blue eyes, had been part of Channon's exclusive circle; she had been a *Tatler* cover girl, and was at Trinity College at the time. "I felt class loyalty to Oli Channon," Mostyn-Owen would recall years later, which made her perhaps less than ideal for the task ahead.

Nonetheless, like Tina, she too had ambition; she wanted to be a journalist. For a fee of £500, she was Tina's guide, rounding up those who knew the dead girl and getting them to talk.

"Well, you can imagine everyone was quite protective," Mostyn-Owen said. The true dyed-in-the-wool tabloids were all over the story, relentless, cornering students. "There was only so much information coming out, and Tina was in a privileged position to get it." She had the distinct impression that Tina was feeling out of her league in this world of class, English class, where she was and always would be the eternal outsider. Part of it was her own background. "She's got a little chip on her shoulder about going to St. Anne's," Mostyn-Owen said. "I mean, it's not one of the historic colleges. It was B-list." And the brusqueness of her! That was hard to swallow, too.

"Her attitude was 'Hello, I'm Tina Brown. Did you know Oli Channon?'" recalled Mostyn-Owen. "Just a little bit too direct." There were ten undergraduates collected to talk with Tina around a lunch table at La Sorbonne, an expensive restaurant famous for its onion soup. She was wearing a straw hat, a silk dress, and—much to the disconcertment of her new acquaintances—sunglasses. Her conversation about the dead girl was strangely distant. What, someone asked, if it turned out that Oli Channon wasn't nice?

"Then that would be interesting," Tina replied.

The unbridgeable distance between Tina and those she wished to interview seemed to have affected her mood. "You know *nothing*," she told her pretty guide, during one of their dutiful rounds. Mostyn-Owen mulled that over in silence.

In June, the *Sunday Telegraph* published TINA DOES IT HER WAY AT OXFORD, a slight story about the awkward luncheon held in the wake of a student's death. It carried Mostyn-Owen's byline, and this was, on her part, a big mistake. She had not been present at the lunch. Boris Johnson, who ultimately became the editor of *The Spectator,* then her boyfriend (subsequently her husband), had been, and had dutifully reported back the details. The piece ended with a thin slice of malice: "and we thought, for the umpteenth time, how pretty she was to be so important. And how clever, and how she was getting exactly what she wanted."

But the trouble was that Tina had received nothing of what she wanted. The article on poor dead Olivia Channon would never appear in the pages of *Vanity Fair.* The trip turned out to be a total waste of time and now a public relations disaster, to boot. A few nights before Mostyn-Owen's piece was published, Ed Victor got wind of its imminent appearance and telephoned the girl's mother, Gaia (at whose house he had stayed on occasion). "You do realize that if this piece comes out, your daughter will never get a job on Fleet Street," Victor said.

Mostyn-Owen learned all about this late night conversation from her sleep-deprived mother. Ed Victor had plenty on his mind, she was told; among other things, "he was waiting for her [Tina's] diaries." These diaries, with entries on the great, the absurd, the outrageous, would presumably one day be published. As Tina's friend and agent, he hoped so. Around London it was whispered that Harry had already glimpsed certain passages concerning various past lovers from her single days and become incensed. Tina, on the other hand, was said to be mightily amused by her husband's jealous reaction.

She was not, however, at all amused by Mostyn-Owen's little piece, when it finally appeared in the press. Sarah Giles dutifully dispatched a letter of complaint to the *Sunday Telegraph*. "I am told that when Miss Mostyn-Owen grows up she wants to be a journalist—let us hope she applies to the *News of the World* and not to a reputable publication like the *Sunday Telegraph*," it concluded in a way that Mostyn-Owen, with her dreams of a writing career, found disturbing. As very likely she should have. "Tina and I both wrote that letter," Giles would later say.

Around *Vanity Fair,* these same undercurrents of dread and possible exclusion became evident to many. There was no feeling among the new elite of having arrived for good; nor, having arrived and briefly prospered at the magazine, any warm welcome in which to luxuriate. Everything was temporary. "It was very high-powered and you had to be young or tough," recalled an editor. "You never felt you could rest on your laurels. *Vanity Fair* never engendered security. Because it was created out of nothing."

It wasn't the money-losing aspects of the publication that promoted this feeling of imperilment. "I knew we were losing money hand over fist. Tina always told us we were," Reinaldo Herrera pointed out. "But she implied always that the world would turn—next week. And the amounts were so vast, so huge, that she always made it seem as though it was *good* we were losing so much. Well, and she had this wonderful personal relationship with Si Newhouse."

In public, Tina's conversations with Newhouse appeared animated, voluble, the essence of charm, as she twisted the torturously shy emperor of Condé Nast around her little finger. Privately, however, she mistrusted him. For one thing, by the late eighties, Newhouse had plucked from English *Vogue* the glamorous and exquisitely dressed British editor Anna Wintour, and brought her to America to become editor of *House and Garden*—renamed, during one flowering, *HG*. "Anna and Tina did not love each other," one *Vanity Fair* writer drily remarked, "as sisters should."

Tina's own efforts in the glamour department were sporadic but valiant. She worked out three days a week with her trainer, Richard Zimet, who arrived at the apartment at 7:00 A.M. Beyond that, however, her dreams of physical perfection did not extend. "The great thing about Islam," she used to tell friends wistfully, "is women can sit around all day in a chador and a veil." That sort of attitude sat ill with some of her own staff. "You are tacky-tacky-tacky, dowdy-dowdy-dowdy and I hope never to see you again in your borrowed designer dresses," the fashion editor André Leon Talley wrote Tina before decamping to Wintour's magazine, according to a fellow staffer. Square-jawed and diffident, Tina's rival seemed wrapped in a kind of mechanized, anxious beauty. It was one of her most potent weapons, lovingly honed.

How many shrewd, good-looking, remote British lady editors was Newhouse going to pack into his empire? Worse, the first issue of *HG* under Wintour contained features on celebrities—Dennis Hopper, Bette Midler, David Hockney—whose rightful home should of course have been *Vanity Fair*.

Tina was deeply mortified by the invasion of this elegant British creature, although the ostensible reason for her resentment, she insisted to friends, went deeper than wounded vanity. It was her contention that her father was on bad terms with Charles Wintour, a prominent newspaper editor who happened to be Anna's father.

"Can you *believe* Si did that!" she hissed to a friend at a wedding. "He's humiliating my father. He knows Anna's father and my father are mortal enemies! He knows!"

Such transparency was, however, rare. She needed Si Newhouse, she enjoyed and used Sarah Giles when it suited her, she liked Herrera. But she kept her options open. It was no accident that gossipy friends were informed by her that Rupert Murdoch, her husband's most ardent enemy and then the owner of Twentieth Century–Fox, had dangled a big producing contract in front of her. She confided in few people, and then mostly just what she wished to see in the papers. She trusted no one outside her close family circle.

For this reason, the sense of fraternity that conjoins beleaguered employees at many money-losing and more desperate publications was conspicuously missing at Tina's shop. "People just disliked other people at *Vanity Fair* so intensely," a former editor recalled. "I don't think Tina cared about this problem one way or the other. She felt that competition was healthy. That's all."

And guarding Tina, protecting her, were her British surrogates—most especially, it was felt, Miles Chapman and Sarah Giles, the latter functioning in a fairly specific way. "Tina had her there to be first friend," said one staffer. "Tina essentially gave her this life as a rich society woman in New York, because she paid her pretty well and Sarah got entree to every party and she was going out every night," an editor remarked. "And she really began to believe that she *was* a rich society lady. And had to have great social aspirations. Including going out with Mort Zuckerman."

And yet this intriguing relationship with Harry's rich friend and patron and her honored place in Tina's affections and the New York social whirl certainly didn't seem to raise Sarah Giles's spirits. "Everyone warned me against Zuckerman, everyone," Giles said. "But I wasn't particularly wounded by Mort. I had no intention of staying with him."

Then, in 1992, having worked for Tina by then for eleven years, Giles was arrested and hauled into court in London for driving under the influence of "excess alcohol." Her excuse, Giles said, as she burst into tears after pleading guilty, was that "I had just undergone a therapeutic abortion. I had a little girl who was a Down's syndrome baby." It was symptomatic of the degree to which she was disliked at *Vanity Fair* that despite her evident pain, a number of uncharitable souls there refused to believe her. "I was, with the full support of my family, going to go back to England and bring up the child there," Giles said in later years. "I thought, 'I am forty-two, I will go through with the baby.' But the baby, sadly, had Down's syndrome and I didn't feel competent to bring her up alone."

Thus, all manner of enmity, all sorts of personal afflictions and agonizing difficulties sprouted at the magazine even as, paradoxically, it found its footing, becoming ever more popular with the public and increasingly contented advertisers, while the coveted parties celebrating its successes grew ever grander. Wilder, too, in certain instances. The parties were the magazine's cement, supplying everything its editor lacked: warmth, surface gaiety, some license. "She would have these parties at these big fuck-suites at the Royalton," recalled one male writer who dragged a girlfriend along and promptly bedded her in one of the rooms. "I don't know if Tina knew about it, but if she did, she probably would have been amused."

At the same time, other equally volatile (and sometimes infantile) forms of acting out began to be evident. The writers and photographers were no longer—as on lesser publications—workaday hacks, but stars, and as such, burdened with some of the pleasurable frailties of Hollywood. But there was a flip side to privilege, and it was stamped with competition, misgivings, and tension. In late 1991, for example, the celebrity writer Nancy Collins was abruptly pulled off an interview she was conducting with Mick Jagger, who had evidently demanded her immediate departure and asked for a male interviewer in her stead.

"She started insulting me about my sex life, asking me, 'Why are you with Jerry Hall?' " Jagger complained to another journalist. Collins denied this, claiming she simply had asked Jagger questions "no one had asked him before." In any event, Tina was worried. "Tina was besotted with Jagger," said a writer. "He complained, so she pulled Nancy off."

At a party celebrating *Vanity Fair* in London, there was another instance of behavior colleagues found unusual. One of their number, who had been taking medication to which she had reacted badly, had sidled up to a famous entertainment executive at a restaurant. There she apparently accused him of having been unfaithful to his wife.

"Get her back to New York!" Tina commanded one of her minions at the party's end.

"Tina, what do you want me to say?" wailed the unhappy employee.

"Tell her, 'You must immediately get back to New York. You have a lot of press appointments!'

"And like that! She was out to that airport and on the Concorde," recalled the employee. "But then she started calling me and saying, 'Where are all my press appointments?' "

There were other tense incidents. The office of David Kuhn, then the editor of the "Fanfair" section, was plastered with homoerotic pornographic photographs while he was away on vacation. Caroline Graham, the magazine's West Coast liaison, came screaming out of the office seconds after she had walked in. It was assumed, because

Kuhn was disliked by certain people, that it was the work of an in-house enemy. A Pinkerton detective was brought in to sniff out the culprit.

Immediately, suspicions landed on Walter Kirn, a young assistant who was in fact completely innocent, but had no use for Kuhn, as was well known, and worked outside his office. "C'mon, between you and me, do you read *Playboy?*" the detective prodded. He was aiming for a confidential tone, without success. Kirn was mortified. This man, he decided, a lumbering, oafish interrogator who perspired heavily, seemed desperate to discover whether Kirn was gay or straight. "*You* like a little porno yourself. Right?"

After the interview, it was clear to Kirn that despite his protestations, he was shunned, a powerless outcast. He was twenty-five years old and completely dispensable, he felt. Deeply offended, he quit. Ultimately, it was discovered that another staffer had been responsible for taping those pictures to Kuhn's office walls, and Kirn was offered his job back. But he never felt vindicated. He had been hung out to dry because he was low-level, powerless. The allegations, false as they were, dogged him for years.

As for Tina, it was easy to see that the terror she inspired, as well as the dread provoked by her minions and surrogates, was no accident. She was a single spigot alternately running hot and cold: one never knew what to expect. Her employees found her famously distant and calculating, equipped with "a rat-like cunning," as Harry Evans himself observed in an interview. Reading this remark out loud at the office, Sharon Delano, *Vanity Fair*'s most outspoken and combative editor, was heard to mumble, "Rat-like cunt is more like it."

And yet it was evident that Tina was, as she told mutual friends, sincerely worried about Sarah Giles, and even about Sharon Delano, who was packed off to Europe when the war of words between them became too much to handle. A number of friends and colleagues eventually realized that there existed in Tina a generously maternal quality, in her occasional bursts of compassion. After Hamilton South, essentially *Vanity Fair*'s "chief networker," was hired by the magazine for $100,000 to promote its cachet among those with clout and money, and to plan and design major *Vanity Fair* celebrations, the young man went through a pretty dismal period. A serious love affair had gone bust and his friend had moved out. One night soon after, he slapped down his Visa card and bought himself a chatty companion— a $2,800 parrot—before discovering that no cage was included in the purchase. For another $48 he got himself an ugly perch, and went home despondent as well as a lot poorer. How he regretted that impulse buy, the ridiculous bird, the unseemly expense.

Two days later, a birdcage arrived at his apartment, although it was really more of a bird hotel. About fifteen parrots could have quite cheerfully coexisted inside, with room to spare. The cage was topped by a gorgeous black pyramid. It had been sent, of course, by Tina.

"Tina saved my life," insisted Fredric Dannen years after he worked for her. In September 1991, he was, he said, "suicidal." Outwardly, no one had less cause for despair. His first book, *Hit Men,* had made *The New York Times* best-seller list and was being brought out in paperback. He had been at *Vanity Fair* over a year and had just completed an excellent article on how the FBI managed to sabotage two court cases against the New York mafioso John Gotti. He had recently come back from a book tour to his building with its Olympic-sized pool. But the woman in his life had ended their relationship, and every morning he went swimming with one thought in his head: *Maybe I'll lose consciousness and just drown.* He could barely get dressed.

One day, Dannen showed up at *Vanity Fair* to talk to his editor, Kim Herron, about revisions that needed to be made on the Gotti story. He closed her door and broke down sobbing. "I'm sorry, Kim, but I'm just too depressed, I can't work," he managed to say finally.

"We need to tell Tina," she said. But Dannen begged her to hold off. "Tina published an excerpt from *Darkness Visible* [by William Styron]," Herron told him. "She knows something about depression." Eventually she relented, or seemed to. "I'll just tell her you're sick."

A few days later, Dannen was summoned to a lunch with Tina. Somehow or other, he managed to struggle into a suit and tie and arrived at the Four Seasons, looking, he decided, "like an outpatient." The same realization, he could tell by watching her, swept over Tina's face when she arrived.

"Fred, I understand you're not feeling well," she said as she sat down beside him. "You're very valuable to this magazine and I want you to take a sabbatical with full pay until you're better."

He wished to take no time off at all. The moment those kind words were uttered, he felt suddenly put to rights, as though someone had administered electric shock therapy. His head cleared. Ideas came flooding into his mind—story ideas.

"What ideas do you have in mind?" Tina wondered. Exactly as though it were an ordinary meeting, Dannen found himself dropping a few gems into her lap. And the next thing he knew, he was flying off to Paris to do a story on Michelle Duvalier, the wife of the exiled Haitian dictator "Baby Doc" Duvalier, a woman who, after her husband had looted the poorest nation in the hemisphere, spent $13,000 on cigarette lighters from Boucheron. Tina loved the story, of course. It was pure *Vanity Fair,* encompassing as it did flagrant excess, beauty, evil, power, and its dissolution—the very traits the magazine valued most in its subjects. Dannen was still in France when, on his birthday, a bottle of champagne arrived at his hotel from the author of his salvation.

It was Dannen's theory that perhaps Tina's unfortunate brother was in some way responsible for her gentle handling of his breakdown: that she had come to understand or at least have sympathy for those who experienced severe psychological stress. And yet he found few credulous listeners. "When I tell that story to people, they don't want to believe it," he said. "Or they believe there was some cynical motive for what she was doing, that this was her way of attaching me to her and the magazine at a time when she thought my work was in demand. But I was *there.* And I remember this very well. She was concerned about me as a person. . . . That was her body language, that was her tone of voice. She wasn't pretending. But you know, I was never that close to her. The only time I felt close to her was that day I came in and she offered me help."

However, Dannen made a point of saying, this same compassionate woman managed just a few years later to turn quite callous. "Brutal," was how he put it. Tina wanted one of his pieces finished "right away" and she had called him on a Friday to insist on it. Dannen decided the rush was absurd; the piece needed two more weeks of work.

"Oh, that excuse is very boring," Tina snapped impatiently. Then she warned: "Fred, you've had a brilliant career. Don't blow it."

Don't blow it. For years, the icy menace of that phrase—especially when contrasted with her previous kindness—haunted and puzzled Dannen. In response, he flew to New Orleans as a "fuck-you gesture," and indulged in a weekend of "great music, food, and sex." Then he swiftly finished the piece. "I'm being an idiot," he told himself. "I owe this woman more than I can ever repay."

As it happened, Tina's mother was vividly aware of the impression her daughter made on others. She worried about it out loud. With the launching of *Traveler* magazine, George Brown had been made a contributing editor from "Iberia," and Bettina sometimes came by the magazine. In her capacity as features editor, Maggie Simmons invited Tina's mother to lunch, and Bettina used the occasion to explain that everybody had it wrong. No one knew her daughter properly.

"A great concern of hers was that Tina was misunderstood, that Tina seemed very cold to the world," Simmons said. "Whereas Tina was really very shy. This was a point she made over and over again."

But the elder Browns were upset over far more than Tina's shyness and the way it inexplicably transmuted itself in the eyes of the world into frigidity. A terrible situation confronted them. Their little grandson, George, then barely three, showed symptoms of a grave, though curable illness.

Learning of this, *Traveler* employees immediately phoned every contact they had. A distraught Harry called on the services of the magazine's medical specialist, Dr. Richard Dawood, as well as any number of old friends, among them Murray and Jenny Sayle, who lived in Japan.

Harry was very grateful, Jenny Sayle recalled, for her efforts in researching the illness and phoning a specialist. "But I never heard another word," she recalled later, "so I'm not sure what happened or if he ever followed up on the advice."

Another contact also called an important doctor. "So I actually played a role in helping his kid," he explained. He too never heard another word, but was, unlike Jenny Sayle, quite miffed at the oversight. "Years later, I met Harry on a plane and I reminded him," this contact recalled. " 'Oh yes, how very nice of you,' he said."

At home, Tina and Harry had a nanny to help care for the fragile child. It was observed at one of their parties that Harry seemed particularly friendly toward the young woman. "Come here, sit by me," he suggested, patting the seat beside him, as Tina chatted merrily with a guest, quite unconcerned. Then, "How's your day been? That's great. Give us a big kiss."

Later, in a cab, one of the guests, who was a witness to that scene and highly incensed, remarked, "I don't see how Tina can put up with that!" It was not immediately apparent to everyone that Harry had enlisted Enid's and his grown daughter, Kate, to care for his son by another woman.

Alas, not all the objects of Harry's affections happened to be family members. The slim, dark-haired fact-checker Sheri de Borchgrave was attracting his interest. She and Harry would exchange kisses in the elevator while she was still at *Traveler.* But one chilly afternoon in early 1989, the pace picked up. Walking around the Condé Nast Building, he slipped an arm around her. "Can I come to your place?" he inquired.

And so he did. Not that day, but soon thereafter. Usually around lunchtime.

By that time Borchgrave was working at, of all places, *Vanity Fair,* although the strangeness of sleeping with the boss's husband didn't put her off. In fact, she confided some details of the encounters with Harry to select friends. "She was dying to tell someone," one of them said much later. However, the interesting thing about her revelations was that none of them seemed designed to enhance her status or exaggerate the regard in which Harry held her. To the contrary.

"I don't think she thought it would be a serious relationship," this friend remarked. "I remember she said he was very British—meaning that after sex, he'd say, 'That was good sport,' words to that effect."

Indeed, Borchgrave insisted, Harry's sole comment about his wife (and it was uttered right from the start) was, "You know, Sheri, I'm not going to leave Tina for you. I hope you know that." It was a warning she tried to heed. Very often he would say, "Let's not get too involved." "Harry," she invariably replied, "this is *fun.* It's fun." She meant she understood his reservations, but why not enjoy the fling while it lasted? *She* was.

And yet, Borchgrave felt, as she would say in later years, "what a daredevil Harry was for getting involved with me in the first place. After all, I had written a steamy memoir about my marriage, it was already in about the eighth draft. And he had read parts of it! He said, 'Send it to Si Newhouse.' And I did. And Newhouse sent it to Random House, where it was rejected."

Harry would tell her little bits about himself, mull over decisions that had to be made from his perspective as the boss. That was exciting, in its way. He was sixty, true, but had, Borchgrave told confidants, strong leg muscles because at the time he was doing quite a lot of riding. He went to ranches on vacation. He was absolutely charming. Unlike Tina, Borchgrave decided, who wore dark glasses around the office—so impenetrable, so aloof. Who wears dark glasses indoors, anyway? Around May 1989, she was fired by *Vanity Fair,* not because of any suspicions of Tina's but because she had made a fact-checking error, and she went off to work for *GQ.* Still, the affair with Harry continued, sporadically, in spur-of-the-moment fashion, she told friends. It was all very "romantic," she thought.

And the thing of it was that Borchgrave knew, without being told by him (after all, she'd heard the gossip), some of the dynamics of his marriage Harry never discussed. She knew, as she commented to friends, that "Tina was getting all the press and publicity so he's sort of in the shadows." Knew that "he's Tina's husband," meaning a man who landed his job partly because his young wife had dazzled Si Newhouse.

But perhaps Harry was not enjoying this interlude quite as much as she was. Certainly he appeared discomfited at moments, Borchgrave noticed, and kept saying, "I don't do this. I don't do this. This is not me." The flowers she received were delivered in person by Harry because he was afraid to use a florist, she felt. The phone calls too were cryptic. He would pretend to be calling about her contributions to the Club Med article. All personal comments were couched in such a way that anyone listening, if eavesdroppers there were, would think the conversation perfectly innocent. "Scared to death, scared to death," Borchgrave decided, mildly amused. She received the impression he hadn't previously strayed outside his marriage, but she found the affair, as she would later say, "an indescribable thrill."

And then, one day, she received a phone call. It was after hours and she had no idea where Harry was calling from, probably not the office.

"You know, this is too dangerous," he said.

"Oh, well. Fine. Thanks. After all this time it's too dangerous?" Borchgrave said. It had been about six months.

"I think we have to break this up," Harry said. There was a pause. "Really. We really do have to break up."

Borchgrave knew she wasn't supposed to ask why. She had known it couldn't last. She said nothing. And yet she had assumed it would be, at the least, an enduring friendship.

Years later, when asked specifically about this end of the affair, because gossip had swirled on the subject for years, Borchgrave would say pointedly: "I had always assumed even when an affair subsides, the affection remains. And I always stay friends with former lovers, except for the Baron. But the friendship with Harry did not continue, even though I was the least difficult and demanding of people. I never demanded to see him or have his attention. The absolute *chaleur*, the warmth of his affection, was just so focused, so intense for half a year—how that glow can be cut off so completely into such a coldness can be very alarming."

Harry, however, was right: it was dangerous. Some years later, a

New York gossip columnist would phone Borchgrave, pleading for details of the relationship. The results were published in a blind item, no names mentioned, but even those bare particulars were enough to fuel yet more gossip. One day, months after this item appeared, a gossip columnist received a phone call from Harry—completely unsolicited, as the reporter hadn't written about him or phoned him in quite a while. "Harry assured me he and Tina were fine, and if anyone said otherwise, I should know they were fine," the columnist recalled. "It was a health report." So all in all, it was just as well that the affair had ended. Harry had other concerns: a career to mold, which he accomplished nicely before the end of the following year; and a family that needed his attention. As luck would have it, both of these grew and flourished around the same time.

On October 22, 1990, Tina gave birth to her second child. Harry was beside her at New York Hospital. Young Isabel Harriet weighed six pounds. There were three godfathers, one of them Mort Zuckerman.

Chapter 11
The Golden Couple

"Once, when he was the most famous newspaper editor in the country, they were known as Mr. and Mrs. Harold Evans. Then she became the most successful magazine editor ever and gossip columnists liked to call them Mr. and Mrs. Tina Brown," a British newspaper reminded its readers in November 1990. "Last week the British media marrieds, Harold Evans and Tina Brown evened up and cemented their remarkable joint conquest of New York."

Harry had, in brief, just been made president and publisher of Random House by Tina's patron saint, Si Newhouse, in whose vast and luxuriant literary garden the publishing company was a golden thorn. "Boy, did he bounce back—and here we go on career number five or six!" a close friend would later remark of Harry's startling reincarnation, his ascent after editing a mere travel magazine.

And yet, it was also felt, there were reasons behind Newhouse's sudden burst of magnanimity, some of which had less to do with Harry's considerable abilities than with Tina's. Within Condé Nast there had been voices arguing for other, less visible and prominent jobs for Harry.

"I regret that move to Random House very much," Bernie Leser, then Condé Nast's president, would later say. He too had once had plans for Harry. Perhaps he should have been made a successor to the brilliant Condé Nast editorial director, Alex Liberman, then seventy-seven. "Alex wanted to semi-retire," Leser knew, and Newhouse was "taken by the idea" of replacing him with Harry. On the other hand, "Alex at that point hadn't made up his mind *when* to retire," Leser said, and not even Newhouse had the temerity to push the imperious Russian out of his slot. Besides, Leser recalled, his boss "had a need for Harry at Random House which was more urgent." As it happened, Leser himself thought Evans could make a success of Random House, a very tall order.

Random House was certainly a messy place at that time, hit-and-miss, barely profitable. Full of comings and goings, firings, plots, rivalries and humiliations, it was a long-running bookish Reign of Terror. Among its latest victims was the recently ousted publisher, Joni Evans (no relation to Harry), pushed aside after three years at the top, the very week she had ten best-sellers, despite assurances from the chief executive, Alberto Vitale, that her work was splendid and her position, scurrilous rumors notwithstanding, unassailable. In fact, Harry was offered her job weeks before she was informed of her fate; and she, in turn, when Vitale gave her the bad news, was advised to tell no one else that Harry would succeed her. Within days, however, the media had the full story.

But Random House had sales of $100 million and a venerable history of publishing some of the best: James Joyce's *Ulysses* as far back as 1932 when it was but a seven-year-old company founded by Bennett Cerf; in later years it published William Faulkner, William Styron, James Michener, and Norman Mailer. More recently, it had garnered media attention for snagging, at great expense, the literary musings of celebrated non-writers: former first lady Nancy Reagan; the real estate magnate Donald Trump; and, most memorable of all, the actress Joan Collins, whose novel the publishing house deemed so god-awful that it refused to honor its contract and actually sued the unhappy actress to regain possession of her $1.3 million advance. It was a sorry decision. In the first place, Collins won the case; in the second, viewers interested in the devolution of "the gentleman's profession" could tune in to the court proceedings on TV and watch Collins as she left the witness stand in tears. It was a company with many of the characteristics of such glorious old-time Hollywood divas as Elizabeth Taylor and Marilyn Monroe, its weepy calamities, fits, and spells every bit as riveting and even glamorous as its triumphs.

This mottled plum was Harry's vindication after years of deflecting the pity and scorn of lesser men in lower places. "He has a proper job at last," trilled a reporter from another British paper. And it fell into his lap one week after the birth of his last daughter. He was sixty-two years old, the father of five. On his advancing years, however, one was not meant to dwell overmuch. "They've put an extra *year* on me," he would later complain about the press. "And it really annoys me when people get these things wrong."

Without a doubt, Harry was still trim and dashing, with the pale, thickly fringed eyes, loping gait, and frantic demeanor of a boy. So much about him was purposefully youthful: the enormous vitality and limited attention span, the overpowering need to be liked, the suspenders and shirtsleeves displayed for newspaper photographers, the invariable impression he gave of being ready to sprint off anywhere. He still swam and played Ping-Pong, gobbled vitamins and vegetables, scorned tobacco and hard liquor, and continued to hold extremely peculiar views on health. "Wacky" was how Graham Boynton would describe these notions. "He made Tina, during her last pregnancy, wear a lead apron during her flights to and from England on the Concorde," he said. But Harry's very quirks and oddities, he himself felt (and he was not alone), were actually his biggest assets. "English people do well in the U.S. because they bring individual, even eccentric endeavor to a superb machine," he said at the time of his ascension.

But was Harry Evans, a man with little experience in book publishing, aside from stints at Mort Zuckerman's small Atlantic Monthly Press and at Weidenfeld & Nicolson, the man to lead Random House? His predecessor thought not. "Harold Evans! He's a magazine person," Joni Evans kept telling herself the day she was informed of her removal. "It's humiliating to me as a book person to be pushed out by a magazine person." She would be given, briefly, her own imprint within the company.

In fact, Harry was perfect in some respects. Who better, after all, to lure famous politicians and actors into Random House's perpetually open maw than Harry, the inveterate stargazer, aided by the contacts of his plugged-in, celebrated, and fashionable wife? Moreover, he possessed other utilitarian qualities. Upset as she was, Joni Evans realized that "Harry was a very good editor." While still at the helm of Simon & Schuster, she had bought Henry Kissinger's memoirs and admired firsthand the work Harry had done for his old friend—for free—on *Diplomacy*. It was the intensity and detail of his editing of Kissinger's ungainly prose that struck her most forcibly. "Line-by-line editing, sentence by sentence," she said.

And at the same time—rare for an editor or publisher—Harry had a visual acuity, a craving for good art, appealing covers, attractive ads. His interest in appearances went far beyond the normal desire of a producer of books or magazines to sucker in readers; it lay at Harry's core and was fundamental to how he approached his work. He loved to look as much as to read. "Harry asked me to illustrate some story for him when he was editor of the *Sunday Times*," David Hockney would recall years later, still impressed by the anomaly of discovering an editor who understood the importance of pictures. "When I turned him down, he said, 'Who can I get? Who can I get? Why can't I find good artists to illustrate anymore?' I said, 'Harry, they don't train them like they used to.' "

Now, as publisher of Random House, Harry could grab practically any big name he wanted—Hockney included. The British section of Random House published *Hockney's Alphabet* in 1992, and Harry selected four of the elaborate colored letters to paste on his office door, which strung together spelled *T-I-N-A*. In the halls of Random House, employees used to tell each other the letters formed a sort of talisman for their boss, designed to keep out evil spirits: there were a number of these about, they believed, biding their time.

But he was too busy to notice this, at first. Within seven months of Harry's arrival, he had concluded ten-year deals to publish the photographs of Richard Avedon and a series of books encompassing the work of Robert Mapplethorpe. He had won a bidding war for the memoirs of the elusive and unpredictable Marlon Brando, a biography of George Bernard Shaw, and a novel by Peter Benchley (of *Jaws* fame) called *Beast*. Nothing was beneath him, no portion of his new fiefdom immune from Harry's meddling or scrutiny. With fortune once again smiling on him, he seemed determined to become a benign monarch, his preferred role. At Christmastime, just a month after his arrival, he pored over a list of names, a few knowledgeable old hands at his side, to determine who among the many employees was worthy of a salary review. On occasion, there were protests. "Alberto doesn't want that person to get a raise," insisted an emissary from the personnel department, referring to Alberto Vitale, the chief executive officer of Random House who, along with Newhouse, had hired him. Harry raised a warning hand. "I was told when I got this job that I had the authority to set salaries for my people," he said. "That person will get a raise." The observers were impressed. "Harry had balls," one said.

He would even, at times, allow an author to sit in on the strategy sessions for his own book, deliberating along with Harry and the publicity department on its future. Should one page or two be purchased to promote it in *The New York Times Book Review?* Shouldn't *Newsweek* or *Time* be the proper venue for first serial rights, rather than a more literary magazine?

Harry edited book jacket copy and suggested promotional schemes. When Gerald Posner wrote *Case Closed,* a book about the assassination of John F. Kennedy which contended that the killing was the work of Lee Harvey Oswald, acting alone, Posner recalled, amazed, that it was "Harry who wrote the advertising for it, absolutely." When Posner's next book came out—a biography of the presidential candidate Ross Perot, which fared about as poorly as the candidacy itself—Harry once again wrote the advertising copy.

"It needs to be re-energized," he declared shortly after taking control of Random House. "The list was too narrow. I want to make this house genuinely 'random' and eclectic. And in a place that has not been a brilliant financial success I would like to be more profitable."

Random and eclectic Harry certainly made the place. But profitable? To the surprise of many of his colleagues, he didn't seem to have, in certain striking instances, the first notion of how to turn a profit. "Harry had no experience in pricing the economics of books," said an editor. "The only way to do it is to work your way up. There is no quick study."

Indeed, at times, Harry appeared to be utterly dismissive of money. When Daniel Menaker, an editor with a strong literary bent, joined Random House after leaving *The New Yorker* in the mid-nineties, a subordinate learned that "Harry said to Dan—quite seriously but also as a bit of a joke—'Dan, your job is to lose money for Random House.' " From this, the subordinate concluded that Menaker "was supposed to *Knopfify* Random House. Meaning give it the cachet that Knopf [a publishing division of Random House] gives to its books. Harry meant that Dan Menaker, who had great discrimination and great contacts, had to promote esteem but not profits."

And yet even some of those books purchased expressly for profit proved maddeningly unreliable. Harry paid, a Random House source said, between $5 and $6 million for Marlon Brando's memoirs and got—what? his employees and detractors wondered: 468 pages of drivel and impertinence. "Hey, you don't want to mention the book, don't," Brando assured television host Larry King. He was the least malleable of authors, as Harry might have known from a cursory glance at the book. "I'm writing this book for money because Harry Evans of Random House offered it to me," the actor explained at the outset of his memoirs. "In his own way Harry is a hooker just like me, looking for a way to make money any way he can."

In fact, it wasn't really money that Harry was after, although the accumulation of wealth certainly counted in his eyes as an emblem of success. He spoke of his earnings at Random House, significantly, in purely symbolic terms. "Not excessively rewarded considering the talent I bring to the job," he told a countryman. He also pulled in between $50,000 and $75,000 a year more from his friend Mort Zuckerman, whose editorials in *U.S. News & World Report* Harry had quietly edited and improved for years. This last source of income, however, involved engaging in a fairly arduous and humbling process; indeed, it demanded considerable labor and enormous discretion, on the part of various participants.

"Actually, it's a process worth describing in detail," said Jim Fallows, who once was the editor of *U.S. News.* "Mort dictates by phone in the middle of the night to a woman in Mexico, as I heard it from old hands at the magazine—from two A.M. to five A.M. He calls a woman in Mexico and she types it up." The Mexican typist, a Zuckerman friend explained, was a former employee who, even after returning to her home country, continued to perform this function.

These early versions of Zuckerman's editorials were described by one staffer as "Nixonian midnight rants." The assemblage of ideas, thoughts, and conclusions proved complicated. "The Mexican typist would fax it to Harry," said Fallows. "And Harry sat down to put it in shape and cut it to size. Most people on the magazine felt they weren't supposed to know about the fact that Harry was involved. From a four-thousand-word stream-of-consciousness thing, Harry makes a column. Then it comes to whoever has my old job."

But the labor didn't cease there. Crucially, the Zuckerman editorial went to someone on the staff who had to "run sentences through Lexis-Nexis" to make sure thoughts and sentences written by Zuckerman had not been accidentally lifted from other publications. One observer to the editing process found this "a richly amusing experience."

If Harry found himself performing odd chores both inside and outside Random House in addition to those normally performed by a publisher of a major company, it wasn't merely because of his natural drive, the energy that had propelled him from a modest job as a newspaper editor into national and now international prominence. There was a new aspect to him, a tight and edgy feeling he gave off, as if nothing was ever enough. Practically the first move he made on his arrival at Random House, according to one top executive at that time, was to "send an envoy to Jason Epstein's office" informing the revered editor of E. L. Doctorow and Norman Mailer's work that he, Harry, would henceforth be occupying that space. "Epstein had had the same office for thirty years, a big corner office on the twelfth floor of Random House," recalled the executive. "Jason had worked there all his *life*. You never do this."

But Harry did. He needed the extra space attached to Epstein's office, he claimed, to accommodate his assistant. He needed, in fact, so many things, tangible and often costly ones, to prove many other things, less tangible but weighty. Brahms playing in the office and a bowl of fruit on his desk, "all to show," a subordinate decided, "that he had a certain taste and discipline." He needed, in addition to the publicity department already extant at Random House, yet another, parallel publicity department, established in 1993, which, one former executive recalled, cost the company $250,000. "It was a significant budget for a shadow publicity department," said the executive. "There was general acceptance of this. But it was also bizarre. Other publishing houses got terribly jealous. 'You've got two fucking publicity departments working on your books, while we have just one!' they'd tell us. But of course one of them was really for Harry."

Nonetheless, with the advent of Harry and this second publicity team, Random House events became a lot like Tina's parties: well publicized, recherché, craftily staged; and above all, useful. There were crowded breakfasts at Barneys, the upscale New York clothing store, where interesting authors would regale select audiences of society ladies, fans, and gossip columnists; there were cozy dinners for celebrity writers. Harry launched an in-house magazine called *At Random*, which promoted the company's books and authors. Word at Random House was that it had a $250,000 budget. "That was Harry's particular baby," said an editor. "There were a lot of young people writing for it, and Harry really got off on it, the journalism of it. And it was a valuable promotional tool."

"I could see he was good, I was absolutely stunned, but he was *good*," Joni Evans herself would later concede. "The showmanship which I truly thought incorrect for Random House started to take hold."

Harry also needed to write a book—an exploration of the country he had embraced—with lots of fine, big pictures. He began it, he explained, "when George was conceived," but despite a battery of ever-changing researchers and a patient photo editor who worked for a time on the seventh floor of Random House, it took thirteen years to complete. It took so long, according to one highly placed publishing source, that Bantam Books finally canceled the contract for which Harry had received, it was rumored, a "substantial six-figure advance." The book was then offered to Random House, where Jason Epstein turned it down. It was to be a massive fifty-dollar coffee table book, shrouded in silver, called *The American Century*. And Harry would dedicate it, when it finally did appear courtesy of Knopf (which substantially increased his advance), to his two children by Tina:

"To George and Isabel, New Americans."

As it happened, by the time the book emerged, Harry was also a New American. It was a step he had been quietly planning, unknown to many of his closest friends, ever since his arrival in this country as a divorced middle-aged former editor, battered and shaken by Rupert Murdoch and, he felt, betrayed by the entire class system of the brutal Old World. "It sounds corny, but I'm in love with this country," he told a British colleague. "I hope this great American body can take this alien parasite and not reject it."

"He fancied the idea of himself as an immigrant," his photo editor Gail Buckland would later explain, "in a nation of immigrants." She had been one of his few confidants on the matter of his pending Americanization. Halfway through the book, Harry had informed her of his plan, only shortly before his naturalization, and she had thought briefly of sending a photographer along to record the moment, but then dropped the idea.

And here he now was, leading an American publishing company, courting American stars, throwing American parties, and simultaneously, after some setbacks, penning a long, very expensive, *Knopfified* love note to his adopted land, as famous and fêted and prosperous an immigrant as one could hope to find. Like the newspaper baron Rupert Murdoch, his old nemesis, he scarcely needed to be naturalized. Harry was one of nature's Americans.

His wife was another.

Indeed, there was an urgent, grabby quality to Harry in those days that, while certainly very American, alternately touched and enraged those with whom he came into contact. Those who were touched thought they understood his drive: it had a childish, almost impersonal quality to it, devoid of any real threat or malevolence. "He has to be in the center of things, he is the publisher of a centric universe," it was decided. But this didn't make life easier for his editors.

For one thing, it was noticed, any credit for a clever purchase, a best-seller, even a minor acquisition, always had to accrue to Harry. No one else was permitted to share in the glory. The original proposal for the best-selling novel *Fatherland,* which was written by his old friend the British author Robert Harris, was given to Harry, who then apparently forgot about it.

"Harry, do you happen to have a proposal for a novel by Robert Harris, called *Fatherland?*" he was asked one day.

"No, no" came the reply.

David Rosenthal, an editor, ultimately got the proposal and bought the book, for which, once it became a hit, Harry claimed full responsibility. As for Harris, much to the despair of more cautious editors, after the author's first triumph, Harry gave him a three-book deal worth more than $2 million. Two of these novels, *Enigma* and *Archangel,* would turn out to be less pleasing to the public.

"I was the editor of *Primary Colors*—Harry acquired it. If he took a deep and passionate interest in it, you could have fooled me," Dan Menaker would later say, drawing a deep breath, because this became a source of friction between the two men. "Until its publication . . . Harry's enthusiasm picked up significantly when the book went through the roof." Harry had bought the book all right, had even paid, according to another subordinate, about $250,000, twice the amount Menaker had suggested. But there apparently Harry's interest had ended. "The first printing was 62,500," another Random House champion of the book would later say.

Published under the provocative pseudonym "Anonymous" (until the media, besotted by the mystery surrounding a roman-à-clef about a philandering southern presidential candidate, finally uncovered the name of its author, the journalist Joe Klein), *Primary Colors* sold 1.2 million copies in the summer of 1996. And that was *before* Klein was revealed as the author, a fact he had previously denied.

But there were larger issues at stake for Random House than the identity and credibility of the book's author. After *The New York Times Book Review* came out lavishing praise on the novel, one Random House employee said, "there weren't enough copies in the bookstores. So we missed days of valuable sales time. They had to print more up. There was a stink. And I think Harry got a bit of a talking-to by Alberto [Vitale]. Alberto was pissed. The book was causing a huge stir. And Harry did have the look of glum contrition afterwards. He looked as though he should have known better."

Worse, as far as Harry was concerned, Menaker, who had immediately recognized the book's potential, was interviewed by *The New York Times* on the history of the best-seller. Harry was seriously displeased. "And he took me slightly to task for speaking in a way that implied a kind of total proprietorship of this novel," Menaker would later recollect. "And I felt that he, in taking me to task, was both right and wrong. He was wrong because as far as I knew, from the minute we acquired it, he had had virtually nothing to do with it. What I was wrong about was in not understanding how important it was that he was the one who had the connection. . . . He was the one who brought it back—physically—into the house. So I didn't quite get that."

Others understood it at once. "Harry's got very Roman sensibilities, he likes ostentatious success," it was ultimately decided by one of his minions.

His passion for staking territory and acquisition well beyond normal boundary lines was by no means confined to best-sellers. It extended to all portions of Harry's new realm. A publishing plan to acquire the rights to the original paintings of the naturalist John James Audubon for a coffee table book was worked up and signed by Douglas Stumpf, the executive editor of Villard Books, a subsidiary of Random House. "But Harry was furious because the letter went out under my signature," Stumpf would later remember. The letter, addressed to the New-York Historical Society, was immediately recalled and Harry's signature substituted.

"Harry was such a figure, people used his name as a verb a lot," a colleague recalled. "If someone was chewed out at work, Menaker said, 'Oh yeah, he's been *Harried*.' "

Harry had been so long in the wings, it was hard, now that he was center stage, not to sympathize. He knew how to occupy space, even how to fill it with all his old allies: brainstorms, ideas, posturing, chatter, and attention. But these so often came to nothing. They were Harry's practiced gestures, as common and facile as a handshake. "Eh Mort, Mort, Mort, c'mover here!" he would call out to Mort Zuckerman, lunching at the Four Seasons restaurant in Manhattan, his favorite spot. When Zuckerman approached the table, Harry pointed to the newspaperman at his side. "The best writer in the *world,* you've never met such a great writer! Worth watching!" The lunch partner would henceforth "walk on air, thinking you're about to get a ten-million-dollar contract on a book." Three months went by.

Then one day the phone rang. "I'm on the Random House jet!" Harry announced. He had two more minutes of time in which to discuss the newspaperman's project, which would come to nothing. So, if Harry seemed awkward and excessive in his approaches, over-certain, overbearing, over-promising, it was as if to compensate for all the years and years of involuntary waiting. Now that at last something had happened—to him—Harry felt it only courteous to suggest it might be a nice idea if good fortune paid a visit to his friends. But it was just that, in many cases: a courtesy, a generalized feeling of good-will. He seemed as delirious as a puppy with a bone—a shake of the head, a wag of the tail. He had a lot to prove, and not only to himself.

"It doesn't bother me if I'm in my wife's shadow," Harry told one British journalist. "She does cast a very long shadow after all. . . . I really am enchanted by her success. She has done extraordinarily well. As for our marriage, the secret is that we love each other and we never stop talking about books, journalism. . . . We're non-stop." No one doubted his affection for Tina. At the same time, few swallowed his protestations over his career—least of all the journalist to whom he confided the secrets of domestic harmony. "Yet Evans is still better known in New York gossip columns as 'husband of Tina Brown,' " he wrote.

Proud as he was of Tina's achievements, and Harry was undeniably proud, who could help noticing that they were invariably detailed in almost every long profile of Harry? And there would be certain fine points added as well: that Tina Brown had, for example, been responsible for the soaring circulation of *Vanity Fair* (from 260,000 to 750,000) "and made herself almost as famous as the people she writes about."

Periodically, sly hints in the press indicated a new degree of restlessness on Tina's part that, not coincidentally, must have been unsettling to Si Newhouse. It was said that Rupert Murdoch, Harry's mortal enemy, "had dangled a big producing contract before the eyes of *Vanity Fair* editor Tina Brown"; that Tina "admits to getting homesick for Britain where she would prefer to educate her children" (in fact, word was spreading around both Britain and the United States that Harry wanted George educated at Eton); and that Tina was, as she put it, "bored with the whole money/status obsession in America, though I also get fed up with the class thing in England." In 1992, Murdoch approached her yet again—this time, Tina confided to a friend, with an even more luscious proposition. "He wanted her to take Barry Diller's job [heading Twentieth Century–Fox] after Diller left," the friend said.

"But I would never take that job," Tina said. "I have small children. It's hard enough to find time to spend with them as it is. If I were to take a job with a studio, I would have *no* time to spend with my family."

And so when the husband of this talented, torn, and restless woman got his big job at Random House, how many publishing executives were surprised by the move? How many genuinely assumed Harry had achieved his exalted post under his own steam? Si Newhouse could read the gossip columns as well as anybody, and Newhouse wanted to keep Tina.

Moreover, these surmises also appeared in print. "Unsympathetic observers say that Si Newhouse was forced to promote Evans . . ." began one of these references, before dismissing the gossip as "debatable." But Harry was not one to dwell on such matters, even with close friends. He did, however, dwell on other intimate issues, as one writer who lunched with him early in his Random House career discovered. He mentioned Tina. "He was very candid in his lunch about their marriage," she would later recall. "There was an allusion to sex within the marriage, something like that."

The woman found her lunch partner "very charming." But she was astonished, and not only by his degree of candor. "He flirted with me—heavily—during lunch. Heav-i-ly. . . . I won't say 'déclassé' is the word. But I kept thinking, does he walk through the world like this? It seems totally inappropriate! He did talk about their marriage—that he took care of the kids." When the conversation turned to the minding of children, Harry seemed particular about who handled that. "I do," Harry told his lunch companion.

Around this same period, another writer, pretty and young, had a meeting with Harry. She had a book to pitch, but when they met in his office, she discovered to her annoyance that Harry's attention appeared sorely distracted. "He looked up my skirt! I was wearing a knee-length skirt, and Harry put his fucking head down to look up it. Then he made some remark about my looks, how attractive I was."

And yet observers of the couple felt there was, despite these flirtations, a resolute solidity to their family life. When seen during recreational outings with the children, in Central Park or at their modest retreat in Quogue with its casual beige beach house furniture, Tina's entire mood altered; the very features of her face appeared softened by love. "Tina just melted," one observer noted. Certainly, she was trying to have it all, and do it all. By the early nineties, she was often spending three days a week on Long Island with her family. Little Isabel, everyone agreed, looked and acted very much like Tina: bright and precocious. George was quite different from other children: bright, articulate, but oddly formal. "He looked like a little genius," Valerie Grove decided when she met him. "And he shook hands like an old-fashioned little gentleman." He detested loud noises; the mere singing of "Happy Birthday" at his own party would cause him to clap his hands to his ears in despair. "Don't sing," he would beg, "I hate singing." Harry wasn't wholly pleased about bringing up either child in New York: "I'd bring them up in England if I had a choice," he told one journalist.

So, there was no doubting Harry's role within the home, nor his partnership with his wife. It seemed unbreakable by anything as frivolous as a casual sexual fling or a wanton look. The very language used by Harry indicated a bond—something professional or contractual—and yet at the same time, he strove for a pretty elastic interpretation of what constituted a violation of that bond.

"I can't see you without Tina being present, that would be an act of *infidelity*," Harry would inform a writer requesting an interview years later. "Infidelity to Tina."

Within these boundaries, the pair flourished.

"Even in those days they were a team—like not an hour went by in that office when Tina wasn't on the phone to Harry, all the time, absolutely," a trusted employee would later remark. Indeed, Hamilton South, Tina's newly hired "networker," would periodically be sent over from *Vanity Fair* to further certain of Harry's pet projects at Random House. There he would be asked for ideas on how to promote the work of some favored author: a humor book by Christopher Cerf, for instance; and then, later, he was dispatched again to help devise the marketing of an autobiography by the star *du jour*, General Colin Powell.

For all its seeming modernity, then, with its spectacle of two scrambling ambitious spouses short of time, there was a distinctly old-fashioned cast to Tina and Harry's marriage. It was as though it had been modeled not on any romantic ideal but on something much older and considerably less American: a royal union. Loyalty, common interests, intermingling kingdoms, heirs, genuine affection, and admiration—these were their ties. There were some who sneered at the obvious flaws inherent in such ties, the jealousy and limited demands. But no one could doubt that the marriage was lasting, that, unlike others haunted by expectations and the specter of untrammeled perfection, it worked. On many levels.

About certain things, Tina was uncanny. "Sometimes she knows something is going to happen and sure enough it does," Miles Chapman said of her. Chapman had the same ability, interestingly enough. But like a number of his colleagues, he was ultimately overwhelmed by the trying and hectic life demanded in New York: "I got out of New York in time, before I went completely mad. In fact, I did go a bit mad. But I got therapy and sorted myself out," he would later recall. In 1989, he was on his way back to a more peaceable London existence.

The nineties, Tina was certain, signaled an end to some of this insanity; it would be a more significant change than most people realized. "I am fed up with the money culture of the Reagan years," she told her old friend Anthony Holden. She was, she maintained at any opportunity, weary even of the "tabloid fodder like Imelda, Leona, Marla and Donald"—the very characters, in other words, who had been the lifeblood of her magazine. "I feel like you do when everyone has been at a party too long and suddenly the lights come on and you look around and everyone looks terrible," she complained.

Nonetheless, the demands at *Vanity Fair* remained the same. "The demand of being not only 'on,' but I had to be wildly intelligent and funny all day long," as one employee put it. "It was grueling! To go there every morning and wait for the phone call [from Tina]. And then—'What did you DO last night? Who did you TALK to? What's going ON?' "

Still, Tina insisted, there was to be a new sobriety on her part, a restraint not merely on eighties-style excesses (those which had initially so delighted her), but also on the figures who had been emblematic of that era. Gone from the pages of *Vanity Fair*, as the decade progressed, were the social staples Princess TNT, Pat Buckley, and Gayfryd Steinberg. Everything even distantly associated with the Reagans and their ilk was thenceforth dropped down a memory hole. The invaluable Bob Colacello, whom Tina had appreciated for his social connections, his Republicanism, and his closeness to the circle that included the former first couple, found himself, now that the usefulness of his friends was in doubt, abruptly exiled. "I think you've had it with New York and are kind of tired," Tina informed him kindly. It was shortly after she had just thrown Colacello a huge party in honor of his book on Andy Warhol.

Then she warmed to her theme. "And the Reagans are out of the White House—this is the nineties now. I think you need to go to LA or Paris, you need a new outlook."

"Maybe," conceded a devastated Colacello.

"Well, decide where to go, Los Angeles or Paris," she repeated.

"LA," he said.

"Oh. Well, I think you should go to Paris." And Colacello did.

On the other hand, the new sobriety wasn't meant to be swallowed whole and undiluted, like a dose of salts. "She killed a story once on the basis of the pictures," said one writer. "Jeff Bridges—who was a little overweight. She told me, 'I don't want an overweight person on the cover.' "

Gracing the covers, almost always, were the un-fat, the un-Gorbachevs: Madonna three times by 1991; Kim Basinger ("Blonde of Blondes," read the cover line), Dolly Parton, Jerry Hall; Demi Moore, famously nude and pregnant, caught by Annie Leibovitz. "I had been looking for a way to make a statement about the nineties, and when Annie brought the picture in I immediately said, 'That is it!' " Tina recalled. "Because it was so natural and it took off the power suits—literally. It said: 'Naked. Pregnant. It's fine to show your stomach.' "

Facilitating the capture of these gorgeous creatures was a "celebrity wrangler" (as the position has since come to be known), whose functions went virtually uncharted until a pioneer, Jane Sarkin, was hired in 1986 by Tina on Colacello's recommendation. The idea was to grab whatever star was hot at the moment and wrap her around, say, an excellent analysis of the desperate state of Haiti by T. D. Allman after the departure of "Baby Doc" Duvalier. Or a fine story on Boris Yeltsin; or a feature on Picasso by John Richardson (whose biography of the artist would eventually be published by Harry); or an intriguing portrait of the British playwright Harold Pinter. The lips, the breasts, the muscles were sugar tits, meant to make the medicine go down.

"I've come close to firing Jane Sarkin a few times," Tina would later confide to a friend, "but now she is one of the three or four people without whom I can't get the magazine out." It was Sarkin who served as liaison between Tina and the Hollywood publicity machines that control access to the stars, she who—to quote a friend—"negotiated the terms." Those terms, however, brought her little thanks from the media world outside *Vanity Fair,* a world in which serious major magazines once had their pick of grateful stars.

Indeed, under Tina, the phrase "celebrity journalism" soon became an oxymoron. There was a lot of celebrity, precious little analysis, as Tina was only too well aware. Part of her cringed occasionally at the star treatment she dished out. "So you see, we're *not* just about celebrity journalism," she would announce at a *Vanity Fair* luncheon honoring some recently acquired magazine award, her steely gaze directed straight at poor Kevin Sessums, her most dependable celebrity writer. To be sure, she was furious with Sessums at the time. He had just informed a reporter that he could always tell when his boss liked a story because "it makes her nipples firm"—a quotation which, alas for him, found its way into *Newsweek.* But the element of celebrity shame was palpable at the magazine. "I'm the trailer park, I know my place," Sessums told a colleague. "They do this celebrity stuff grudgingly, but the flak they get for it! They hate dealing with it. Anyone who does celebrity journalism for a magazine is finally going to be looked down on."

Nonetheless, it was serious business. In fact, it was pure business. As the daughter of a producer, Tina had few illusions about the commercial value of pretty faces and excellent bodies. "Fifteen hours for a photo shoot, one hour for an interview," grumbled one *Vanity Fair* writer. When celebrities were dismayed with their coverage, when they even thought they *might* be, Sarkin would receive a call. Conversely, the star or her agent might have a favored writer in mind, which neither would be shy about mentioning.

"I was asked for by Madonna, so obviously sometimes things got said," recalled the *Vanity Fair* writer Lynn Hirschberg. "Sure that happened. And Tina is interested in the quote that gets picked up by Page Six or Liz Smith. I think at first—as with Gay Talese's famous piece 'Frank Sinatra Has a Cold'—Tina was fascinated with the nature of celebrity in America. She took one class system and brought it to another system. And then she changed. Tina understands that pull, the desire in a democracy of people who want to anoint stars. . . ."

Buried beneath the stars, as time went by, were the more serious stories she had originally wanted, especially those occurring abroad. Some guilt was evident on Tina's part over their gradual diminution. "You'd go into her office, and Tina would say no about nine times to a foreign affairs story. And the tenth time she'd say yes because she felt so badly," recalled an editor. "Then it would come in, and she'd kill it. This was all very depressing."

For a respectable magazine to anoint celebrities—no one, at first, could accept that. Tina's pioneering concessions to Hollywood (similar to those she had once accorded society lionesses) would eventually set the stage for the even more egregious courtier magazines that followed, most notably *In Style*. Even Hirschberg, a journalist fond of interviewing Hollywood actors and actresses, found the transmutation of traditional reporting, the suspension of critical faculties by a few of her peers, "pernicious." It had never before been thought necessary. It had, in fact, been thought pernicious.

"We could get anybody we wanted on the cover, Jane Fonda, Ann-Margret, Jack Nicholson, whomever," said Tom Hedley, an *Esquire* managing editor of the seventies, who eventually went on to become a Hollywood screenwriter (*Flashdance*) and then a book publisher. "Agents could never dictate terms. Now they're dictating camera lens, dictating quotes. Then they were not like that." On the other hand, Hedley realized, "I think Tina just understood the times. She recognized we had moved into a star system and you either played to the star system or you lost it."

Tina thought so, too. "If I were to start packaging this magazine with a serious cover," she said at the time, "I'd kiss off at least twenty thousand sales on the newsstand—which means," she hastily added, lest anyone think fluff still prevailed at *Vanity Fair,* "twenty thousand people are not going to read the piece about the MCA deal."

In case this infusion of high tone wasn't quite enough, Tina relied, as she always had and always would, on the literary establishment to provide sanctuary for the rest of her less worthy endeavors. Norman Mailer was hired as "writer-at-large," and just before going off to report for his new employer on Cuba (and then on Warren Beatty), he sent one journalist a note explaining his decision to sign on. It was helpfully entitled *"Quote"*:

"*Quote: Vanity Fair* is open and lively, occasionally wicked and sometimes pretty adventurous. That's not bad for a mass media magazine." Then the tone turned slightly dubious: ". . . And I expect I look forward to writing for them."

To accentuate this new, more purposeful mood, in the summer of 1989, just as Nancy Reagan pulled out as patroness of Phoenix House, a foundation that set up effective drug rehabilitation centers in Los Angeles and New York, Tina assigned a piece on its founder, Mitch Rosenthal. Highlighted in the article was the defection of the former first lady, ostensibly the nation's most virulent anti-drug crusader, from his cause. It was Tina herself who decided to take up the slack.

"She realized—the way Nancy Reagan realized—that she had to get a cause, and she got drugs," one observer to this process concluded. "Tina realized right away that the Steinbergs and the age of ostentation were over."

But perhaps not entirely. Or rather, the noble cause and the large, glittery gathering might, in some happy circumstances, be combined. Tina threw a huge lunch for Dr. Rosenthal in Los Angeles, leaning heavily on the friends of Norman Lear, the television producer, to get him to buy a table, which Lear did.

Inevitably, Lear requested a return favor. Not too long after Tina's dinner, he called to ask for her assistance at a charity event, a live television broadcast called *The Environmental Media Awards*. "Now, he could have said he was involved in cleaning gutters in South Central, he was Norman *Lear*," explained a harrowed employee who had to help organize the television tribute. But there were few fond memories of that evening, at which one thousand people were in the audience, a meandering rat on the soundstage, and, as a distraught Tina herself pointed out to her subordinates after telling them they were ruining her party, no air-conditioning.

"A disaster" was how one organizer characterized it.

To begin with, decided the *Vanity Fair* employees corralled into the endeavor, the Environmental Media Awards weren't exactly the Oscars. "It was like Mary Steenburgen handing out an award to like some daytime soap opera that had some story line about deforestation," said one. Tina Brown, Donald Keough, president of Coca-Cola at the time, and Peter Guber, then running Columbia Pictures, were the event chairs. Robert Redford gave the keynote address.

Jane Sarkin, Hamilton South, and Sara Marks, the magazine's party organizer, all utter novices to television studios, soon found themselves helping concoct the California event, living at the Beverly Wilshire Hotel for almost a month and working out of a trailer on the Sony lot. Guber gave them the use of the studio; there were two soundstages, one for cocktails, one for dinner, and garlands of sunflowers had to be hung from a fifty-foot ceiling. "I thought I was going to have a nervous breakdown," said one of those involved in the planning. "We were wheedling union workers—this was a union soundstage—to get it done." Tina had insisted her crew incorporate the society florist Robert Isabell (who supplied her own parties as well as those of Gayfryd Steinberg) and the famed hotelier Ian Schrager. As one *Vanity Fair* staffer noted, "Tina just couldn't bring herself to face the fact that it was a TV show. For her it just had to be glamorous and Robert was the component that brought glamour to it."

It was Isabell who came up with the environmentally friendly idea of hanging recycled paper on a soundstage, but this inspiration, it would later be recalled, quickly ran into trouble. "The union crews walked in and said, 'Are you out of your fucking mind? This hasn't been fireproofed!' " However, "since it was recycled paper, when he sprayed it with fireproofing, it dissolved. Like putty! So it was a calamity of just epic proportions." New paper that was flame-retardant had to be swiftly shipped in. The Environmental Media people considered the party an enormous success, but Tina was another matter.

Still, despite her manifest displeasure, a case of champagne arrived on the doorstep of one organizer. "See, Tina gave aspirational gifts" was the verdict of the recipient. "It was always one step above what you thought you could actually have."

So Tina's charitable impulses continued to flourish. Around Christmastime 1991, yet another big bash would be thrown for Phoenix House by Tina, this one in New York at the old Customs House. It was to be a major event, Jessye Norman singing, Ian Schrager co-chairing, and the invited shelling out $1,000 a head. One of the invited approached Tina before the event with some sobering insights about the guest list.

"Tina, I don't want to burst your bubble, but the co-chair, Ian Schrager—he was once arrested." And jailed. The former owner of Studio 54 had, along with his partner Steve Rubell, plunged into a fair amount of hot water with the IRS years earlier; both were briefly incarcerated on tax charges. The guest then named another person on the list whom he believed to be a cocaine supplier to a certain entertainment executive.

His hostess laughed. "Oh, that is rather inconvenient," murmured Tina.

But the guest walked away, mirthless, thinking, "This woman doesn't have a conviction in her body. There is no cause other than

Tina Brown. . . . Despite the fact that I had seen Tina be incredibly disingenuous in the past, for me that was a radar moment."

And yet these parties, which set Newhouse back roughly $1 million a year, had a finely crafted purpose. They were not merely another offshoot of *Vanity Fair*'s rapidly evolving publicity machine, which performed as expected, sending, for example, a Gail Sheehy political profile "to the right people in Washington—so it gets admitted to the *Congressional Record* and then Liz Smith would run that." The large and gorgeous gatherings were more sharply focused. They were planned, as one staff member would later explain, to distinguish *Vanity Fair* from its rivals.

"Because magazines are magazines. And what Tina did that no one ever did before was she reanimated them through people. The magazine meant more when Henry Kissinger was dancing with Vendela at a party. Tina knew that. Tina knew it was worth it."

Who could quarrel with her success? Quibble though one might about Tina's methods, her undiluted pragmatism, her sometime loyalties, her lack of conviction, her withered passions, her need to win at any cost, she had, in fact, won. And won not only for herself but for every last one of her charges, the writers, editors, photographers, bosses, friends, and associates who depended on her, and were alternately smitten and repelled by their dependence on such a woman. By the end of 1991, *Vanity Fair* would be in the black, its second such year, with almost $50 million in revenue and over $1 million in pretax profit.

However meager that figure might appear, it must be compared to the sums of earlier years, during which about $63 million of Si Newhouse's money had gone straight down the drain. This trend had begun before and continued throughout most of Tina's tenure. In 1983, *Vanity Fair* lost $11,320,186; in 1984, when Tina arrived at the helm and circulation was at a pathetic 274,000, it lost over $14 million; in 1985, it dropped $10,136,077; and a year later, it lost more than $9 million.

But those days were over. By 1991, *Vanity Fair* had 1,444 ad pages and a readership calculated at almost two million, a bit more than double its circulation. The October issue alone had a 116-page supplement for Calvin Klein jeans, which cost the designer roughly $1 million. By the end of the following year, the magazine's pretax profit would swell to over $5 million on a total revenue of $60,549,040. The circulation would be well over one million (60 percent of all readers women), and the ad pages would have fattened to 1,501. After nine wintry years, Si Newhouse was not exactly coining money, but he was making it.

The more clever among Tina's writers figured out the secret of her success pretty quickly. *Vanity Fair* was no tabloid. It simply used and then subverted the traditional subjects of tabloid journalism for its own purposes, much as it used and then subverted Norman Mailer ("I grew up thinking I would marry the first woman I had sex with!" Warren Beatty confided to the author of *The Naked and the Dead* in the profile Mailer wrote of the actor), or indeed the paintings of Picasso. "I think one reason *Vanity Fair* became so successful is that smart people didn't have to feel guilty reading it," explained a contributing editor. "It wasn't like junk food, like *People* magazine. You could feel you were doing something smart reading it—and it informed you about significant things like Gorbachev. And then you could also do the Demi Moore thing. You could always get the good gossip but you didn't have to feel guilty about it because it wasn't ever tacky."

This veiled intelligence which from time to time descended on the magazine, informing its writing, draping its fluff, and burrowing deep into one or two articles per issue, was due, people understood, at least to some degree to the man behind the throne. "Because Tina—partly because of Harry—is a person of genuine intellectual curiosity and depth and breadth. And they're internationalists, and they're in the world."

But it was also due to Tina, who supplied no single visionary force, but a chocolate box of temptations. "Sometimes you think she's Lucille Ball, she can be so flighty and batty," Sessums remarked. "But there's a genius to her madness. The whole way she edits, she throws everyone she wants into the magazine—and at the very last minute, that's what's in. The last thing lying at the printer's—that's what's in."

Last-second changes, the despair of her subordinates, were never construed as emanating from self-doubt or fear, however. Tina appeared supremely confident, secure enough to reevaluate periodically her own first impressions and flashes of reverence, or, when the mood struck, revoke previous infatuations for any of her hirelings. These reversals of fortune would often come without warning. Practically anyone was dispensable, or at least likely to be deemed less worthy than initially suspected. "For a year and a half Kevin Sessums was the golden boy, then the bloom fell off the rose," it was recalled. "She didn't mind if he was thrown to the dogs."

In any event, there had never been anything like *Vanity Fair*. It had an old title, but it was an ingenious new product. Even Tina's rivals were forced to concede as much. "What they couldn't get their heads around—and what Tina did that no other magazine seemed to be doing, the modern thing that is now totally acceptable—was that the magazine is not just a niche," explained her admirer Miles Chapman. "It is not just aimed at one particular reader. It's aimed at people who are interested in everything. If you are a man of forty, you are not just interested in cigars and motorbikes. I mean, we have grown up in a time when the media, television, tells you everything you want to know about the past, the future, science, art. It's all there at your fingertips. That's what's modern about our generation. We're the television generation."

What else was there by way of competition? *New York* magazine had, at that period, lost its verve. *Esquire* was a sliver of its former self, moribund, appealing exclusively to men, and very dull men at that. *GQ* was select in its readership, fond of motorcycles, Italian suits, and the cigars clenched in the jaws of muscled stars.

As for the weekly *New Yorker,* however cherished, it was losing circulation. Like *Vanity Fair,* it was a Newhouse property and had been since May 1985, when he paid $168 million in cash for it. Like most men who overpay, the new owner was inordinately proud of his purchase. He was also at wit's end. In 1987, Newhouse had fired the revered editor William Shawn ("*Mister* Shawn," as his writers invariably referred to him, no matter how long they had worked there), replacing the seventy-nine-year-old gentleman with the benign Robert Gottlieb, a Newhouse friend who had previously run Knopf. But this move, traumatic as it was, had proved of little value. The magazine was still generating income just before Newhouse bought it, $60 million in advertising revenue, netting it $5.5 million. But it was losing fans.

"I think every time a hearse went down Fifth Avenue, they lost another reader," a top Condé Nast publisher said. "It was being written for whoever worked there. It became a publishing museum."

Yet despite all that, Tina Brown wanted it.

Not that she gave any sign. She was busy planning the tenth anniversary issue of *Vanity Fair,* her mood especially buoyant and involved. "What I'm really thinking of," she told Ron Galotti, her balding publisher, who had a much vaunted fondness for an assortment of women (he was the model for "Mr. Big" in *Sex and the City*), "I'd like to have a 500-page issue with 250 pages of ads."

"Well, you know, I'd like to be six feet tall and have a full head of hair," replied Galotti.

"You think I'm being unrealistic?"

"Yeah."

Who could imagine that Tina was going anywhere? Graydon Carter certainly couldn't.

In June 1992, a forty-two-year-old Canadian named Graydon Carter assumed that he was about to take over the editorship of *The New Yorker*. He had had meetings on the subject with Alexander Liberman; many of the details had been ironed out; he was ready and thrilled at the prospect. The new job was supposed to be announced that month, after Si Newhouse had spoken to the magazine's editor, Robert Gottlieb.

In its own way, it was as risky an appointment as the one eight years earlier of a young British woman whose only previous experience had been editing a puckish society magazine. Carter was editor of the *New York Observer,* an irreverent weekly newspaper chockful of media gossip. Before that he had been a founding co-editor of a deeply impertinent publication called *Spy.* In this latter capacity, he had supervised the skewering of, among others, Tina Brown, Donald Trump, *The New York Times,* Mike Ovitz, David Geffen—and, intriguingly, Si Newhouse. *Spy*'s editors called Newhouse "a dwarf"; he possessed, the magazine suggested, "famous aversions to leisure and interaction with other human beings."

So the notion of placing Carter at the head of this hallowed waxworks publication was unusual. Tina, for one, wasn't thrilled by the idea; it was Carter's *Spy* that had published her smarmy mendicant's letter to Mike Ovitz just a few years earlier. Moreover, she did have an idea as to who should be running *The New Yorker.* And so did Steve Florio, the magazine's publisher.

"Give me Tina," he begged Newhouse at their 6:30 A.M. meetings. "Send Gottlieb back to Random House."

"I'll think about it and get back to you," Newhouse promised.

Then Florio met with Tina herself.

"What does Si say?" wondered Tina. "I'd love to work for you, but what does Si say?"

Newhouse informed Florio that he would tell him his decision the following Monday. It was the tail end of June, there was a Metropolitan Museum of Art gala on that Monday night, and Florio found himself milling around. Newhouse grabbed him from behind. "Gottlieb's

JUDY BACHRACH

going to Random House, he's okay with it," he said. "I want to give *The New Yorker* to Tina."

Carter swiftly discovered that instead of receiving the coveted *New Yorker* as his prize, he was about to be made editor of *Vanity Fair*. It was a prospect he regarded with genuine revulsion. *Spy*, his brainchild, was everything *Vanity Fair* was not: funny, wicked, disdainful of the establishment. This last sentiment, as everyone at *Vanity Fair* knew, was returned in kind. How could Carter function in such a milieu? How, wondered one editor with close West Coast contacts, was a magazine that depended on the kindness of Hollywood supposed to survive with Carter, who had spent his career trashing it?

"Graydon had a really bad reputation in Hollywood," the editor said. "They wanted nothing to do with him. And it wasn't the agents who hated him. It was the really *powerful* people who hated him. Loathed him."

But what choice did he honestly have? Carter had three children and he needed the money badly. Anyway, word had already leaked out that Tina was to get *The New Yorker*.

"*You've* got a big mouth," Harry informed Carter the next evening, the moment he stepped inside the door of the Evanses' apartment. It was an accusation that deeply affronted Carter. Aside from his immediate family and his best friend, he insisted, he had told no one.

Carter occupied the sofa, downcast, speaking little. He was to write his own press release, saying how pleased he was to be awarded such an honor. All the people who mattered were assembled in the apartment, jubilant, talking excitedly: the delighted *New Yorker* publisher, Steve Florio; his younger brother, Tom Florio; another Tina fan who would also eventually become the magazine's publisher, Ron Galotti; Tina—and Harry banging away at a typewriter. He too was writing a press release for his wife, phrased largely in superlatives.

The next morning, the troops were rallied. *Vanity Fair* writers and editors were telephoned one by one and asked to attend a special meeting. Ron Galotti was present. No one knew ahead of time what would be discussed at this gathering. "I'm here to tell you some sad news," Tina began, bathed in tears; and indeed there was, after she delivered her speech, genuine dismay over her departure. She wasn't allowed to take many people with her to her new place—everyone was told that, and many a listener hoped (a longing fanned in a number of instances by Tina herself) to be among the few thus chosen. But what could she do? Everyone knew her heart was at *Vanity Fair*. Si had wanted this to happen, Tina told her friends. It was Si who had

222

asked her to take over *The New Yorker*. And with that, she went around the room, hugging some of her old employees. With one of them, she was prescient.

"I think they're going to hate me over there," she said.

Graydon Carter arrived at *Vanity Fair* the following week and found—nothing. There was a backlog of stories that had been sitting in a "kill pile," articles previously considered by Tina or her editors that were, for one reason or another, deemed unfit for the magazine. But aside from this cache, Carter was left with no immediate resources: there was no indication of what pieces might go into succeeding issues, no drawerful of ideas. *Vanity Fair* always planned months ahead, even if those plans never materialized.

"Nothing, nothing, nothing" was the description of what had been left behind.

Chapter 12
Synergy and Its Discontents

The decision to place Tina Brown on the back of this horned and mutinous mythical beast—to hand her the reins to *The New Yorker* and (as it would later be said inside Condé Nast) a salary approaching $1 million—was decidedly terrifying, the old pampered hands decided. Their fragile nerves had never wholly recovered from Gottlieb's invasion as editor five years earlier when, the writer Renata Adler felt, "the magazine had begun seriously to slide"—in part, she maintained in her memoirs, because of the automatic assumption "that *New Yorker* pieces were too long" and that "cutting means improving." But Gottlieb was a pale, temperate, almost deferential figure compared to what followed in the magazine's sixty-seventh year.

"Seriousness will be sexy again," Tina declared on her ascendancy. "Substance is back in style."

The writers shuddered. An "evil blond headmistress" had taken over, one of them was heard to mutter. Was the exquisite repository of fiction and thoughtfully crafted non-fiction articles doomed to an eternity of naked and pregnant Demi Moores and quotations from Brad Pitt? Would the cutting of pieces grow harsher or more indiscriminate? Would treasured journalists, habituated by years of indolence and hazy, far-off deadlines, actually be expected to cough up the goods? On time? Attached to a news peg? Sixteen calls a day came in to Tina from contributors and subscribers the summer of her ascension.

"When I heard Tina was coming, I couldn't believe it," said one member of the staff. "Because, well, there was a running joke when Gottlieb took over: *Next time it will be Tina Brown!* I mean, people were just laughing about it. Just laughing. It was a *joke*. It was not to be taken seriously."

Fairly quickly, however, the regular contributors had a chance to see how grave and sweeping the transformation of *The New Yorker* was going to be. Elizabeth Drew, famous for her sonorous, implacably earnest political commentary, was no longer the Washington correspondent. Ray Bonner, who wrote a two-part, 40,000-word piece on Indonesia, found his contract wasn't to be renewed; Tony Hiss, Milton Viorst, James Lardner; John Newhouse, who had written for the magazine for twenty years—all disappeared sooner or later from its pages. Tina was also no fan of John McPhee, but he far from alone. Her favorite put-down for some of those whose work she found wanting was "a B-writer."

On the other hand, as one employee soon discovered, certain individuals were not meant to take their rejections personally, or even indefinitely. "It's interesting, sometimes Tina would 'forget' she disliked a writer," he said. At one meeting she decided, 'We need more coverage of Washington. Shall we call Elizabeth Drew?' We said, 'Tina, you let her go.' She said, 'Oh, that was *then*.' "

Others quit in anticipation of catastrophe, among them the writer and radio host Garrison Keillor, whose departure precipitated, for almost the first time in his career, genuinely funny remarks. "If some ditzy American editor went to London, took over *The Spectator*, and turned it into, say, *In Your Face: A Magazine of Mucus*, there would be a big uproar," he said. "Here, a great American magazine falls into the clutches of . . . a British editor who seems to know this country mainly from television and movies and nobody says much about it."

But the thing was, everyone was saying a lot about it. And although there were those, like the fine fiction writer Jamaica Kincaid, whose initial response was "I wished her well. I thought it was an amazing joke that Si Newhouse had sent us a woman," this was by no means, as Tina had prophesied, a universal reaction. The bright old things were out to get her. As one of her early allies put it: "The storyline for Shawn was 'Reclusive Genius, Friend of Writers.' The storyline for Tina was 'Vulgarian, Lowering Standards.' "

Those same vivid fears that had plagued Tina when she took over *Vanity Fair* returned now, redoubled. Only this time her terror was prompted not simply by the backbiting of subordinates and rivals, but by her own feelings of jealousy and inadequacy, more difficult to vanquish. Yet again, she was feeling "besieged," her old London friend

Alexander Chancellor realized when he breakfasted with her early on, overwhelmed by the extraordinary history, talent, and richness of *The New Yorker* that once was.

But she certainly hadn't lost the ability to arouse a man's protective instincts. Tina was almost thirty-nine, sparer and more fragile than Chancellor remembered from her London days. In her square-shouldered pale suit, her hair freshly cropped and combed, she looked more professional, and yet vulnerable too. Despite his sympathy, a few of her notions tickled him. "She seemed to fear that the people around her were conspiring to make her fail in her great task—some even by the cunning device of writing bad articles," he wrote in his book *Some Times in America*. Indeed, her resentment of the magazine had some of the elements of a class struggle: the sharp unbridgeable divisions, the presentiment of long-running strife. "She reminds me of Margaret Thatcher," said Chancellor. "Margaret Thatcher, when she was in government, always talked about 'Them.' Tina had that same quality."

In order to vanquish the beast, Tina tried her best to diminish it. "The old *New Yorker,* this great myth," she would sneer. "There is a lot of faux puritanism out there. It's all part of the *New Yorker* fakery. Good taste in the prissy sense has never been of interest to me."

That was Tina's solace when she took over the magazine, her constant mantra. The mythical *New Yorker;* what was it, after all?—pompous, wordy, and dissolute, in Tina's eyes scaly with age. "Balls-aching screeds about the life of the fruit fly," Bettina, her mother, would loyally remark to Tina's friends. She and George, whose health was declining, had moved from Spain to New York, where they occupied the same building as their daughter, and often cared for her children.

"Why did dinosaurs perish?" read a Lee Lorenz caption for a cartoon that Tina gave as a gift to a valued employee. The drawing showed a dinosaur standing in a prehistoric landscape, gazing in dismay at a letter: "We are sorry to say your submission does not meet our editorial requirements."

In her crusade to eradicate the Ur-*New Yorker,* Tina had allies. Harold Brodkey, the novelist and short story writer, chimed in with yet more comfort, using language Tina would borrow. "Oh, don't pay any attention to the *New Yorker* fakery," he told her. Until his death from AIDS, Brodkey would act as her godfather in her new realm, whispering those magic words into her ear. And Tina would cite them at staff meetings as proof that the spell was broken. The past was unworthy of reverence. Harold Brodkey, a famous writer, had said so.

But inwardly, some of those around the magazine—especially James Wolcott, plucked by Tina from *Vanity Fair* with a mandate to write about popular culture—marveled at her reliance on such unthinking consolation. Whatever its faults, the old *New Yorker* wasn't so easily dismissed or abandoned. Who was Brodkey, with his "oily charm," to trash it? "Tina likes this kind of guy," said Wolcott. "You know, Tina is very into people who are betrayers."

For herself, however, she demanded absolute loyalty. When Hamilton South, her director of special projects, decided to remain at *Vanity Fair* under its new editor, Graydon Carter, rather than jump to *The New Yorker* after a six-month hiatus, as had been originally planned, Tina flew into a rage. South had been not merely her party packager but a prized sidekick, with important contacts in the world of advertising, publicists, and Hollywood agents. Daily, he was fielding calls from Tina and Steve Florio. "We have a new ad campaign," they would tell him. "You have to come take a look at it."

So, his defection, after Carter offered him a $15,000 raise and a new title, was a serious blow. Moreover, Si Newhouse refused to intervene in the matter. "I can't force you to go to *The New Yorker*," he told South, "but you have to make the call yourself. You have to see Tina."

Tina kept South in her office for an hour, twice almost reducing him to tears.

"You're not going to be able to accomplish anything without me," she said. She had made South what he was. Then she took a step back. "I can make you the Jeffrey Katzenberg of *The New Yorker*." But even then, South realized that if there was any job that shouldn't exist at the magazine, it was that of Jeffrey Katzenberg.

To defuse a general mutiny, Tina had sent letters, Federal Express, to those she wished to stay on, expressing admiration and extending large raises—$30,000 wasn't unusual—when contracts were renewed. Meantime, she put into place a cadre of her own lieutenants, "the shadow government," John Lahr, son of the actor Bert Lahr, would call it. He would become her new theater critic. On the shabby sixteenth and seventeenth floors of the West 43rd Street building (*The New Yorker* remained separate, and in theory inviolate, from the rest of Condé Nast on Madison Avenue) were boxes of old *New Yorker* issues. The new executive editor, Hendrik Hertzberg, and Gottlieb's protégé, the writer Adam Gopnik, helped supervise the transition. It was their job to bring in the rest of her troops.

"In fact, Hertzberg was, I assume, given the job of helping Tina hold things in place," explained one longtime editor, who was on vacation when the news came that he was about to report to Tina. "Rick called me; he was going on about how wonderful Tina was. What fun we could have. And we could be assigning pieces that were traditionally not done. There was still some concern among Tina and her people that there'd be defections."

As it happened, Hertzberg was in no position to assure people about the wonderfulness of Tina. He barely knew her, having met her initially at a party thrown by Katharine Graham, the publisher at that time of *The Washington Post,* and then subsequently only when Tina hired him after a lunch at the Harvard Club. But he had history. He had started at *The New Yorker* in 1969, writing for "The Talk of the Town," and then drifted away in the mid-seventies, becoming Jimmy Carter's chief speechwriter; later, he served as editor of *The New Republic,* and, subsequently became a freelancer. He had no notion where he would end up until Tina called with her tempting offer, long desired by him, to return to the fold.

Paradoxically, it was his connection to the glory days of William Shawn that Tina valued in Hertzberg, his ability to confer the legitimacy she craved. Hertzberg could be reassuring to staffers, and yet (since he had left Shawn and didn't especially like Gottlieb) simultaneously loyal to her.

Equally important, he might instruct Tina on what was feasible and what was impossible. "Pull quotes"—the mainstay of *Vanity Fair,* where quotations from the subject, executed in bold type, decorated a page, inveigling the reader into the text—were not feasible in *The New Yorker,* Hertzberg informed a disappointed Tina. "That would be against the magazine's DNA." Cover lines were also a bad idea: too much of an affront to the past. On the other hand, it *was* a good idea to have a see-through flap on the cover (this innovation lasted a year, after which the magazine ran out of see-through paper). Shorter articles were fine, too. Large, provocative photographs—Richard Avedon became the first photographer hired in the magazine's history—would likely prove acceptable.

Not that Tina needed continuous instruction. She knew what she was after: loyalty, passion, clever writing enhanced by brevity, smart, hungry staffers—her crew.

"Tina, I'm really hot for this job," Lahr told her, after Gopnik phoned him in London, where he had been living on "a hundred pounds a week."

"I like that word hot," said Tina. "That's what I like to hear. Come see me."

Their conversation lasted ten minutes, but it was filled with significance. "Tina was unhappy with theater criticism, in fact, didn't like criticism at all," Lahr recalled. "She found it, as it was practiced, tedious and hidebound, and boring. That's how both she and I found it." Indeed, the goal was to "make criticism more 'inside,' " a radical departure for a magazine once peopled by such devastating critics as Dorothy Parker and Robert Benchley. Lahr was "to bring into the discussion of theater the artists who were making theater—not just my opinion. The whole idea was, she was hiring someone who was inside, who was raised in the theater, who knew the practitioners."

Moreover, the coverage was not to be confined to New York drama, but designed to be international in scope, including of course London. Such expansiveness had other advantages. Within a year of his arrival, Lahr observed, "our goal for the theater section had been accomplished—we were taking a lot of money away from the *Times*." As for the reporting itself, it was backed by lots of *New Yorker* galas. "Tina raised a lot of money for the National Theatre, the Almeida Theatre, the Royal Court—now she of course had her own vested interests in doing that," said Lahr. "She wanted to be a presence in England. I fronted a lot of it."

How New York-ish was *The New Yorker* supposed to be under such a regime? Her old friend Alexander Chancellor had occasion to ask himself just such a question when, in the summer of 1992, Tina wanted him to edit, of all sections, "The Talk of the Town," a column rife with brief sketches of intriguing Manhattan characters and doings. Even Chancellor was taken aback.

"I don't know anything about New York," he told her bluntly. "How does it work, 'Talk of the Town'?"

"Oh, I think there's a dozen people or something attached to it," she vaguely replied.

Chancellor got the distinct impression that this swarming hive of worker bees would be "rushing around New York, going to parties, panting back with all their copy, their scoops." He, in turn, was hired

229

to "give it Old World elegance, give it some style, make it acceptable to the literati," although he suspected Tina of other motives as well. "I thought I was moral support in some way," he said. In later months, even when he discovered that, far from having a dozen eager bees at his disposal, he had but four, and that other staffers were actually resentful of working for "Talk of the Town" (the pieces were unsigned in those days), he exonerated his boss. "She was perfectly sincere. I think she had no idea about 'Talk of the Town.' "

And neither, as it happened, did Chancellor, a charmingly self-deprecating but fumbling presence during Tina's first trying year. "Stockdale," he was dubbed by colleagues, after Ross Perot's bewildered running mate, Admiral James Stockdale, a war hero who became a national joke after he launched the 1992 vice-presidential debate with "Who am I? What am I doing here?"

Some of this perplexity seemed to have found its way into Chancellor's stories. Practically his first inspiration on arrival came in the form of a November 1992 press release revealing that a large fir tree was about to be put up at Rockefeller Center, a not unusual occurrence in New York around Christmastime. Nonetheless, Chancellor, after viewing the tree ceremony, wondered "if I could find a way of describing it amusingly." (He couldn't, another editor decided.) Certainly, Tina consistently failed to find his work amusing. "She had this habit of reading everything, but she read it quite late, more or less on press day," Chancellor discovered. "And then she'd kill two pages, saying, 'Boring, pathetic.' 'Pathetic' was one of her favorite words. So was 'wet.' "

What she wanted, Tina explained to everyone, was news. Scoops. Christmas trees didn't thrill her. Neither did another Chancellor story on the suspicious death in rural New York State of a prize Holstein cow, which led to the subsequent suicides of two farmers.

"Pathetic!" Tina would snap over the telephone. It was especially provoking, Tina swiftly decided, how recalcitrant some of the old staff was proving to be. In March 1993, she asked John Newhouse, another Washington writer (no relation to Si), to file a profile on the British prime minister of the day, John Major. "Not a good idea, he's a dull guy," Newhouse told her.

"Well, I *am* British," Tina reminded him.

Nonetheless, Newhouse preferred to profile Chris Patten, the former governor of Hong Kong, who was fiercely critical of the circumstances in which the British government agreed to hand over the former colony to an undemocratic mainland China. In the end he wrote about both men. But by the time the piece on Patten appeared, the *New York Times Magazine* had already beaten *The New Yorker* to the punch.

"Look, John, it's no use pretending people don't read *The New York Times Magazine*, they do," Tina told him reprovingly. Timing was everything, she added. In vain did Newhouse protest that the competitive *New York Times Magazine* had cobbled together its own piece on Patten, very likely, only after it heard he was about to write one himself. Furthermore, the *Times Magazine* profile was far weaker than the one that appeared in *The New Yorker*. Clearly, he didn't understand the problem.

Excellence was by no means the sole criterion at the new *New Yorker*. "Don't you see?" pleaded Tina. "The gilt is off the gingerbread!"

Newhouse understood what she meant by that archaic expression; he had to be first with the story, any story. Otherwise, it was no use. And he had tried. For instance, Newhouse had learned quite early that the CBS program *60 Minutes* was also after the outspoken Hong Kong governor, and he had, at Tina's insistence, successfully hurried the story along to declare victory over Lesley Stahl. Of course, the old *New Yorker* wouldn't have given a damn about beating a television show. Everyone knew that.

Everyone but Tina. Sitting in her office, stunned and distraught after her lecture, Newhouse couldn't think of a word to say in reply. Things had changed so suddenly. Very likely, Tina took his silence for disapprobation. He was part of the old guard, she swiftly decided: "Not hip." After two years under her aegis, he found his salary sizably diminished. Then he was gone.

And as for Chancellor, "There were all kinds of slight scandals to do with me in one way or another," he would later say. In January 1993, "Talk of the Town" ran a longish piece by Irene Dische on the trial of the eighty-year-old former East German dictator Erich Honecker, who was accused of permitting the killing of thirteen people who had tried to escape his country. It was just the sort of "scoop" Tina coveted: an intimate glimpse into a difficult trial brimming with complex issues, and best of all, closed to the public. And it was intriguingly sympathetic to the defendant, who was mortally ill at the time. But Dische was, alas, the wife of Honecker's own lawyer, Nicolaus Beeker, which accounted for her unique access to a closed courtroom.

No mention was made of this unseemly relationship in "Talk of the Town," as all of the column's items were then unsigned, but Chancellor decided "that this didn't matter." In days to come, he was to regret that decision. *The Washington Post, The Wall Street Journal,* the *Columbia Journalism Review*—all three tore into *The New Yorker.*

Nor was that the end of the episode. "Do you have a photograph of yourself?" Maurie Perl asked Chancellor shortly thereafter. She was a new and indefatigable presence at *The New Yorker,* forever in conference with the boss. Perl ran the magazine's publicity—Tina's publicity, really, as her staff soon realized.

"No, why do you want something like that?" asked Chancellor. It turned out that *Newsweek* also wanted to run "a sort of unsavory story" about the incident.

"They want to publish a picture of Tina. I'm not going to have them publish a picture of Tina over this shit," said Perl. "I want *yours.*"

He was a white-haired, "fifty-something Brit they'd never heard of," Chancellor explained. Better to send *Newsweek* a pretty photograph of Tina. "She was famous." They would run a picture of her anyway.

"But they *can't* do that," Perl protested. "I haven't allowed Tina to say anything." But they did. And Tina, relenting, finally consented to discuss the problematic article in a vague way. She believed, she told the world, in journalistic integrity.

The problem was that Tina's notions of journalistic integrity were, on occasion, at variance with the norm. And it derived not from calculation, but from a daffy British unawareness, despite her years in the field, of what constituted the rules of the game in respectable American publications. These rules were pretty simple. You identify any possible conflicts of interest. You don't use a publication to settle scores. You keep a salutary distance from subjects, however powerful or potentially useful. You clean up your own messes.

But the application of these rules, in Tina's case, had been at best spotty. At *Tatler,* when she was young and seeking advancement, the rules didn't apply. At *Vanity Fair,* those rules had been bent, without consequence, to please potent friends and advertisers. At *The New Yorker,* so many items were being tossed out the window—the precious opening fragment, "A friend writes . . ."; much of the quota of fine short stories; the hegemony of the cartoon Regency mascot Eustace Tilley, with his silly monocle—that one hardly had time to sort through all the garbage.

Quite early in her tenure, Tina directed a British writer, Francis

Wheen, to review a biography of Rupert Murdoch written by the talented journalist William Shawcross. It was, from any angle, an assignment of doubtful wisdom. The book, not then out in the States, was overwhelmingly kind to its subject, and especially critical of Tina's husband, whom Murdoch had fired years earlier. In a brief and gossipy article in *The New Yorker,* however, the review blithely ignored the fact that Tina's husband had been unflatteringly displayed in the Shawcross biography, choosing simply to savage its author for being overly well disposed toward Murdoch.

"She should have acknowledged the relationship—'Harold Evans, who is the husband of the editor' should have been in the piece," Shawcross insisted years later. In vain did Tina deny animosity toward Murdoch or Shawcross for trashing Harry. Few believed such protestations. David Cornwell (the real name of the spy novelist John le Carré) also entered the fray.

"Within weeks of taking over *The New Yorker,* you have sent up a signal to say that you will import English standards of malice and inaccuracy," he wrote Tina. "New York doesn't need them and funnily enough, the Brits don't either." Le Carré then warned against "the entry of the degenerate British standards of journalism."

Such protests about a British invasion swiftly multiplied. The work of Tina's old boyfriend Martin Amis and her Oxford friend the novelist Julian Barnes became staples of the new *New Yorker.* "One thing that would make America better is if all British journalists were forcibly repatriated to England," said Jamaica Kincaid, who found herself increasingly alienated from the magazine. "They are a horrible curse on our country. They, first of all, are completely undemocratic. They bring this chatty nonsense. They can't write. Martin Amis is a *terrible* writer. Then she brings over Chancellor, a man who knew *nothing* about America, and inflicts him on us. . . ."

But how valuable were these American writers to *The New Yorker,* really, Tina wondered. "Huh! These *American* journalists— so conceited!" she would grumble, albeit only within earshot of her compatriots. American writers gave themselves such grand airs, they were forever lecturing their bosses, and they had no notions of deference. British journalists were fortunately more malleable. "Because they are superficial and quick," one of them explained. "And they don't have airs. They can't afford to. They are a despised section of the population."

It wasn't only this segment of her native land that tugged at Tina. "Oh England, I miss it so!" she would erupt, dwelling on odd evocative details: the unmown grass; the coziness. "You know, Harry and I—we must have a holiday in England!" In 1992, they had tried, really tried, said Tina, even going so far as to rent an old mill house in Oxfordshire.

And yet, none of her listeners put much faith in these periodic bouts of yearning for the home country. The rented Oxfordshire house remained resolutely empty; Tina and her family ended up spending their vacation in Montana. Besides, it was felt, Tina needed to operate on a vaster and more variegated plain. "I would never go back," staffers heard that she once said. "There are no Jews in Britain."

Nonetheless, she needed England, the welcoming comfort and dependability of it, in the same way certain offspring persist in seeking, long after childhood, the beaming approval of a parent. In her second year at *The New Yorker,* she brought a trove of her most treasured finds to Britain's Cheltenham Arts Festival: John Lahr, Sidney Blumenthal, David Remnick, and Christopher Buckley. There, the last three were asked to debate a group of *Daily Telegraph* journalists. It was certainly a novel experience, as Lahr discovered. "If you are on Tina's team, you felt very much like Mae West with her muscle men," he said. "You stood behind her."

The subject of the debate was "The Sixties Should Never Have Happened," and the new *New Yorker* crowd drew the long straw, arguing, significantly, that the sixties were in fact a boon to all mankind. The *Telegraph* participants felt so defeated that they never showed up at the celebratory dinner. Tina walked in, elated, with a brief announcement honoring the competitiveness and vulgarity culled from her years in foreign parts.

"We kicked ass and took names!"

Her trips to the home country, her reliance on her compatriots to provide counterpoint, debate, and fodder for her magazine were, in effect, her public armor. If they were not *New Yorker*-ish, they were at least proof that she was no barbarian within the gates, but a friend of men of letters. Of course there was also another side to her, as became evident when the first Tina issue was published. On the cover of the genteel *New Yorker* was a drawing of a hansom cab, and inside it, a punk rocker with a purple Mohawk haircut. That punk, it was generally conceded, was a stand-in for Tina, defiant, vulnerable, itching for change. Any change.

In quite another way, the Washington writer Sidney Blumenthal, a friend of the Clintons, whom he viewed most tenderly, was also a sort of armor. "The facilitator of Tina's vision," the writer Peter Boyer thought. "Tina really liked to get in that door." Not that she understood particularly well where any door would lead. At the January 1993 Clinton inaugural, Tina had importuned everyone, desperate to discover which of the mobbed parties Jacqueline Onassis might attend, an unlikely social event for someone of her stature.

Boyer had been one of the few asked to follow Tina from *Vanity Fair* to her new perch, so he understood her pretty well. At *Vanity Fair*, Tina had had special editors at her disposal whose sole function was to grease the publication's access to the power-wielders on both coasts. At *The New Yorker*, although there were certainly editors with this function, the chore was increasingly shouldered by select writers. In this sense, Blumenthal, with his reverence for the presidential couple, was ideal. He met with Hillary Clinton once a month at the White House and he could get Tina the special invitations she required. He would end up hosting a party for Tina and the future British prime minister, Tony Blair, on whom Tina and Harry had specific designs, and he had, according to a British newspaper, informally introduced the Blairs to the Clintons. Blumenthal was Tina's ambassador to Clintonia. In fact, *The Washington Post* suggested in 1994 that his political column should be renamed "In the Tank."

Naturally, there were those who worried about Blumenthal's closeness to the White House—and worse, entertained serious doubts about where his loyalties lay. Jeffrey Toobin, whose first piece for the magazine was on Health and Human Services Secretary Donna Shalala, discovered that right before his article was to appear, Blumenthal had gone to the boss to complain about the piece: Toobin simply didn't *understand* Shalala.

"The White House knew a lot about what *The New Yorker* was doing because of Sidney—that was the assumption of my colleagues," said Boyer. It was also his assumption. In the course of probing the White House Travelgate scandal, which involved scrutiny of the Clintons' close friends Harry Thomason and Linda Bloodworth-Thomason, Boyer gave the couple a call. As it turned out, they were already fully apprised.

"I spoke with one of the Thomasons, who told me they heard I was working on a hatchet job and they have been warned by their friend Sidney to stay clear of this," Boyer recalled. It was a deeply troubling piece of news. After all, if the couple had been told by another staffer that a "hatchet job" was in the works, they might, once the article appeared, consider suing for libel. At the behest of his editor, John Bennet, Boyer wrote a memo complaining about Blumenthal to Tina. Blumenthal's editor, Jeffrey Frank, called the Thomasons inquiring if the writer had tipped them off; they denied it. So, for that matter, did Blumenthal.

However, in short order, said Boyer, the magazine realized that Bob Bennett, a lawyer for the Clintons, had been hired to represent the Thomasons. A threatening letter was duly dispatched, warning that Bennett's clients knew a hatchet job was in the works. There was no doubt in Boyer's mind that it was an attempt to get *The New Yorker* to back down on the article. It didn't, and in the end Bennett phoned Boyer to praise the piece.

But the worst of it was not Bennett, Boyer decided, but that "he had been aided by an employee of the magazine. That is my gripe with Sidney—was my gripe. He was wearing the habiliments of a journalist working on *my* magazine. It was an utterly inappropriate behind-the-scenes slither." Blumenthal's response to that was cursory. "Peter Boyer spread all sorts of apocryphal stories about me, and I don't know what his motive is," he said. Beyond this, he refused comment.

In July 1994, Blumenthal was out of his columnist's position, but remained on the magazine, albeit not working out of its Washington office. His replacement, Michael Kelly, insisted on this before taking the job. Even in his absence, phone calls continued to come twice a week from the first lady to Blumenthal. "Her incompetent staff couldn't get it through their heads that he wasn't in the office any longer, and we would give them his home number," it would later be recalled. "We went through this ritual every week."

How could Tina bring herself to part with such a valuable employee?

There were those on *The New Yorker*, good friends, who could never manage to understand why she kept Blumenthal on; but Boyer, for one, understood her motives. Tina wanted to possess Washington in the same exhaustive way that *Vanity Fair* had, under her aegis, colonized Hollywood. And the Clintons, after all, were Hollywood, in a way. They possessed huge potential, not necessarily for the benefit of the country, but *story* potential. "Great new soap opera," Boyer would call it. "She had a great intuition about our business and what was going to become an epic yarn." In however raggedy a fashion, Blumenthal, because of his access, could help spin that yarn.

Of course, "it was a diminishing of our politics to view it as entertainment." But that was Tina. She had, as a very close ally observed, "no interest in Washington and she is afraid of it, because she doesn't know it." She had never cared in a deeply personal way about American politics. For that matter, despite her strong Yankee temperament, she had never cared much about America.

"I don't think Tina likes America," Harry was told, shortly after his wife took over *The New Yorker.*

"Of course not," he replied. "She's never been here."

What he meant, his listener realized, was that Tina possessed a strange, errant conception of the United States. She was invariably taken around Manhattan by limo and was barely aware of the rest of the country, Los Angeles excepted. "You know, Tina invented a country that was called Trans-Atlantica, and it had all of the virtues and none of the vices of England or America," Harry once said wistfully. He would have liked to live there. Tina already did.

She was entertainment. She was theater, film, Trans-Atlantica. That was what she was born into and how she had begun. She could never really change.

And yet, there was an interesting part of her, during those first years anyway, a cerebral side about which, as Harry once observed, she was "more shy." This was the other Tina: the one who occasionally seemed to perform acts of penance for her crasser, messier parts. In 1993, she published Janet Malcolm's impressive and lengthy distillation of the lives of the poets Sylvia Plath and Ted Hughes—just the sort of literary jolt *The New Yorker* needed. Readers could also immerse themselves in two distinct but engrossing pieces on AIDS or, alternatively, the work of Philip Gourevitch, who traveled through Rwanda to write about genocide. If Tina Brown was perceived in certain circles as the Antichrist just then, she was at the beginning at least only a spotty Antichrist: one of considerable flair and breadth of interest. How long these qualities might prevail over the rest of her was another matter. But there was little doubt about her abilities. "I think she saved the magazine," said one of her editors.

Tina's showbiz side, however, provided unanticipated bonuses at times for the wilted magazine. Steve Florio, its publisher, would host a luncheon for perhaps three hundred potential advertisers out in Detroit, and then Tina would get up and talk about her "vision" for the magazine. "She was kind of the Madonna of publishing and people wanted to meet her," one of those assembled would later remember. The head of Ford's advertising department would thrill to her presence. Who wouldn't? "She went at it with great passion. She was funny and charming and at the height of her popularity. She knew what she wanted to do with *The New Yorker*."

Within four years, the magazine attracted 140,000 new subscribers, bringing it to a circulation of 868,851. But there was a problem. Subscriptions were deeply discounted. Initially, new subscribers to Tina's *New Yorker* could get it for beggarly rates: just $16 a year, or about 32 cents an issue. This cost the magazine millions, although within four years rates rose 25 percent. The number of annual ad pages hovered around 2,200. At the height of *The New Yorker*'s commercial success, which was in 1966, it had 6,143 ad pages. Under publisher Steve Florio and later his brother Tom Florio, the publication was bleeding money—roughly $20 million and $25 million *a year* during Tina's first two years. Then it improved. Somewhat.

But Si Newhouse didn't run a public empire; there were no anxious shareholders clamoring for profits. And he patently adored Tina. She had utterly transformed the image of the short, withdrawn publishing mogul. Newhouse was now the stuff of gossip columns, a corporate sugar daddy who backed pretty, ambitious British women and their magazines, a potential source of quotations (which, however, he hardly ever gave). To what extent Tina reciprocated this affection is open to question. Certainly, she appreciated aspects of him. A phone call to Si was, in the early days at least, all it took for Tina to get what she wanted.

"That's what I like about Si. He doesn't get muddled, he acts with spontaneity," she told an editor right after she got Newhouse's consent to run a fiction issue. It was exactly the sort of gesture that would impress her critics, she hoped. "Anybody else, I would have had to have a meeting. I would have had to figure out what the advertising would be."

In Newhouse's presence, the cold shoulder and icy distance that even closest friends and treasured employees could periodically, and always without warning, expect from her evaporated utterly, replaced by smiling animation, volubility. "But she was quite detached in her attitude toward him," Chancellor observed. Like her husband, Tina knew who really owned the vast domains over which she and Harry ostensibly reigned, knew with what swiftness such cherished territory could be demolished or abandoned. They were simply well-paid celebrity squatters.

Newhouse, whose empire was by then worth an estimated $11 billion and whose dreams were sometimes antithetical—or at least impervious—to the bottom line, had bought *The New Yorker* from more touching motives: a yearning to bask in the great publication's literary prestige. That desire obscured more traditional corporate values. "You know, when Si bought *The New Yorker* in 1985, I don't think he realized what kind of financial shape the company was in," a Condé Nast executive would later recall.

And so Tina wasn't weighted, initially at least, by the primacy of hoarding pennies, as she certainly would have been in any other shriveling magazine. In fact, a Condé Nast executive found her "pretty good about budgets." Nonetheless, she could be generous. Spurned old-timers departed with generous severance packages. Newcomers enjoyed big salaries; among them, her longtime editor David Kuhn, who had not been widely loved at *Vanity Fair* but was famous for his loyalty to Tina.

Nor was she overburdened by the truth—at least not to the extent of feeling compelled to lighten the load by releasing to the media the full extent of *The New Yorker*'s fiscal anguish. TINA BROWN: *NEW YORKER* NEAR PROFIT, the *New York Post* informed its readers in August 1996; and indeed, in the first paragraph of the article, Tina was full of assurances that the magazine would turn a profit "by the end of next year." By her side was her second publisher, Tom Florio (who had replaced his brother), explaining that ad revenue was up about 26 percent "since Tina came in."

True, mistakes had been made, Florio conceded: "In the past, many people in this industry treated Tina a bit like a schoolgirl, they wouldn't show her the business side of publishing. But we did. . . ." Editorial costs had been reduced by 15 percent since 1992; even the car service bill was down "sharply." Newhouse, Florio declared, was pleased.

But Tina was not. She regarded both Florio brothers with equal disdain, but was especially indiscreet about Tom, whose abilities she belittled to subordinates. Within publishing circles, it was whispered that she had campaigned for her old *Vanity Fair* publisher Ron Galotti to replace him. Privately, the air was thick with quarrels between her and Florio, disputes about the costs of the paper, the publicity and parties. There were fights about how much the magazine should charge for ads. Tina wanted more of them and didn't care how deeply discounted they had to be. Their mere existence, fluffing up the magazine, was emblematic of her success as an editor. Worst of all, despite

JUDY BACHRACH

Tina's brave fiscal forecasts, *The New Yorker* was very far from profitable, as she well knew. By 1996, the year she declared imminent victory to the *Post,* it was still losing well over $10 million a year.

Who could blame her for aching for old England, for armor, for loyalists? Never, in her unimpeachably successful career, had any goal remained so distant from her grasp. She was going home every evening at five-thirty to attend to her children, but writers and editors would routinely receive faxes at 1:00 A.M. from her home. And Tina, in turn, would think nothing of demanding that a writer fax her the next morning at her doctor's office. "Whenever I saw Tina, she looked really unhappy, really tense," one of her employees said. "I always felt somehow that *The New Yorker* was suborning her."

What exactly was preying on her? "People were wondering if there was something going on between her and Harry," said James Wolcott. "But nobody really knew anything."

Certainly, she had become brusquer, more remote in her new venue. "More inflexible," as Fredric Dannen, who followed her to *The New Yorker,* observed. "*Vanity Fair* was a small place. The door was open, you could walk into her office, she was accessible. *The New Yorker* was a big place." With David Kuhn at her side—"her Haldeman," thought Dannen—the atmosphere altered significantly. Kuhn's role, too, had changed since his *Vanity Fair* days. Where once he was merely one of Tina's editors, now he acted as her double, her echo.

Few doubted that Kuhn spoke for Tina, parroting her every command, no matter how hopeless or absurd. "Tina wants to know, what happened to the cunt quote? She loved that cunt quote," Kuhn demanded in a call to John Seabrook. In an early 1998 draft of a story, the writer had attributed that epithet to David Geffen, who had used it to describe, in fairly jocular fashion, Ahmet Ertegun, the founder of Atlantic Records. But a transcript of Seabrook's tape somehow or other failed to contain that specific word, and a *New Yorker* fact-checker had therefore deleted it.

Kuhn had reason to pine for the word's reinstatement—a desire that remained, as things turned out, resolutely unfulfilled, owing to its mysterious disappearance. This was provoking. Tina's *New Yorker* was now supposed to be, among other things, a repository for all the risqué language that had never before made it into the magazine.

So this was the new Tina. In her zeal to remodel the magazine, and her worries about the consequences of such a venture, she had little time—for anything. Surrounded as she was by sycophants, publicists, writers nervous about their longevity, she was increasingly clueless. "Tina's problem was she never became her own person at *The New Yorker*," one editor remarked. "She never preserved the old *New Yorker*, although she felt to a great extent bound by tradition. And, at the same time, she was so terrified of making mistakes that she never created her own *New Yorker*."

Wolcott, for his part, could "see her develop real tunnel vision, she didn't watch TV, she didn't know contemporary culture. So everything that was coming to her was funneled into her from the outside. It was like she had no interests. She had no hobbies. No safety valves. That was part of it. But part of it was also this sense—*Once again I have to save the magazine.*"

The magazine needed spice to be saved, she was certain. And yet every time she gave it a sprinkling—an April 1995 cover cartoon of the Easter bunny crucified on a tax form, which enraged not only the Catholic Church but a number of Tina's own employees; another showing two male sailors smooching on V-J Day; a third, by the cartoonist Art Spiegelman, depicting a Hasidic man embracing a black woman—all she caught was hell. Not that she had anything much against hell.

"You're Jewish, aren't you?" she asked Dan Menaker, one of her fiction editors.

"Well, I'm only half-Jewish," he corrected her.

"Well, what do you think of this?" Tina showed him the Spiegelman cover of the interracial couple, soon to be published.

Menaker glanced at the Hasid. "Well, if he marries her, he'll be cast out of his community, you know that."

"No, I didn't know that. Will I get in trouble?"

"Yes," said Menaker. "But that's what you want, isn't it?"

By 1994, Menaker was gone from *The New Yorker*. Harry Evans, of all people, had phoned him one day, requesting that he come by for an interview at Random House, but with no clear notion of what title he should give him at the publishing company. "I know it's going to be difficult for you to leave after so many years at *The New Yorker*," said Harry. "Has it been six or seven?"

"No, it's been twenty-six," said Menaker, amazed that his would-be boss hadn't done his homework—startled, in fact, by the entire notion of a husband's decision to hire his wife's employee. Of course, he figured that there had been private discussions between the two of them about the proposed job at Random House, but the odd thing was that Tina never mentioned a word about it, until broached on the subject.

There were good reasons for him to leave, Menaker felt. Fiction at *The New Yorker* was diminished, a half-starved second-class citizen at the back of the book. Tina no longer even read it, although she had done so at first. Menaker had enjoyed her early comments. "They were astute in an amateurish sort of way—but that's what you want," Menaker said. She loved the superb short story writer Alice Munro, putting her impressive "The Albanian Virgin," which ran almost forty columns, smack in the middle of the first fiction issue. You couldn't fault her literary taste; not that.

On the other hand, Menaker decided after he accepted Harry's job offer, he hadn't really left *The New Yorker*. It had left him. Long before he ever walked out of the building, the magazine he knew had disappeared. Perhaps, given the nature of Tina, that was inevitable. "Now I get to be the mistress instead of the wife," she scribbled on a cartoon tendered to Menaker at his good-bye party—meaning, he felt, now their relationship would no longer be one of difficult obligation but pure pleasure.

Anyway, this shuttling of employees between husband and wife was nothing new. Michael Kelly, Tina's new Washington columnist, had earlier written a book on the Gulf War for Harry at Random House, where his editor, Sharon Delano, had found refuge after being exiled by Tina from *Vanity Fair.* Joe Klein, after writing the best-seller *Primary Colors* for Random House, was hired by Tina, also as a political analyst. The editor Jeffrey Frank was talking to Harry at Random House, only to find himself recommended to Harry's wife. The former prosecutor Jeffrey Toobin, who wrote consistently about the O.J. Simpson trial for Tina, turned his research into a book for Harry. The British art connoisseur and Picasso biographer John Richardson delivered his work to both shops. So did Christopher Buckley, whose comic novel *Thank You for Smoking* was fêted by a 1995 Random House party in which smoke machines that were set up for ambience were tripped off, bringing in the Washington, D.C., fire department. Of the twenty-six books that were excerpted or reproduced whole in *The New Yorker* during 1996, more than half were from Random House.

"Synergy," the popular press dubbed the relationship between the two halves of the power couple. But among themselves, those who knew Tina recognized what provoked this great fusion. Fear.

"Tina is entirely dependent on Harry," an especially prominent *New Yorker* writer explained in those days, in an unguarded moment. "Both for psychological support and for help in what she was doing. Because she is insecure about it. She is not really experienced, and he is. Now he is sort of eclectic and has a limited attention span. The Random House–*New Yorker* relationships are getting closer and closer and more corporate-like, as far as I can see."

But the upshot of this synergy was something more invasive, far-reaching, and invidious within the network of opinion molders. By the mid-nineties, the number of people who owed dual allegiance, at times dual paychecks, to Tina and Harry was practically incalculable.

As a result, the Brown-Evans media coverage was almost invariably pleasing and tastefully wrought, shot through with such recurrent phrases as "premier socializers" and even "glitterary." Whatever resentments Tina and her husband incurred, either singly or as a couple, were generally buried beneath the ambitions of any given writer. Case-hardened journalists who wouldn't think twice about shredding a U.S. president to pieces or insulting his wife, laid down their weapons and stilled their tongues. After all, how many reporters, aside from Sidney Blumenthal, were likely to find employment in the White House? Where else might they double their current salaries? Tina herself would refer to her largesse with unusual candor when discussing a rare critic, Andrew Sullivan, who had the temerity to lash out. "He's mad at me because he's the only writer at *The New Republic* that I never approached," she said.

It was only in September 1996, when Tina invited Dick Morris to breakfast with seventy advertisers, staff writers, and editors at *The New Yorker,* that for the first time, a startling onslaught of criticism erupted. Despite Tina's determination to attract ads at any price, the idea of selecting Morris as bait demonstrated a breathtaking lack of judgment. A trusted Clinton adviser—until it was revealed that he consorted with a prostitute (he sucked her toes for $200 an hour, she claimed to the *Star,* and permitted her to eavesdrop on a phone conversation with the president)—Morris represented everything the magazine had a long tradition of shunning. Vulgarity, treachery, bad form.

"What on earth is Morris doing here, and why would any vaguely respectable magazine even stoop to dangling him as a bauble to attract advertisers?" thundered John Leo in *U.S. News & World Report.* "Morris betrays his wife with a hooker. The hooker betrays Morris to the *Star.*"

JUDY BACHRACH

"Ms. Brown bestowed literary legitimacy—or whatever literary legitimacy *The New Yorker* has left to bestow—on Mr. Morris . . . ," wrote the *New York Times* columnist Maureen Dowd that same month. "We live in a time when infamy sells. . . . There is no honor, no reticence, no loyalty."

It was by no means the first time Dowd had attacked the Evanses: Harry's publishing decisions had earlier come under her scrutiny, after which the columnist was made to see the error of her ways. In May 1996, she was skewered in a long article by James Wolcott in *The New Yorker,* derided as "increasingly kittenish. . . . She rubs up against the reader's leg. Her work lacks any sense of social dimension. . . ."

Such observations, however heartfelt, were by no means spontaneous. Tina had walked up to Wolcott at a Christmas party. "She did ask me to do a piece on Maureen Dowd," he affirmed. "And I said, 'Sure!' because it was something I was thinking about anyway."

"A teensy bit of payback," was the verdict of a *New Yorker* editor.

As for John Leo, he was phoned by his boss Mort Zuckerman before the column appeared. "I'm not going to censor your column because I don't do that," Zuckerman promised, referring to an agreement the two had made the day Leo was hired. "But would you mind if I gave Harry a heads-up?"

"He's your friend," agreed Leo. And sure enough, he got a call from Harry about the forthcoming column. "He wanted me to change it or drop it," said Leo.

Harry's motives here were not merely to protect his wife. Synergy was once again at work. Tina wasn't the only one interested in Morris's moneymaking possibilities. Random House had agreed to publish a book by him on the Clinton presidency, months before the president himself was apprised of the matter—or Morris's intimate life had been unearthed by the tabloids. "Before a toe had been sucked," in Harry's unfelicitous phrase.

But once the servicing of those toes became public, Morris ended up, courtesy of Harry, with an even grander number of digits: $2.5 million for a memoir entitled *Behind the Oval Office.* "I mean, not only did Harry pay too much for Dick Morris's memoirs, he then—without needing to—paid even *more* to Dick Morris," explained a Random House editor. Word was that the reckless Clinton adviser, now that he was hot, had been considering marketing the book elsewhere. "Welcome to public morality 1996," wrote John Leo, whose column was neither changed nor dropped.

244

Publicly, Harry maintained a posture of resolute defiance, calling this unaccustomed rash of opprobrium "cultural fascism." He simply could not understand the fuss over a public man's private life; that was the sum of the flap over Morris, as far as he was concerned. "We're all sex addicts, for God's sake!" he consoled Morris. Moreover, the notion that he was working in collusion with his wife was, he said, ridiculous.

"There are people who don't understand . . . that it's possible to be in love with a woman, to be married to her, to see her every day, to have her children and yet regard her in the journalistic area as a competitor," he said. "Or put it a different way, if there's one thing in the world that you would not do for your wife, it is something that would damage your career."

But he *had* wrought damage with this public embrace of Morris. They both had. Privately, the couple's friends agreed, Harry was severely shaken by such mass indignation. In America, his chosen country, he was perceived as the publisher of a dirtbag, a purveyor of shameful, and shamefully overpriced, memoirs. And he was, more than ever, Tina's husband. As Harry told an Oxford crowd on a trip back to England, he sometimes felt like the *New Yorker* cartoon of a cocktail party where the wife urges her abashed husband, *Tell them who you were, Henry. Tell them who you were.*

If only the Morris book had been a *succès d'estime,* Harry, if not his bosses, could have lived with whatever financial losses it incurred. Or had it been a tell-all blockbuster, then the criticism wouldn't have mattered quite so much, and Harry might easily have ridden out this shocking and completely unexpected wave of derision. But even the Random House sales force wasn't behind the book. It was estimated that, given its audacious advance, *Behind the Oval Office* would have to sell 500,000 copies to break even. Morris, alas, had delivered exactly what Harry promised, "a book about politics and policy, not sex," and the sales were so pitiful that even the best marketer—that was Harry—couldn't spin. "Random House may have lost somewhere close to $1.5 million," it was estimated by one reporter. It was a terrible year for the book industry all around. In 1996, hardback sales were down and returns of unsold books were way up. Harry's lofty advances stoked the general conflagration.

Such talk infuriated Harry. "Almost every single thing is judged by money, money, money, money, money, money, money," he barked at Suzanna Andrews of *New York* magazine when she had the nerve to broach the subject of the sales of Dick Morris's book. He would have preferred the press to be interested in "literature and the value of the word."

But just how interested was Harry in literature? His biggest score was Colin Powell's 1995 autobiography, *My American Journey,* for which the former chairman of the Joint Chiefs of Staff (and future secretary of state) received an advance of $6.5 million and a Random House–financed tour of the nation, which fueled speculation of a presidential bid. That made money. It also made great copy—for a while, although Maureen Dowd attempted to throw a damper on the interesting alliance between commerce and a potential presidential bid. "Don't worry about a conflict of interest," she wrote in the *Times.* "What's good for Random House is good for the United States." But such carping was barely audible over the din of adoration. A New York lunch for over one hundred people honoring Powell brought out the television tycoon Barry Diller, Si and Victoria Newhouse, Bob Woodward, Barbara Walters, Bianca Jagger, and Jessye Norman. "Electrified" was how gossip columnist Liz Smith, who always managed to settle herself in Harry's corner, described him at this gathering. The very asparagus served at lunch was "beautifully bound." As for the book, after Powell decided not to run for president, sales dropped.

Still, to some extent, what Harry said about himself was true. He was not immune to "the value of the word," and had a knack for communicating that significance to others. In 1992, the three imprints he oversaw had nineteen books on the best-seller list, of which eleven were signed under his aegis. *A Civil Action,* a book by Jonathan Harr about a crusading lawyer, insolent polluters, and leukemia victims, received, despite its initially dreary sales, an insistent push from Harry, who was convinced it would be a hit. "He said, 'You've done your job—now it's our time to do ours,' " Harr said. Four months later, the company republished the book, replacing its dull jacket with a more compelling one; copies were given away, and ultimately it was made into a film starring John Travolta. Such acts were simply its due, the likely fate of any project that became known as "Harry's baby." In the same way, John Berendt's *Midnight in the Garden of Good and Evil,* although the prize pet of editor Ann Godoff, also received, at Harry's urging, an arresting jacket that contributed to its success. Harry regarded Godoff with genuine admiration and promoted her ambitions—for quite a while.

However, books in which he evinced little interest, specifically upscale fiction, were treated by him with all the expert disregard of which Harry accused the press. *CivilWarLand in Bad Decline,* a group of brilliant short stories by George Saunders, got very short shrift, to the disappointment of the author's in-house admirers. "It was the kind of thing that would have appealed to the critics, and it didn't need much of a push," said one employee. "Jay McInerny called it the best thing since Barry Hannah's *Airships.*"

Random House did publish, and fairly good-naturedly too, a very funny novel by Harry's old colleague Philip Norman called *Everyone's Gone to the Moon.* In it, a British editor of considerable ambition is wooed by an inscrutable young woman with literary yearnings and a pronounced knack for sexual advancement. It escaped no one's notice that these characters bore a resemblance to Harry in the old days, and the lady who deftly acquired him. "There is some verisimilitude," Harry acknowledged in a gracious note to Norman. "The characters pop out of the page."

To some degree, however, Harry concentrated on precisely the kinds of books that were bought mainly to make "money, money, money, money, money, money." When his interest was piqued, he spared no effort to acquire them, however meretricious. From the first, he craved Madonna's tome on sex.

"He was just totally obsessed with Madonna. Harry is just obsessed by ballsy women," said one Random House editor whose orders were "to find out every little detail . . . all that could be found out about Madonna." To accomplish this, the editor found himself contacting a handsome man on whom the singer evidently had designs. "This guy kept all his phone messages from Madonna, and he would play them for me, and I would report them to Harry."

The purpose of this hopeless mission ultimately failed: the Madonna book on sex ended up in the arms of Warner Books. But the more immediate result was, in its own way, almost as impressive. Harry called his subordinate for two months regularly—with a focus and an application that would never be repeated. "The whole phenomenon was his titillating desire . . . ," the editor said. "What could be a greater coup than Harry on the arm of Madonna? It was kind of like a wet dream."

The undiluted concentration expended on this venture was rare enough. As Peter Gethers, who ran Villard, the Random House subsidiary, put it, Harry had "a hysterical personality. He carries hysteria with him. Frantic. He has a very short attention span." As usual, subordinates observed, he was moving "a million miles a minute." The journalist Henry Porter observed in an article in *The Guardian* that "during our talk, he suddenly got up and wandered out of the room. . . . I didn't want to lose him so I followed.

" 'I'm going to have a pee,' he said somewhat testily."

This perpetual frenzy—"He's here, there, somewhere else"—was the description of Harry's daily trajectory, an echo of the activity he used to immerse himself in during his newspaper days in England. Only at Random House there was less tolerance for galloping executives. "People aren't used to the fact that publishing is a very stodgy, boring profession," said Gethers. Certainly, Harry seemed destined to defeat that image. Rumors of his famous flirtatiousness abounded. There were, it was said, two women whom he admired. One of them, Helen Morris, an attractive grandniece of Edith Wharton and editor of the promotional company magazine *At Random,* would confide to a colleague that she had deflected Harry's attentions. A second rumor concerned a younger woman, widely regarded within the company as "a pain in the ass." The gossip eventually made its way to Harry himself, who appeared eager to discuss it with one of his top editors.

"Have you heard what they're saying around the office? That I'm fucking"—and here Harry mentioned the name of the young woman with whom he had been widely linked. "Can you imagine anything so preposterous?"

"Yeah, Harry. Preposterous," agreed the editor. Privately, however, he felt that the display of outrage was manufactured. "He wanted me specially to know about this, though."

Meanwhile, there were bouts of evaporating attention and a yawning distance from matters at hand. "I was in Harry's office at a meeting, and I was looking at his desk, at the in-tray, where my father's book was—Harry had published my father's book," recalled a British executive whose father was a well-known dignitary. "I said, 'I see you have my father's jacket there. It looks really great.'

"And Harry says, 'Why? Is your father a jacket designer?' The man actually thinks my father is a *tailor.*"

The writer Suzanna Andrews, on a visit to Random House, discovered that President Clinton's former national security adviser Anthony Lake was also on the premises—in fact, sitting in Harry's office for forty-five minutes, twiddling his thumbs. Lake himself wasn't in the least offended by the experience. But Andrews was startled. "He had arrived thinking he had an appointment with Harry to talk about a book. And Harry wasn't there," she said. "It was an embarrassment. He wasn't there at all."

Indeed, at times it seemed as if the old Harry had been hijacked. In his place was someone of borrowed sensibilities and blunted intellect. The disastrously expensive Brando book, which ignored essential parts of the star's life (including the guilty plea of his son, Christian, on manslaughter charges), was one example. "Everybody knew it was bad at the time. That book had been circulated before Harry bought it—I mean, people had seen it and didn't cough up the dough," said Gethers. "So when he came in and bought it, that was a surprise. And people always do that when they come in because they want to make a splash. It's just that the stakes were a lot higher with Harry. He definitely escalated prices."

Harry protested that most of the advance from *Brando: Songs My Mother Taught Me* had been recouped by sales of the rights to foreign publications, book clubs, and paperbacks. Some within the company believed that, but word persisted that foreign rights had earned but a fraction of the advance. "I'm sure they lost three to four million on that book," a former Random House employee would later say. "When you make that kind of mistake, that's your whole year, no matter what else you publish. It will sink your profit line for the whole year."

And so Harry's hold on the company grew ever more tenuous. That became evident in 1996 when a book by Mary Schiavo, the former inspector general of the Department of Transportation, and a brave and harsh critic of both the Federal Aviation Administration and careless airlines, was bought for $600,000. *Flying Blind, Flying Safe*, it was called. "We thought it would be one of those celebrity-driven public affairs books we do so well at Random House," said a champion of the book.

As celebrities go, Schiavo was relatively new. But David Rosenthal, the Villard publisher who agreed to purchase her book, was certain of its success. Harry, too, was supportive; he thought the book "promotable," and its advance justified. On the other hand, others in the office were not so optimistic. "That was the year of Incomprehensible Decisions—I could never fathom any of it," said a top editor. "We have to fly, and we certainly don't want to know how dangerous it is. So that was a book no one would buy."

That was also, as it happened, the surprise verdict of Alberto Vitale, CEO of Random House. "This is a fucking disaster! No one wants an airline safety book," Vitale said.

In vain was he told that having made the deal, the company couldn't very well unmake it; that was unheard of in publishing. Vitale was adamant; he was going to retain "fiscal authority" over the advance. The offer was quickly rescinded and Random House was threatened by Schiavo's agent, Suzanne Gluck of ICM, who said she would never do business with them again.

So there were decided limits being imposed on Harry. His independence was being thwarted from the top. It was considered a warning sign.

And those who owed him allegiance—where were they? The synergy on which Tina and Harry had for so long counted was beginning to backfire; the degree of indebtedness among some of their friends and subordinates diminishing. Jeffrey Toobin, for example, became seriously unnerved when he discovered in 1996 that his O.J. Simpson book, *The Run of His Life*, was going to encounter serious competition *within* his chosen publishing house. Lawrence Schiller, an author of dubious credentials (he had earlier written Simpson's self-serving best-seller, *I Want to Tell You*), was co-writing yet another book on O.J., and like Toobin's work, it was destined for Random House. Or such was the common wisdom.

Yet, Toobin told friends, every time he and his editor, Ann Godoff, approached Harry on the matter, he would assure them he was not going to publish Schiller. The Schiller project was "dead . . . not viable." Eventually, Toobin learned that the dead had been mysteriously brought back to life. Harry explained he simply wanted to control the second book's timing, as indeed he did. One month after Toobin's book appeared (it was a best-seller), Schiller's *American Tragedy* popped up under the Random House label, much to Toobin's disgust.

John Richardson, a friend to both Harry and Tina, who was in the process of writing a four-volume work on Picasso, discovered around volume two that Norman Mailer was working on a rival book on the same subject for Random House—a book that drew on some of Richardson's own insights. He couldn't believe it. Mailer, of all people! "I think of Norman as the Leroy Neiman of American literature," he said. "Neiman does paintings of prizefights and horse-racing things, very brightly colored with a palate knife. Every dentist's office all over the Midwest has one." Mailer's book was ultimately published by Atlantic Monthly Press.

As bad, Richardson decided, was the scathing review Adam Gopnik of *The New Yorker* gave him in December 1996 on the publication of volume two of the Picasso biography. Richardson had contributed to the magazine, and before that, to Tina's *Vanity Fair.* Indeed, the very week the bad review appeared, Tina and Harry were hosting a little party of eighteen in Richardson's honor—at his newly decorated apartment—to celebrate the publication of his book. It was not an event Tina was looking forward to, she informed a friend. She wondered if she might try to back out as hostess.

For his part, Richardson was wondering if he might back out as guest of honor in his own flat. He had the feeling, distinct if unprovable, that the reason *The New Yorker* had panned his book was to drive home a point to critics of the couple. Appearances to the contrary, Tina and Harry were not in collusion, the bad review would assure skeptics. A book published by Random House might well fall on hard times in Tina's shop. In fact, Tina said as much shortly before the Gopnik review appeared. "This is what I find funny, this idea of collusion," she told Eleanor Randolph of the *Los Angeles Times,* using the review of Richardson's book as a sterling example of her utter lack of complicity. Harry, she said, was "not going to like it."

And despite the parties and the power, increasingly Harry found himself isolated, the triumphant notes of the buzz he generated drowned out by bottom-line discord. "Alberto Vitale blamed Harry for what was going on; Harry blamed Alberto," it would later be remembered. "There was no interest on the part of Si or Alberto to keep Harry." Jason Epstein himself would later describe the friction between Vitale and Harry in similar terms. "The tension between them was horrible; you could just sense it," he told *New York* magazine.

In June 1997, Random House issued a press release announcing that Ann Godoff, Harry's erstwhile protégée and a prodigious selector of best-sellers, was being promoted from editorial director to editor in chief. That was not good news. Whatever allegiance Godoff may have once owed Harry had been sorely tested over time. "I'd rather sign authors with multiple books rather than one-shot celebrity authors," she would declare meaningfully some months later. "You can't sucker a reader." Godoff had no serious aversion to making news with her books, she declared. "But celebrity for celebrity's sake? I'd be pretty cautious." With such goals, she had won over Vitale, who was no friend of Harry Evans. Word spread that Harry had been asked to take an emeritus position as an editor at large twenty floors away from the action. Both Vitale and Harry vehemently denied it: "I have a three-year contract and I am very happy with my relations with everyone," he insisted to a reporter. But there had been for some time industry speculation that he was, in one way or another, going to leave his top job. "Harry knew what was coming, we all knew," a Random House editor would later say.

By November, it was all over. Around Random House, rumors flew that Vitale had had a word with the embattled executive; that Harry had been in fact pushed—or as the *New York Post* would describe it within a year, "pushed out." Epstein himself would later say, "Si had no choice" but to let Harry go, "because Alberto was running the company." There were variations on this: "Harold Evans . . . has jumped from Random House . . . ," the *Daily Telegraph* reported in London, "but the rumors in New York are that the push would not have been far behind." In any event, Harry was leaving. There had been, it was also said, considerable feuding between the newly promoted Ann Godoff and Harry over lines of authority. "The struggle had apparently continued right up to the timing of the resignation, with Random House pressing for an earlier announcement than the day before Thanksgiving," *The New York Times* reported.

For public consumption, events were cast in a somewhat different light. Officially, Harry had "just thought it was the right time to go" in order to indulge in "my original love affair with newsprint." Once again, the invaluable real estate and publishing magnate Mort Zuckerman, godfather to Harry's daughter, was riding to the rescue. But Harry was firm. "Mort Zuckerman has been pressing me to join him for ages," he insisted to one reporter. Since April, he told another. Harry was to return to *U.S. News & World Report;* he was also to improve another Zuckerman property, the New York *Daily News.* He was getting wonderful new titles. He was filled with untrammeled joy.

Nonetheless, it was hard going.

The very week of Harry's announcement, Toby Young, a young British journalist, was throwing a wrench into the publicity machine. "Harry is one of the grandmasters of spin, but even he had trouble persuading people that his new role as editorial director of Mort Zuckerman's publications is a step up," Young jeered in *The Spectator.* "Would anyone believe he had left voluntarily?" In fact, Young wrote, his prospects were slim: "The only person left for Harry to turn to was his old friend Mort Zuckerman."

Within a few months, Harry responded in a series of letters; these were followed by still another onslaught via his British lawyer, Theodore Goddard, citing a litany of alleged inaccuracies and brimming with outrage. *The Spectator* and Young were both put on notice: "The picture you paint of Mr. Evans is of a failure who has reached the end of the road. What you are telling your readers is that our client is a liar; that he is dishonest." Damages, unspecified, were demanded ("to be paid to a charity of Mr. Evans's choice"), along with legal fees, a correction, and most amazingly, a promise that the writer would never again cause either Harry or *Tina* to be "defamed, denigrated and ridiculed." Harry, in other words, was fashioning an all-purpose silencer.

This contretemps went on for weeks, went on, significantly, in Great Britain, where the libel laws were, as Harry well knew, infinitely more draconian than in the United States. Harry had spent a considerable amount of effort almost two decades earlier deploying lawyers against the British magazine *Private Eye,* finally demanding, as its editor Richard Ingrams recalled, "that neither he nor his wife Tina Brown should ever be mentioned in the magazine again." Toby Young was genuinely appalled by the possibility of a lawsuit. "For someone so closely identified with the virtues of American journalism . . . to do something which the First Amendment would prevent him from doing in the United States—it seems so flagrantly hypocritical," he said.

Who could doubt Harry's passion for the freedoms of the New World? Just ten years earlier, living in his beloved America, he had composed an ardent defense of an author sued for libel. In an editorial for *The New York Times,* he expressed his immense delight in the First Amendment: "As the Supreme Court has said, there is no such thing as a false idea, however pernicious an opinion may seem. . . ." In 1985, a jury ruled that *Time* magazine had not been guilty of malice or libel in a lawsuit brought by General Ariel Sharon, who would one day become the Israeli prime minister. Even though the jury foreman added that certain *Time* employees had "acted negligently and carelessly in reporting and verifying the information," Harry greeted the verdict with enthusiasm. "America rightly gives greater latitude than Britain for honest debate," he said. "The jury's verdict is a triumph of common sense: *Time*'s journalism was sloppy, but there is no doubt they believed what they said is true."

Now Harry proposed to muzzle a fellow journalist, and for good measure, any number of future opinions concerning him or his wife.

The First Amendment, no question about it, was a powerful shield that won Harry's unmitigated admiration—in America. It was simply his good fortune that in Britain the libel laws provided him with a sword.

He was in no mood to dispense with whatever weapon was at hand. Harry was sixty-nine when he ordered his lawyer to impale an impertinent young journalist and a magazine on a bunch of words. He was, yet again, out of a glamorous, powerful job, one that had given him so much of what he craved: respect, equal standing with his wife, a chance to mingle with celebrities. And he was, if not at the end of the road, at least slogging along, battered and much older, into the unknown.

Chapter 13

Appeasing the Gods

If Toby Young and others came to the conclusion that Harry was thumbing through the "Help Wanted" ads well before his announced departure from Random House, it was partly because of certain urgent social and financial signals he and his wife were perpetually sending to a British politician, Tony Blair. He might have plenty of jobs to hand out in short order once he became, as they correctly assumed, Britain's next prime minister. "Harry is playing for Britain now," a friend remarked, after observing him at a party in Blair's honor.

With at least one confidant back in England, Harry talked about becoming a kind of culture czar: rumors had already circulated that he might be named chairman of Britain's Arts Council. True, the attached salary was pitiful—$50,000, barely lunch money at Random House—but with a $250 million budget and the world of British culture at his feet, it might provide a soft landing after the setbacks and humiliations of his publishing years. Or if not the Arts Council, Harry's confidant was told, then "something important in the Blair government." Rumors of Harry's imminent ascendancy to this prestigious post, along with the possibility of a peerage, were duly floated—along with his dutiful denials.

"It's all bullshit, put a stake in it," said Harry in one breath. In the next, however, Britain's onetime preeminent newspaper editor was boasting that he was "now a card-carrying member" of the Labour Party.

Of course Blair was grateful for such support from across the

Atlantic. Who wouldn't be? At the April 1996 party for Blair thrown by Sidney Blumenthal at Tina's behest, Blair mentioned that back in his Oxford days, an invitation from Tina Brown was a sign that one had truly arrived. "I know this," he said, "because I never received one."

She had every intention of rectifying such an oversight. In September 1996, she and Harry were hosting a Labour lovefest at the Royalton bar in New York. "Tony Blair's Britain sounds an exciting place and I would like to spend a lot of time in it," Tina confided to a gathering that included Bianca Jagger. In February 1997, after Harry solicited money for the Labour Party at a fund-raiser held at the Century Club, where guests included Felix Rohatyn and Glenda Jackson, a letter made the rounds of British expatriates in the United States exhorting them to send yet more money to the Labour Party. It was signed by, among others, Harry Evans.

In June that same year, Tina was throwing a private dinner for her new best friends, the prime minister of Great Britain and his wife, Cherie. There were 150 people in attendance, among them Anjelica Huston and Lauren Hutton, Henry Kissinger (who lectured Blair about how to deal with Hong Kong), Jesse Jackson, Martin Scorsese, and the invaluable Mort Zuckerman.

"The New Camelot" was how Harry referred to Blair's government in his introductory remarks. But this was faint praise, compared to his review of Blair's qualities a month later. ". . . Tony Blair is getting what he deserves," Harry wrote in an impassioned column in the *Daily Telegraph*. "The mood in Britain, it seems to me, is in part a reflection of his own goodwill and grace, and in part a gratified astonishment that Mr. Blair's government might very well have the capability to do all the things it said it would do, and then some." Among Blair's probable triumphs, he told an audience on another occasion, "a press almost as free as the American."

Oddly, however, nothing ever came of these fond, insistent approaches, not for Harry. "Tina didn't want to leave New York and George was very happy in his school," said a friend of the couple. But it was also true that once comfortably settled, Blair's closest advisers somehow chose to ignore Harry, their benefactor. When approached on the matter of Harry's ambitions in the new regime, a close Blair ally instantly replied, "I can tell you he doesn't have a hope in hell of doing anything for the Blair government."

There were rumors, too, concerning Tina: according to the tabloids, she was destined to become Blair's ambassador to Washington. But these, alas, had even less substance. "I started that rumor. Absolutely," Toby Young would later confess. "So they would look bad when it didn't happen. I completely made it up."

Nonetheless, Tina remained loyal to the new prime minister, or perhaps it was simply loyalty to Harry that kept her perseveringly kind to a potential patron of whom the couple had not yet despaired. On the pages of *The New Yorker,* Blair received a welcome occasionally every bit as warm as the one Tina and Harry extended at their home. It was a new home, too, decorated in cautious floral fabrics, and located close by the old apartment, but far grander. Worth $3.7 million, it contained four bedrooms, a library, three maids' rooms, a large garden (in which the Blairs held court), and six bathrooms. Indeed, the recentness of its acquisition and its massive expense were often cited by Harry as indications that he was not ready to fly home to Britain forever; that his heart, like Tina's powerful job, was in New York.

Tina's job was secure at that moment, true. But would Si Newhouse have parted so willingly from her husband had Tina still been the golden girl of her *Vanity Fair* days? Fortunes had changed, and not just for Harry. The world had to be convinced, however, of just the opposite.

Seven days a week, every week, during the first years of Tina's *New Yorker* reign, Maurie Perl and Melissa Pranger, her publicity assistant, would work steadily into the evening, beating the drums for the magazine from its sixteenth floor. There were a couple of others on the publicity side as well, but it was Perl, the best in the business, on whom a certain amount of wonderment focused. At five feet one, she was often described as "the little woman running." A resolute keeper of secrets and a "force of nature," according to admirers, she somehow managed to be everywhere at once—on the phone with television host Charlie Rose, who wished to interview Tina for PBS, conferring with Tina one floor above, badgering editors to look at press releases, fielding disasters. Occasionally, the exhaustiveness of the process, along with Tina's demands, would reduce her to tears.

"Tina would ring and Maurie would run," one editor remarked. Late at night, Perl would start from a standing position and end up in a full headstand because, as her assistant noted, "it was just something to do when you're working seven days a week." Such hours were by no means unusual, as far as Tina was concerned. She herself rose each morning at five-thirty, then worked out on her StairMaster. She averaged about five hours of sleep a night.

There were so many to placate, and so much Newhouse money went into it—"a fortune," one of those involved would later say. The magazine went to the printer on Friday. By Saturday morning, the CNN news desk in Atlanta was already apprised of any breaking stories that might be contained within its covers: an early excerpt from Edmund Morris's book *Dutch* about Ronald Reagan's Alzheimer's, for instance; or a piece by Seymour Hersh. On Sunday, the publicity department's most frantic day, a major courier shipment of about a thousand copies went out to the select. The cloakroom of the Senate and the House of Representative got boxes of *New Yorkers*; Clinton received his copy on his doorstep, as did Mike Ovitz, Peter Jennings (a particular Tina friend), Barbara Walters, and their assorted television producers.

This early warning system was Perl's invention, and it got *The New Yorker* what it had never before pursued or even coveted: buzz, comment, praise, outrage. These last two were more or less the same to Tina.

"If it was derogatory, fine," Melissa Pranger soon realized. "Tina is remarkably thick-skinned, honestly. This is what is so complicated about Tina, I think. Tina is really all about Tina." In fact, in many respects, Tina was "like a man," her subordinates felt. This was not to be construed as criticism. Tina possessed a remarkably powerful and rare characteristic in a woman: she honestly didn't care whether or not she was liked. It was the work that counted. She *was* the work.

Of course, *The New Yorker* under Shawn would never have dreamed of harboring anything so raw and unseemly as a publicity machine. But Tina's blue-eyed gaze was unwavering. She had, if truth be told, a pretty grim and unflattering view of *The New Yorker.* "We had to take it out of its benighted decline," she said.

Part of the general acceptance of this internal revolution derived from its manifest necessity. *The New Yorker* was, much like Maurie Perl, standing on its head, a novel posture that started with Roseanne.

In July 1995, John Lahr wrote a profile, very long and highly flattering, of the comedienne, dwelling on her life, work, and thoughts, none of them especially surprising to those with access to a television set. "Roseanne holds nothing back; whatever emotion overtakes her, she expresses. 'I'm pure id,' she says."

The piece also arrived at certain conclusions. These *were* startling. Roseanne was, Lahr implied, essentially a severe ideologue summoned from more revolutionary times to smash centuries of injustice and oppression; her predecessors were Charlie Chaplin and, for good measure, Martin Luther. "Roseanne's rejection of manners and clean language," Lahr wrote, "is both a critique of and a revenge on the decorum of patriarchy, which assures that women collude in their own destruction." That analysis was illustrated by Roseanne herself: "I love the word 'fuck.' . . . It's a verb, a noun, everything, and it's just infused with intense feeling and passion, you know, negative and positive. And women aren't supposed to say it, so I try to say it as much as I can."

The idea of writing about Roseanne had, of course, been Tina's, but Lahr accepted the assignment within "six seconds." He knew Roseanne was "extremely important in the culture . . . representative of a constituency that had never before been seen in the magazine," and also "in a way, just terrific." Beyond that, the comedienne had her uses. "We wanted to cross over and get another kind of readership for the magazine." And it worked, Lahr thought. "Everybody read it," he said. "The point is—people who chose to argue how *The New Yorker* had declined by discussing women like this—that is an absurd and blinkered view. I mean, in its heyday, *The New Yorker* was writing about people like Walter Winchell!"

In its heyday. Even Tina's staunchest allies on the magazine, of whom Lahr was one, seemed to imply that despite her considerable efforts, that heyday had passed. Batty or inspired, it was Tina's notions that almost invariably prevailed, leading one editor to exclaim, "There's no secret to succeeding here. Just find out what Tina wants and give it to her!" After a while, no one in authority presumed to argue with her or express a different voice. It was observed, for instance, that when David Kuhn, her handpicked editor, phoned a writer, he would begin and end the editing process by saying, "Not that I don't have my own concerns, but *Tina wants* . . ." So who was there left to tell Tina that the downtrodden "constituency" that hailed Roseanne, and whom she hoped to inveigle as readers, would never buy *The New Yorker,* not in any incarnation?

As it turned out, Roseanne's contributions were not confined to a laudatory profile. One month after her innermost thoughts were aired on its pages, *The New Yorker* announced that she would become "a contributing editor and consultant on an issue about women." That was news to lots of the staff. Roseanne a contributing *editor*? A *consultant*? A woman who dispatched her ex-husband on *The Tonight Show* with: "I've had the Tom Arnold touch, and, let me tell you, what he lacked in size he made up for in speed." A boss who posted a potential hit list of employees "who are going to be fired if they're not nice to me."

Almost instantly, Maurie Perl's minions attempted to backtrack. No, Roseanne wouldn't actually be editing the publication. Nonetheless, the furor that this caused among the magazine's readers and writers was unending, especially when it emerged that Roseanne would, in fact, be doing . . . something or other. What that was would shortly be decided. Tina herself and a host of staffers were flying out to the West Coast to confer with Roseanne. Ian Frazier, a longtime contributor, resigned, nor was he alone. George Trow had also tendered his resignation after the appearance in *The New Yorker* of a sixteen-page photo spread celebrating the O.J. Simpson case which starred, among others, Kato Kaelin blow-drying his hair. "For you to kiss the ass of celebrity culture at this moment that way, is like selling your soul to get close to the Hapsburgs—1913," Trow wrote Tina. His gesture, however heartfelt, failed to impress her. "I am distraught at your defection, but since you never actually write anything, I should say I am notionally distraught," Tina wrote back.

She was certainly in no mood to brook rebellion over Roseanne.

"Don't do this, she's a horrible person," Jamaica Kincaid begged.

"I'm going to do it, I don't care what you say," Tina replied.

In vain did Kincaid inveigh against "this disgusting piece of garbage, this cruel woman." She would have vastly preferred the magazine to cozy up to Larry Flynt, the pornographer. "I'm serious, at least he's an interesting person," she said. Roseanne, on the other hand, was merely "vulgar." And Tina? "Joseph Stalin in high heels with blonde hair from England," she told the *Sunday Telegraph*. It was the end of the line for Kincaid. "That's when I knew I was going to leave. It was a very hard decision. My health benefits ceased. They kept my health benefits but they lost their minds."

In any event, Tina and her group, David Kuhn and the editor Deborah Garrison among them, did indeed go to the Coast, where they met with Roseanne, Carrie Fisher, and Mary Daly, the feminist theoretician. They all listened as "Roseanne would go off on a spiel about something," and then Tina would murmur, "Yes, but how are we going to turn this into an article?" The participants emerged from the session exhausted, perplexed. Where would all this lead?

Only on the faces of Tina and Kuhn was utter bafflement absent. "They were like two birds chirping to each other, they were consumed," one participant reported back at the time. "They were not wound down at all. They were working up to the next phase. They were this inseparable unit."

Tina loved Roseanne, who represented, the staff was informed, "raw candor." As indeed she did. The comedienne was even asked to express a few more of her opinions for a subsequent article in the magazine, a piece encompassing what Lahr subsequently called "her ideas of Woman-with-a-capital-W," which needed serious surgery: "I think I was sent out to salvage the thing," said Lahr. Alas, this wasn't quite feasible. His colleague James Wolcott, who glanced at the article, remembered it best for the star's deathless passages, once again, on Tom Arnold. "So many nasty, libelous things, they couldn't possibly run it," he remarked.

But that decision was also fraught with peril. Would Roseanne go on *Jay Leno* and dump all over *The New Yorker* for rejecting her second batch of musings? Would Maurie Perl be spending the next few months spinning yet another disaster? The next thing Wolcott knew, he was designated to write an apologia, explaining *l'affaire Roseanne* to the readership—and to Roseanne herself. "We really need you to pull our coals out of the fire. This is an emergency!" Tina told Wolcott. He dutifully wrote a few columns on the influence that Roseanne had exerted on the magazine by having "lambasted P.C. pieties" and encouraged "us to get women to write pieces in which they owned up to the scary parts of themselves."

"Yeah, I was embarrassed, but I really felt I was doing it for the magazine," Wolcott would later concede. "You don't want to say, flat-out, no." He did try to don a bit of camouflage by suggesting that the byline should read "From the editors." That was swiftly vetoed. "Too late. We've already sent out the press release saying you've written it."

But who could deny that Tina had done exactly what she set out to accomplish? Or that she was, with twenty-eight new journalists under her belt, exerting an impact? *The New Yorker* was changing—hourly—becoming ever more controversial, a creator of buzz. Bit by bit, the old mythical *New Yorker* that so haunted Tina was being cunningly dismantled.

By 1998, this process was well under way. That was the year the writer Lillian Ross came out with a hapless memoir entitled *Here but Not Here,* published by Random House, in which she detailed her years as William Shawn's mistress and employee. "Bill was attracted physically to all kinds of women," Ross wrote. "He lusted for beautiful women pictured in magazines . . . for fat women . . . for elderly women who resembled his mother. . . ." So much for the ghost of Shawn.

"I know Tina was a supporter of Lillian Ross's book on Shawn," said one staffer. There certainly appeared to be a mutuality of back-scratching between the two women. ". . . William Shawn and Tina Brown, the current editor, are indeed similar," Ross wrote in a passage that flabbergasted the protégés of the reclusive and withdrawn Shawn. They shared "naivety, insight, and sensitivity." Whatever Shawn's defects, "he did not deserve this," Renata Adler wrote.

It was a hurtful book, and quite unnecessary, the old hands decided. Few among them still harbored illusions about the great Shawn. Under him, "*The New Yorker* was tremendously infantilizing," one of their number would later say. "It was a closed world. The outside world never intruded."

Under the new regime, there was no world separate or inviolate. The outside had invaded, camping itself, in fact, right inside the *New Yorker* offices. One day Steven Spielberg walked in, with the proviso that "somebody has to ride with me on the elevator"—he was scared of elevators—and begged to see the famed *New Yorker* library.

"Fine. Let's do that," Tina agreed. Then she turned to John Lahr, helpless. "She didn't know where it was," Lahr would later explain. That, however, was a generic disability, not confined simply to the library of her own magazine. Like many before him, Lahr would discover Tina to be geographically dyslexic.

Sharon Stone also sashayed into *The New Yorker* (Lahr had been assigned to do a piece on her—Tina's idea, once again), after getting into such a snit, Lahr said, about some outfit she was asked to wear during a Richard Avedon photo shoot that she actually stormed out. Star in a huff, rejected gown, photo shoot in tatters—it was the kind of new *New Yorker* moment that should, by rights, have appeared in *In Style.* Lahr was dumbstruck. What to do? He phoned Tina and was directed to follow the actress to Cipriani's, rope her in, and bring her straight back to the office. Tina very much wanted to meet her.

As it turned out, Stone also experienced an overpowering urge to make a pilgrimage to the *New Yorker* library. Gravely, she wandered the hallowed premises while weary writers and editors watched "gob-smacked," as Lahr would later describe them. Inside the small library, her eyes lit on an ancient volume.

"Sharon picks up a Dorothy Parker poem, reads it, tears come to her eyes," Lahr said.

To remain in Tina's inside world exacted certain sacrifices. Those endless columns of *New Yorker* prose were swiftly chopped; merci-lessly, some thought. "By the end, my articles, which used to be about 35,000 words, were cut down to 10,000–12,000 words," one of the writers would recall. Then the demand came in for 5,000 words. "They no longer had the telling detail. They no longer had the rich-ness of an internal story, as seen through the eyes of an individual. They were different, that's all."

And sometimes, much better for being different. Those who couldn't bring themselves to be brief found their utility to the maga-zine had vanished. "At the end of '96, Tina sent me a letter saying it was best we part company, she felt it best if I didn't enter into an ex-clusive contract with the magazine, although she said she wanted me to continue writing pieces," Fredric Dannen would later recall. "The explanation was she needed me to write shorter pieces, and I obvi-ously wasn't going to do that. And I agreed with her totally."

No one could argue with Tina's talent. She was a fine story editor ("within her own framework," a writer hastily amended), certain of her powers, which were considerable. *That* came as a surprise to her detractors. "She could look at a piece of prose, good, bad, whatever, and write, 'It needs more of page 20 on page 5' "—and she would be right.

And as for her consultations with Roseanne, they bore fruit. Or rather, they were merely a raucous affirmation of Tina's own goals for the magazine, which would, even without Roseanne's participation, likely have been put into place. Some of these changes were gratifying and subtle. "Is this a bad time for you?" Tina would always ask a writer with young children whenever she phoned. Others were bla-tant, more rowdy, and decidedly feminine transformations.

Women certainly were, on the pages of that august magazine, ar-dently and often owning up "to the scary parts of themselves." In fact, the scary parts inhabited a kind of literary whoopee cushion: squeals of outright sex, exquisitely rendered, blaring from silvery prose. In the women's issue of February 1996 that had been so widely touted, there was Daphne Merkin writing in a most cerebral vein about spanking as a sexual practice, which derived from "a deeply pleasurable sense of exposure, brought about by the fact that enormous attention was being paid to my bottom."

It wasn't an easy piece to run in such a publication. The legal department of *The New Yorker* initially wanted confirmation from Merkin's sisters that her depiction of certain formative spanking events was not the product of the author's fevered imagination. Ultimately, after her protests, the magazine decided to take her at her word.

Alison Rose wrote "How I Became a Single Woman," an episodic saga of affairs with an adulterous man, a man who "was a little like King Kong," and a Greek "who was better at sex than any of them." A busy dominatrix was profiled by Paul Theroux: "One novelty was her sewing a man's foreskin together at the end and then sewing a button to it. The man loved it. She was amazed by the pain levels he could endure."

Inevitably, there were those with whom Tina came in contact who liked to talk of "prestige." They were not particularly criticizing her ambitions for the magazine, but conveying its importance, both as a resource and a goal.

"Prestige is dead!" Tina snapped back. And here she had, one particular listener realized with a pang, "correctly picked up something about our culture."

Prestige *was* dead in America. In its stead was money, which had come to interest Tina a great deal—and not just as an antidote to poverty, which had been her greatest fear in her Oxford years. Tina liked to compare her lifestyle, the millions spent on the new maisonette on 57th Street, her daughter's private school, not to their parallels among her colleagues and competitors but to the accoutrements of tycoons, men of power. In their assemblages of material wealth, she maintained an unflagging interest.

On the other hand, the goals of writers were beginning to perplex her. If they really wanted money, as they always said they did around contract renewal time, they should go to Hollywood, Tina said. And as for women, there were only two ways for a woman to get rich. One was to marry big money—either that, or work for Si Newhouse. Those were the only options available, said Tina. And in this regard, in the bareness and simplicity of her desire, more than one associate at *The New Yorker* felt that there was something amiss in her. Her drive was overwhelming and yet, in a way, so limited. "Something insatiable," a writer would say, "something damaged, like long ago she

264

gave up on ordinary gratification." Tina didn't appear interested in love, or not driven by it, anyway. Food left her cold; she ate chicken salads and drank diet sodas.

Of her daughter, Isabel, she spoke in invariably loving terms. The child suffered from asthma, and during an early bout, Tina spent a night in the hospital with her. The time she allotted to both her children was apportioned seriously, consistently, and without deviation. After she left the office, her home phone remained off the hook for at least three hours while they dined with their parents and grandparents. And yet with George, the older, she seemed somehow more objective and analytical, one confidant felt. The whole family had been Americanized, Tina said, except for George, "who walks around in his Little Lord Fauntleroy suits."

As for Harry and marriage itself, she wasn't exactly candid about either. At the same time, Tina never lied. "Who's to say what a married relationship consists of? There are all kinds of marriages, there are all kinds of complications," Tina would remark. Her listener was impressed and later said, "She never pretended to have the perfect marriage." That became evident when the subject of the Clintons came up. "Oh, Bill Clinton—what a rogue," someone would comment at a story meeting.

But Tina never chimed in. She found such conclusions unsophisticated, hopelessly puritanical. Once she mused, perhaps thinking of earlier days, "When a man marries his mistress, he creates a vacancy." It was a steal from Sir James Goldsmith, the late British tycoon who had acquired both types of women. But on the whole she understood men well and her sympathy was doubtless conveyed to them in some fashion.

"Tina came into the office, and the thing that fascinated me is every man in the office sought to take care of her," a female staffer recalled with marked scorn. "She charmed them." The writer and senior fiction editor Roger Angell, the editor Bill Buford, the newer hires—"They had the feeling they stood between her and the Deluge. They thought she was a fragile flower. They *had* to take care of her, or everyone would take advantage of her. And women were flabbergasted . . ." And miffed. "She would abandon a woman talking to her if a man came along."

And yet women were by no means immune to her charm. "Tina rattled me, she rattled me totally because she had been so incredibly crazy and seductive," said one, who had previously felt secure in the belief that Tina "understood" the distinctiveness and purpose of her writing. That assumption was ultimately shattered. "She wanted me to stop a piece I was writing, one that came from my heart, and do a *celebrity.*" How could she even dream of such a thing? "She *knew* I wasn't an interchangeable commodity!"

More and more, it was noticed, Tina found herself identifying with Hillary Clinton and her travails. It wasn't simply the imperfections of marriage that united them, although here Tina clearly empathized. It was the animosity—cataclysmic in its ease of ignition—that both women managed almost effortlessly to arouse. Some of this derived from their ability to alienate friends and associates. The writer Marie Brenner, who had been close to Tina since her London years and was godmother to George, abruptly left *The New Yorker*—"A very swift disenchantment between the two of them" was how the process was described—and returned to *Vanity Fair* (although subsequently the affection between the women was reignited).

"Because she is attractive and female," Harry once said, "Tina has been forced to put up with more silly criticisms than I have. There is always someone who thinks that you're not supposed to be intelligent and inventive if you're also pretty."

But these were simply the cue cards of correctness that Harry flipped. They had little basis in fact. For one thing, Tina wasn't especially pretty. The soft contours of her youth had receded. There was a heightened sharpness to her features, a bolder definition to her jaw that made her appear more striking, and yet redoubtable. As ever, observers were struck by the extraordinary beauty of her eyes, which were deep-set and still luminous. "You could be literary and call them 'haunted,' " said an associate. But there was something untoward in the bright power of her gaze. "It's like what Warren Beatty said about Madonna: 'There is no *on* when the camera isn't on.' I kept thinking, is she ever passive?"

Tina's sense of sorority with the first lady (one-sided, as it turned out, because Hillary certainly didn't reciprocate the sentiment) began when the magazine's women's issue appeared. To celebrate the event, *The New Yorker* threw itself a disastrous Washington luncheon during which "all the Washington gals were kind of mean to her," as one of her writers explained. "The *Washington Post* Style section the next day reamed her a new butt-hole."

Tina's response was one of displaced sympathy. "Poor Hillary," she said. "I don't see how she can live down there with all those awful bitches."

Part of her emotional intertwining with the first lady was pragmatic in origin. "She doesn't want to be against the Clintons when the Clintons are hot," her confidant realized. But much of it stemmed from a shared temperament, a nervous impatience and insecurity which, when given vent, often produced untoward results. Like Hillary, Tina occupied a small and claustrophobic domain, "a tiny cockpit, with no door and only slits for windows on the real world," in the words of one subordinate. Moreover, they were both insulated from the results of brusqueness and betrayal. "I'm easily bored," Tina would boast. Those articles that were arrayed before her underwent, without apology, a Darwinian trial. "And the weaker things don't make the cut," she said.

More and more, the loyalty on which Tina had always unthinkingly relied—her reward for big salaries and generous publicity—was beginning to wane. In the first place, the large sums of which she had once been a pioneer and generous dispenser were now more commonplace. *Vanity Fair*, under Graydon Carter, maintained that tradition. In the second place, the Dick Morris and Roseanne gaffes were swiftly eroding the aura of inviolate triumph that had previously enveloped her. Far from being grateful for her largesse, certain writers were proving as intractable as Teamsters. Her taste was openly questioned.

"My joy of working for *The New Yorker*, because I am a fairly un-hip guy, is this glorious curiosity about the subworld of America, the unspectacular, the unheralded," the writer Bryan Di Salvatore would later say. He had been dismayed that a long, previously approved story about a small-town Montana man who was raising a 700-pound black bear named Buffy "flew back at me" after Tina took over.

"Okay. Who are the characters? What's the plot? I don't want just another small town," Tina snapped at Di Salvatore on another occasion when he pitched an idea, exactly as if he were a screenwriter. Di Salvatore noticed that all around him, "people were panicking and freaking out." So was he, for that matter. Topicality, currency—they were not his strong suits. He had an idea, a good one, but it wasn't hot. Not then.

Di Salvatore wanted to investigate "a closed, potentially violent, frightening and relatively obscure society" called the Constitutionalists. The group's approach was more theoretical than violent, but they were very right wing. They operated out of Montana, suing law enforcement authorities and refusing to recognize federal currency because it wasn't based on the gold standard. Indeed, Di Salvatore wrote

Tina, the group dwelt "in a perpetual dusk of paranoia, where the only light comes from the fires of perceived national and world-wide conspiracies." Quiet and unknown though they were, Di Salvatore had a feeling about some of their members. They were "going to make big headlines one of these days. Maybe big bloody headlines," he warned.

In February 1994, Di Salvatore received the go-ahead and an advance of $1,000 for research. Then he launched "an intricate, extended, fraught dance with up to a dozen extremely paranoid people," one that carried with it the possibility of physical danger. Four months later, Tina made another decision. "I don't think it's going to go. I don't think it's right. I don't think it's interesting. It's boring. Tell him," she ordered Nancy Franklin, one of the editors.

"I went Sicilian," Di Salvatore recollected. It wasn't the killing of the piece—Tina hadn't even seen it, as it was still being drafted. It was the agony of four months' work (for which he received $5,000, plus expenses) and the reasons behind its stillbirth that upset him. "My people, they weren't sexy. Nobody had ever heard of them," he said.

In April 1995, another sort of extremist named Timothy McVeigh blew up a federal building in Oklahoma City, killing 168 people. At that point, Di Salvatore received a phone call from Tina, most apologetic. This was not her first foray into patching up differences. During an initial call, Tina had, quite astonishingly Di Salvatore felt, informed him that the decision to kill the piece on the extremists was not originally hers. She blamed Nancy Franklin, his editor, for the bad decision.

"I took Nancy's recommendation to kill it. . . . It was not represented to me," Tina insisted, while Di Salvatore tapped out notes of the conversation on his computer. Nancy was, she added, "negative and confused. . . . I'm fond of Nancy, but quite honestly . . . I made her a theater critic for a reason."

So an underling was made to bear the brunt of Tina's bad executive decision, Di Salvatore thought to himself. Nor was this a solitary instance of her scapegoating. Another disgruntled *New Yorker* writer, peeved that a promised assignment had fallen into someone else's grasp, was informed by Tina that the decision was none of her making. "It was John Bennet's doing," she said.) The next thing Di Salvatore knew, once Oklahoma City blew, Tina wanted him to write yet another story about the subterranean world of the extreme right wing.

"You're a marvelous writer, marvelous. Love your stuff," she said.

268

"I don't know whether to tell you to fuck yourself or go piss up a rope," he replied.

Of what possible use was he to the magazine Tina had reinvented? Perhaps, as Si Newhouse had indicated, the old magazine had been losing its relevance. "But so much baby was thrown out with the bathwater." It was time to leave. "When she goes, I return," Di Salvatore promised.

"How sad (and how unable I am to enter the fray) that *The New Yorker* is going to roll up its sleeve and react, sending someone out to battle the hordes of journalists down there right now," he wrote a *New Yorker* colleague. "My plan, my preference, was always to get to folks before or long after they were in the spotlight. Now, good fucking luck. . . . Every swinging dick in the bighouse is camped there. Not for me. Not for me."

"Do come to the Anniversary party," begged Tina.

She meant the seventieth anniversary party, which was held at the Hudson Theater, its seats ripped out for the event and tables substituted in their place. Tina had worked on the party for an entire month. John Lahr had been designated to write an amusing revue and special sets had been constructed. "Focus groups"—magazine personnel roped into service—were brought to the Evanses' new flat to judge the revue's contents. Trooping in and out were Debra Winger, John Lithgow, Anne Meara, the director Gregory Mosher. No one was spared. Lithgow performed the role of the writer George Trow, who had abandoned, on principle, a boss who was "kissing the ass of celebrity." Winger played Tina, weary of principle, dishing out her saucy retort.

What did money matter? The event cost $100,000, but it was "not a waste of money," Lahr thought. It was a form of magic, a new spell the sorceress cast on behalf of an ancient magazine. Among the six hundred guests were Brooke Astor, Harrison Ford, Anna Wintour, and Tina's parents, Bettina and George. The clipped bon mots spouting from the pretty mouth of an accomplished actress were the essence of Tina. That distance was essential, Lahr decided. "I was raised in a household with a star, so I understand that," he said. "Glamour has to do with distance. You can't see it too close because then you see the flaws. So the whole point about Tina was to hit and run. She understood it. That's why Tina is glamorous She comes and leaves the silver bullet—which is the event."

This sort of gathering was fast becoming as commonplace a *New Yorker* event as it had been at *Vanity Fair*. In fact, the two were growing practically interchangeable. In March 1994, for instance, Tina flew to Los Angeles to host a party in celebration of a special issue devoted entirely to the film industry.

It was there that Robin Williams, the subject of a highly flattering profile in the magazine, stood up in the garden of the Bel-Air Hotel, under a white tent illuminated by five hundred white paper lanterns. Behind him was a collage of Richard Avedon photographs of Marilyn Monroe. The *New Yorker* publicity department had spent the entire previous week planning the event.

"I would like to thank Tina Brown for the puff, I still have a hard-on," Williams said. And so saying, he broke into a Jack Nicholson drawl. "Or as Jack would say, a major chubby." After this revelation, Williams snatched a camcorder from Caroline Graham, the magazine's West Coast organizer, and stuffed it in his trousers. "That's the Bobbitt home movie," he said. "I will be playing the part of the penis. It's a small part, and it may be cut."

Then Tina walked to the podium to give her pitch. Arrayed before her, among others, were Steven Spielberg in a pale suit, United Artists studio chief John Calley, Kate Capshaw seated next to Michael Ovitz, Annette Bening nuzzling her husband, Warren Beatty, Whoopi Goldberg in dreadlocks, Glenn Close, Raquel Welch, and Ralph Fiennes. Even Lassie showed up to promote a line of Lassie products.

"This issue is not about Hollywood glitz at all," Tina said to explain her mission. "We're celebrating the work with this issue, not the money, not the lifestyle, not the planes, not the limos." There was more. She was horrified, Tina told her audience, by those magazine editors who entered into slimy agreements with agents and publicists over star profiles, determining what is written and who gets on the cover. Such sellouts had to stop. In return, she assured the famous faces at her party that she hated the "snide puff pieces"—the seemingly innocuous celebrity pieces that always end with a sneer.

This was the Tina Brown who had launched her career on a sneer, balanced it on celebrity profiles, and kept it in spin by the assiduous courting of stars and magnates—all the people in the Bel-Air Hotel garden, in other words. They were now not simply fodder for her magazines, but her people. Her friends. Her contacts. Guests at her parties. She was, at long last, one of them.

And yet—not completely. There was still, despite her magic, her many triumphs, a sort of aspirational quality to Tina that persisted into middle age. The journalists with whom she dealt were made vividly aware of that. "Courtney Love's lawyer says she's a very nice person," Tina would tell them, straight-faced.

"Tina had a crush on Peter Jennings," a *New Yorker* writer noticed as time went by. "She would tell me sometimes, 'You know, Peter liked what you wrote.' She used to tell me, 'Peter says this is important.' Just like any young woman with a crush on a man, who wishes to hear the man's name repeated, so she says it herself."

And so when, in February 1998, a Tina Brown report on a White House party for Tony Blair and his wife appeared in *The New Yorker,* the degree of almost universal amusement and derision that poured forth came as a genuine surprise. The assumption had always been that despite her love affair with celebrities, Tina was a sophisticated, hard-bitten journalist, too *glamorous* to be easily seduced. That assumption, it now became evident, was flat-out wrong. She was, in Peter Boyer's words, simply "a schoolgirl." Her decision to extricate both Blair and Clinton from any political context and plant them against a backdrop that might just as well have been the Bel-Air Hotel was very likely not calculated, not even, perhaps, a conscious decision at all. It was Tina. She had evolved. She was no longer a journalist.

"See him instead as his guests do: a man in a dinner jacket with more heat than any star in the room," she wrote of the president of the United States. Every sensuous detail impressed her: "his height, his sleekness, his newly cropped, iron-filing hair and the intensity of his blue eyes. . . . He is vividly in the present tense and dares you to join him there." As for Blair, his tense was never fully explicated, but he did possess "a kind of elfin glow."

Tina's own people at *The New Yorker* couldn't bring themselves to bask in the elfin glow. "You know what *did* surprise me? The Blair-Clinton piece. That did," one of them would say years later. "That she thought of the president as a star from *Photoplay,* that she wrote about his sex appeal instead of the issue of governance. That she didn't know there has to be a distance between the journalist and her subject."

But this staffer did understand how Tina's White House Valentine came to be published in a magazine that had always prided itself on that reasoned separation between subject and observer. "Because there was no one around to say no to Tina any longer. No way to stop her."

. . .

Harry returned to Mort Zuckerman's publishing empire as editorial director and vice chairman in January 1998, a lithe, cheery presence in suspenders, probably destined to run into trouble. There were several who were elated by the prospect of having a genuine hero, a slayer of monsters (for this was how Harry was still perceived), on the masthead. "I thought, Oh great! This will inoculate us from Mort a bit," recalled one staff member. The temperamental Zuckerman had a well-established propensity for removing editors—five in all—from *U.S. News & World Report,* for "messing with cover stories," as one subordinate noted, and cutting budgets. Harry's reputation as "a whirlwind" reassured those who felt he would probably serve as a buffer between them and the unpredictability of a hardheaded, imperious owner. Why shouldn't he vanquish Zuckerman? After all, Harry was the dauntless journalist who had once shamed the makers of thalidomide, the publishing executive who had, by pure force of will, ensured the success of the initially unpromising *A Civil Action,* a book, essentially, about idealism.

And at first, such hopes proved well founded. "Harry came in, and his attitude was 'Mort is doing all these incredibly unprofessional things, and it's got to stop,' " one early admirer recalled. Harry didn't like Zuckerman's budget cuts, for instance. Precious funds earmarked for stringers seemed to evaporate and he saw that kind of interference as "an insult to Harry." On the other hand, although many were familiar with the Harry of legend, no one was quite prepared for the man Harry now was.

His very appearance came as a shock. "Poignant. . . . Here was this guy as old as my father, slowing down; he seemed a very sad, old, tired character," one *U.S. News* staffer reported. "Actually, he walked very quickly. But he seemed mentally tired." James Fallows, the energetic new editor of the magazine, also marveled at Harry's perseverance. There he was, a man of extraordinary attainments and reputation, but almost seventy. "What I couldn't really understand is why somebody who has all these achievements behind him should subject himself to this kind of scrambling," Fallows said. "He doesn't need to! He acts as if he still needs the money and the position."

No one was quite sure what Harry was supposed to do for the New York *Daily News.* His first task was to redesign the newspaper, but it was, staffers thought, a very risky proposition: readers were used to the gritty look of the tabloid. As for *U.S. News & World Report,* after an earlier rise, its total paid circulation was down 1.6 percent within months of Harry's arrival, its ad pages down 9.88 percent. Only its newsstand sales had risen—7 percent.

Certainly, part of his mission was to maintain an uneasy truce between Zuckerman and Fallows, a much admired and thoughtful magazine editor, but acerbic and headstrong. Fallows was never one to keep his opinions to himself. He had worked two decades earlier as a speechwriter for Jimmy Carter, with whom he fell out publicly. And in 1996 he wrote *Breaking the News: How the Media Undermine American Democracy,* a harsh attack on the laziness and arrogance of journalists. Zuckerman's decision to reduce the number of foreign bureaus and cut down on coverage of news from abroad was anathema to Fallows, and at first Harry seemed to stand in his corner.

"I stood up to Murdoch, you're standing up to Mort," Harry would tell Fallows. Nonetheless, his patronage was by no means assured—and not simply because Zuckerman had lately tired of Fallows and was clearly itching to get rid of him.

Harry and Fallows, too, had history. About a week after he started at *U.S. News,* Fallows was asked by Zuckerman to look at Dick Morris's ill-fated Random House memoir with an eye to excerpting it for the magazine—if he chose to do so, Zuckerman added. Harry had obviously been in touch with his old friend Zuckerman, and when Fallows phoned the Random House publisher, he was struck by his calm assumption that excerpting *Behind the Oval Office* was, in fact, a done deal.

"When you use this . . ." Harry would say. And, "We are so excited that this will happen!" That was distressing. "Nobody at the magazine wanted this to happen," Fallows later recalled. "Everybody was against it."

Still, Zuckerman's word was law, so he reluctantly conceded. Fallows consented to run the Morris extract, but not unaccompanied. What he specifically had in mind was a companion article, "an anti–Dick Morris piece" written by the columnist Gloria Borger. Harry, apprised of this idea, was aghast.

The next thing Fallows knew, he was having "quite a starchy conversation with Random House lawyers. They were talking about how there was this Implied Agreement to present [the Morris excerpts] in a compatible setting." Fallows held firm. There was no such agreement, he said. "But even if there were, they couldn't control the contents of the magazine."

Another idea dawned on Fallows. If some other publication

quoted extensively from the Morris book shortly before its official publication date, it would be worthless to *U.S. News* as a magazine exclusive, in fact, needn't be run at all.

"Gee, wouldn't it be a shame if somebody got hold of this book," Fallows told his associates, who immediately recognized that as "a signal to start the search for a copy." Staff members fanned out to bookstores, attempting to convince salesclerks to sell them a copy of Morris's book before publication date. A similar effort was conducted by the *Daily News,* which emerged triumphant.

On learning this, Fallows called Zuckerman. The "honor" of *U.S. News* was at stake, he informed him. Very soon excerpts from the book would be made public. The magazine had to call off the deal.

Another person who was likely to have problems with Harry was Fred Drasner, Zuckerman's partner, who "couldn't understand why Mort was bringing this person in—as this *supra*-editor," in the words of one *U.S. News* editor. There were consequences for Harry. "Fred seemed to have made sure that Harry wasn't put on the third floor [the site of the *Daily News*] and was instead put on the eleventh floor," said another Zuckerman employee. "Which is far removed from everything." A large work space was made available for Harry's secretary; but, it was observed, "because Harry didn't keep very long hours, she was sort of like the Maytag repairman."

On so many levels, the Harry Evans of *U.S. News* would have been unrecognizable to his old admirers in the newspaper business, or even at Random House. He would fly down to Washington to participate in story conferences—and then fall asleep in the middle of a meeting. That happened twice, according to three individuals who participated in those conferences. With women, Harry was sprightly and amusing; but American men, unlike their British counterparts, were far less tolerant of such gender-based discrepancies in behavior. "He's one of these guys you hate as a male," said one. "He sees a woman at the magazine, he yells over to her, he flirts like mad, a big kiss." Moreover, this burst of charm and energy, rather than erasing earlier impressions of a subdued and tired Harry, served merely to heighten the contrast.

His ideas, too, seemed weary and flat-footed, as if he couldn't quite wrap his mind around the implications of certain national news events. After Monica Lewinsky emerged as a political liability for the president, who had lied about their sexual liaison, it was noticed that "Harry was always pushing the Clinton-as-victim line at meetings. . . . He didn't seem to get the gravity of the story." In vain would the Washington staff of the magazine attempt to explain that the story was "all about perjury." To Harry, "it was all about sex." With Fallows, he was even more direct. "He was all over us to move faster in exposing 'the anti-Clinton conspiracy,'" Fallows said. Much like his wife, Harry seemed to empathize with the first couple, beset by issues he considered private and of negligible consequence. "I always lie about sex and never lie about money," the *New York Post* reported he told Lady Weston, the wife of the British ambassador to the United Nations, at a dinner party.

In any event, Harry's value to *U.S. News,* along with the quality of his insights, was increasingly questioned. "He huddled with the investigative team, but I never heard of any investigative project that came of it," Fallows would later maintain. Other contributions seemed downright peculiar within the context of a newsmagazine, more consequential for Harry than the interests of the reader. He was particularly anxious that the magazine run an article about the problems faced by the paraplegic actor Christopher Reeve, whose book had been signed while Harry was still at Random House. A multipart serialization of a forthcoming book by Harry on American history was also proposed. Zuckerman had bought the rights and Fallows was, according to a friend, "struggling with his conscience" about running a lot of excerpts. The *U.S. News* columnist John Leo was among those who disapproved of the project. "I don't think that people in authority should use that authority to promote their own book," Leo said. He thought Harry "would have been better off if it had appeared elsewhere."

What was Harry's purpose at the magazine? Even his protestations of friendship and advocacy, while doubtless sincere at the time of utterance, were of small worth. Again and again, Fallows would later insist, Harry consoled him: "He'd tell me how he liked me. That we were great friends. I was like him at that age. I was doing a great job and had such character. That sort of thing."

In fact, Fallows found signs in Harry of a rebellion in his long and complicated relationship with Zuckerman, but they took a subtle form that required some decoding. "You could tell there were times when Harry was fighting with Mort," Fallows said, by the quality of Zuckerman's own journalistic forays—specifically, the Zuckerman columns that Harry was being paid a small fortune to edit, and which occasionally he somehow neglected to edit quite enough. When tensions developed between Harry and Zuckerman, said Fallows, "Harry turned in the copy raw. You'd get something that had not been cleaned up for exposure to polite society."

One instance concerned a Zuckerman column which Fallows would later describe as "a defense of the rich." The wealthy were unfairly criticized by the envious was its gist, especially those who had worked hard to amass their great fortunes. "Harry passed this on with a snort, saying that he was pissed at Mort," Fallows said. "He hardly needed to say it, given the way the column looked.

"I was mad at Mort too, at the time, so I didn't clean it up much, either."

Then Harry's tone began to change. There were increasing problems with Zuckerman, Fallows was told. Zuckerman resented the relatively brief coverage—just one page—that the shooting of the famous fashion designer Gianni Versace had received in *U.S. News,* while the networks and other news magazines were blanketing it. Zuckerman wanted Bianca Jagger, a former girlfriend, to act as a consultant for an article on Hispanics. Nothing wrong with that, Harry told the press, although he was unaware of the proposal at the time. "She's a smart lady," he said. "I wouldn't think that was horrible at all." But Fallows, who loathed celebrity journalism, disagreed. That did not bode well for him.

"There's a problem with Mort, I don't know that I can pacify Mort," Harry would tell Fallows. Or, "Great cover! But Mort didn't like it. Isn't there a way to do more of what Mort would like? I don't know if I can *control* Mort."

Fallows had every reason for concern. In February 1998, Harry approached him about signing a confidentiality agreement. "Something we have to do is make an agreement that all of our discussions are in confidence," Fallows was told.

"Harry, that's fine," he said. "About twenty years ago I had a public fuss with Jimmy Carter. Since then, I've never given anybody any trouble. And I wasn't the one who wrote a book about Rupert Murdoch!"

Harry had the grace to laugh. But the next week, Fallows received from the British-born champion of free speech a document to sign that he found "just incredible." Again and again in weeks to come, Harry would impress on Fallows the necessity of signing this agreement—without results. What it demanded, in essence, was a promise from Fallows never to reveal any particle of his experiences at *U.S. News*, no syllable of any conversation with Zuckerman, Harry, or just about anybody. Fallows asked around, but no one he approached claimed to have been asked to consent to such an agreement. Worse, Fallows found, "there was no reciprocity" in the agreement, "it was all one-sided." Of course, he knew what that meant. "It was literally my first step to moving out the door," he said.

In the late spring of 1998, Harry approached Fallows once more, this time with unimpeachable candor: "Well, I think, my boy, you need to start looking for other things. Let's prepare for an orderly transition." It wasn't orderly and there certainly wasn't much of a transition. On the morning of June 29, 1998, Fallows phoned Zuckerman. "I understand from Harry you want someone else in this job," he said.

Zuckerman was nonplussed. "Oh, I have nothing to do with this, it's all Harry's decision. It's entirely out of my hands. I've given Harry free rein." But when pressed, he conceded, as Fallows would later recall, that a dismissal was in the cards that Harry would soon be dealing.

"Five minutes later, I went and told everybody I was fired," Fallows said. In fact, he imparted something more critical to his staff. "Mort Zuckerman has decided that I should leave the magazine . . ." That was particularly galling to Zuckerman, and for good reason. Zuckerman was not overly anxious to see a headline (as indeed he shortly did, in *The Wall Street Journal*) that read: ZUCKERMAN OUSTS ANOTHER EDITOR AT *U.S. NEWS*.

Nor was Harry especially happy with Fallows's announcement: Now he was faced with the humiliating task of convincing the rest of the staff that *he* was the hangman. Refrain from insisting on his executioner's role and he would look like a wimp. "As Editorial Director and Vice Chairman, I have the responsibility, by contract, for appointment and dismissal of editors, and the decision here is mine," he insisted. But the proclamation rang hollow, especially after an e-mail circulated indicating that as late as April 1998, Harry was telling Tom Evans, then the magazine's publisher, that he had "become a big fan" of Fallows and that he was "still working on Mort, admittedly with limited success."

No one sincerely believed Harry was in charge. The writer Timothy Noah informed *The New York Times* that Harry was "a papier-mâché boss," who is "frantically trying to look like he's not taking orders from Mort." Stung, Harry selected a most unfelicitous rebuttal. "I have not been known simply to be a lap-dog," he told *The Washington Post*. It was the phrase that resounded long after all the combatants had laid down their arms, a remark akin in its poignancy, its flailing, hapless denial, to Nixon's "I-am-not-a-crook."

So Fallows left, Timothy Noah left, and Harry stayed behind, his titles intact. But how comfortable was this fast-emptying berth? Shortly before his departure, Fallows had complained to Zuckerman about Harry, referring to him alternately as "the wee Yorkie" and "a certain little Englishman."

"I'm onto the 'little Englishman,' " Zuckerman replied. Fallows was struck by his employer's appropriation of the term and the almost audible quotation marks he placed around it, like a fence.

Chapter 14

"Somewhere in the Dark"

Nothing worked.

In an effort to return to profitability, *The New Yorker* cut one page per issue from its editorial content, a measure that was supposed to save $500,000 a year. Then it trimmed the width of a spread by ⅜ of an inch. Over time, operating costs went down $20 million. By mid-1997, the magazine's cost per page was about $10,000, about half the amount expended by some of its rivals. And still it was bleeding money, although certainly not as much money as before. Tina had a $35 million editorial budget, which had to be fed, occasionally in a manner unthinkable in previous eras. Publisher Tom Florio hit upon the idea of selling the magazine's sophisticated crossword puzzle to Mont Blanc, so that an ad featuring that brand of pen always appeared on the page next to it. The book column was placed catty-corner to a Barnes & Noble ad.

Nor were the tastes, or what Tina imagined to be the tastes, of new readers neglected. In September 1997, shortly after the death of the Princess of Wales in a car crash, a Diana-dominated rush issue appeared, published on a Friday, three days early for the first time in the magazine's seventy-two-year history. In it, Tina published the details of her own tête-à-tête with Diana, a woman she had accused twelve years earlier of having "pussy-whipped" Prince Charles "from here to eternity."

Their encounter had taken place the previous June over lunch at the Four Seasons, by which time Diana seemed to have vanquished any grudges she might reasonably have harbored and grown extraordinarily confiding to both Tina and Anna Wintour of *Vogue,* who had set up the meeting. Prince Charles just didn't have the right stuff to be king, the princess told the two editors. Had she, Diana, only been permitted to become queen some day, "We would have been the best team in the world. I could shake hands till the cows came home. And Charles could make serious speeches. But"—she shook her head—"it was not to be." Listening to her, Tina recalled, "I feel a great sadness for England. She is right: they would have made a great team." And so on. Word around *Vogue* was that Wintour, the luncheon hostess, was by no means pleased to learn that these revelations were being published by Tina. Others had more expansive objections to its appearance. "It was an exercise in self-display, so odious as to shame everyone in journalism," Jonathan Yardley wrote in *The Washington Post.* Shame, however, was not on the front burner. Newsstand sales jumped 175 percent.

What Tina exacted from herself, she demanded of others. All sorts of writers of demonstrable talent and intellect found themselves pressed into the service of celebrity, although the degree of goodwill, rebellion, or resignation varied with the author: Salman Rushdie gamely poured forth more verbiage about Diana. John Seabrook consented to write about the Hollywood mogul David Geffen (the very piece from which "the cunt quote" ultimately evaporated), all the while realizing that "other writers had been offered it and prudently refused, because taking the assignment would obviously mean acting as a relationship broker between Tina and Geffen." Of course, Seabrook was curious about Geffen. But equally important, as he wrote in *Nobrow,* a book that contained his memories of that era: ". . . I think I wanted to please Tina, to impress her as someone who could write about the kind of people she was really interested in, to be included among the inner circle of writers who went to her house for dinner and got faxed in the middle of the night."

The anxiety to please Tina was a consuming force at *The New Yorker.* "I want a *blockbuster,*" she would say. Even her words seemed hijacked from Hollywood. Valiant attempts were made in that direction. Writers learned that the best way to grab her attention was to beg editors to hand in their stories at the very last minute, thus gaining Tina's regard for their freshness and novelty. The need to propitiate stemmed not merely from Tina's force of will, the triple-strength potency of her demands (which Seabrook described, memorably, as being accompanied by her "quick, thrilling, high-octave glance up from the Diet Coke"), but from the necessity of averting other, more unpleasant scenarios.

Everyone seemed to understand, if only implicitly, the likely repercussions of giving voice to too much dissent, of rejecting yet another request from Tina for a newer, "hotter" celebrity profile. Even the losers won. Richard Reeves was paid an estimated $50,000 to write on the Clinton presidency, a piece that was ultimately killed; Gay Talese received at least that much for another spiked article, on John Bobbitt. Favored members of the staff received incomes of $200,000 or more, among them Ken Auletta, whose well-disposed portraits of media bosses and Hollywood giants won Tina's approval (and who was the husband of the powerful literary agent Binky Urban). His writing had "to go through a lot of heavy lifting," according to one editor. But Tina felt he was worth the strain. "Oh, what are we going to *do?* We've just cut off Ken's balls," she said, sighing, after a massive bout of editing had left Auletta fuming and he was threatening to withdraw his byline. "I've got to go make nice to him."

These salaries were, however, always at risk.

"We were in an odd courtship, the writers and Tina," said one old hand. "Tina had paradoxical strengths. She can be charming and make you feel very good. And then be unkind or cold. I got the latter a couple of times when I was asked to do things I said no to."

Mark Singer, after considering and then aborting an article on the hairdresser Frederic Fekkai and rejecting out of hand both Ted Turner and the designer Karl Lagerfeld, ran out of excuses and consented to explore the aftermath of the arrest of Heidi Fleiss, the Hollywood madam. "Listen, I did the piece. And my sixth-grade teacher, retired thirty years, wrote me, 'That was beneath your abilities. Don't ever do that again.' " Singer was "impressed by that letter." But he never blamed Tina. "I blame her *idea.*"

And yet the odd thing was that none of these ideas brought the magazine what it had two years earlier so jubilantly predicted: a profit. True, Tom Florio had managed to stanch *The New Yorker*'s fabled losses. In 1997, they were reported to be roughly $11 million, down from $14.4 million in 1996 and $17 million the year before that. And true, the number of readers was up, to almost 808,000. Even ad revenues had inched 0.7 percent higher, to $28.3 million. The industry as a whole, however, was enjoying a rise of 7.7 percent.

But in January 1998, an ominous squib appeared in the press. Steve Florio, now president and CEO of Condé Nast, had, at Si Newhouse's request, "been examining the books." In fact, Newhouse was giving serious thought to moving the previously independent magazine under the supervision of Steve Florio.

That was not good news, not for Tina and certainly not for an irate Tom Florio, who, after reading the article, was reported to have promptly informed his older brother that if he ever spoke about the magazine publicly again, *The Wall Street Journal* would learn the precise losses incurred by *The New Yorker* under his earlier nine-year reign: about $100 million, *Fortune* magazine maintained, although Florio disputed this. It was a contretemps that was minutely dissected by the press. Tom was having a hard time. His big brother had embarrassed him and Tina was spatting with him. She was under increasing pressure, everyone knew, and not only from Newhouse and the powerful critics of her magazine. Despite all her frantic efforts, her blockbusting demands, and her 1:00 A.M. faxes, *The New Yorker* was still, perversely, swimming in red ink.

Moreover, all around *The New Yorker,* and outside it as well, among the professional gossip columnists who confided their gleanings, "whispers about Harry and his philandering" were circulating, one editor said. Tina, it was observed, rarely smiled around the office.

She had a lot on her hands. Her son, George, was attending a school in Greenwich, Connecticut, and in 1998, Tina and Harry bought a house in nearby Bedford. One of the child's teachers lived in a cabin on the grounds; in another lived Kate, Harry's grown daughter, and her new husband, who helped fix up the place. And Bettina, Tina's witty, ambitious mother, her champion and best friend, was ill with cancer—dying, Tina soon realized. It was from her mother that she first learned how to throw a good party. She used to love "to watch the transformation of my mother because she and I were very alike, really," Tina would recall after Bettina's death. "She was also very reserved, a very private woman. But when she got in a social situation, she sort of flowered. It was really quite interesting. Suddenly the bubbles would rise to the surface and she would be this sort of incredibly witty, very vivid personality."

With friends, she talked about Bettina, a woman who had clung to youth, to Tina's youth really, with such bright, impenetrable insistence that her later years almost parodied her daughter's earlier ones. Bettina's gossip columns, scribbled in middle age, her friendships with fading film stars, her radio show, her journalistic stunts and sherry parties in the expatriate community of Spain—Tina understood what all these signified, what she, Bettina's daughter, had clearly meant to such a mother all these years. She knew, said Tina, that her mother "had devoted her entire life" to her, had developed and molded her. "She said she was her mother's project," one friend recalled.

Conversely, Tina had dedicated much of her life to the dreams of her thwarted mother. That eagerness to partake, to sprout roots among the celebrated, was part of her legacy. Even Bettina's passion for cats had been passed on to her daughter. Not to the extent of welcoming lame pets, of course, that wasn't Tina's way. But she had objected, strenuously, to an anti-cat column written by Calvin Trillin.

Now the mother who had often cared for Tina's children, who had soothed her ruffled vanity when her stewardship was under attack and been a sparkling, chatty presence at her New York parties, was abandoning her—and at a critical and most miserable period of the daughter's career. Bettina herself had never been an undiluted fan of the magazine. "She kept telling me that I didn't have enough fun," her daughter recalled, and more than fun, some element of independence: "Something I had started myself." Life at *The New Yorker* was a harsh affair for its editor. Tina was at once lonely at the top, and yet the position itself was strictly illusory: she was not really at the top at all. Above her were the men who needed to be placated. Below, all sorts of intractable types, who resisted her efforts to alter the publication in ways they found unsuitable. Practically no one understood what she was trying to accomplish. "I spent too much time appeasing elements of the magazine that . . . were really holding it back," Tina would say a few years later. Some stalwarts remained, grateful she had saved their magazine from perdition, but not enough. Her allies, her support, were dwindling fast.

She still thought advertising rates at *The New Yorker* too high, and wanted them reduced, however much they had to be discounted, because an increase in advertising would be emblematic of her success. "It's never about the magazine," Tom Florio would complain to his older brother. "It's always about what's best for *Tina.*" At Condé Nast, executives were made vividly aware, as one of them later said, that Tina was something more than anyone else in the company: "She had just become such a *star.* Her image is everything to her. That's all she cares about."

Her star status gave her, Tina believed, enormous leverage with Newhouse, and that she increasingly deployed. "Tina would quite vociferously complain about the publisher, whether it was Steve Florio or Tom, to Si," said a friend of the publisher. "He was definitely Big Daddy." Of course, everyone realized, "Si loved her." He said as much himself in a rare interview: "I think Tina Brown is superb . . . Tina has turned the magazine around." But as Tina's complaints mounted, Newhouse's attitude, too, experienced a slight change. In disputes over the magazine, "Si defended those Florio boys."

Meanwhile, Tom Florio conceived another idea for a special issue, one that arose directly from Tina's strengths as an editor. Like so many who had worked with her, Florio had been struck by Tina's uncanny ability to forecast the next hot trend, or more precisely, the individual who would embody it. Thus was "NEXT," *The New Yorker*'s most solemn, desperate, and fattest issue in twenty-five years, brought into the world. One hundred seventy-eight pages of ads and three months in the making, it appeared at the end of October 1997, a would-be primer on what the future held, devoid of humor or surprise, but packed with hubris.

Within its pages was an amazing amount of prophesying and preposterous insights. From Henry Louis Gates, Jr., a profile of "an un-Republican named Elizabeth Dole" who would be, the headline assured readers, "The Next President." From David Remnick, glowing words on the Disney empire and its leader, Michael Eisner. "Here we were going to predict the future, and in just three months!" remarked one of those involved with the issue, with the dry disdain that became widespread. "I felt like I was choppered into a war zone." It was not, in other words, a happy time. "You could almost hear the sphincter muscles of the editors tighten as Tina clickety-clacked down the hallway toward the offices," said one editor.

David Kuhn was the editor of that special issue, but as usual it was Tina's ideas that prevailed. These were forever changing, except in one instance. She wanted, over the vigorous protests of several on her staff, an article by the writer Tony Schwartz ("The kind of writer the old *New Yorker* wouldn't have considered in its darkest days," it was pointed out). Schwartz was working with Michael Eisner on his autobiography, entitled *Work in Progress,* and Tina's employees received the distinct impression that it was this valuable connection to Eisner that accounted for her urgent need to use Schwartz. He turned in a piece on the desire of certain aging Americans to lift weights, which was deemed risible even by Kuhn.

"I'm sorry, but you're just going to have to make it work," said Tina, when yet another detractor caught up with her. But even after thirty seconds of pleading, Tina was utterly unmoved: "You have to make sure Tony does not go away unhappy. Because he's been enormously helpful to us in the Conference."

Indeed, there was to be a NEXT conference to accompany the NEXT issue. It took place at Eisner's $35 million Disney Institute in Orlando, Florida. Tina had persuaded Si Newhouse to pay for the event, as well as the accommodations for all 150 guests. Most of the guests arrived by corporate jet, and their identities provided certain clues to the conference's raison d'être; really, what would happen next—for Tina. Harvey Weinstein of Miramax was there; Barry Diller, the chief executive of USA Networks; Vice President Al Gore; Michael Bloomberg; ICM chief Jeff Berg; and Steven Rattner of Lazard Frères—along, of course, with Eisner himself, who hosted the event.

When it was over, Tina slipped into Weinstein's Miramax plane. The two would soon have certain ideas to hash out that could be advantageously discussed only in private. "With hindsight, it became clear. It was all part of some master plan," it was later observed. "To ease the transition into another world."

The press was not invited to the conference, but its bewildered attendees were amazed at the change in the woman who had arranged it. The Tina who previously had evinced no interest at all in her clothes now indulged in frequent, if unsuccessful, changes of wardrobe. "I kept thinking it was a little off," a guest recalled. "The shoes and the hose—the hose was pink. Like secretarial pink. No visual appetite."

And the purpose of the conference was a mystery. Still, a few of the more perspicacious had their suspicions. "She was getting a job. It was totally clear to me that's what it was about at the time. It was clear to me when I saw who was there, it seemed so movie-oriented."

In their rooms, baskets of wine and bottles of vinegar awaited the attendees. The writers conferred among themselves. "We all discussed how much it cost," said one: $500,000, claimed the *New York Post*. Why was Newhouse picking up the tab? What could it possibly have to do with the magazine?

And so in her last years at *The New Yorker*, the Tina perceived at work and at parties was a markedly altered woman. She had grown colder and more abrupt, ever more distant. Her insights into the history of the magazine she had acquired—"They used to fuck like rabbits around here!" she remarked—seemed especially telling and out of place.

She was sadder too, and everyone considered her immensely brave for coming into that barren and frosty office day after day, despite her load of personal anguish. Bettina died, at seventy-five, on June 30, 1998, leaving her daughter and son around $40,000 each. Tina inserted a small, apt notice in her memory in the papers: "Do not stand at my grave and weep. I am not there. I do not sleep. I am a thousand winds that blow. I am the diamond glint on snow."

The daughter was stranded, desolate. Her invincibility was fast evaporating, and with it, her associates felt, the pleasure of basking in her sizzle and brightness. She "didn't listen in her last years," James Wolcott would later say. "She would pay lip service to what you said, but she didn't listen."

Wolcott took his leave from *The New Yorker* to work for Graydon Carter at *Vanity Fair,* which was particularly galling to Tina, as the two magazine editors cordially detested each other. "I thought you were happy here," Tina protested.

"Well," Wolcott replied, "one can always be happier." Then he watched as Tina performed an odd gesture. She moved aside a coffee table book that was lying on her desk, her arm snaking protectively around it.

"You'll find you don't have the freedom there you think you'll have. And the stakes aren't as high," she warned.

"At that point I just sort of shrugged," Wolcott said. "As I was leaving, I moved my arm to shake hands with her. She didn't budge. She looked at me. My hand sort of hung in midair. I looked at it. It was good-bye."

Wolcott recalled, as well, the look of Tina's office. "She never had the blinds down. The light is coming at you. And you feel as if your face is melting as you're sitting there. You're plastic, man. You're melting."

Tina, too, was fast diminishing. In February 1998, rumors were circulating that she was going to be ousted from her perch. Si Newhouse himself felt compelled to deny them, but there was no doubting the precariousness of her situation. Condé Nast had announced that the precious and much vaunted distance between *The New Yorker* and its parent company was completely at an end. The magazine was folded into the rest of the empire. Physically too, it would move: into the new Condé Nast Building that was going up in Times Square. From that moment on, Tom Florio was to report to his older brother, the CEO. "All of a sudden they were going to have this bureaucracy looking over their shoulder," it would later be explained, "looking at every paper clip they bought."

"I'm fine with it," said Tom. But really, word had it, he wasn't. He saw the move as wrongheaded, counterproductive. Even though gross margins had improved 100 percent, there was still impatience on the part of the parent company to make *The New Yorker* profitable. He wanted out of the magazine.

As for Tina, who didn't have much use for either of the Florios, she too was anything but fine. "Being part of Condé Nast somehow represented her failure as an editor," one of the corporation's executives would later remark. "And there was a lot of negative press about her and the product and the business of *The New Yorker.* And she felt she was unfairly tarred by the same brush."

Yes, the magazine was losing less money and had risen 30 percent in circulation since her arrival. Yes, it was attracting, thanks to Tina's passion for lowbrow ideas veiled in up-market prose, a lot of talk. "But *she* wasn't doing okay. *Her* reputation was on the line. And I don't think she wanted to hitch her star, you know, to a loser."

Tina read what the critics were saying. What had happened to all her years of deft courting? The media that used to nestle snugly in her pocket, the gossip columnists who sang the praises of her parties, the writers who had owed her and Harry dual allegiance as well as dual incomes (and equally, the writers who yearned to). So many of these had gone astray. Harry had fewer plums to offer anyone. And as for Tina: "They were lined up to knock her off that pedestal," said one Condé Nast executive. "And they did."

To Newhouse, Tina begged for Tom Florio's removal, and by the end of May, that was accomplished. Tom Florio left *The New Yorker,* fired by his big brother, said the press. Both Florios would later deny this. But there was no doubt that it was the elder Florio who came up with the suggestion of moving his brother and appealed to Newhouse, saying, "Look, give Tom another assignment; he was doing great on *Traveler* before you pulled him off. Let me talk to him."

Newhouse demurred, at first: "He'll never report to you, there's tension between you." Nonetheless, he caved in, and Tom Florio was made publisher of *Condé Nast Traveler,* the magazine where he had started out as advertising director under its first great editor, Harry Evans.

"She hated Tom. Tom hated her," a top executive at Condé Nast said. David Carey, formerly publisher of *House & Garden,* was dispatched to *The New Yorker* without Tina's consultation. She found out about the move the day before it was announced, a mortal slight. "And she pretty much hated that, too. She was dying to get out."

"Tell me about the magazine," the PBS host Charlie Rose asked her that year during an interview; ". . . you feel like you've got it where?"

"Under control," said Tina. And that was about as exhilarated as the Queen of Buzz would permit herself to get on his show. But there was one other telling point she chose to make, a coded message to Newhouse probably. "You know," she said, "we generate so many stories that go into the movies anyway. It might have been fun, at some point, for the magazine to get involved in doing that."

"Why do you say 'might have,' as if it can't be done now?" Rose wondered.

Over and over in an effort to avoid reporting to Steve Florio, as she was now supposed to do, Tina "was constantly trying to end-run to Newhouse." Hadn't she done what she set out to do—raised the circulation of the magazine by a third? Newsstand sales had risen 145 percent. Under her six-year aegis, the magazine had won nearly two dozen major awards. What had her various publishers done for their part? But with each sally, she was making larger and larger withdrawals from her dwindling store of star power. Tina told Newhouse what she wanted: more writers, more cartoonists and artists. And Newhouse, in turn, kept Steve Florio apprised of all their conversations. His heightened awareness of Tina's quiet end runs didn't improve relations with Florio. He insisted she defer to him.

And Newhouse, too, was troubled. Tina wanted *The New Yorker* to be a base from which ancillary sources of revenue might be created and promoted; perhaps it might publish its own books. That notion was nothing new. "From what I understand, she asked every year," said an executive. But Newhouse wasn't interested. There was no money to be made in books, he felt, after long, bitter experience in the field. Moreover, he had little desire to mollify his editor with any fresh concession. To the contrary. "What he did," said one Condé Nast source, "was to create an atmosphere where Tina would be relentlessly under pressure to control expenses and produce a profitable magazine."

Even though Tina was dillydallying over a new five-year contract, not signing it and yet not refusing to sign either, no one was seriously alarmed. A draft of that contract was sitting on the desk of Tina's agent, Mort Janklow, whose client claimed to want about $1.5 million a year to continue at the magazine, along, it was reported, with a share of corporate profits. Those profits, however, were a sticking point; they were unavailable to non-Newhouses. Tina had to learn her place. Once Newhouse had said, in reply to a press question about Tina's future, "In my opinion you can't go higher than being editor of *The New Yorker*." He wanted her exactly as she was: an employee.

No longer was Newhouse a suitor. Indeed, it seemed to those who knew him that he would prefer to dispense with Tina's services rather than bend to her will on every issue. Ever since he had first laid eyes on her, Tina had been like a luxury car, beautifully styled and polished, expensive to run, but worth every nickel to a rich man with a craving for cachet. Lately, however, she had developed bad engine trouble.

Month after month Newhouse backed his executives, while Tina bridled. He was weary of *The New Yorker*'s losses, tired of the squabbling. In his view, the golden girl had to be brought into line. "Si had his threshold and she crossed it," said one of his lieutenants. By May 1998, the *New York Post* ran yet another prescient headline: TA-TA TIME FOR TINA?

It was more than likely, thought an executive close to Newhouse; in fact, very likely. "Because after all these years, she made it clear she wasn't going to change." Besides, there were other factors at work. "When Harry was pushed out," a Condé Nast insider told Rupert Murdoch's *New York Post* in July, "the ground turned very slippery for Tina."

On July 8 at 10:00 A.M., Tina announced her decision to quit *The New Yorker*—and something else besides. She was about to start a new magazine, she said, in partnership with Harvey Weinstein of Miramax, the same Harvey Weinstein who had whisked her off in his private plane after the NEXT Conference. As Miramax was owned by the Walt Disney Company, her new venture would also fall under the umbrella of Michael Eisner, the very same Michael Eisner who had hosted her NEXT Conference at the Disney Institute and received such fine treatment in Tina's *New Yorker*.

Left unmentioned was Bettina's death, which occurred just over a week before Tina jumped ship. At the time she would intimate that her bereavement had much to do with her starting out on a new, more promising life, and one of her own making. "I surfaced after this terrible five days," she said. "I felt strangely strong at the end of that experience. My head began to clear for the first time in a long time and I began to feel a tremendous desire to have my motors raced." Tina gazed at the contract with Condé Nast on her agent's desk, she told a friend, and said to herself, "I just can't marry this. I just can't do five years."

But the notion of teaming up with Weinstein had been brewing a good month before Bettina's death. In the weeks succeeding the loss of her mother, after the announcement of her new venture, Tina seemed bent on escape from solitude and reflection. She plunged into activity: press conferences, interviews, babble. "I'm exhilarated by my change—*exhilarated*," she told a reporter over the phone. "I'm having a fantastic time. I've never had such dynamic meetings in my entire nineteen years of being an editor. The meetings are so exciting right now." The reporter listened, amazed. "Ms. Brown sounded as if she were about to lose it," he wrote.

The new magazine Tina had in mind (it still didn't have a name) was to be everything she had sought to wrench, without success, from Newhouse. It would be part of a journalistic venture that would also produce books and movies. "For example," *The New York Times* speculated, "the magazine might do an article on the Italian automobile executive Gianni Agnelli, while Miramax produced a companion biography to run on the Arts & Entertainment cable channel." As important to Tina, she and her new publisher, Ron Galotti, would receive a share of the profits.

The small, intense world of power, celebrity, and publishing over which Tina then reigned was very much taken aback by all this commotion. But not the people at Condé Nast, who had received an early warning. Over the Fourth of July weekend, Steve Florio received a call from Ron Galotti himself. Galotti had a history at Condé Nast, having first published Harry's *Traveler*, then moved on to *Vanity Fair*, before ending up at *Vogue*. There he had spent many years as a lady-killer, a rough diamond, admired by men, adored by Tina.

"I'm going to ruin your weekend," Galotti told Florio. "I'm leaving." He explained that he wanted to start a new magazine with Tina and also to be in the "movie business."

"Haven't you seen this movie before?" friend Florio reminded him. Galotti, along with his peers, had been famous around Condé Nast for muttering, "It's nevah about the magazine. It's always about fucking *Tina!*"

"This time it's gonna be different," Galotti swore.

Tina said good-bye, too, in her own way. Within the publishing empire, word spread that she had given Newhouse as a parting gift a rare and costly first edition of *Vanity Fair*, not the magazine but the wry British comedy of manners written by the great nineteenth-century novelist William Thackeray. The book details the crafty odyssey of its anti-heroine, a dazzling little adventuress named Becky Sharp. By dint of her own remarkable powers of seduction and the expenditure of a great deal of other people's money, Becky progresses brilliantly from forlorn obscurity to society queen (and then, alas, back again).

Whatever tender feelings Tina had once harbored for her benefactor were now, with the disposition of this gift, at an end. Si Newhouse, who had brought her to America, crowned Tina the queen of two successive domains, and Harry the ruler of two others, was from then on a figure considerably less beloved. In public pronouncements, this was not immediately apparent. "I loved working with Si, I absolutely adored him for 14 happy years, which is a long time to be with anyone," she informed the *New York Observer*. "But I'm afraid the entrepreneurial gene that seems to have been in the American *Zeitgeist* entered my bloodstream. . . ." In private, however, no such puzzling imagery plagued her listeners, and she was known to speak ill of Newhouse and Condé Nast when the subjects arose.

"This is my last hurrah in newsprint," Harry had said at the start of his latest career. But the cheering had died. At both *U.S. News*, the magazine, and the *Daily News*, the newspaper, Harry was a bustling but sporadic presence, fading in and out. He would show up at the *Daily News* days in a row and then, seemingly, vanish. "You wouldn't see him for a few weeks," a colleague remembered at the newspaper. The magazine people, for their part, would ask the newspaper staff, "What's Harry doing?" The answer was often, "Well, we think he spends most of his time at *U.S. News*."

Certainly, Harry harbored decided ambitions for the paper, but these were not necessarily shared by the staff. He viewed the *Daily News*, he explained, as "a serious newspaper in a tabloid format," which it really wasn't. It was a provocative tabloid in tabloid format. For the man who had once been Britain's preeminent editor, that was a hard pill to swallow. Harry wanted to oversee the kind of paper that would be eagerly devoured by his friends, or at least by those who enjoyed lofty incomes. His subordinates, on the other hand, knew that

"*Daily News* readers average $32,000–$35,000 a year in income. They are not going out every night. They do not go out to lunch every day."

They were, in short, precisely the kind of readers that Harry, when he was earning a comparable income in the depressing British town of Darlington, used to court as a young editor on the *Northern Echo*. But for all his talk of democracy, for all his burning passion for America, such a constituency was now completely foreign to him. The workingmen and -women of America didn't come to his dinner parties, nor did they labor by his side. They didn't earn, as it was rumored Harry did, a salary of $750,000. "Harry didn't understand the paper nor the audience, nor did he *like* them," one editor remarked. He was, despite his trumpeted change in citizenship, a man without a country.

With his staff, Harry would argue that the newspaper's circulation could be expanded by appealing to finer, more exalted appetites. His listeners knew better. "People on the Upper East Side are not going to rush out and buy the *News*," one said.

Another of Harry's functions was to carry out the directive, which sprang from Zuckerman, to fire people. "Let's go over the staff and find out who's bad, who's good, who to let go," Harry would say. But that didn't sit well with Debby Krenek, who as a *Daily News* editor was unwilling to participate in the excision of talent from the paper, and effectively resisted it. "Harry came in as Mort's agent," felt a staff member. On one notable occasion, when the subject of whom to let go came up yet again, one subordinate piped up, "You know, Harry, if you were let go from your job, we wouldn't have to cut anyone."

From time to time in an effort to improve quality, Zuckerman asked Harry to hold mini-seminars for the newspaper staff on writing and photo display, subjects on which he had once written authoritative books. No one thought the points he made in these lectures were exactly foolhardy or wrongheaded. Indeed, one staffer found him "a professor of a kind, insightful and genial." But others saw these talks as demeaning to those to whom he preached, and worse, irrelevant. Harry would retrieve some article written two weeks earlier and examine all its flaws in the light of new facts that had subsequently emerged. Two weeks, he seemed not to realize, was an eternity in the world of tabloid journalism, where pieces are banged out in twenty minutes. He had grown insensitive with age.

And his recent displeasure with the press had substantially accelerated: *The Spectator,* which had published Toby Young's impertinent review of Harry's down-spiraling career, received six weeks' worth of letters promising legal consequences from both Harry and his lawyer—

until the beginning of March 1998. When all sorts of amused columnists on both sides of the Atlantic learned, as *The Spectator* made sure they did, of the threatening letters from his lawyers, Harry remained defiant. "There is something to be said for British libel law because it encourages better journalism," he informed the American press.

Oddly, no one reporting his threats, even in England, seemed much cowed by his wrath. "The words 'sledgehammer' and 'nut' come to mind," suggested the London *Evening Standard.* As for *The Spectator,* when Harry sent off a windy letter, refuting its allegations point by point and demanding the publication of every word, he received a very curt reply. "Your letter is rather long. In fact it's longer than Young's article," Frank Johnson, then the editor, wrote back coolly. The letter was published in a shortened version. No damages were paid or apologies given. And that was the end of the matter.

There was a new Harry abroad. In a newspaper column he regularly wrote for *The Guardian,* he would still champion free speech. "Nowhere is there a freedom to match the American freedom to find out what the hell is going on," Harry observed. But at other moments the very depth and breadth of such license sent a shudder through him.

"If there is to be freedom, it is freedom for what?" he wrote in a vitriolic attack on what he saw as the miserable state of the press in the United States, in which he invoked the specter of Senator Joseph McCarthy. "Freedom to pay for a video of the Princess of Wales and her supposed lover?" He remained heartbroken over American coverage of Dick Morris's book, feeling that the author's "sexual misconduct made him a non-person," and incensed by newspapers that "do not hesitate to use a supermarket scandal sheet as the source and pretext for the most scurrilous stories." And there he was at the *Daily News,* which although no purveyor of trash, nonetheless demonstrated few serious objections to reporting a major scandal.

Little by little, all the tenuous strength and authority that Harry had tried so hard to marshal were being eroded, and not just by an English magazine or an obstreperous newspaper staff. At *U.S. News,* an employee remarked that on certain occasions when he found himself in Mort Zuckerman's presence, Harry's demeanor altered sharply: "sycophantish" was the verdict. He would accompany his boss, and listen carefully to Zuckerman's critique of some story that was being planned for the next week. If Zuckerman said, "I'd be very careful, extremely careful with that story because we're not sure what's happening really," Harry would swiftly chime in. "You know, Mort's right! I would listen to what Mort says." It made his listener cringe.

And so Harry became, after an initial show of energy and rapt attention, invisible. Not simply invisible in the figurative sense of rendering himself less forceful or constructive in his stabs at leadership on Zuckerman's various publications, but often enough, physically invisible.

"They say he's *here*," Fred Drasner would explode when Harry evaporated from the newspaper. "Other people tell me he's at *U.S. News*. Where the hell is he?" Zuckerman, too, wondered about that as time went on. At the newspaper there was a certain amount of sympathy for his absences; it was recognized that Harry spent a lot of time with his children. "He would pick them up at three P.M. You could not call him after five or six o'clock at home," said a staffer. "He was good and sweet with his children." But it was also said that "he loved to have dinner out, lunch out."

"... Where is Harry anyway?" asked *The New York Times* early in his tenure, noting he was "not much of a visible presence at the publications."

"I'm the invisible man," Harry replied. "And if people say Harry's doing nothing, that's fine with me."

It was around this time that Harry ran into his old friend James Glassman, the former executive vice president of *U.S. News*, and gave him a lift from La Guardia. Glassman was struck by his old colleague's industry during the journey into Manhattan. He seemed very much absorbed in what was going on at the newspaper. Evidently there was a story about to go concerning a Zuckerman friend, and Harry was speaking to an employee on the car phone: "We're going to do this story anyway!" Glassman wondered about that. "He may have been trying to make a point to me," he would later reflect. At the very least, Harry was giving "the appearance of someone who was not a figurehead."

He had his plans, said Harry. He was studying the field of journalistic talent, for instance, seeing who was up to snuff and who wasn't. As for himself: "I don't know how to spell the word 'retirement.' My attitude is, I keep running. And somewhere in the dark there's a cliff.

"And I don't want to see it before I fall off."

Chapter 15

Immigrants at a Party

Harvey Weinstein was a movie mogul famed for high-quality films produced on trim budgets under a tight management—and also for his explosive temper. *The Piano, Pulp Fiction, Good Will Hunting,* all were made by Miramax, where a flair for salesmanship had produced thirty Academy Awards by the time of his partnership with Tina. Although he had his admirers, this reputation for excellence did not necessarily extend to Weinstein himself.

In 1996, when Weinstein learned that *Shine,* a movie he coveted, had been bought out from under him, he confronted Jonathan Taplin, who had sold it to Fine Line. Taplin would later tell *Fortune* magazine that Weinstein shouted profanities at him, grabbed him by the shirt, and referred to one of Taplin's female friends as "a bitch" ("Harvey is a passionate guy" was how this encounter was summed up). At other moments, Weinstein was less obtrusive in his demeanor. He liked to say, "For a big studio an expensive movie is $100 million. For us an expensive movie is $40 million." The latter sum, he suggested early on, would approximate the cost of Tina's new magazine. Such a tightfisted pronouncement might have been expected to give Tina pause, but she remained, outwardly at least, unfazed. In later months she would describe Miramax, admiringly, as "a mobile cardiology unit . . . a three cell phone culture," as if such a climate suited her down to the ground. Perhaps it did in a way. She needed a change after the fusty, recalcitrant world that she believed had stymied her progress at *The New Yorker.* "I just felt that this job would be tremendous fun," said Tina.

Certainly, such a high-octane world suited Weinstein. He was a tough negotiator, whose motto was "Always ask for it because you might get it. And if you don't ask for it, you're certainly not going to get it." In contract negotiations, Miramax people soon learned to ask for the earth. Sometimes they got it. Agents, worn and battered from protracted negotiations with Miramax, would come back to their clients and say, "What could I do? That's Harvey." That was Harvey. You never had to wonder what he was thinking. Business matters he played close to the vest. Emotionally, he was as transparent as glass.

For at least four years Weinstein, who read voraciously (the trades and the morning papers had been masticated and devoured by the time he arrived at work) and required only four hours of sleep a night—about as much as Tina—had been pining for a magazine of his own. It was to be a smallish venture, perhaps $5 million, a simple Weinstein pleasure. "The greatest train set anyone ever had," one of his subordinates figured; its mission was to grant its backer "an expansion of the playing field," where "the people you want to play with now have more room to play." The people Weinstein liked to play with were the Clintons—he was a devout Democrat—and movie stars.

It was very simple really, as far as the movie mogul was concerned. "You want to keep Tom Stoppard in the fold, but he doesn't want to write any of your screenplays? He can do an article!" explained the Miramax subordinate. "You keep Gwyneth in the fold by giving her a cover and letting her dress in fun costumes. Sure, *Vogue* could do it, but it's satisfying to Harvey that it's in *his* magazine. It's great to always have one magazine that can always run something for you on the cover, can always run an article by someone you're trying to smooth talk. Plus it's just fun! It's fun to be Tina Brown's backer."

A year or two before approaching Tina with this idea, Weinstein had assigned the magazine project to Lynn Hirschberg, the New York writer who had once worked for Tina at *Vanity Fair* and subsequently written two articles, neither ever published, at *The New Yorker.* Hirschberg did a magazine prototype ("For no money," she would later recollect), which she called *Bluff,* after her dog, and Weinstein, in turn, took it to Michael Eisner, his boss at Disney. Here, however, the project stalled. "Great, but I don't want a magazine," said Eisner. "*You* do it."

Then, three days before the world learned that it was Tina whom Weinstein had selected as a surrogate mother for his embryo,

Hirschberg received a call from Weinstein himself. "You're the first person Tina wants to hire," he informed her by way of consolation. That turned out to be an exaggeration. In the short run, it was Tina's ever loyal subject David Kuhn (destined to be the new magazine's executive editor) who called Hirschberg with a story assignment so mystifying and vague that it was almost impossible to take on. Hirschberg never did figure out what the piece was to be about because "Tina would not tell you, would not even tell you what the money was."

Tina was very afraid, Hirschberg gathered, that "people would say no to her," grand ideas would be robbed, and word of her doings and plans would somehow spread to the legions of people still nursing bitter grievances against her. Some of these people were already carping. Randy Cohen, a former *New Yorker* writer, summed up the sentiments of the old guard in a sentence: "I assume we can now look forward to Miramax becoming the shallow, celebrity-obsessed money loser she made *The New Yorker*." Jamaica Kincaid, who was married to William Shawn's son, Allen, said the very week of Tina's surprise announcement of a job change, "I hope Mr. Shawn, wherever he is, is happy. I will dance on her grave for him."

Her rivals certainly were learning a lot about the venture long before it even had a name. Tina was not wrong in mistrusting them or fearing their stealth, but she might have been astonished by who was providing them with fodder. In early February 1999, publishing executives learned that Harvey Weinstein had called Si Newhouse, of all people, with a proposal:

"Hey, Si, why don't you go fifty percent with us on the magazine?" Weinstein suggested. He wasn't, Newhouse decided at once, joking. But he did not want such a magazine just then, and explained that to Weinstein.

In fact, the magazine, now that Weinstein realized its true and impressive costs ($50 million at least), was being shopped all over town, without results initially. No major general-interest magazines had been started in a long time, as potential partners realized. And for all Tina's delight in her newfound equity—"I get to be an owner, not an employee; the key is a new magazine in which I have a stake," she said—no one could imagine her stake was worth a nickel just then. Nor would it be until the day the magazine made a profit, and that day would be far off.

In search of more funds, Ron Galotti, president of the new project, Weinstein, and Tina had paid visits to David Pecker, president of Hachette Filipacchi Magazines; to Norman Pearlstine, editor in chief of Time Inc.; and to Frank Bennack, Jr., and Cathleen Black at the Hearst Corporation. But such ferreting begged the question: Why wasn't Disney, Miramax's corporate parent—a company Tina had winsomely described as being "as solid as the Bank of America"— throwing more cash at the project? The answer proved touchingly simple. The company didn't want to. "Michael Eisner didn't want to spend a lot of money on this," a senior Disney executive explained to a reporter.

By mid-February, despite the indifference of Time Warner and Newhouse, this orgy of begging produced results. Hearst consented to take over "office support"—circulation, newsstand distribution, and direct mail—in return for 50 percent joint ownership in the magazine. Moreover, it would pour $25 million of its own money into the venture. Thus equipped with fresh funds and improved possibilities, the magazine could become what everyone involved assumed it was meant to be: a knife poised at the throat of Condé Nast.

Equally important, the magazine eventually acquired a name: *Talk,* initially with the subtitle "The American Conversation," although this would be dropped. Other titles had, of course, been considered and disposed of: notably, *Reporter, Profile,* and most sagaciously, *Brown's.* But the title selected had special resonance, and not simply among Tina's backers.

"It has been lost on no one what the name of her magazine is," a *New Yorker* writer declared with some energy. " 'Talk of the Town' is the best-known feature of *The New Yorker.* It is referred to exclusively in the magazine as 'Talk.' And fairly widely outside the magazine. I don't think this has escaped anyone's scrutiny." Certainly, David Remnick, a writer handpicked by Tina herself and now *The New Yorker*'s new editor, was made unhappy about that choice of title, a friend remarked. Within short order, he learned some of his staff were being courted by his former boss, but without success.

"Tina is competition," it was said around her old haunts, even among those who once had cause to love her.

And yet here they were wrong. For one thing there was, it quickly became evident, the issue of money. *Talk* wasn't offering enough, some insisted; and the Weinsteins were by no means inclined to break tradition and become as open-handed as Si Newhouse: "Every dollar they spend, they bargain," a *Talk* editor complained. In fact, there was every reason for Tina to fear hearing no from those she courted, even when the sums offered soared appreciably, as they did to a few select journalists. Don Van Natta, Jr., a *New York Times* investigative reporter whom Tina had offered a $200,000 salary to become a senior writer, and Jeffrey Goldberg, who contributed to the *New York Times Magazine,* both turned her down. Again and again, established writers were approached, often by Tina herself, using all her remarkable powers of persuasion, with pleas for stories. "You *must* write for us, you must write. I *need* you," the new editor in chief and chairman of *Talk* would say. Or alternatively, a less inspired pitch: "The magazine will be a combination of *Slate* and *The New York Times.*"

Then freelance writers would hear from David Kuhn and certain harsh details concerning remuneration would be communicated: $7,500 . . . $10,000 . . . $12,000 for three months of work. Such sums were depressing enough for journalists whose lifestyles had been improved and expectations first raised by Tina herself more than a decade earlier. The irony of all that was not lost on anyone.

TINA BROWN'S INNOVATION? CHINTZING THE WRITERS read a headline in the *New York Observer.* It was a reference to another unwelcome *Talk* novelty: its boilerplate contract, the source of startling new demands—almost Weinsteinian, one might say, in their daring and vastness of scope. Except that Tina had experienced similar cravings.

"I commissioned a piece by Michael Korda about author Jacqueline Susann," she would recall of her *New Yorker* days, when Korda was asked to write about the late novelist. "The movie rights sold for $700,000. Michael took me to lunch and said, 'Thanks.' "

At *Talk,* gratitude would be expressed contractually and in ways more substantively beneficial to the magazine.

"You hereby grant to *Talk* the following rights to the Material throughout the universe . . ." a contract read. One of these new universal rights included allowing the magazine "an option for all motion picture, television, allied and ancillary rights," based on an author's article—for up to thirty-three months, and a payment of as much as $20,000 in at least one instance. Similar rights (but for a much shorter period) were demanded by *Talk* for any book that might arise from a piece. Of course a writer might consider, after six months were up, going to another publisher who was more generous. However, at least one version of the *Talk* contract insisted, those authors who entertained such notions were advised that they would have to hand over to *Talk* "10 percent of any advance that you receive over $200,000." At *Talk,* this rights grab was called "one-stop shopping."

At the literary agencies, it was called something else entirely. Conflict of interest.

It did not escape the notice of agents, who traditionally received a hefty chunk of a client's fee (from 10 to 15 percent) for performing these very functions, that *Talk* had set up its own book division headed by Jonathan Burnham, late of British Viking Penguin. Or that it also now had a TV development person, Gabé Doppelt, formerly editor of *Mademoiselle* and an old friend of Tina's from her London days. In whose interest exactly was it to abrogate the freewheeling whims of writers lucky enough to sell stories to other film companies or publishers? Not the authors', and not the agents', whose goodwill Tina now needed more than ever. The William Morris Agency flat out refused to allow clients to consent to these provisions. Other agents followed suit.

And Tina's much vaunted ideas for stories, the ones she wished to shield from the fierce gaze of her competitors, were they honestly worth the stealing? They seemed to derive their inspiration from the last frantic days of Tina's *New Yorker*. Confessions in relief was what she wanted now, but divested of the veils of eloquence that once shrouded their glare. The gossip columnist Liz Smith was approached. "Wouldn't it be great if you could 'come out' for the first issue!" Tina importuned, but Smith declined to write about her private life, reserving a portion of it for her own memoirs.

A passel of "widow profiles" was suggested to a well-known reporter: the widow of Sammy Davis, Jr., and when that idea was discarded, the widow of Frank Sinatra. An article on the drug Ritalin, prescribed to control attention deficit disorder, was offered to the *Talk* writer Walter Kirn after he informed Tina he had once taken the medication.

"Tina wants that Ritalin piece for the first issue," David Kuhn told him.

But on due reflection, Kirn decided he didn't want to write the article. In the first place, he had taken the medication as an adult, not as a child, which Tina seemed to have misunderstood. And secondly, he told Kuhn, he thought writing such a story would be "self-exploitation."

"Kuhn got really upset with me," Kirn would recollect. "He accused me of being a liar. A liar to Tina. To get the job at *Talk*. I really didn't appreciate that. He accused me of manipulating Tina with a story I wasn't going to deliver."

With one deft phone call to the writer's house, Tina managed to smooth his feathers. "It's all a misunderstanding," she said. "Won't you please work for me?" Kirn was not really averse. He had only one peeve; he didn't want to do celebrity profiles. Nonetheless, that was what kept pouring in: the comic actor Adam Sandler, the cherub-faced star Leonardo DiCaprio, the television writer and producer David Kelley. Gradually, Kirn understood. "This magazine was not going to be a combination of *The New York Times* and *Slate*," he said. "I thought, tabloidy."

To make matters worse, Sandler wasn't cooperating. "He doesn't like the press," Kirn said. DiCaprio at that point wasn't interested, and neither was Kelley. "These were people on her wish list who were not coming through," Kirn realized. By the summer, before a single issue of *Talk* appeared, he had defected to Condé Nast.

So there was Tina. She was exhausted and shattered after the death of her mother, and her older friends felt that taking on a diffi-cult new project just then was exactly the wrong thing to do. "Some-one should have told her when you have that kind of emotional upheaval you can't make that kind of decision," one friend said. She had also lost the rest of her old support system: a billionaire backer and a company where, all things considered (even the Florios), she had been looked on with an indulgent eye.

In their place, she had an as-yet-unpublished magazine in crammed, untidy offices on West 57th Street, guarded by a reception-ist with an iMac, and a highly wrought, nervous, and overworked staff, a few of whom were actively thinking of bolting. And she had Harry to give her advice and to help shape certain pieces (to their detriment, insisted one editor). On Ron Galotti's desk was a framed mock-up of a *Talk* cover depicting Tina and the publisher, and below their merry grins, the headline read: SI YOU LATER! There was no end to this sort of send-up of Newhouse. Louis Vuitton, a prospective advertiser, received a garbage can from Galotti with copies of *The New Yorker* and *Vanity Fair* jammed inside. Attached was a note from the publisher: "I have taken the liberty of selecting the trash, the garbage, on your media schedule. I suggest you put it out on the curb."

For the rest, there wasn't much. Not enough space, for one thing. Her secretary had to work in Tina's own office. On the floor below her, Lesley Vinson, the new art director, discovered two non-functioning computers but no technical experts, and she had to mock up the dummy in twenty-eight days. There wasn't enough money to tempt hordes of fine writers and not enough cachet to lure a number of celebrities. "Tina Brown is the junk food of journalism," declared Hillary Clinton to a writer who encountered her at a party.

Tina also had David Kuhn—and his value to her through their years together at three magazines, although significant for its undistilled devotion, was not always reciprocated. "He's just like a little lapdog," Tina once informed subordinates, demonstrating some canine panting for effect, after Kuhn left a *New Yorker* meeting. At the new magazine, Kuhn received a rumored $300,000 salary and all the angry sentiments employees were fearful of exposing to their more formidable boss: "The henchman of some of her destructive capabilities," one said.

He was useful to Tina that way, his subordinates felt, a voice box for the remote and androgynous blond goddess who "adopts masculine characteristics in her toughest moments." It was one of her triumphs that Tina managed to compel, as indeed she had at other magazines, a considerable amount of empathy for what she was going through. First glimpsed, "she looked seriously depressed," it was decided. And although this impression would be slightly revised as time went by, Tina often did appear sad and vulnerable to her employees, her weariness edged with desperation and also an endearing sort of awkwardness. On a day when Michael Eisner himself showed up at the offices, she emerged in a white suit, her hair slicked back and her pale complexion flaming with cosmetics she had no notion how to apply. "Her face was a completely different color," said an observer.

None of this affection for her frailties transferred, however, to the man who did her bidding. Kuhn become known at the magazine as "Mini-*She*." A new writer, after accepting an assignment, discovered that "David Kuhn kept telling me he was worried about whether I could do it—but this was after he hired me, not before. Every time I saw him, I thought his head would explode from the stress." He had "a constant need for reassurance."

Worse, the article assigned, a business story about a start-up company in Los Angeles, was burdened by the ceaseless involvement of the company's public relations firm, which insisted on being present "in every interview . . . with a person from the PR company writing everything down," the writer said. "So of course it was intrusive." Indeed, few better publications would have allowed such intervention. Even the writer realized that, although *Talk* remained sanguine. "It was so compromising," the writer said. "The whole deal. Because the way they negotiated access was with the PR company."

Complaints about such an assault on traditional journalistic standards proved useless, the writer decided. "When I told this to David Kuhn, he got really, really defensive. And angry. And said, 'You know, this is an unbelievable story. We wouldn't be getting it otherwise, and you should be so thrilled.' "

In the end, the story was killed and the writer received $5,000—after three months' work. "Blood money," it would later be described.

Appeasement of the subject, however, would prove to be an inalienable part of the package. It was Tina's method of improving access to the previously inaccessible. The successful courting of Hillary Clinton, for example, despite her initial reservations, would be a vital component. "A Clinton fanzine" was how Kirn described the magazine's birth, especially after Tina hired the former Clinton aide George Stephanopoulos to write for her. As ever, these decisions were not construed as an accurate reflection of her political beliefs. Tina had none, or at least none that stood in the way of getting what she wanted.

For those who thought of reporters as outsiders in a fundamental way, as people who ask questions for other outsiders—the readers—*Talk* was not the place to be. Walter Kirn might look askance at his former boss and protest her view of journalists as "cronies of the powerful who manage to serve their interests at the same time as they are pretending to give information." On the other hand, he realized, "That's her game. She's entitled to it."

Besides, where was Tina to go? What was she to do? Despite all Harvey Weinstein's power, the stars who had been her traditional standbys weren't exactly stampeding to her magazine. The staff was mutinous with resentment and jealousies, and often sleep-deprived. The breakfast cereals and small packets of coffee offered by *Talk* to bleary-eyed employees were regarded with special loathing: they were ominous portents of just how many hours in a day were due their employer. As the time for the launch of the first issue approached—the first issue that was to include, if one was to believe Tina's promises, practically every article ever mentioned, desired, or thought of—editors were urged to meet 6:00 A.M. deadlines, then the following day 7:00 P.M. deadlines. Up to ten full drafts of varying lengths of the same piece were demanded so that Tina might pick which among them best suited her, before engaging in another rewrite. Two and three editors were assigned to the same task. Money was, to say the least, tight. The smell of panic was in the air. Harvey Weinstein became a regular, examining the covers, puffing his cigarettes.

Within the small, brittle world Tina knew best, certain top writers were laughing up their sleeves at her. Even in dear old Britain, that sort of dismissiveness prevailed. At a London dinner party attended by, among others, Gore Vidal, Tom Stoppard, and Clive James, one of the guests was overheard asking the rest, his tone amused, "Well, were *you* asked to write for this magazine, *Talk?*" As it turned out, Stoppard did eventually throw Tina a bone—an article on his Jewish ancestry. But that night, there was a good deal of laughter at her expense. A few of the guests maintained that the publication, when it finally came out, would probably resemble *Empire,* a good British fan magazine.

Something had to give.

In every respect, *Talk* was to be different. It was going to look like *Paris-Match,* said Tina, or the German magazine *Die Stern,* with thin paper. "Scrunch it," suggested Tina. "Everything is so fast, people don't have time for a big marmoreal glossy that sits on a coffee table anymore. This is meant to be really used and flung around. I want it to be stuck in a gym bag and left in a car seat."

It would also be an oversized magazine, which automatically presented added difficulties for a newcomer. Condé Nast had tried that years earlier with *Allure,* a woman's publication, and discovered, as one executive said, "it was a disaster because it cost $7,000 extra per advertising page to make film that unique size." And where on a newsstand could an oversized new magazine be positioned? "The only way to do that is to pay enormous sums to the newsstand dealer, and frankly, no one can afford to do that."

In the midst of this confusing set of prerequisites was Tina. She was nearly forty-five, no longer the perpetual *wunderkind* of limitless energy. At home were the demands of her children, competing desires and needs: "Motherhood is the hardest part of my life," she said around this time. "Very often your head is completely wrapped up in something else and yet the children need you." At the maisonette, she and Harry would greet certain employees as early as 7:00 A.M.

There were dark circles under her eyes. "A person suffering in some way," a new subordinate quickly decided. "And massively insecure—just because she doubts everything everyone says." Indeed, she was very bitter.

Her feelings toward Newhouse still rankled, and at least one listener assumed that this was due in part to Tina's loyalty to Harry, her resentment over his experiences at Random House. But she herself still harbored grievances even more recent. Steve Florio and Newhouse, a confidant was given to understand after talking to Tina, were particularly egregious: "She said they fucked up the business in such a way that there was nowhere to go. They were unchallengeable. She said that she brought *Vanity Fair* up by the tacks and she supported and she nursed it. And then Graydon Carter got all the credit. The same with *The New Yorker*. . . . And then when the time came for her to get support from Si, none came for her." She had sacrificed almost every portion of her life for those magazines and the men who controlled them. "When I worked at *The New Yorker,* I allowed myself just one night off a week," she told a friend. "I worked every other night."

In her new incarnation, that single free night seemed to have evaporated. Tina was working maniacally, impervious to the needs of her staff. "I can be cold and difficult when I don't like a person much, and I probably am difficult to work with," she said nonchalantly. "I don't have any apologies for that. I think if I wasn't difficult I wouldn't be any good."

But how good was she at this exacting point in her career? "She was just paranoid about failure," said one employee. "She had this Prussian attitude. She believes you work on every single thing insanely until the end of it, that's the only way to get success."

In fact, it paved the road to failure. Tina's fatigue was no longer confined. It became palpable, widespread. Once crisp and lucid explanations of intent had overnight turned to babble. "*Talk* is a cultural search engine," Tina would say. It was hard to tell what that meant. "Heat is quality," she informed a reporter, before swiftly retracting: "No, quality is heat." A sixty-second compilation of equally mystifying Tina pronouncements on *Talk*'s qualities, all articulated in her strange mid-Atlantic accent—"Conversation! Discussion! Chatter! Context! Emotion! Intimacy!"—was filmed and edited by MTV artists over a hip-hop beat. Dubbed "The Tina Rap," this ad was then inserted into two video duds, specifically *Little Voice* and *Wishful Thinking*. All in all, it was not an inspired notion. "The very reason for renting a videocassette is you fast-forward past the commercials," a surprised publishing executive said.

Over and over again, Tina kept assuring prospective readers as well as her own staff that she wanted *Talk* to be "a quality magazine." That was not a new ambition. It had been Tina's earnest profession even during the most incendiary, lowbrow years at *The New Yorker,* when she insisted that her "passion is to put, for example, El Salvador on the cover, and still have strong newsstand sales." At *Talk,* similar protestations of seriousness were aired and, initially at least, to some extent met. The first magazine cover was an ardent and confused reflection of what Tina had always called "The Mix," and what her artistic director, Lesley Vinson, had in mind: no simple shot but a jumble of them spread against a black field. It would showcase Gwyneth Paltrow, a Miramax star, crawling about in black leather underwear, but framing her wiry body were the political figures of George W. Bush, shot in meager black and white, and Hillary Clinton, spread across the top in three identical shots, a visual stutter. "It was sort of a joke," said a staff member. "It was meant to be ironic and funny."

Within that odd fusion, it was the long-awaited saga of the first lady that claimed precedence, although not for reasons of substance. "The Intimate Hillary" it was called, and the reader was not meant to consider it as anything more than a confession of the parlous state of a marriage seemingly under repair. The story was finally completed, once the first lady's objections to Tina had been successfully overcome, by Lucinda Franks. As the wife of New York district attorney Robert Morgenthau, Franks possessed excellent Democratic connections. Morgenthau was much admired by the first lady; and she had met Lucinda Franks socially a couple of years earlier on Martha's Vineyard. This, along with Tina's efforts and Weinstein's, went a long way toward securing the writer the access she wanted.

Nothing went smoothly, however. The accompanying photos, meant to be charmingly informal, were neither. Some of the staff arrived with a pile of chic outfits for the first lady's shoot, but nothing turned out as expected. "Tina wanted her to pose in a taxicab, at a New York Yankees game, but unfortunately that never happened," said a staffer. "She hated the first round of photos." Those were snapped by Michel Comte. He was given, it was claimed, roughly fifteen minutes to accomplish his mission. "I don't think he was happy with our choices of the photos we ran," said one staffer. Nor did the article meet with instant approval.

After multiple drafts, Tina herself set to work. The article was to be modified—"simplified" was the explanation—in a breathtaking manner. "Tina inserted a long comparison between Hillary and the Princess of Wales," it would later be remembered. Two full paragraphs were expended on this unlikely coupling of an undereducated, pretty princess with a fine wardrobe and a bad marriage and a ferociously intelligent, ambitious politician, who also happened to have a cheating husband. "Lucinda had a fit."

Clearly, she had not yet fathomed Tina's ambitions for the publication. It was to be a mirror held always at the angle most advantageous to its editor. As editors wilted through scores of drafts and redrafts, one staffer realized, "She really wants every story to sound like her voice. She really wants the magazine to be her vehicle." Although by then the question of whose identity was being explored was up for grabs. Was it Tina's? Hillary's? Diana's? The three fused into one.

So, there were more revisions. A few days later, the verdict was clear. "Tina disliked the new draft and wanted to go back to hers, with the comparison of Hillary to Princess Diana." By then, editors were ordered not to talk to Franks, who was phoning despairingly from her hotel in France where she was vacationing. She not only loathed the notion of comparing Hillary to the late Princess of Wales, she also disapproved of Tina's flippant description of the first lady: "The velocity of her changing hairstyle," it read. Among *Talk* staffers there was a fear that Morgenthau might call *The New York Times* to describe the mangling of the article. And then what? *Talk* couldn't survive such a disaster. Staffers were on the phone with Devereux Chatillon, *Talk*'s in-house counsel and vice president. Eventually, Tina caved in. The article, when it appeared, remained Diana-free.

The intensity and darkness of those panicked days were reflected in practically every aspect of the magazine. "You write about us and I guarantee there'll be no cooperation down the line," a spokesman for Tina warned a London newspaper in June 1999, before a single issue had appeared. *Talk*'s vision of itself had irretrievably and finally mutated. It had no intention of being perceived as a hungry magazine with an uncertain future and synergistic yearnings for books and films. It was giving itself the airs and conceits of an old-time Hollywood studio, flush with power. Tina might as well have been Louis B. Mayer. When the *Sunday Telegraph,* which had booked an interview with Tina six months before *Talk*'s first issue, decided to switch reporters, David Jenkins, the more hard-hitting substitute, phoned the magazine at once, and was assured of a rendezvous.

But once Jenkins arrived in the States, matters became more complicated. "No, it's not going to be you," said a spokeswoman for Tina. "It's going to be who it originally was." With resignation, the *Telegraph* flew Jenkins home to London and paid the extra airfare for He-lena de Bertodano, the first reporter assigned. She, in turn, arrived at *Talk*'s New York offices only to meet "a PR magnate, an elderly man with a cut-glass English accent," who "insisted that 'everyone will be more comfortable if he stayed.' "

In vain did de Bertodano protest that "only prime ministers and monarchs have needed baby-sitting."

"I'm *advising* Tina," said the public relations man, "and I think it is better like this." The public relations man stayed, but Tina ultimately apologized, and gave de Bertodano a second interview.

That same month, Tina threw a party for her staff at her maisonette. After the hors d'oeuvres, people collected on the patio for a speech from their boss. It was doubtless meant to be a rallying cry, several of those who heard it would later claim, but the tone was grim and disheartening. "What you're about to face is like a Hell's Angels initiation. Everybody is going to urinate all over us," she told her shocked company. "There was this sense of persecution," said one of the guests. "That *they* were going to be against us. That *everyone* is going to be running us down, and don't listen. 'We are inventing the American literary magazine and *nothing* like this has been done in thirty years,' she told us."

Furtively, some of the invited guests glanced at each other, perplexed. "I had no idea what precursor she was talking about for this 'literary magazine.' There was this paranoia going on," said one of them. "I didn't understand where all the confrontations were expected to come from. I didn't understand why the magazine had all these enemies or where they were coming from."

But Tina did. "After twenty years of being an editor, I've fired a lot of people and killed a lot of stories," she said. "I don't make friends that way."

In late June 1999, Rudy Giuliani learned that *Talk* had shot a cover of Hillary Clinton, at which point the New York mayor, who had serious hopes of running for the Senate on the Republican ticket just then, decided the magazine was unworthy of the Brooklyn Navy Yard. That was the site selected for a massive party, to celebrate the launch of Tina's new magazine, and it had not been an idle choice. A $150 million film studio was being planned there by Harvey Weinstein and Robert De Niro. Giuliani, who suspected (correctly, as it turned out) that *Talk*'s first fully dressed cover girl was entertaining similar senatorial ambitions on the Democratic side, suddenly saw no reason for the city to pay for the policing of the Navy Yard lot.

"A week ago, we heard they were going to put Mrs. Clinton on the cover, and we thought that would lead to an event possibly becoming politicized," complained Randy Levin, the city's deputy mayor for economic development. "There was the possibility that this thing would turn into a circus."

Thus it was that one of the canniest Republican politicians around managed, through a combination of hypersensitivity and general pigheadedness, to cement that possibility into a certainty. The media circus now began in earnest. When *Talk* managed to snag Liberty Island as an alternative site, Tina was not loath to create certain analogies. "We're thrilled to have the Statue of Liberty," she told *Daily News* writer Celia McGee. "Nobody can knock this Lady."

The magazine's forthcoming gala made headlines across the country. Giuliani, one of those invited, looked like a prime bully. Tina at that juncture of her career couldn't have paid for the breadth of publicity he had just handed her.

Nor did she have to. Once the twelve-acre site run by the National Park Service had been established for the party, the *Daily News* boasted a front-page headline: PARTY ON! it read. "Now Party's on Liberty Isle." Inside was McGee's article on Tina's coup: BASHING BACK AT MAYOR was the headline, followed by: "Mag Big to Throw Party in Hil Flap on Liberty Island." It ran complete with an assessment of the catering tab ($200,000 or more) for the picnic-style dinner that would be served, and the cost of two ferryboats ($9,000), which would bear the elite to and from the Battery.

The story was illustrated with an arresting front-page shot of the Statue of Liberty. Except it wasn't quite the Statue of Liberty much of the world had come to know. In place of the familiar blank-eyed bronze head, a photograph of Hillary's smiling face had been substituted. That was odd, decided Mort Zuckerman, when he opened his paper. At first, he was under the mistaken impression that it was Tina's familiar features he was glimpsing. But even when corrected, he was not at all pleased. He couldn't understand why it was leading the newspaper.

It was not unusual, of course, for both Tina and Harry to perform little favors for each other and their friends within the discrete realms of their publications. But for the longest time, especially during *Talk*'s planning stage, Harry didn't interfere with coverage of his wife's magazine at the *Daily News*. Occasionally he dropped by the paper's business desk to discuss morsels of *Talk* news. It was pretty much left at that. *Talk* would receive far more intense and brittle analysis at the hands of other publications, but there was no directive at the *Daily News* to proceed gingerly, and Harry's influence wasn't directly exerted.

But in July 1999, just as *Talk* was planning its big launch, a story ran in the *Daily News* after feeling the weight of Harry's heavy hand. In the Sunday *News,* an article about Michael Eisner was being reported by the feature writer Edward Lewine, new to the paper. There had been, as Lewine learned, "rumblings" that the Disney chairman was leaving the $70 billion company, where profits were sagging. Those whispers in the end proved untrue and Lewine himself never suggested the Disney chief was leaving. But there was ample reason at the time to speculate on his standing within the company. Eisner had been involved in a wildly expensive breach-of-contract lawsuit with his former studio chief, Jeffrey Katzenberg ("the little midget," as Eisner called him), who eventually received a settlement of roughly $200 million. After eighteen months at Disney, the super-agent Michael Ovitz was also forced out of Disney and given $100 million. Critics wondered at the costly successive bloodletting at the parent company of Miramax.

Harry read the article on Eisner's tribulations without much pleasure and dealt with its author over a period of several days. Then he rewrote the piece—much to the annoyance of Lewine. Only a week on the job, Lewine wasn't about to make a fuss; he wasn't, after all, an entertainment reporter. Privately, however, a thought crossed his mind: He was aware of Disney's importance to Miramax. Later Lewine would tell colleagues, "Harry's married to Tina, Tina works for Michael Eisner." He didn't pretend to know what Harry's motivations were. Lewine was worried about his own reputation. "This looks terrible," he said.

Harry explained. He knew Eisner, he said, as well as other people involved in Disney. He could help. The quotations Lewine had received from sources didn't back up his contention that there was anything amiss with Eisner, said Harry.

The published version of the article on Eisner and his company, although dotted with their well-known misadventures, was gentled into a long tribute to both. "You'd be perfectly right if you said that the vast majority of what appeared in the newspaper came from the pen of one Harry Evans," said a *News* writer. In fact, the article began with a particularly tender tribute:

Disney Chairman Michael Eisner is like the hero of his new animated box-office hit, "Tarzan."
Just as the teeth of tiger and croc go snap, snap, he swings through the Hollywood treetops, away from critics predicting his imminent demise because of sagging profits, defecting executives and that nasty court case.

Those opening paragraphs were supplemented with a "resounding endorsement" from Sid Bass, whose family owned the largest share of Disney stock, and whom Lewine had been prevailed upon by Harry to call: Harry gave him the phone number. Bass evidently needed no prodding to praise Eisner. "He's a terrific executive, and has built an expanding company," Bass said. Moreover, "There are always bumps in the road. But, in the long run, the successful trend behind us will be duplicated in the future." The piece closed with yet another reference to "this Tinseltown Tarzan" who "swings from vine to vine."

And who knew? Lewine, in his first week at the paper, certainly wasn't acquainted with the powerful executives with whom Harry had contact. There could be some justification for his intervention. But the reporter was by no means happy with the massive editing and rewriting. There was no byline on the story. Lewine, deciding it bore no relation to what he had written, had withdrawn his name.

The other circumstance in which Harry was said to have intervened concerned the *Daily News* story on *Talk*'s festivities by the Statue of Liberty—the very piece that had arrested Zuckerman's attention. Harry was evidently interested in the coverage himself. He wasn't giving the reporters any scoops on the subject ("Oh, how can you do this to me?" he said, before confirming the big party's change in locale). But in deference to the great tradition of tabloid competitiveness, one staffer heard, Harry had said, "The *New York Post* is going big with it."

As for the notion of affixing the smiling face of the magazine's future cover girl, Hillary Clinton, to the torso of the Statue of Liberty, that, as best can be determined, was the result of group consultation, done in Harry's absence, significantly. All sorts of inspirations were floated. Should Tina's face be pasted on the statue? Or Hillary's?

There wasn't any dissension among the staff when the idea came up to give the story such prominent placement, either. They all seemed like good ideas at the time.

But Mort Zuckerman was another matter. The next morning, the newspaper's proprietor gave full vent to his outrage in a phone call to Debby Krenek, the editor in chief. Just why was Tina's face placed atop Lady Liberty? And why was the headline of the story leading the paper to begin with? And who was responsible for putting it there? Krenek, who happened to be in Seattle attending a conference at the time, called around.

She was the first female editor in chief of the newspaper in its seventy-eight-year history, a small, personable woman, but with little use for Harry. The two had once had "a knockdown, screaming fight," witnessed by several in the newsroom. Nonetheless, her first words to Zuckerman might have been expected to improve his mood toward everyone, including Tina Brown's husband.

"No, Mort, that wasn't Tina's face. That was Hillary's," she assured her boss when they next spoke. But even with that correction, Zuckerman's anger was not assuaged. "I know for a fact Mort went ballistic," one Zuckerman employee would later recollect. "He felt Harry was serving his own personal interests with this story rather than the newspaper's."

To determine where responsibility lay for turning the *Daily News* into an arm of Tina's publicity machine, Krenek rang her deputy editor, Robert Sapio, who was on duty in her absence, and learned something interesting: Harry had apparently made a morning call to Sapio. "Basically Harry said to Sapio, 'I had nothing to do with any of that.' He was agitated," a *Daily News* source would later recall.

Krenek had yet another conversation with Zuckerman. Krenek told Zuckerman she believed, after checking, that it had been Harry's idea to have the story on Tina's forthcoming party lead the paper.

Several months later, various Zuckerman employees learned that Harry's contract, which was up in December, would not be renewed. There were those at the newspaper who thought that the fuss over the prominent piece on Tina's party was the final straw. But the issues between the two men were clearly more substantive, provoked by more than a single incident. "He or Mort decided it wasn't working," said Fred Drasner. "Mort was very upset with him in the end."

And perhaps Harry himself was not so very surprised at this turn of events. As an old British friend would later write, "[T]he only evi-

312

dence I saw that he was actually editing anything was a crumpled piece of paper which he proudly produced from his wallet to prove that Mort Zuckerman authorized him to describe himself as such."

He had not, however, been idle. In the waning months of 1998, Harry's long-awaited book on his adopted country appeared to largely impressive reviews. Entitled *The American Century,* it was coffee table–sized, cloaked in a gleaming silver cover that bore the stamp of approval of his best-paid Random House author ("A book every family should have"—General Colin L. Powell), as well as a $50 price tag. The great Indian chiefs Sitting Bull and Geronimo, General Douglas MacArthur, the journalist Edward R. Murrow, the environmental legacy of Teddy Roosevelt, Jimmy Carter's efforts on behalf of peace in the Middle East—all these and more were dispatched in a series of paragraphs or pages.

It had not been a quick or solitary endeavor; anything but. The project had been ongoing for thirteen years, and Gail Buckland, the book's photo editor, explained that part of the reason for its endless gestation was that "we really didn't want to make compromises. I mean, Harry, when he cares about something, is a perfectionist. He would read the most phenomenal amount, unbelievable. Every sentence he writes with authority." Tina, too, was admiring. Almost a decade before the book's appearance, she was marveling at his industry.

"It's typical of Harry that he must have read something like 750 books on the subject," she said. "But when did he have time to read these books? He stays up all night, he reads in the car; he reads history when he's on the Exercycle."

The length of the pursuit was nonetheless wearying. "Oh my God, I'll never get this written," Harry told Buckland. And in fact she realized "he was tempted maybe for a second" to get some help from a writer. But at this suggestion, she took him aside and said, "There are two things we need. One is quality. The other is your voice." With that, she recalled, "he threw out the idea of someone else writing it."

For a short period, Buckland worked on his book on the seventh floor of Random House, over which Harry was then presiding. Among his colleagues there was considerable speculation about its fate. "No one ever thought it would ever come out," one assistant editor said. "It was taking so long, people thought he was undoing it at night." But Harry was, in fact, weaving together a lot of disparate strands—too many, as it turned out, and (here his detractors were dead right) for too long. Had he managed to meet a more timely deadline, his book might have met with greater success. And yet, he couldn't help himself. As another collaborator would point out, "This was a labor of love. Harry's Valentine to America."

Harry kept his promise to Buckland. "I wrote every word of that book myself," he would later boast, and the truth of that was buttressed by the familiar style, stamped on every chapter—much of it sturdy, earnest, and trudging, as though marching home from battle. "The long debates of the thirties and early forties reflected divisions about the nature of America that remain," Harry wrote. A single paragraph contained the phrases "interventionist mind-set . . . faint heart . . . harsh reality." It was that sort of style, unobjectionable but bearing the imprint of too many edits, revisions, and consultants. "He would send his text to whoever was the leading expert in the field," Buckland explained. "John Kenneth Galbraith, Arthur Schlesinger, Bob Woodward on Watergate."

It was not insights but the sweep of conflicting ideologies and movements that drove the narrative. Hollywood, his wife's domain, was barely discussed in the six-pound volume; the birth control pill never got a major role. And yet the book had considerable merit. Its photographs were extraordinary, shedding an intimate and reflective light on the steady and impressive compilation of historical detail. In the last pages, the best of its author emerged, as Harry wrote from the heart on a matter dear to him: the GI Bill of Rights, which gave veterans scholarships, allowing even the least affluent among them to get the education they needed. "And every time one of them stepped up to receive his diploma, a lightbulb lit up in everyone's mind: What a waste of this country's talent we had endured by limiting higher education to the well-off, what an undemocratic denial of a citizen's potential we had tolerated!"

In December 1998, *The American Century* moved to No. 8 on the non-fiction best-seller list of *The New York Times*. From its perch a full seven rows above it, *The Century,* a similar work of history by Peter Jennings, gazed down in triumph. The ABC anchorman whom Tina so admired came into America's living rooms every evening.

Harry flung himself into a round of promotions and parties. Liz Smith reported the news that President Clinton possessed "a well-thumbed copy of Harry Evans' dazzling new book" and was "evidently riveted by it." And still the book failed to seduce the nation to whom it was dedicated.

It was a hard blow. "I can't go on ABC to do promotion because of Peter Jennings," Harry complained to David Westin, the network chief. His listener was distinctly unsympathetic. "Don't be paranoid," Westin said.

But how could he not be? Jennings, with his easy access to ABC's *Good Morning America,* distinctly outmatched Harry; within short order, ABC and the History Channel were planning a twenty-seven-hour series based on Jennings's book. By February 1999, it was out-selling Harry's almost six to one, and had earned nearly $9 million in royalties (which went, however, to the network). In all, Harry's coffee table book sold 125,000 copies; not bad. The timing of its appearance, on the other hand, was.

For its disappointed author, friends felt a rush of sympathy, born of many elements: the work, the many years he had "poured his heart into it," the man himself. Although American, Harry's photo editor had once been a curator at the Royal Photographic Society of Great Britain, and during those years, a passionate admirer of the old Harry in his glory days of courage and leadership at the *Sunday Times.* Gail Buckland knew the Harry few Americans had ever met, an editor who had been an inspiration, who through his crusades had altered the course of journalism in his native country, for a time anyway.

"The paper had so much energy, people couldn't wait to go out and buy it," she recalled. "Harry's brilliant. Most people don't know that," she added. "Harry was a hero. . . . Nobody gave him anything."

And here her memory was, of course, perfectly accurate.

The evening of August 2, 1999, was balmy, with soft breezes jostling the colored Japanese lanterns that dipped and swayed from the trees of Liberty Island. From 7:30 P.M. onward, some fifteen hundred guests were transported by ferries across the river to the *Talk* festivities. Once on land, their paths were illuminated by ushers, *Talk* editorial assistants mostly, equipped with headsets and large flashlights. There were fireworks. "This one's for Harvey and Bob Weinstein!" proclaimed George Plimpton as a pair of rockets exploded. He was serving as a kind of emcee for twenty minutes. And Queen Latifah, the rapper who had won a Grammy, begged the assembled to "give it up for Lady Liberty."

"Queen Latifah is the only queen I'll ever have to curtsy to," quipped Tina. "I mean the Statue of Liberty—America—this is what it's all about."

She sounded, understandably, just a bit addled. And yet at the same time cocky, enchanted by everything that transpired at her own party: the forces of nature that contrived to give her a fresh, rainless night; the brightly painted lanterns brought in by Robert Isabell; the swarms of guests who devoured the contents of Glorious Foods baskets, sausages, fried chicken, lamb chops, containers of corn salad.

Through the looming dark, the semifamous could just manage to pick out the completely famous as they foraged through the baskets or lounged with wineglasses on striped cushions arranged in pretty little groupings. Hillary Clinton, alas, wasn't among them. But there was solace in the quantity and rank of substitutes: Madonna on the arm of Rupert Everett; Sarah Jessica Parker, Salman Rushdie, Paul Newman, Kevin Bacon, Pierce Brosnan, Lauren Bacall, Demi Moore, Elizabeth Hurley, Liam Neeson, and Natasha Richardson.

Against a triumphant blaze of television lights, Tina greeted them all. She was wearing a white silk dress decorated with small crystal beads, and for once, was not unaware of the impact and importance of her attire. "Thank you, Donna Karan, for making this dress," she said, "and then I had to pour myself in it." Just about everyone else in the world was thanked by Ron Galotti, cynics noted: Evian for providing the bottled water; Mondavi (a *Talk* advertiser) for the wines; Tommy Mottola of Sony for the music. "And of course the writers are never mentioned," one of their number later muttered.

But these were trivial dissents, barely heard above the din of buzz. It was an astoundingly impressive party, eloquent in its studied informality, not a hair out of place, not a celebrity nose out of joint. Even Weinstein appeared supremely happy with his investment. "You're fucking great, kid," he said by way of congratulating the art director on the magazine's complicated European-style cover.

Talk was to hit the stands the next day at $2.95 a copy. It had, just then and despite its early setbacks, a fair prospect of success. Inside the first issue were 107 full pages of ads and some very intriguing articles, at least two of which were bound to generate a lot of publicity. The stars who had earlier snubbed Tina were, it now became obvious, making tracks to Liberty Island, the expensive writers reconsidering their earlier verdicts, and her exhausted staff as yet in abeyance. They were there, weren't they, present at the creation? The first lady, who had belittled Tina, was now in her pocket. Despite months of mounting panic and the scorn of her rivals, Tina had accomplished just what she had promised. She had molded something out of nothing: an infant magazine.

"An editor can see only the flaws, but she's our baby and she's breathing," she had written. From experience, Tina knew all about the fragility of new life. It was her moment. She had earned it.

Beside the proud mother on that magical night was Harry, a gallant Zeus bidding a jovial farewell to the worshippers who stepped onto the ferry that would bring them back to Manhattan. One of those hailed was Dan Menaker, the editor who had worked successively for both halves of the famous couple, and one of many who would write about that evening. He had been among those petitioned by Tina to write for the new magazine, but did not.

"By the way, congratulations," Menaker told his host.

"On what? I haven't done anything," said Harry.

"Um, on your book?"

"Oh that. Well yes, thanks."

Chapter 16
Deep Wounds

"This is an unbelievable response to the debut issue of *Talk*," declared Cathleen Black, the tough-minded president of Hearst Magazines, who was not inclined to coddle editors. During her three years at the top, Black had eased out the editor, Ed Kosner, from *Esquire* and somehow managed the retirement of Helen Gurley Brown from *Cosmopolitan*. Tina, on the other hand, looked pretty good to her just then, which was, all in all, a salutary signal, considering the idea for half ownership of the magazine had, it was suggested, by no means been her own but that of Frank Bennack, Jr., the CEO of Hearst.

"Hearst isn't where Tina Brown meant *Talk* to end up," wrote Michael Wolff, *New York* magazine's noted media critic. "As for the Hearst Corporation, if becoming an icon weren't in itself a vulgar media thing to do, the company might be an icon for blandness and facelessness in a glitzy, high-profile world." At this less glitzy corporation, there was evidently all sorts of conjecture about whether or not Bennack would "get" Tina, meaning understand what she was trying to accomplish. As for Cathie Black, Wolff wrote: "Tina Brown is either the opportunity of a lifetime or some major, major pain in the ass."

Three days after the magazine appeared on the stands with an initial run of one million copies, *Talk* went back to press for an additional 300,000, so for that moment it looked as though Black wouldn't be feeling much pain in any portion of her slim physique. It was, as Hearst's press release pointed out at the time, the fastest-selling title in the company's history.

The popular response was driven in large part by the first lady's confessions about her husband in the first issue. "You know in Christian theology there are sins of weakness and sins of malice, and this was a sin of weakness," she told Lucinda Franks. Her husband's infidelity, she claimed, was understandable when placed in context. She had thought, mistakenly, that his passion for other women "was resolved ten years ago." But fortunately, "He has become more aware of his past and what was causing this behavior." Bill Clinton had at the age of four been "scarred by abuse"—a muddled accounting that was evidently not to be taken literally in any of the usual meanings of the term, but to refer to the "terrible conflict between his mother and grandmother."

That was titillating enough, but by no means the only theme of the piece. Melanne Verveer, Mrs. Clinton's chief of staff, was summoned to the text, where she did some hasty mending. "[W]e've slowly seen a physical passion come back into their lives," she said. "And it's not just for show." Among the staff was a certain constriction of throats when those remarks were included. "I thought it too unbelievable and stupid. I think Tina originally wanted to use it as an ending," said one. On the other hand, as at *The New Yorker*, there was a view that she was assigning articles with a specific purpose: to explore herself. In another woman, that sort of endeavor might have been taken as evidence of narcissism, except it was found that Tina no longer saw herself as merely Tina. In her discussions of story ideas, one listener was struck by the gradual displacement of her identity. It was as though notions and suggestions considered suitable for future issues of the magazine had somehow assumed a corporeal form, after which they experienced a physical relocation.

"She seizes on something where there's a personal association. You know it in your body that the conversation has shifted and has become about Tina. You know you are no longer having a conversation about the ostensible subject. You're shocked—because you don't even know her. She is so obviously talking to you about herself in the guise of Hillary. . . . Everything talked about is strangely associative: in her mind, Hillary is Tina." There was specifically, this *Talk* employee added, the matter of "the marriage."

Sometimes this psychic association with Hillary received its fullest amplification in the expression of where the two women—and their husbands—differed. "The Clintons have a passion for politics, Harry and I have a passion for print," Tina informed subordinates. But the very contrast cemented the analogy; that, and the cool command she displayed, which alternately compelled and deflected admiration. "She's got incredibly beautiful skin, but she's kind of androgynous," said one of her employees. "Sometimes she bends over and you think, Who is that professional golfer from Sydney, Australia? And yet, she has a lot invested in sex appeal."

Her identification with women of regal and unapproachable bearing was also apparent in social contexts. Just a few weeks before her first issue, Tina had attended a party in Britain thrown by her friend the novelist Julian Barnes. Once inside the house, she was approached by one of the guests, a Frenchwoman passing around the hors d'oeuvres, who offered the platter to the visiting celebrity. "Tina's face didn't flicker, didn't change," recalled her friend Stephen Glover, who was also among the guests. "She didn't pick up the hors d'oeuvres, she didn't decline them. She didn't ever acknowledge the woman. It was as if she weren't there." That was not wholly unusual behavior for Tina. Many a subordinate, especially women, had been blasted by that touch of frost. But now, accentuating her usual distance was a disassociative quality. It was as if Tina wasn't entirely there. Someone statelier and even more important appeared to have taken her place.

The magazine had accomplished more than wresting words from the first lady that had previously been locked inside. The presidential candidate George W. Bush, in the issue's less publicized piece, also spoke the unspeakable. " 'Please don't kill me,' " he whimpered, mocking Karla Faye Tucker, the convicted murderess who was about to be, with his complete approval, executed in the state of Texas. It was a revelatory display of callousness ("Odd and cruel," noted Tucker Carlson, the conservative author of this story), and an adumbration of what the electorate might expect from this aspirant president.

Of course, quibblers might note that the Bush article was totally empty of hard *political* detail. A passage hailing the Texas governor's ability to forge with the Democratic lieutenant governor, Bob Bullock, an alliance so strong that the two men "worked out compromises on legislation" failed to mention what that legislation encompassed. *Talk* was aimed, just as Tina said, at "a real intimacy of access"—meaning that little else, politics included, counted. Just as Tina's fans had predicted, the magazine managed to slide in, at the last second, a photographic tribute by Peter Beard to John F. Kennedy, Jr., who had died with his wife, Caroline Bessett Kennedy, less than a month earlier in a plane crash. And yet here, Tina, who had imagined a far more encompassing "intimacy of access," found herself thwarted, not for the first time, by her own staff.

David Kuhn, who was intimate with some of the Kennedy inner circle, suddenly reared up, said an acquaintance, refusing to divulge the conversations and reactions of his friends. Danielle Mattoon, a *Talk* senior editor and close friend of Kennedy's cousin Rory (who was about to get married), also received an urgent call on Martha's Vineyard from the office. "Talk to everyone" were the instructions. She too refused. "I was impressed by Danielle," said Lynn Hirschberg. "She told me, if Tina fires her, she understands."

At that early date, Tina was firing no one, nor could she afford to. The first issue was a triumph. The *New York Observer* pronounced that there was "something new here . . . a certain informality, an underproduced, casual feel, a warmth even, that you don't usually associate with other products turned out by that cold, calculating, control freak, er, I mean Ms. Brown."

But after that first success, there was another issue to get out. And the next month, still another. Paradoxically, because of Tina's well-established urge to control almost everything, an atmosphere of confused effort prevailed. The photography editor would discover, after the fact, that certain photographers not of her choosing had been assigned to stories by other editors. The art director would be ignorant until quite late of the success or failure of shoots. The writers could not fathom what was expected of them, precisely because the only expectations that counted were Tina's, and these were not always imparted straightaway to editors, but were supposed to undergo an almost telepathic conveyance based on what she had rejected. Thus, the same article would endure an agony of revisions, sometimes by several editors, each competing with the others and fearful of displeasing Tina. That last was relatively easy to do. Knowledge was precious, compartmentalized, unshared; responsibility and lines of authority ambiguous. "There was total disorganization," one editor remarked. Secrecy was everywhere.

The difficulties at *Talk* arose in part from the exalted expectations raised by its first issue; but most especially from the fears of its creator. They were vivid and constant, and occasionally Tina would give them voice. "What's the alternative? To be a flop?" she had asked at the birth of her magazine, when a journalist wondered how she dealt with the envy of her peers. The question was strictly rhetorical. She had never failed before; it was imaginable but unaffordable. "She certainly looks at life in terms of failure and success in an almost killing way," one of her old employees observed. How many more chances would she have? None, Tina suspected. "This is definitely the last big roll of the dice as far as I'm concerned." She had staked everything on it.

And yet, as inexperienced as she was in the field, she knew what defeat engendered. The mere prospect of it already tickled the competition, and a simple touch might so easily trigger the long slide. Around Condé Nast, there were few well-wishers. It was accepted wisdom that rumors concerning Graydon Carter's early and very difficult days at *Vanity Fair* had been abetted by Tina in conversations with favored reporters. Approached on this, Tina would stoutly deny being the source of such gossip. But she knew its power, and, better than anyone, how easily the tables might someday turn. That fear of failure was direct kin to her old nightmare, the one she had harbored as an Oxford girl, that she might in old age be afflicted by poverty. Poverty was now not a likely option. But failure was. In fact, it was already sitting on her stoop, pale, haggard, waiting.

Tina was seen after the first few issues of *Talk* (surprisingly, an acquaintance thought, considering her workload) at a film showing of a Weinstein picture entitled *Music from the Heart*. She looked sad. She was asked about *Vanity Fair* and *The New Yorker*, whether she missed them. "Well, I like to leave them after I fix them," Tina replied, "and they're on their feet."

But *Talk* was something wholly new, built from scratch. Unlike *The New Yorker* and all her previous publications, there was no structure or staff, however flawed or misdirected, in place when Tina arrived to "fix" it. Every last atom of it had to be created—by her. And then, as another month approached, recreated. "It was a vicious cycle," said one of the top staff. "You know how it is when you're a child, running down a hill and you just can't stop? The momentum just builds? It's too steep?"

And what did Tina have to work with? "We really went into a major launch with a very small and quite young staff," she would later say, when what was actually needed was "some more seasoned and additional people to get things done."

But how exactly was that miracle to be accomplished? In October 1999, to enormous fanfare, Harvey Weinstein consented, after a plea from Tina, to plow an extra $5 million into the publication—this on top of the $12 million designated for the first year's budget. But the popular press learned that his partner, Hearst, was by no means eager to part, after its initial investment, with even a fraction of that kind of cash. Cathleen Black assured everyone, "We are three thousand percent behind Tina"—and that, given her company's frugal reputation, was about the only substantial figure it was likely to award her.

There were, said one editor, rumors of "production cost overruns—a $15,000 overrun that Hearst was giving her shit on." Fifteen thousand dollars! Such a sum would have barely bought blue pencils at Condé Nast. Problems she had never dreamed of now plagued her. Even Tina's supposed coups, the miracle of snagging Gwyneth Paltrow in provocative leather for the first cover, for example, were promptly expropriated and laid at the feet of the more powerful. The "First Lady of Miramax," as Harvey Weinstein dubbed Paltrow, had decided to pose on the magazine's first cover only "when Harvey asked me to do it." It was Weinstein who commanded loyalty, acquiescence. "It wasn't about 'Hey, everyone, check this out,' " Paltrow said. "It was more, 'Here's another thing Harvey's making me do.' So let's not do Grace Kelly pictures; let's try something different."

In the name of independence, of acquiring her own brand, Tina had dumped Newhouse, a shy and doting sugar daddy, and gained . . . what? Weinstein, who couldn't manage to stay quietly in the background; and Hearst, a notoriously unsentimental outfit, which was two-timing her with a recently announced new magazine under the banner of television star Oprah Winfrey. In the face of such competition, of what practical use were all of Tina's much touted connections, her glamour? Who was there on her meager staff of fifty, many short on experience, to inform her of the likely new hit on Broadway, the coming trend? At her command was younger, cheaper merchandise, tentative and untried.

"Tina is going to get stuff at *Talk* and she's going to have heart attacks at what she sees," an expensive *New Yorker* writer predicted early on, with smug but perfect accuracy. "There's a reason why we're paid what we are. We've been writers for years."

Tina's current stable of writers and editors were uncertain of what their boss wanted—until draft after draft of the same story flew back, rejected. "She's pretty rarely pleased. Because she's so wound up, I never understood what her expectation was," said one of their number. "And then five minutes later she tries to seduce you again. She shines her light on you and you suck it in. She's a charm. And it works. Until it doesn't."

Those miscommunications were not wholly the result of much of the staff's combined inexperience. Tina herself hardly knew what she wanted. For the first time in her impenetrably self-assured career, she was feeling manifestly insecure and much aggrieved. "The Mix," Tina's potion for success in all previous incarnations, had become all mixed up. It was as if a spell had been cast. Everything backfired. A soggy article entitled "In Praise of Housekeeping" was succeeded by a macho profile of Vince McMahon, the chairman of the World Wrestling Federation. A promised jump to page 213 in a piece on New York governor George Pataki refused to leap to its intended destination; on the assigned page, readers found a picture of a white-haired Liz Taylor clutching her white-haired dog, Sugar.

"Except for the article about Hillary Rodham Clinton in the premiere issue, nobody is talking about *Talk,*" the *Boston Globe* informed its readers.

"I often felt sorry for Tina," said her art director, Lesley Vinson, who had worked in Germany. "If only we'd had the luxury of putting out a market-tested magazine—a *Nullnummer,* as they call it in Germany, where it's a standard procedure. But Tina felt she didn't have that luxury. If she'd had the option, it could have been different. But she was in an untenable position. She had too many masters to serve and I could see she was being pulled in a million different directions."

Tina would take the layouts home and study them. "Almost every article that came in had to be edited and laid out in three ways, as a feature, a department, and a smaller story in the back of the magazine," a staff member said. "She had to see it in layout form to figure out which it was going to be. So it had to be edited to three different lengths, illustrated or photographed in three different ways." Often Harry came to her aid. He was seen at *Talk*'s offices, on occasion as late as 1:00 A.M., offering his opinions on the layout and the typeface. Vinson found his suggestions invaluable. Harry's advice, born of years of experience, was, she said, "lucid, clear—he was a wonderful guy, somebody I learned a lot from." His demeanor, too, was a comfort. "He never talked down to people, he was good with graphics and a great concept man. Harry and I thought much alike."

In fact, the covers, dark and intriguing as Vinson had intended them to be with multiple photographs, were attracting a lot of comment, some of it not wholly flattering. "The most beautiful magazine ever printed from behind the Iron Curtain," sniped a member of the staff. "It looks like the *Belgrade Weekly.*"

Part of the problem with the look of the magazine, it was felt, was the limited participation of Vinson herself in the process—not her choice, as it happened. When the decision was taken to make the aging movie star Elizabeth Taylor the cover girl of the second issue, a peculiar choice in any event, as she hadn't done much at the time to warrant such placement, Vinson opted for a contemporary photograph. It was vetoed by Tina. Puzzled readers saw on the cover an old photograph of Taylor as she had been perhaps thirty years earlier, hair cropped pixie-style and as black as tar.

Nonetheless, a photographer was dispatched to shoot Taylor for the inside pages. Vinson was not asked to come, which, she complained, left her clueless. But in her feelings of exclusion she was far from alone. "It became a private agenda, more like Moscow, there was too much stuff that was unknown," said one employee.

New story ideas were tossed around, many as bewildering as their forebears. The wife of Christopher Reeve was one; another was an article by Betsy Israel on young mothers who took Atavan or Valium, which, amazingly, did make it into the magazine. Time and again, Tina's once infallible instincts appeared to fail her. When the young agent Jay Moloney, a protégé of Michael Ovitz, hanged himself in November 1999, the dead man's mother immediately received a letter from Tina.

It began by offering the author's "sincere condolences for the death of your son," and then moved seamlessly to the point of the exercise. "I wondered if you would care to write a piece for our magazine that would remember your son and the struggles that he endured," wrote Tina. She was specifically interested in the young man's addiction to drugs, as well as in "the people who led him astray," and the press, which "must have played a malignant role in all this." The terrible irony of a "malignant" press seemed to have been lost on the author of this note. But it was not lost on the grieving mother, who received it on the very day of her son's funeral. In short order, the contents were faxed around Los Angeles and New York.

Nothing seemed to work, even though a frenzy of non-stop activity was the order of the day. "That fax, my God!" said one employee. "Every single person got a fax and a computer. There was no choice. They came to your house and installed one. And it really burned her if you didn't have a cell phone." As for Tina, where once (during her

New Yorker days) she religiously quit the office around 6:00 P.M. in order to see to her family, and worked from home, now after a break with the children, she returned. Eleven o'clock at night would find her back at *Talk;* sometimes she could be seen there until two in the morning. "I thought she was very there, too much there," said one colleague.

It was the frenzy that was her undoing. There was no time to pause to reflect on the consequences of her actions or how certain ventures and decisions might be perceived by the world outside the office. Tina was like "a hen in a barnyard pecking frantically," a subordinate remarked, "saying, 'When am I going to see the next draft of that?' "

But her oversight was spotty, at best. In January 2000, a special glossy advertising supplement to *Talk,* wrapped in plastic, was provided by the Italian fashion house Benetton and its creative director, Oliviero Toscani. Entitled "We on Death Row," it featured a series of murderers, and next to each photograph, an interview of questionable skill and sensibility ("What is different about your life since you've been on death row?"). Its ostensible purpose was somehow or other to end the death penalty. Ron Galotti would claim in December that Benetton had spent "seven figures" to achieve that goal in *Talk.*

But how was an advertising supplement in a celebrity magazine supposed to accomplish such a mission, especially when it turned out the project itself was riddled with ethical lapses? Benetton would concede that payment was made to two inmates for the rights to their likenesses. Prison officials in five states and at least one of the condemned claimed to have been misled: "We thought it was a magazine story," said Theodis Beck of the North Carolina Department of Correction. "We never expected to be involved in an advertising campaign." Jay Nixon, Missouri's attorney general, sued Benetton, also claiming that Toscani and an associate entered the prison under false pretenses, pretending to be journalists to hide the purpose of their campaign.

"I was surprised Tina didn't have that checked out more," one of her ever-changing employees would later say. "I always wondered about that insert. What's going on here? I mean, did the magazine need the pages that badly to thicken it? And what was her deal with Toscani?" Galotti would deny any deal at all. Only one thing was certain. Tina decided that "the bad boy of advertising," as Toscani was known, was just the boy for her. Shortly before the supplement appeared, *Talk* hired the man who had once compared himself to Michelangelo (and Benetton to a medieval pope) as the magazine's new creative director. Toscani would work there two weeks of every month, then fly back to Milan for an equal amount of time.

Even those subjects under the editor's direct control were unsettling. The profile of Liz Taylor was plaintive and uneasy, as if the magazine was strapped for subjects, any subject, no matter how weatherworn, as indeed did appear to be the case. Where was (to borrow Tina's favorite adjective) *hot*? Whither *buzz*? Written by Paul Theroux, the Taylor profile even contained the author's own reservations on the assignment, dismissive and harshly rendered:

"What puzzled me was—given the facts that she is not in films much anymore, that her workload is light, that she doesn't seem to read, that she has little more to occupy her mind than her dates and her dog . . ." That certainly begged the question of what anyone was doing spending time on the piece. It began in vague and discursive fashion with a long description of Neverland Ranch, the property of the unappetizing singer Michael Jackson, who was Taylor's particular friend. It ended in a manner more pointed, but self-referential and cruel. "After a particularly good session of talk at her house, I went away. Soon after, speaking with a mutual friend, Elizabeth asked, 'Is Paul married?' "

Inside *Talk*, objections were raised about such a self-congratulatory ending; in vain. "Tina and David Kuhn thought the piece was great just as it stood," one editor said. "Kuhn said, 'It's brilliant. Brilliant.' " For once the edits and reedits that afflicted other writers were held in abeyance. "She won't touch Theroux because he is a name."

Talk was certainly in crisis by then, but it was hard to fault Kuhn for every misstep. There was a hit-and-miss quality to the whole operation. In an interview with *Mediaweek,* Galotti seemed to blank out on where *Talk* was printed and had to consult briefly before coming up with the answer: Salem, Illinois. He was a different Galotti, everyone noticed, "so nice," less outwardly aggressive, more good-natured now that he was married and a new father. "The savageness was gone," said an impressed member of the staff. "He was very much about making a community out of the staff."

At a champagne party, reference was made to the "new Ron Galotti." It did not go over well. "I liked the *old* Ron Galotti," Tina mumbled under her breath. Everyone understood what she meant. "She liked the tough guys."

* * *

What was *Talk*? Who was its target audience? Hot on the heels of Elizabeth Taylor came the next cover: Arnold Schwarzenegger. "What kind of old news is that?" wondered a staff member. Surely not the sort of bait with which to hook the young and the hip.

There was a wobbliness to the enterprise, symptomatic not of start-ups but of start-ups without direction, governed by fear and indecision. An interview with Theodore J. Kaczynski, the murderous Unabomber, was completed by Stephen Dubner, edited by *Talk*'s Lisa Chase, and ready for publication. Then: "Tina told Lisa that she had 'moral problems' with the piece." That argument was met by one employee with some cynicism. "If you know Tina for fifteen minutes, the words 'moral problems' are not something she can get away with."

Nonetheless, Tina was insistent. "My problem with that story was that I felt it was a puff piece about the Unabomber and I thought it needed some balance," she said. Certainly the Unabomber's brother, David Kaczynski, was made unhappy by the prospect. As it turned out, the "good" brother had been negotiating to sell the rights to his own story to Disney. But members of the staff came to learn that piece of news only gradually. Tina would later claim that this film deal "had zero to do with anything," and in fact, there were some staff members who genuinely believed her. But others didn't know what to think. "Tina won't be square with an editor to even hint on the political things she is dealing with," said one. "You have to guess it."

Dubner ended up selling his scoop to *Time*. Lisa Chase, the editor, quit.

It was not a lonely exodus. The staff was exhausted, fed up with Tina and David Kuhn. "If you have people who are not particularly well paid and working seven days a week, twenty-four hours a day, my inclination would be to at least be polite to them," said one of the disgruntled. "But they're Mr. and Mrs. Charles Dickens really. They're beyond it."

By the end of 1999, there were nine defections from a magazine that had been publishing exactly four months. Of the top twenty on the masthead, seven had left, "a top management turnover of 35 percent," the *New York Post* pointed out. Among the missing were Howard Lalli, the managing editor; George Hodgman, a special editor; David Randall White, the production director; Lesley Vinson, who returned to Germany—and Kuhn, who simply, friends said, "couldn't take it anymore."

This last departure came as no big surprise. Word had been going around for some time that David Kuhn was anxious to leave; in fact, he had been in job negotiations for over a month. Meanwhile, Tina had hired Bob Wallace, late of St. Martin's Press, as the new editorial director of her magazine. Her most loyal servant had been summarily handed what one writer called "a real fuck-you."

After Kuhn told Tina he was leaving, he went to Galotti's office, where he found both the publisher and Devereux Chatillon. There was a fifteen-minute conversation. Then Galotti told him, "I think it would be best if you left today." That came as a surprise. Kuhn had expected to give two weeks' notice. After twelve years off and on in Tina's service, he left the office in an hour and a half.

"I liked George Hodgman, and when Lisa Chase left, that contributed to my feeling of unease," recalled the culture writer Manuela Hoelterhoff. She, too, resigned. "I tried to explain to them I wanted more serious things to do." Despite Tina's pleas, she was adamant. "I'm pushing fifty. And I thought, 'I just can't do this.'"

Outwardly, Tina tried hard to be sanguine about all these many departures. "Most magazine launches in the first six months have more people vanishing than Idi Amin's cabinet," she said—not an entirely felicitous comparison. And then her wit failed her. She made a mistake—a large one, as it turned out, and fraught with impact. To a question about the staff defections posed by the on-line magazine *Salon,* Tina replied: "Some people find it too hard. . . . Some people don't like hard work. Some people are too inexperienced to handle it. Some people are out of their depth."

A bit later, she phoned Susan Lehman, the reporter at *Salon,* attempting a desperate retraction. "The editors who left had all worked incredibly hard under a lot of pressure because our staff was so small," she amended. David Kuhn would be "great" in his next job—he was signing up with an on-line venture. Howard Lalli, who was moving on to become editor of *Atlanta* magazine, "deserved the promotion."

If these hasty encomiums were meant to appease the nettled, they failed. A lot of those who joined *Talk* had been asked to sign confidentiality agreements, meaning that in theory the world would never learn just how they felt about their employer. Wounded and incensed, people formerly at *Talk* started talking.

Of course, at varying intervals there were also small spikes of satisfaction. In February 2000, much to the displeasure of *Vanity Fair,* which had been under the distinct impression that its cover that month would feature the movie star Leonardo DiCaprio, *Talk* got him instead. "Harvey Weinstein did arrange for Tina to meet Leo in

New York on one occasion to get that cover," a magazine employee recalled.

LEO RISES was the headline, although the body of the accompanying story by Aaron Latham failed somehow to substantiate such a promising claim. " 'My stomach's killing me,' he grimaces. 'I have to go to the bathroom real quick.' Leonardo runs out of the room, down a short hallway, into the men's room and throws up."

But was that successful celebrity wrangling a tribute to the power and appeal of Tina? Or just a sop to the movie company that controlled her magazine? Just three days before the young actor had agreed to appear on the cover, Miramax consented to become a distributor of DiCaprio's grim and violent new film, *Gangs of New York*. That movie was, according to the press, "having some trouble getting financing when Miramax stepped in." However much Tina and DiCaprio's new agent denied any connection between the two events, the impression remained. Harvey Weinstein was at the helm. He was calling a number of the shots—specifically, the big shots.

In fact, the weight of Weinstein's influence was more subtly exerted at the magazine. He was by no means running the whole show. "Harvey definitely had an influence," said a *Talk* employee. "But he was not as hands-on as people think. If we select a cover subject in which Miramax is involved, then he becomes more involved. It's his film, and publicitywise, he wants to do that. If we get a star, it's less because Harvey desired someone than Tina desired that someone, but if there needs to be pursuit, it would be Harvey who does the pursuing. He definitely wields influence and has the last word, but that last word is wielded rarely. In a sense they get a bad rap, because *Talk* is owned by Miramax."

All the more reason, then, to tread carefully, and pursue celebrities from other studios. But that was difficult. *Talk* was a mendicant magazine; it got the desirable people Weinstein could get precisely because he could get whomever he wanted. That was ultimately a gift of suspect and dubious value. As the *New York Times* reporter Alex Kuczynski pointed out, after four issues were out, of twenty-two articles "written by people in the film industry or about people or characters in the film industry, 11 featured people recently or currently affiliated with Miramax or Disney projects."

"All those Miramax and Disney people they've got to get on there," one *Talk* defector said. "I sometimes think they should just call it *Miramax* magazine. Just do that, make it a movie magazine.

Make no bones about it. Say, 'We're doing an in-house product,' and be successful."

And in one area at least, the magazine was undoubtedly a success, of sorts, even a trailblazer. It honed and burnished the oxymoron "celebrity journalism." It was, of course, an area that Tina had pioneered, albeit in slightly less dissolute form, at the very start of her career. Her *Vanity Fair,* like her *Tatler* before it, had assiduously massaged the egos and ambitions of those it needed (and simultaneously dispatched or mocked the characters and prospects of those it did not). That was the game, expertly and dangerously played. It was left to the reader to figure out where the truth, or some fraction of it, actually lay.

But if earlier profiles in Tina's *Vanity Fair* might have contained some wickedness or at least a spot of bad news for the subject and his publicist—an on-set lapse into adultery, a previous, undisclosed marriage, or a nasty tantrum—newer versions of these pieces in *Talk* glossed over or bypassed such indelicate episodes. The magazine needed access, instantly, before Weinstein grew impatient or Hearst checked its balance sheet. "It's taken time to organize our approach to Hollywood, which is very much organized around the world of celebrities," Tina told *The New York Times.* "I am afraid I am partly to blame for that because I kind of invented the concept of the celebrity wrangler and now everybody is wrangling away."

Talk was by no means the only publication that indulged in unblushing and mirthless treatments of potentates and stars. Under Graydon Carter, *Vanity Fair*'s Hollywood coverage could certainly be laudatory. *In Style* was famous for acts of reverence toward those who consented to drop into its pages. The difference here lay in each magazine's pretensions. *In Style* had none. *Vanity Fair* offered monthly penance for its star profiles in the form of stories, columns, and investigations where all bets were off and certain verities—ugly ones at times—were exposed. *Talk,* on the other hand, didn't seem to be able to come to terms with the identity fashioned by its own creator. It was, Tina insisted at the outset, nothing less than "very eclectic and, you know, in depth at the same time . . ." And yet with each succeeding issue that depth eroded and critical analysis was held in abeyance. Most of *Talk*'s subjects—even those who lived far from Hollywood—had grown too important for its survival. Film idols were worshipped with a religious fervor.

"His two eyes are different," a director remarked in its pages of

DiCaprio. "The left eye is very soft and empathetic. The right eye is more analyzing. One eye oozes warmth, while the other is more pene-trating. One eye is psyche, the other is intellect." Illustrating those re-markably diverse ocular qualities was a passage from the actor's notebook, dealing with the environment and the sorry fashion in which, DiCaprio wrote, "the human animal is predisposed to trample paradise."

Other media outlets were, as ever, watchful, alert very likely to the new path being beaten by Tina at *Talk*. Within two months, ABC News sent DiCaprio to interview the president of the United States for an hour-long special on the environment. "We are not making this up," wrote Howard Kurtz in *The Washington Post*. Nor was he. In the ensuing flap, however, the network edited the interview down to two and a half minutes, reprimanded two producers, and the show bombed in the ratings, where it finished second to last of all network programs.

As for Tina, who had promised to provide her readers with "good writing" marked by "a little bit of a brainier twist," she was clearly facing a similar defeat. It was as plain as the left eye on DiCaprio's face.

In search of the "brainier twist," she seized on Arianna Huffing-ton, the Greek-born adventuress of considerable charm and an eye for a string of powerful men who had helped her throughout her writing career and in her climb up the celebrity ladder. The two women had other elements in common. At the precise moment when Tina was the toast of Oxford, Arianna Stassinopoulos, as she was known back then, was the hit of Cambridge University and the president of its de-bating society. She had written a biography of Maria Callas and then married Michael Huffington, heir to an $80 million oil fortune, quite undeterred, he would later say, by his revelations about his homosex-ual past. She wrote another biography, this time of Pablo Picasso, and a few years later she was by Huffington's side when he financed an uninspired California campaign for the Senate with $28 million of his own money. Soon after he lost, she was no longer by his side.

Arianna Huffington joined up with her old comrade Tina Brown, she would later say, "because I could write about those people that would interest me." One evening, Huffington found herself in Tina's Manhattan maisonette. It wasn't long after Bettina Brown had died, and her daughter was feeling particularly downcast and vulnerable. "Look at this place," she said plaintively. There were large numbers of books stacked against the beige walls; long English flowers fell from the window boxes, and beyond those was a lovely garden. But for all that, it was extremely impersonal, as formal as an embassy. "It's a career woman's apartment," Tina concluded, without joy. She meant that with the death of her mother, the best friend Tina had in the world, that's all it was.

On October 20, 1999, *The New York Times* broke the story that certain people at *U.S. News* and the *Daily News* had known for three months: Harry Evans was leaving by the end of the year. He was, he told the press, going to be writing books again. "Two major American historical works," Harry said, one on business innovators and the other a prequel to *The American Century,* both of which would perhaps be turned into documentaries. None of this information was couched in particularly glowing terms. "At *U.S. News,* Mr. Evans's most public action was taking credit for the dismissal of its former editor, James Fallows, who had fallen out of favor with Mr. Zuckerman," wrote Felicity Barringer of the *Times.*

It was pretty well established by then that the aging editor, too, had fallen afoul of Zuckerman. And yet, even in those last months at the *Daily News,* it was noticed, there was a palliative and complicated aspect to their relationship that occasionally belied those tensions. Zuckerman was godfather to Tina and Harry's daughter; he had proved his friendship in hundreds of ways over the years. "There was a closeness, too, between the two men. It was a funny relationship. Even after Mort had said, 'Harry's going to be gone,' there was that friendship," remarked an employee.

Harry and Tina, for their part, had been among the first important editors to embrace Zuckerman in the eighties, when he was widely considered little more than a real estate barbarian who had the temerity to storm the sacred temple of journalism. Harry especially had offered him, for a very long time, the respect and protection the businessman craved. And Zuckerman, who found Harry brilliant, had offered his for an even more extended period, sheltering him after the storm swept through Random House. "In a lot of respects they were close," one Zuckerman employee said. On both sides, more than a touch of that gratitude and admiration remained. But on Harry's there was something more: a placatory element.

Late in his tenure, he learned that MaryAnne Golon, *U.S. News*'s director of photography, had decided to quit. Harry approached her with his usual endearments; the two were fond of each other, sharing a passion for the visual aspects of the magazine. In the seventies, Golon had devoured Harry's classic book on the subject, *Pictures on a Page*. When they lunched together and his cell phone rang, Harry would whisper into it, excitedly, "I can't talk to you now. I'm lunching with the *most* gorgeous girl. Don't tell my wife."

But endearing and talented as he was, Golon was under no illusions about Harry. He was a survivor above all else. "I imagine you're upset, MaryAnne," Harry had acknowledged, after he insisted on taking credit for the dismissal of Jim Fallows. "Harry," Golon had replied at the time, "I don't know that 'upset' quite does it." Despite Harry's urgings, she found his role in that instance "kind of sad." She knew how much "he wants to be liked . . . to be loved and respected."

In fact, Harry had guessed right. Golon was irredeemably disaffected. Six months after Fallows departed, even though Zuckerman himself wanted her to stay, she made her own announcement.

"Oh dear, oh dear, you *can't* leave, MaryAnne darling," Harry said to her. "Why are you leaving?"

Golon told him she was leaving Washington to join the staff of *Time,* in New York.

"Oh okay," Harry replied, resigned to the inevitable. "But if Mort asks, please tell him I tried to dissuade you."

Those attempts at regaining Zuckerman's goodwill were unavailing, however. On the whole, it was felt, Zuckerman's disappointment in his onetime mentor was so severe that however deep the original debt, it had been, of late, more than repaid. Amity alone was not likely to secure Harry's continuance.

"There was a period of time when we couldn't find him," said Fred Drasner, who was Zuckerman's partner.

For all his pique over Harry's unexplained absences, Drasner too experienced mixed feelings about the anticipated departure. "Harry is a genius," he would later say. "A brilliant man about print. On the merits, he's as good as anybody I've seen." Drasner himself had learned a lot from Harry. "He was a most astute observer," he said. "He's an interesting and sometimes difficult character. But on raw intellectual horsepower, he's as good as I've seen. . . . And yeah, he wasn't as hands-on as we'd anticipated. But if I were starting another publication, I would put him on as consultant. I don't think I'd put him on as an employee or an editor, though."

But Harry's feelings of enthusiasm for his waning position were decidedly mixed. It was "a non-job" by the end, he would inform his old friend Murray Sayle, months after he had left Zuckerman's employ. He was "getting too old for this sort of thing." Anyway, his mind seemed elsewhere, as it had been for some time. *U.S. News* received a list of its cover sales sold on newsstands and for a while the results were disheartening. The magazine's newsstand sales, said an editor, were "down nearly ten percent in the new regime, compared to the Fallows era. That was a pretty big drop." Harry read these figures, the editor would recall, walking down the hall.

"Oh, this is quite impressive," he declared. "We're doing really quite well."

The editor tried to set Harry straight. "We're *down* ten percent," he said.

"Really? That's not good. Not good."

Harry had many things besides Zuckerman's empire on his mind. One of them was the issue of his advancing years, which appeared to have struck him with a special force.

"If you could wait a *very* short time," he pleaded with a prospective biographer, asking for a long interview, "you wouldn't have a living subject to write about." It was not merely a lighthearted stab at deflecting substance. It was a bleak rumination, at age seventy, on what he expected from his future. "I'd rather wait till they close the pine lid. Also—I see the grave opening up," said Harry. "Life must be closing. I'll be dead soon. Why don't you wait? Till then? I'll be dead."

Moreover, said Harry, "for the last five years," he and Tina had not granted interviews jointly. "Because we have individual lives. Tina and I never let *People* magazine photograph us together." He was quite tenacious on this point.

It was a disturbing conversation, but there seemed more involved than a dark mood, or Harry's insistence on his own looming mortality. There had been at least one other would-be biographer interested in unraveling his life, Harry said, but apparently nothing had come of it. Harry simply said, "You'll probably see his whitened bones in the desert, as you pass."

More than a year later, the first portion of that conversation would be eerily echoed by Harry's first wife, Enid. She was living alone in North London (her three children now grown), a slight, aging woman, trim in trousers and a loose floral blouse. Behind thick glasses were alert blue eyes. She had high, ruddy cheekbones set in an intelligent, good-humored face, framed by a short cap of graying hair. There was no glamour to her. It was a face innocent of cosmetics or indeed any touch of vanity. Although retired from her teaching career, she still had the brisk, starchy manner of someone in the habit of compelling the interest of others. A glance at the compact house with its garage painted in bright blue enamel, the small, neat hallway, bespoke the obvious. No two lives could have become more different than Harry's and Enid's. They had started out, young and much alike in England, northerners both, left wing and educated. There it ended.

Enid Evans was leading precisely the kind of existence—obscure, cheerfully modest—that her former husband had fled. And yet, distant though they were by then in almost every sense, the same mortal thoughts articulated by Harry clearly passed through her mind. "Couldn't you possibly wait just a little, until we're all dead?" she inquired politely. Had they managed to stay together, Enid and Harry might have shared these worries and been comforted by, if nothing else, a commonality of experience.

But back home in the impersonally decorated apartment in New York there was Tina, forty-six just then, and although she was certainly facing down a number of demons and disasters, and bravely too, age and death weren't among them.

Chapter 17
Twilight

She was feeling very bitter. Condé Nast and Graydon Carter especially, she told friends, were out to destroy her. Carter, she insisted, had hired a special publicity woman at *Vanity Fair* with this exact goal in mind. In late February 2000, just as an issue was about to appear featuring on its cover the singer Jennifer Lopez (finger mischievously cocked as though it were a pistol), her feelings of persecution were voiced. "This is going to make Condé Nast come after me again," she said. "This issue is so socko, they're going to try to destroy me again." Tina's listener found her remark at once "paranoid" and "endearing." On the one hand, at that relatively early date in *Talk*'s fortunes, it was patently faltering. The March issue featuring Lopez had forty-four full ad pages (discounting those sponsored by Talk Miramax), less than half of any of its four predecessors. On the other hand, there was still something unsinkable about its editor, at least in the awkward and Yankified passion of her rhetoric. "She talks like Batman. Pow! Socko!" said an editor.

And Tina did have ample reason to feel aggrieved. It was absolutely true, for example, that a substantial portion of Condé Nast no longer wished her well; and to some extent she herself had fostered such a widespread sentiment, and not just by leaving the company. Tina had described Hearst as "the greatest publisher in the industry." Si Newhouse was said to have been deeply offended by such a calculated snub. Steve Florio was convinced that a highly critical article about him that ran in *Fortune* two years earlier had been fed by Tina. "I ran into Steve Florio at a magazine conference," said Steven Cohn, the editor in chief of *Media Industry Newsletter*, "and every other word about her was four letters."

So, yes, the general hope among Tina's many ill-wishers at Condé Nast and *Vanity Fair*, the formidable giant into which she had once breathed life, was that *Talk* would run into bad trouble. But they had to exert themselves scarcely at all to see their hopes fulfilled. As one of Tina's own employees would later concede, "Although they were very nervous and competitive over there, by the third issue, they had written her off. That was like her worst punishment. To be written off."

Almost as terrible were the stories still being written about *Talk*. Buzz was in its death throes, suggested columnists. From February to June 2000, ad pages dropped sizably; by contrast, the industry overall experienced a 24 percent increase, and *Vanity Fair*'s ad pages during this slower period rose 40 percent. *Talk*'s March issue contained just 41.3 pages of ads; the April issue 70.8 pages; and June–July 36.1 ad pages. When these dismal figures were released, Ron Galotti reverted to the old pugnacious Galotti Tina had so admired. He had out-advertised *Vanity Fair* and *In Style*, he insisted. "I have kicked their fucking asses, and you can quote me on that." How could anyone be stupid enough to compare the four first launch issues to a bunch of spring-summer issues, he complained? *Talk* had racked up 828.9 pages in its first year; *Vanity Fair*, by comparison, had 556.8 pages. He loathed reporters who were too lazy to "do the homework." By spring 2000, Galotti predicted, there would be a total rate base of 650,000, and average newsstand sales would be as high as 247,000.

Meanwhile, the press indulged in a fair amount of snickering at Tina's expense: Arnold Schwarzenegger ("who hasn't had a hit movie since the mid-'90s," one reporter pointed out); Farrah Fawcett ("a '70s bombshell"). What kind of readership could Tina possibly expect after dishing out such warmed-over fare?

They couldn't know, as Tina's staffers certainly did, how desperate the magazine was for the unattainable. "Julia Roberts said no. From what we heard, she didn't like the look of the magazine," explained one *Talk* subordinate. Even Tina's special coup, Jennifer Lopez, in an issue that was supposed to bring rivals to their knees, was a disaster of sorts. Snapped by Oliviero Toscani in that playful shooting pose with a cowboy hat clapped on her pretty head, Lopez had no way of knowing the odd turn her life would take. Just days after the photo session, she and her boyfriend, Sean "Puffy" Combs, had engaged in a high-speed escape from a New York nightclub and Combs was later indicted (although ultimately acquitted) after a shooting incident that had occurred there. Then she spent fourteen hours in jail, and testified to a grand jury that she hadn't seen any gun at all on her boyfriend. What a stroke of luck—for *Talk:* ". . . The pose would seem strangely prescient," Bob Morris, author of the profile, reported. But Lopez and her publicity agent, Elaine Goldsmith, were evidently made unhappy by such prescience. "They felt it was an example of back-stabbing, that kind of thing," said a *Talk* staffer, "especially since Elaine had worked to give Tina the Lopez cover after her other client, Julia Roberts, said no."

And in Tina's selection of celebrity profile subjects, there was still another factor working against her, some of her staff thought privately: "Not having her finger on the year 2000," one said. "Some of those people who are sexy to her—Demi Moore, Daryl Hannah, Schwarzenegger—that's the *past.* Those years she spent at *The New Yorker,* even though she used some stars back then at the magazine, she was out of the glitzy celebrity culture. That may have affected her. That's how I see it."

That's certainly how she was seen by her younger staff members, 70 percent of whom had less than five years' experience in the field of journalism. Tina was out of it, "hopelessly and inexcusably out of touch with the culture," in the words of one of the aggrieved. A whole new generation was scrambling into journalism, quite ignorant of who Tina had been: the youngest, brightest, most plugged-in editor anyone could imagine at three successive magazines. All they knew was Tina in middle age. There she was, fast approaching forty-seven, and as ancient as some of their mothers, only considerably less doting. "You know how she is. Use and abuse," one of them remarked.

Some of her ideas would arrive like missiles aimed at a writer immersed in other, more serious projects. It was Tina's way of indicating that the writer should immediately abandon all previous endeavors and shift course. To duck such assignments, a great deal of ingenuity and quick thinking were required.

One writer described Tina's mode of operation. The phone would ring, and it would be Tina's secretary. "We have Tina on the speakerphone for you," she would say. The recipient of the call would then start talking, not without apprehension. "While you are talking, you sense other presences. It's terrible," the writer said. " 'Dev [Chatillon, the in-house counsel] is here,' you'll hear. Or some editor. And also other presences. And it's awful. You have no idea what faces they are making to each other, what they're indicating to each other while you're on the phone. It's dreadful."

But at a certain point, while speaking to yet another editor from those disembodied voices grouped around the speakerphone, the writer would realize that the initiator of the phone call—Tina—had mysteriously vanished. She was no longer speaking, no longer there. "She's gone out to lunch. She has gone out of the office. Something," the writer said. "It's like a call from Mount Olympus. And meanwhile your only goal is to get off the phone as fast as you can, and that's all you are thinking about. Mainly, you don't want to have to deal with Tina's next awful idea."

Tina's ideas at this juncture tended to be as dismal and bleak as her mood. They were slightly different from their predecessors. Gone were the obscure widows of celebrities and the homosexual urges of a particular writer. In their place was disaster and misery. The untimely death of Lee Radziwill's son, for example, was one of her notions. The difficult life of the daughter of the plastic surgeon Elizabeth Morgan was another. Morgan had spent twenty-five months in prison for civil contempt rather than allow her small daughter unsupervised visits with an ex-husband who, she said—although the former spouse denied this—had sexually abused the girl. A cancer victim who was the sibling of a television personality was yet a third. It was awfully difficult to understand how such inspirations might appeal to the thousand-eyed, squidlike creature Tina claimed as her reader. "She's a woman in her thirties who wears Prada," Tina said, "watches Miramax movies, and uses Urbanfetch to order a Harry Potter book at midnight for her children."

The saga of successful marriages also intrigued Tina. And yet, here again her selections were found peculiar: Helen Morris (Harry's old friend from Random House, where she claimed to have deflected his attentions), who had in the intervening years married the director Martin Scorsese; Allan McKeown and Tracey Ullman, the producer and the comedienne who had hired—and then fired—Tina's brother after he appeared in court on charges of assaulting women on London trains. These pieces were executed in breezy, unanalytical fashion, bolstered mainly with approving quotations from the parties concerned. And that was odd, one of those who dealt with Tina found, because the marriage stories were conceived as something more intriguing. Tina had originally wanted incisive analyses of these unions from a writer, not a human tape recorder.

So the waiting world lost its patience. Whatever breaks might have been extended to another start-up publication with a more modest or less publicity-hungry editor at its helm vanished. That magical night on Liberty Island, when the colored paper lanterns and the brilliant fireworks were outshone by all the stars who had come out just for Tina and Harry, seemed, in retrospect, a prime example of hubris. All sorts of newspaper accounts included variations on the phrase "A little more than a year ago, at the feet of the Statue of Liberty . . ."

In vain would Tina protest, with perfect justice, the impossibility of instant success for a new magazine. She had stumbled, she freely conceded. Her magazine had its faults. But no one was giving her a chance. No one was allowing her to regroup her forces and forge ahead. It was just as her employees said. She was suffering the worst of all punishments. She was written off. And worse: dispatched with a fair degree of glee. As ever, she felt she knew what accounted for this unseemly satisfaction. "I have had three successful magazines," she said, "and I think people just don't want to give you a fourth."

Moreover, she had been through all this before at *Vanity Fair*, when everyone was predicting its imminent demise. "It's not an overnight situation, nor will it be," she maintained. "Nobody seems to be particularly surprised by our arc. The only difference for us is that for every single sneeze in the magazine, the whole world waves a handkerchief."

By "the whole world" she was talking about her former friends, the ones who wrote for a living. Gone were the legions of ardent admirers, the decades of devotional pieces lauding Tina's talent, her beauty, charm, tireless industry, and the huge salaries and potential for literary stardom she and Harry had once proudly dispensed. A few stalwart champions remained in her corner—the gossip columnist Liz Smith, most notably. But the media world itself had changed so very much since Tina's first miraculous days in America, when she had managed to vanquish an entire industry. "In 1998, there were 60 wholesalers routing magazines to most of the nation's newsstands; now there are just four," wrote Alex Kuczynski of *The New York Times* in January 2001. *Talk,* she added, was conceived "long before the magazine industry entered its own version of recession."

Equally to the point: many of the newer on-line columnists had never partaken of the Brown-Evans largesse. They owed her nothing. Certain others, older writers who had warmed themselves for years in the refracted light of Tina's success, glamour, and generosity, felt, as they looked back, a mixture of fondness and alienation, emotions that would alternately advance and retreat, one trumping the other, according to the mood of the speaker. Some remained steadfast in their admiration of her abilities, which only served to heighten the contrast between what she could produce and what she did produce. Others saw, in retrospect, a slow decline. What Tina had always needed was a structure to build on, a portion of this group said. *Tatler, Vanity Fair, The New Yorker:* all existed before she ever stamped them with her own unmistakable imprint. But *Talk* was wholly hers, beginning to end, and therein lay its problems, said this contingent. Nothing should be entirely Tina's. Part of their willingness to explore their disenchantment was attributable to simple pique: most of the more established writers had endured, along with the delightful rewards, years of slights, killed stories, and unaccountable mood swings. It was just as one of Tina's newer subordinates remarked: "Anybody can become her favorite. And then all of a sudden, you're out of favor."

But much of the disappointment expressed went deeper. There had developed in the intervening years, behind Tina's back, a vast chasm of critical distance. Now that many of her old staff members were in the employ of other freehanded editors of note (often the very editors who had followed in Tina's footsteps and then assumed her budgets), a desire emerged to explore that distance. Who was this woman who had once controlled all their destinies? What had accounted for the length and breadth of her reign, the near unanimity of a courtesan press? How to explain the inviolate power she once wielded over a peculiarly expansive and yet restrictive kind of journalism, one modulated in part by Tina's unflagging desire to please those who counted? In the faltering first year of *Talk,* the heat had been turned up under that long-simmering desire, fueled now by desperation. Where Tina's old *Vanity Fair* had featured such powerful potential advertisers as Calvin Klein or Ralph Lauren on its covers, *Talk* often hunted for smaller prey, but with the same goals in mind. How else to account for a small, unsigned piece on Helene Mercier ("an intensely private woman"), who just happened to be the wife of Bernard Arnault, the head of the luxury empire LVMH? By the end of the year 2000, Valerie Muller, a senior vice president for MediaCom, was acknowledging that LVMH was extremely interested in *Talk.* "Not all the brands in that company are advertising, but many," she said. "They are definitely buying." Just months later, in its April 2001 issue, Arnault himself was discovered by the magazine to possess "a surprisingly nuanced sense of beauty."

Tina foraged through the landscape of her life for justification. Once she had been a witty, irreverent writer, famed for sending up the pretentious, she acknowledged. Then her fortunes had changed. "An editor has to be more responsible, has to go out and network and make friends for the magazine, and you can't be too controversial in a sense, as an editor," she said. But the best American editors have always been controversial. Harry, for that matter, had once been just that, and not because his newspaper pages displayed Demi Moore, disrobed, in her seventh month of pregnancy, but because of the true substantive curiosity which is the petri dish of great journalism—and controversy. Little by little, magazine by magazine, compromise by compromise, the light had dimmed.

"One's betrayals here have to be rather more subtle," Tina had said near the outset of her American career. Just how subtle was that? Who could have failed to heed such an explicit warning? What had happened to the powerful, independent Yankee world she had penetrated, embraced, and then refashioned in her own image? Why had they let her do it?

With the perceived decline of her latest venture, some of both her old and new colleagues were ready to talk. Gratitude was, of all human qualities, the most swiftly discarded among journalists. The statute of limitations was up. Besides, there were, since her defection from so many writers' lives, other soft landing sites for those Tina left behind. After Graydon Carter took over *Vanity Fair,* the magazine's advertising pages eventually rose by more than 60 percent and it evolved into a most profitable publication (the second most profitable in the Condé Nast realm, in fact, with over 2,000 ad pages and almost $12 million in ad revenue). David Remnick, her successor at *The New Yorker,* was a more muted presence, but the quality of the magazine became more consistent.

Meanwhile, Tina was seen as having dropped the torch, and the press, here and abroad, has never been able to resist the spectacle of flames.

Following Tina's determination to blame her staff for the defects of *Talk* ("Start-ups are not for kids," she told *USA Today,* unwisely. "If you can't take the stress, my advice is to go to work for a magazine that has been there for 35 years, and your life may be much easier"), her press got, if possible, a lot worse. A number of *Talk* defectors raced to their computers, from which they sent anonymous e-mails to an on-line media critic.

"In the *USA Today* article, Tina Brown contends that start-ups aren't easy but they are fun. For who?" wrote one of the defectors. "Anyone involved in the first few issues of *Talk* knows that it was one of the most miserable places on the planet and that the problems started at the top."

TALK STRUGGLES TO FIND ITS VOICE read one headline. "Is *Talk* magazine making a last stand?" inquired the *New York Post* in June 2000, on the occasion of another makeover for the magazine. It was its second face-lift in nine months, requiring heavier paper, a different form of binding glued to a hard spine, and the abolition of the dark Euro look that had earlier given the first issues some distinction. The large-sized format was shrunk by about 20 percent, permitting a reduction in paper costs and allowing it to fit more easily into newsstand racks.

There was cheerier news as well. Harvey Weinstein would be footing most of the bill—$13 million—for a roomier set of offices in New York's Chelsea district. In April, Galotti estimated advertising revenue at around $19 million. A few months later, he promised a gratifying circulation increase to 650,000 copies, up 100,000 from *Talk*'s inception. Of these, the publisher said, around 250,000 copies would be sold at newsstands at the new price of $3.50. If accurate, it was certainly a felicitous signal to advertisers. (And indeed by spring the following year, 2001, Galotti's optimism was very nearly justified. The magazine's circulation jumped to 619,000.) But newsstand sales, often the litmus test of just how cherished a publication is in the eyes of the consumer, slumped 23 percent from the previous six months—to 115,447. Earlier statistics on newsstand sales had been embarrassing enough: just 150,674.

Even worse, *Talk*'s sell-through rate during that earlier period—meaning the number of copies that actually are purchased from the pile at the newsstand—was almost 19 percent, and found to be very low; indeed, half the industry's average. For most of the year 2000, the number of *Talk* copies returned on average was 645,901. "Horrible, horrible," said E. Daniel Capell, a consultant to the magazine industry, who estimated these sizable returns cost *Talk* "about $400,000 per issue, not including editorial costs."

Despite his evident pleasure at reeling off rosy figures, Galotti was clearly wearying and growing thin-skinned from the bad press. "Eventually," he said with a sigh, "everyone will get tired of shitting on us and shit on somebody else." About the increasingly disappointed staff, he was less upbeat: "We have over a hundred people on our staff, and unfortunately some of them are idiots," he told a reporter from *Media Life*.

As for Tina, her nerves were in a state. In June 2000, even Talk Miramax's book division came under assault. John Connolly, a former New York City Police detective, had originally been assigned by the division to do a book entitled *Insane Clown Posse,* a work for which he received an estimated $100,000. Its ostensible purpose: to report on twenty-four hours in the life of the Monica Lewinsky scandal. Apparently, he soon tired of this task, deciding instead to unravel, with the help of a private eye, the sex lives of various Clinton critics, among them independent counsel Kenneth Starr, some of his subordinates, and the extravagantly blond conservative columnist Ann Coulter.

This project came to an abrupt end when the on-line gossip columnist Matt Drudge received a working manuscript of the book, which read in part: "There are no less than six gays involved in the [Lewinsky] case. Two of the 'elves' and three of Starr's young male protégés were gay. . . . ' " As for Ann Coulter, she had had trysts with "playboy" Geraldo Rivera at his "oceanfront retreat in New Jersey," Connolly wrote. "On the basis of the excerpts about me, I'd just like to say I'm looking forward to owning Miramax if it ever publishes any of this," Coulter replied in her column. "The sad truth is, my affair with Geraldo at his 'oceanfront retreat' was compromised by the presence of my brother, Mrs. Rivera and several other guests." Talk Miramax's response to Drudge's revelations was less than enlightened; it threatened to sue. But the book project was shelved.

However, compared to the magazine, the book division was doing brilliantly. Talk Miramax might point with pride to more impressive acquisitions, and vast sums were paid to some of its better known authors. The memoirs of Queen Noor of Jordan, for example; the revelations of David Boies, who had been Vice President Gore's advocate and the vanquisher of Microsoft; the ordeal of Dr. Jerri Nielsen, the physician at the South Pole who diagnosed and treated her own breast cancer—all these were acquired by Jonathan Burnham to much fanfare. The South Pole saga shot up to the best-seller list. The queen's autobiography was purchased for $1 million, $800,000 of which was recouped when German publication rights were sold.

Even Mayor Giuliani decided to bury all past animosity toward Tina, in return for a $3 million, two-book agreement; Secretary of State Madeleine Albright, until then noticeably reticent about her private life, consented to delve into what Tina called "an epic personal odyssey" for a deal estimated in the low seven figures. But the wisdom of such sizable purchases would not be known for some time. And the company lost out on Hillary Clinton, Harvey Weinstein's most ardently cultivated friend, despite all of Tina's efforts to snag her memoirs. The great Harry Evans himself would be editing Hillary, Tina promised, but the first lady's memoirs went to her old publisher, Simon & Schuster, for $8 million. In subsequent months Tina would tell friends, "I was the one who told Harvey, we mustn't do the book on Hillary Clinton. We are a young company, and it would have been two years of distraction."

Indeed, it was noted that she took a vast amount of credit for those literary triumphs that had come her way. It was because of "my contacts," said Tina, that Dr. Nielsen's "*Ice Bound* became a number one best-seller. I got the author on all the major television shows . . . I brought television producers to be on my editorial team. They know where the action is." Her listener soon realized that Tina had "hitched herself to the book division." And perhaps for good reason: in certain circles it was assumed it was the Burnham publishing division, which was flourishing, that might sustain *Talk*. That, and Weinstein himself. "What I tell people," said Steve Cohn, "is *Talk* has a sugar daddy with Weinstein, just as *Vanity Fair* has a sugar daddy. Weinstein will do anything till hell freezes over for this magazine."

A raft of new people drifted in to replace those who had abandoned *Talk*. Some came, as had their predecessors, to encounter the mythological Tina, a remote and shrouded figure whose mere touch, history had proven, could cure a lame magazine. Others joined up for the money; there was certainly more of it being dispensed ($15–$20 million, according to industry estimates), especially to the well established. A piece by Richard Reeves, for example, commanded $20,000. Contract writers received six-figure salaries. Besides, Tina was still talking about "a magazine of voices of intelligence, good writing, smart commentary." But exactly how serious were such aims?

Star profiles underwent a surgical change, evolving from flimsy text and mild probes (with all the threats to future access implied by such ventures, however gently contrived) into safe question-and-answers. "We decided to avoid the typical reporting of celebrities to keep things more adaptable," as a *Talk* employee delicately described the evolution. At a stroke, the perceptions and judgments of the reporter, the traditional filter through which celebrity conceits had been poured, were practically exterminated. "I don't want to hear what journalists think," said the editor who had once attracted some of the best writers on two continents. "I want to hear what the real people think . . . I want to hear what the celebrity has to think." Beginning in April 2000, Chris Connelly interviewed Tom Cruise with very little benefit of commentary. Tina was delighted with the results. "I think she developed a real comfort with Connelly, whose expertise is Q&A," said one *Talk* employee. "He came on like the savior. PMK and the other agencies loved the fact Connelly was very light, very friendly with people and gets good answers from stars."

"When that Tom Cruise Q&A came out, it was *extremely* well liked by his publicist and by him," said another employee. "And then you'd hear from all the publicists: 'We want something comparable to that.'"

And from then on, that's what they got.

"Oh, it's going the usual route of a new magazine, it's regularizing itself," Tina's former lover Martin Amis said. "It's finding its audience, simplifying its look, streamlining itself. And I have no doubt Tina will make it successful."

His was not an objective view, however, and not just because of his old ties to the editor. Amis had received a widely reported million-dollar deal from Talk Miramax to publish *Experience,* his memoirs (in which Tina was, inevitably, mentioned), as well as a collection of essays and an excerpt from the book in its magazine. Then he would get the chance to write a screenplay for Miramax Films, for which he would be paid yet more money.

The glow and substance of the first issue never returned. By the summer of 2000, it was rumored that Oliviero Toscani too, frustrated by a lack of creative freedom, was ready to leave. The rumor was stoutly denied by *Talk*. In November, he was back in Milan, having decided to "cut back" (in the words of the *New York Post*) on the time he spent with the magazine, and concentrate mainly on its photography.

In a peculiar way, it was Tina's parties that became at this point her most impressive accomplishments: unstoppable ambition incarnated as revelry. But where once social events were, literally, the embodiments of a "hot" publication, now they were a substitute for it. There appeared to be a frantic, off-target element to certain calculations: more than ever, she and Harry were jockeys in desperate pursuit

347

of a winning horse. But how likely was it that the earnest and pallid political figure on whom they pinned their hopes was the right one?

In November 1999, the presidential candidate Al Gore was fêted at the Evans household with Barbara Walters, Howard Stringer, head of Sony USA, and Catherine Zeta-Jones and Michael Douglas in attendance. Harry held forth "practically weeping tears of joy, he was so proud," in the words of one guest, though "he'd had like three glasses of wine," and his words were "a little slurred." But his performance with Gore was "brilliant," according to another of the guests. Harry was used to turning dinner parties into salons and he was perfectly comfortable in such a partisan milieu. In columns he still wrote for British newspapers, Harry was proving a devoted and unquestioning fan of the Democrats and, by contrast, quite a critic of the American press—"such a hunger for sleaze," he wrote—which had had the temerity to rummage through Clinton's sex life. "There was a conspiracy, no doubt about it," Harry insisted, "and the herd fell for it. . . ."

Guests plied Gore with questions, which the candidate answered in a relaxed and amusing fashion. Even though the microphone didn't work very well and guests had to strain to hear, it was a spirited evening, all the more cherished for being off the record, and a little store of social capital on which the Evanses could draw in the event of a Democratic victory.

As with so many other hopes in their lives, that one was dashed. There were compensations, but these were momentary. Exactly a year later, on the evening of election day, Weinstein and Tina presided at a more spectacular and public display of power at Elaine's, the watering hole of New York's literati. But really it was Weinstein's show. He was "the big impresario of the evening," in the words of one guest. Tina was more than usually subdued, in the background, friendly but withdrawn; what little she said seemed purposefully bland, as if designed to be unquotable. Harry, by contrast, was so bouncy and ebullient that at least one guest believed "he was in his cups." When the networks flashed a visual indicating that Gore might be the winner, Harry announced, "I feel liberated!" All about him swirled a host of instantly recognizable faces: Gwyneth Paltrow, the director Sydney Pollack, Uma Thurman, Ethan Hawke, the television interviewer Charlie Rose, Barry Diller, Ben Affleck, Chevy Chase. Even Jennifer Lopez, momentarily divested of both "Puffy" Combs and her earlier animus toward Tina, was found nibbling from a platter of fried chicken.

Like the rest of the company, as well as the Secret Service and its sniffing dogs (which lunged for the hors d'oeuvres), Lopez was waiting for Bill and Hillary Clinton to make the party complete. "I have plans for them to come tonight," Weinstein said confidently. The first couple, after all, had debts to repay: to Weinstein, their friend and supporter; and to Tina, whose magazine had helped humanize the first lady in her successful bid to become a senator from New York. "The last time Harvey Weinstein was this happy, Shakespeare was in love," the *New York Observer* pointed out. "He had just helped elect his first United States Senator."

By 12:45 A.M., however, word reached the hosts that with the election results in doubt, the Clintons would remain at their suite at the Grand Hyatt, but were more than happy to invite "sixty of the faithful," as Weinstein put it, to their rooms. It was Tina whom Weinstein designated to pick the chosen, and she performed this important function with her usual astuteness; at least three of those so honored were, significantly, gossip columnists. The rest, who jumped into waiting cars, included Jessye Norman, Ben Affleck, and Uma Thurman. Then the Evanses took off in their chauffeured sedan, Tina crowded into the back with a small clutch of friends, Harry up front with what one observer described as "a babe-elicious girl in his lap."

Eventually, the group joined the first couple in their suite, with crusted cheese platters and large buckets of bottled beer on ice their only source of nourishment at that hour. The lovely Thurman breathlessly recounted to the president how much the Gore-Bush debates "made me really miss you." Clinton busied himself by enumerating the states where Green Party candidate Ralph Nader was making inroads on Al Gore's doomed chances.

"I want to kill Nader!" Harry exclaimed.

"That's not a bad idea," Hillary joined in with a big smile. She was still wearing her vibrant turquoise green pantsuit, very much in her element now that she had won her Senate seat.

The next day, when this lighthearted exchange was reported in *The Washington Post*, Lloyd Grove, the writer, received a furious phone call from Harry. Didn't the reporter know every word spoken was off the record? Grove was quite cool in reply: "(a) I believe you know what I do for a living, Harry; (b) No one told me it was off the record, until after the fact; (c) You took me up there in your own car."

"Oh, okay, I withdraw my objection," Harry conceded, mollified, and that day he phoned Ralph Nader to apologize. How could he honestly complain about the coverage? He and Tina had been reported among such august company, hadn't they? In all their transient glory.

"The question about *Talk* is—is it something that should be allowed to continue? Or not?" said a source close to Hearst executives in December 2000. "Will Hearst leave? Is it a question of fuck it and throw her overboard? No one knows yet. But I can tell you that meetings on the subject are taking place as we speak. Right now it's basically a question of money."

This was a very sticky point, to be sure. In an interview with *The New York Times*, Tina insisted that Hearst had agreed to produce *Talk* a total of five years. However, that very article also noted that "Ms. Black, the Hearst executive, would not comment on the length of the contract or if Hearst Magazines had included a clause allowing it to pull out of the relationship."

The problem, as Hearst saw it, was not simply *Talk*, but its comparison to *O*, also published by Hearst in partnership with the nationally adored television hostess Oprah Winfrey. Actually, there was no comparison, or at least not much. Both were read mostly by women, and both publications had experienced early personnel changes: *O*'s original editor left after the first issue. And there all similarity ended. The triumph (if not the splendor) of *Talk*'s debut seventeen months earlier was easily surpassed by *O*'s in April 2000. Its initial issue had a printing of 1.6 million, over 900 ad pages sold in the first five issues, and Cathie Black suspected it might be profitable in 2001. Very likely it was not intended for the woman who wore Prada while simultaneously diapering her infants and surfing the Internet. *O* was unabashedly about "personal growth": there would be Oprah summits devoted to this, according to the ads; and Oprah's dog, her favorite books, as well as her chef's recipes made cameo appearances. Its trajectory provided a most unfair contrast to the fortunes of poor *Talk*; but then life, as Tina had by then discovered, wasn't wholly evenhanded. Personal growth for some, as it turned out, was a personal disaster for others.

In any event, Black must have been only moderately happy to discover herself listed, as she did in October, among *Fortune* magazine's fifty most powerful women. "Her high point: The O-so-successful launch of Oprah's magazine," read the squib. "Her low point: Let's not Talk about it."

Fairly quickly, Black's champions rallied to her side. "Oprah's magazine was very much a Cathie project," one of them said. "*Talk* is the product of Harvey Weinstein and Frank Banneck, who then said, 'This is a good thing to do.' Cathie is very much a corporate girl, and if Frank says, 'Get involved,' she will get involved. But Cathie's compensation is predicated on how well the magazine division is doing. The launch of Oprah was very expensive, but at least it will generate a lot of money. But *Talk?* You tell me. Let's put it this way: Tina was not known for making a lot of money for anyone."

But she was known for conjuring it out of their pockets. By December 2000, she had quietly inveigled another $5 million from Weinstein. According to gossip in publishing circles, it was going to be needed. *Talk* was racking up annual losses of about $25 million, word had it, and all Galotti could say when confronted with this estimate was, "This was never intended to be a two-dollar magazine. All expenses are under control."

And so, who knew about Tina? She still had a dose or two of buzz up her sleeve. She had just received, courtesy of the Queen of England, a CBE—Commander of the British Empire. It was the sort of honor that had a lot more currency back home in London, where she made sure to collect it, than in New York, where there were those under the impression that she was navigating a warship. In a sense, that was exactly what she was doing. Anyway, it was a start.

And as for Harry, he was writing his books on American history, and serving in at least one instance as a liaison to *Talk*. Right before the presidential election, Harry telephoned an astonished journalist to ask for an article on Bush for his wife's magazine. For the rest, he was in a particularly critical frame of mind. He had received complaints, he informed an editor at a publishing company, about a rude author who was writing a book on him and had phoned a number of those he knew with questions. Friends had told him they had been "harassed beyond mere polite inquiry," and Harry felt it necessary to write on their behalf. Indeed, he seemed in general put out by quite a number of the very practitioners of the trade he plied. What particularly irked him, he told an interviewer, was "the press," which "has also come to the cult of celebrity and the pursuit of individuals without very much to add to human knowledge."

But this cult of celebrity, he was asked, wasn't it to some extent Tina Brown's doing?

Harry groaned. "Am I my wife's keeper now?"

Tina, less reflective and analytical by nature, had a few old scores to settle, and at this task she was laboring with some skill by year's end. In the February 2001 issue of *Talk,* readers were treated to the saga of a Texas billionaire named Shelby Bryan, a network communications high-flyer in the midst of "one of the ugliest meltdowns to hit Wall Street in the last year." Bryan was better known, however, for being the boyfriend of Anna Wintour, the elegant and long-reigning queen of *Vogue,* whose marriage to a child psychologist had collapsed. Wintour had pleaded with Tina not to run the story, without success. But what kind of leverage did she have? Besides, the published article on Wintour's boyfriend could be viewed, in its most charitable guise, as just the sort of helpful hint one well-disposed girl-friend, anxious to improve readership, might offer to another: constructive criticism of Wintour's taste in men. "He behaves appallingly with women, I hear stories about what he says to women at dinner parties," a socialite remarked of Bryan in the article. "He asks nineteen-year-old girls and forty-five-year-olds at parties in Southampton if they want to fuck him."

Tina was good enough to send Wintour a copy of the published article, a "With Compliments" card attached, but this did not apparently do much to improve relations. When the article's main points were repeated in the *Daily Telegraph,* Bryan decided to sue for libel in Britain, but settled with the newspaper after it withdrew its allegations and agreed to pay a sum to charity. He was, it was said, particularly upset about being depicted as a lothario by the newspaper.

It was not, of course, the February issue's lone allusion to sexuality. The cover story on the actress Heather Graham reminded readers of the splash she had made in the film *Boogie Nights,* wearing nothing but a pair of roller skates. The cover itself featured an impressive amount of Graham cleavage pouring from a body crunched in the manner of a praying mantis. *Talk* that month had the charmless desperation of a teenager willing to do just about anything to attract the notice of suitors. But somehow or other, that notice was secured. In that area, at least, Tina Brown hadn't lost her touch.

So, no one was willing to count Tina out, least of all Si Newhouse. "Si is tempted to buy *Talk,*" one executive confided. Tempted he was, but by no means certain to rush to Tina's side and, with one stroke of the knife, free her from bondage and the oncoming train. A proposal had been made near the end of 2000, claimed the executive. The asking price of the magazine was very high, but you never knew with Newhouse. "Frankly, Si is always tempted by magazines," the executive said. "Always. He was tempted by *Fast Company* and it was a ridiculous price. This is a man who is a private company. If he likes and wants it, sometimes he will go very far to make it make sense."

"Is it competitive?" Newhouse wondered aloud.

"Yeah, it's competitive, but one of the reasons it's competitive is because of the low ad rate charge and the high sizzle factors," he was told. "Consequently, it could be a long time or never before they get the average rate up to sustain the cost of a magazine selling that many copies."

That seemed to have its effect, and no more was heard of Newhouse's suggestion to rescue his fallen angel. Nonetheless, Tina might have been surprised by some of the reactions to her magazine from Condé Nast executives, even the ones who considered her "an albatross" to any potential deal. The magazine was evolving, said one of them: "It's looking and reading pretty good now. The cover design is strong, she's changed the stories she's selected." In its pages could be found, from time to time, a fairly interesting piece on Osama bin Ladin's bomb-making guide, discovered by an ex-CIA agent, or even—and this was an interesting departure—a tough piece on Tina's former sponsor Calvin Klein.

But was any of this quite enough? It was as though with this new venture something precious had been extinguished in its creator: a certainty of mission, an immutable identity, a power.

One by one, some of the more essential parts of Tina's life quietly took their leave. "I don't really care what people say about me, as long as the twenty people I love reciprocate," she told a journalist in the midst of her troubles with the magazine. "If you've got twenty people you love and they love you, that's a lot. Who needs more?" In January 2001, she lost the most stalwart member of this close circle. George Brown, Tina's father, who lived in her building and dined nightly with his daughter and her family, died at eighty-seven. He had been very unwell for a long time, had never anticipated living longer than Bettina; like her, he had always been his daughter's fiercest champion and refuge, an unquestioning source of sympathy even when he least understood her. "She has changed curiously little," George once told an interviewer, when Tina was fighting for *Vanity Fair*'s tenuous young life back in 1984. "Now and then I look at her and see the child I remember. Those wide eyes and that brow. You never quite know what's going on behind it." Unlike so many others, he loved her for that.

And with these losses came other disappearances: a portion of the crowd of well-wishers who had occasionally relied on her largesse. The British writer Francis Wheen, for example, whose biography of Karl Marx had so thrilled Tina that she had brought it to the attention of Weinstein, was ecstatic when he learned that Miramax was considering turning the book into a film starring Ralph Fiennes as a possible Marx, with Tom Stoppard as a potential screenwriter. A bit too ecstatic, perhaps. Wheen went out and bought himself a boat. "Bit of a shock for poor Francis," said a mutual friend after the project came to nothing, and Wheen learned that the idea had simply been "one of Tina's enthusiasms." He had to settle for the BBC as his new patron. Of course, some of his Marx material made it into *Talk,* but he didn't seem satisfied with the results. "A complete mess," said Wheen.

So there was a solitary aspect to Tina's new life, a long series of defections. About Newhouse's moment of temptation to buy her magazine, Tina likely knew nothing. All she knew was what was staring her in the face. She still had Weinstein to placate, Hearst to mollify, advertisers to inveigle, readers to win over, celebrities to wheedle, her own mounting panic to subdue. And her dissolving mystique—that needed some surgery as well. Most of the time she revealed little about her true sentiments, but every once in a while her resolve broke, the veil drooped, and some fragment of candor or pain would become audible. This happened in Milan, when she called on the Italian designer Giorgio Armani, a *Talk* advertiser. They were sitting on the low pale chairs of his starkly decorated villa, coffee cups in their hands, and Tina was talking of her awful year. "It's all *Schadenfreude,*" she said. "The pleasure people take in someone else's misery."

And very likely, she was right. There were those who derived a certain delight from her raft of difficulties, plenty of them, but even they were cautious in their forecasts. After all, *Talk* was releasing the list of those it had invited to a conference in Santa Barbara, California, organized with PaineWebber—"Innovators and Navigators," the event was called. Summoned to Tina's side were new beneficiaries, old standbys, authors, TV stars, the rabbits once unfailingly pulled from Tina's hat. "Get this," wrote Liz Smith, as she ticked them off: Queen Noor, Peter Jennings, Rudy Giuliani, Christiane Amanpour, George Weidenfeld, Michael Eisner . . . But Jennings dropped out, and Hearst executives Cathleen Black and Frank Bennack both were absent—in Paris, attending a board meeting.

Who would stand by her? Whom did she wish by her side? In media circles, gossip swirled that Tina's feelings toward Weinstein

("She finds him incredibly vulgar," it was said. "She doesn't know how she got into this in the first place") were undergoing the sort of downsizing that was, once again, afflicting her magazine's ad pages. Right after a particularly fat April 2001 issue that boasted over a hundred full-page ads, ads in the May issue of *Talk* dropped to less than half that number and included one for the organization Jews for Jesus.

Tina "can take care of herself," Harry promised an interviewer. It was a safe enough prediction. She had always done that. That diary she had begun as a plump, drab girl of whom nobody took any notice: it was, Tina assured anyone who inquired, full of sharp portraits of those she had encountered in the long and eventful journey to fame she shared with Harry. "My old age insurance," she called it. The fiery brilliance of her that had once so dazzled two nations—possibly it could still be found, singeing those pages.

In any event, she was poised on the precipice, Tina's favorite perch.

And Harry was not idle. In 2001 he found another in a long set of bosses, joining up with Felix Dennis as consulting editor of *The Week,* a weekly news digest that was originally launched in Britain. "Brevity is the soul of wit," said Harry. There would be a $17 million budget for the American version, and an initial circulation of 150,000, costing subscribers $75 a year. Dennis, also the publisher of the risqué magazine *Maxim,* was an unlikely employer for such a renowned editor, but Harry was by then used to—if nothing else—unlikely employers. And there was quite possibly a certain satisfaction to be derived from the notion of thumbing his nose at *U.S. News.*

But even with this new job, the memory of his years at Random House, the dimming of glory days, clearly nagged at him. "He felt underappreciated at Random House," an acquaintance quickly realized. A writer inquiring about Ann Godoff, Harry's replacement at the publishing company, was given a list of people who, his listener realized, might have "different views" of her proven abilities.

There they were then, Tina and Harry. The all-important race was still being run, but in altered, less vivid fashion. There seemed to be no finish line. The buoyant, fascinating adventures into which they had once flung themselves with such infectious joy and energy along with the legions of anxious disciples—many of these had vanished. In their place were newer, more fragile pursuits, often quite lonely ones, and all around them, the gradual stilling of cheers. Whatever the fate of *Talk,* it was still, despite the most valiant efforts, a more muted endeavor, its proportions in certain ways more modest and bearing little resemblance to the gorgeous sweep of properties over which Tina and Harry had once held sway. "Let me put it this way: I think this is my last magazine," Tina said. "At the end of this one, I hope to have built a great asset and a great magazine, and then I will melt into the European sunset."

Everything was different for them, then, even their choice of sunsets. They hadn't of course "melted," but the temptation to do so, to quit the scenes of her remarkable triumphs, the hard-bitten country she and her husband had so fervently embraced, was clearly passing through Tina's mind even as she labored on what she suspected was her last magazine. The reign of the couple, alternately brilliant and hapless, was over. And it ended like a lot of Victorian novels, in part because of the overweening ambition that originally fed it, but mostly because every so often for no apparent reason destiny shrugs its shoulders, takes a look around, and then tosses its darlings, the gods who once believed they ruled it, to the winds.

Acknowledgments

Acknowledgments are inadequate here: the generosity, care, and understanding of my colleagues and friends on both sides of the Atlantic are worthy of far more. As I received no help at all from the subjects of this book (which did come as a surprise), I had to rely on the kindness of those who knew them. Or alternatively, on those who knew me and, often enough, recognized those tendencies of the author which had to be curbed or enhanced in this book

I owe a huge debt of gratitude to, among others: Joni Evans, Fred Hills, Michael and Margaret Crick, Fredric Dannen, Tom Prince, James Wolcott, Nicholas Monson, James Fallows, Tony Palmer, Stephen Glover, Lucy Nichols, John Lahr, Valerie Grove, the late Auberon Waugh, Angela Huth, Bernie Leser, Alan Brien, Philip Oakes, Bryan Di Salvatore, Philip Norman, Magnus Linklater, Don Berry, Lynn Hirschberg, Martin Amis, Jamaica Kincaid, Hunter Davies, Reinaldo Herrera, Joan Collins, Daniel Menaker, Bruce Page, Ian Jack, Toby Young, Sarah Papineau, Phillip Knightley, Alexander Chancellor, and the magazine *Private Eye,* which gives great lunches.

And to Dick for his bottomless reserves of patience.

And to the Columbia University Graduate School of Journalism, which gave me, some time ago, two precious gifts: a year of pure joy, and the profession I love.

As for all those who, for one reason or another, I cannot thank by name: Thank you.

Index

INDEX

INDEX

INDEX